THOMAS AQUINAS
ON THE IMMATERIALITY OF THE HUMAN INTELLECT

ADAM WOOD

THOMAS AQUINAS

ON THE IMMATERIALITY OF
THE HUMAN INTELLECT

The Catholic University of America Press
Washington, D.C.

Copyright © 2020

The Catholic University of America Press

All rights reserved

Library of Congress Cataloging-in-Publication Data

Names: Wood, Adam, author.

Title: Thomas Aquinas on the immateriality of the
human intellect / Adam Wood.

Description: Washington, D. C. : The Catholic University of America
Press, 2020. | Includes bibliographical references and index. |
Summary: "The author offers a comprehensive interpretation
of Aquinas's claim that the human intellect is immaterial and
assessment of his arguments on behalf of this claim, also positioning
Aquinas's thought alongside recent work in hylomorphic metaphysics
and philosophy of mind"—Provided by publisher. Identifiers: LCCN
2019042035 | ISBN 9780813232560 (cloth) |
ISBN 9780813232577 (ebook)

Subjects: LCSH: Thomas, Aquinas, Saint, 1225?-1274. | Intellect. |
Hylomorphism. | Philosophy of mind.

Classification: LCC B765.T54 W625 2020 | DDC 128/.2—dc23

LC record available at https://lccn.loc.gov/2019042035

CONTENTS

	Acknowledgments	vii
	Abbreviations and Notes on the Text	ix
	Introduction	1
1.	Forms as Limiting Principles	7
2.	Forms as Essences, Structures, Truthmakers, and Powers	48
3.	From Incorporeality to Incorruptibility	90
4.	Aquinas's Theory of Cognition	152
5.	Aquinas's Arguments for the Immateriality of the Human Intellect	193
6.	The Immateriality of the Human Intellect and the Life to Come	255
	Selected Bibliography	295
	Index	313

ACKNOWLEDGMENTS

This book began as a doctoral dissertation under the direction of Gyula Klima at Fordham University. I am very grateful for Gyula's support, encouragement, and guidance as the project has progressed. His influence is present throughout, even where we disagree. I thank Giorgio Pini and William Jaworski for their help developing many of the book's ideas while at Fordham. Earlier still, I am grateful to Joshua Hochschild for directing me in studying Aquinas's *De anima* commentary and inspiring my fascination with this topic. For helpful commentary, criticism, and discussion as the book progressed I thank Josh, Jeff Brower, Therese Scarpelli Cory, Greg Lynch, Peter Hartman, Brendan Palla, Shane Wilkins, Ryan Kemp, James Gordon, participants in the 2015 and 2018 Cornell Summer Colloquia in Medieval Philosophy and the 2015 JHP Master Class at the University of Toronto (as well as Scott MacDonald and Peter King for making these events possible), and the two anonymous referees from the Catholic University of America Press. Much of this book was written while on leave from Wheaton College in the beautiful city of Querétaro, Mexico. I wish to thank its residents for their warm hospitality toward my family, as well as Wheaton's Center for Global and Experiential Learning and Philosophy Department for making the leave possible. I also wish to thank Sadie McCloud for her keen editorial eye. My father, W. Jay Wood, is chiefly to blame for getting me into philosophy, for which I am (usually) grateful. Above all I thank my wife, Caris, for supporting me through the writing process with her calm, steady, reassuring presence and her many sacrifices so that I could puzzle through metaphysical minutiae. This book is for her.

ABBREVIATIONS AND NOTES ON THE TEXT

A few words about texts and terminology. Translations from Aquinas are my own, based on the editions listed in the bibliography. References to Aquinas's works follow standard textual divisions. When chapter and/or paragraph numbering in the critical edition differ from that of another widely referenced edition (e.g., the Marietti editions of Aquinas's Aristotelian commentaries) I include both, separated by a slash. I employ the following set of abbreviations:

CT	*Compendium theologiae*	
DEE	*De ente et essentia*	
DMC	*De motu cordis*	
DPN	*De principiis naturae*	
DUI	*De unitate intellectus contra Averroeistas*	
In 1 Cor	*Expositio super Primam Epistolam S. Pauli ad Corinthios*	
In DA	*Sententia super De anima*	
In DC	*Expositio super librum De causis*	
In DCM	*Sententia super libros De caelo et mundo*	
In DGC	*Sententia super libros De generatione et corruptione*	
In DH	*Expositio libri De hebdomadibus*	
In DSS	*Sententia super De sensu et sensato*	
In DT	*Expositio super librum Boethii De trinitate*	
In Met	*Sententia super Metaphysicam*	
In Meteor	*Sententia super Meteora*	

In NE	*Sententia super libri Ethicorum*
In PA	*Sententia super Posteriora analytica*
In Peri	*Sententia super Perihermeneias*
In Phys	*Sententia super Physicam*
In Pol	*Sententia libri Politicorum*
In Sent	*Scriptum super libros Sententiarum*
QDA	*Quaestio disputata de anima*
QDP	*Quaestiones disputatae de potentia Dei*
QDSC	*Quaestio disputata de spiritualibus creaturis*
QDV	*Quaestiones disputatae de veritate*
QQ	*Quaestiones quodlibetales*
SCG	*Summa contra Gentiles*
ST	*Summa theologiae*
TDSS	*Tractatus de substantiis separatis*

Aristotle's works are cited according to their Bekker numbers along with volume and page numbers from *The Complete Works of Aristotle*, edited by Jonathan Barnes (Princeton, N.J.: Princeton University Press, 1984), from which all translations are taken. Commentaries and disputed questions by authors other than Aquinas are cited according to standard abbreviations and textual divisions for the works in question (e.g., Ordinatio as Ord., Quaestiones de anima as QDA). Footnote references to editions of Thomas's works employ the following abbreviations:

Leo.	*Sancti Thomae Aquinatis, Doctoris Angelici, opera omnia, iussu impensaque Leonis XIII P.M. edita* (Rome: 1882–)
Marietti	*Sancti Thomae Aquinatis, Doctoris Angelici*, various works and editors (Turin/Rome: Marietti, various dates)
Mand./Moos	*Scriptum super libros Sententiarum*, ed. R. P. Mandonnet and R. P. Maria Fabianus Moos (Paris: Letheielleux, 1929–47)
Parma	*Sancti Thomae Aquinatis, Doctoris Angelici, opera omnia ad fidem optimarum editionem* (Parma: Petrus Fiaccadoris, 1852–73, repr. New York: Musurgia, 1948–50)

Brackets within translations indicate something I have added for the sake of clarity, or the Latin text of certain especially important or controversial phrases. For claims regarding the dating of Aquinas's works I rely throughout on Jean-Pierre Torrell's study of Thomas's life and works cited in the bibliography. Some of Aquinas's terms are notoriously difficult to translate. I have left some—such as *species*, in psychological contexts—untranslated. I translate others in ways that seem the least likely to mislead English-speaking readers as to Aquinas's meaning. I render *esse* as "act of being," for instance, and use "cognition" as a generic term for what both the senses and intellect do when it is not clear that Aquinas has some more specific cognitive act—such as understanding or reasoning—in mind.

Finally, I refer to specific arguments/concepts with the following abbreviations:

IA	argument from the intensity of intellectual operations
MA	argument from the mode of intellectual operations
OD/E	ontological dependence/explanation
RA	argument from the reflexivity of intellectual operations
SA	argument from the scope of intellectual operations
SPR	argument for survivalism based on the possibility of resurrection
SS	argument for the separability of human souls from bodies

THOMAS AQUINAS
ON THE IMMATERIALITY OF THE HUMAN INTELLECT

INTRODUCTION

Thomas Aquinas frequently claims that the human intellect is immaterial. It is a crucial claim within his philosophical psychology. For Aquinas, the immateriality of the intellect is tightly related to our power to make free choices, our capacity for self-knowledge, our ability to think and reason abstractly, the possibility of our souls surviving after death in a disembodied state, and other important matters. That the human intellect is immaterial is also a highly controversial claim. Critics from Aquinas's day to the present have charged that it renders his philosophical psychology incoherent, that his arguments supporting it are failures, or both.

It is not hard to see why his claim should have aroused such controversy, given the host of perplexing questions it invites. Consider three. First, Aquinas takes the immateriality of the intellect to supply grounds for holding that human souls can survive in a disembodied state. Yet, following Aristotle, he also thinks that a human's soul is her substantial form. And he is happy to borrow Aristotle's examples to illustrate what he means by form: the form of a bronze statue is its shape, as opposed to the bronze itself, which is the statue's matter. Presumably, though, there could not be a "disembodied" statue-shape existing apart from the bronze. So why suppose that there could be disembodied human souls, however immaterial their intellects might be? Second, Aquinas thinks that in normal cases intellectual activity depends on the brain, at least to the extent that when the brain is injured, the intellectual soul cannot function. And of course very many philosophers nowadays would agree about there being some tight connection between thinking and brain activity, even if they disagree about how exactly to specify this connection. Given this tight connection, though, how can there be disembodied intellectual activity apart from the brain? And how can Aquinas claim, as he often does, that due to the intellect's immateriality no bodily organ shares in its operations? Third, because he claims that intellectual operations are incorporeal and that human souls can exist in a disembodied state, it is easy to understand Aquinas as a substance dualist, and to interpret the "immateriality" of the intellect to mean "nonphysicality." Aquinas adamantly opposes the sort of substance dualism that he associates with Plato, however, and it would be anachronistic to interpret the immateriality of the intellect as an antiphysicalist doctrine if we define "physicalism" in terms of contemporary physics. So what kind of dualism, if any, does Aquinas endorse? In what ways does the immateriality of the intellect imply a rejection of physicalism?

These difficult questions concerning one of its central doctrines notwithstanding, Aquinas's philosophical psychology has received considerable attention in recent years. It has garnered many supporters, some of whom argue that it provides resources for a mind-body theory, occupying roughly the same theoretical role as familiar views like Cartesian substance dualism or physicalism, but superior in various ways to its competitors. Dubbing Aquinas's theory "Thomistic hylomorphic dualism," or using similar terms, some are optimistic about the prospects of its threading the needle between "the Scylla of materialism and the Charybdis of dualism."[1] The general idea is that Aquinas inherited the

---

1. David Oderberg defends a view he calls "hylemorphic dualism" and ascribes to Aquinas in "Hylemorphic Dualism," in *Personal Identity*, ed. Ellen Frankel Paul, Fred D. Miller, and Jeffrey Paul (Cambridge: Cambridge University Press), 70–99, and *Real Essentialism* (London: Routledge, 2007). Edward Feser argues on behalf of "Thomistic dualism" in *Philosophy of Mind: A Short Introduction* (Oxford: Oneworld, 2005). J. P. Moreland and Scott Rae defend "Thomistic Substance Dualism" in *Body and Soul: Human Nature and the Crisis in Ethics* (Downers Grove, Ill.: Intervarsity Press, 2000). The reference to Scylla and Charybdis is from Gyula Klima, "Aquinas on the Materiality of the Human Soul and the Immateriality of the Human Intellect," *Philosophical Investigations* 32, no. 2 (2009): 163–82. Others proposing that Aquinas offers a mind-body theory worthy of serious consideration include David Braine, *The Human Person: Animal and Spirit* (Notre Dame, Ind.: University of Notre Dame Press, 1994); C. Stephen Evans, "Separable Souls: Dualism, Selfhood and the Possibility of Life After Death," *Christian Scholars' Review* 34, no. 3 (2005): 327–40; Patrick Lee and Robert George, *Body-Self Dualism in Contemporary Ethics and Politics* (Cambridge: Cambridge University Press, 2009), chap. 2; James Madden, *Mind, Matter and Nature: A Thomistic Proposal for the Philosophy of Mind* (Washington, D.C.: The Catholic University of America Press, 2013), chap. 8, and Alfred Freddoso, "No Room at the

hylomorphic basis of his psychology from Aristotle, but developed and refined Aristotle's views in various ways which, among other advantages, allowed him to demonstrate the possibility of postmortem human existence.

These positive appraisals of Aquinas's philosophical psychology are premature insofar as there remain lingering questions about what exactly Thomas means by the immateriality of the human intellect, along with concerns about this central doctrine's coherence and defensibility. Despite its contemporary relevance, however, and its significant and controversial status, Aquinas's claim has yet to receive book-length scrutiny. Certainly there have been many fine books and articles touching on aspects of Aquinas's metaphysics, philosophy of mind, philosophy of science, and philosophy of religion that comment helpfully on the human intellect's immateriality. But no single work provides a comprehensive look at what Aquinas means by his claim, combined with an analysis of his reasons for making it. The present work aims to fill this gap in the literature.

I begin by developing an account in the book's first three chapters of what Aquinas means by calling the human intellect immaterial. To make sense of the way in which Aquinas thinks there can be forms without matter, I argue in the first chapter, we must move beyond simple characterizations of matter and form as "stuff and structure" or as "referent and truthmaker of predications," and instead appreciate Thomas's conception of forms or essences as principles delimiting or determining an act of being (*esse*) into various modes. Immateriality, I claim, is one such mode in which Aquinas thinks that various forms have their acts of being. By calling the human intellect immaterial, he primarily means that it is a form with its act of being in an immaterial mode. In the second chapter I expand upon this claim by examining the relationships between some of the different roles Aquinas assigns to forms: essences, structures, truthmakers, and powers. Thomas thinks the intellect and will are powers that, unlike all others we possess, do not structure our bodies into organic parts. In that sense, our intellectual powers are in-

---

Inn: Contemporary Philosophy of Mind Meets Thomistic Philosophical Anthropology," *Acta Philosophica* 24, no. 1 (2015): 15–30.

corporeal. Their incorporeality does not, however, extend so far as to preclude any sort of correlation whatsoever with bodily parts, states, and processes. Indeed, as I mentioned, Aquinas thinks that intellectual operations depend in normal cases on the brain. In the third chapter I argue that one additional way of understanding Thomas's claim that our intellectual powers are immaterial and incorporeal is as maintaining that their operations cannot be explained in terms of coordination between bodily parts, states, and processes, including brain activity. If Aquinas can show that the human intellect is immaterial and incorporeal in this sense, I argue, he is entitled to the further claim that human souls are incorruptible, and hence capable of survival after death in a disembodied state.

Having established an understanding in the first three chapters of what Aquinas means by claiming that the human intellect is immaterial, chapters 4 and 5 examine Thomas's arguments for thinking this claim is true. Does Aquinas succeed in showing that intellectual operations cannot be explained in bodily terms? Because Thomas's efforts to prove the intellect's immateriality and incorporeality hinge crucially on his theory of cognition, chapter 4 sets the stage for considering his arguments themselves by offering a selective overview of his cognitive psychology, focused on those features most important for understanding Thomas's claims concerning the human intellect's immateriality. In chapter 5, I consider his arguments for the human intellect's immateriality themselves, and in particular examine three types of argument that I take to be especially significant. They are based, respectively, upon the scope, reflexivity, and mode of intellectual operations. That is, one is based upon the potentially infinite variety of different objects that the intellect is able to cognize, another upon the intellect's ability to cognize itself, and a third upon the "absolute" or "universal" way that it cognizes its objects. I think the first type of argument probably fails, and Aquinas's few brief presentations of the second argument-type leave its success questionable. In addition, many of the ways in which the third type of argument has been interpreted in the literature leave it vulnerable to criticism. I argue, however, that on one plausible (though somewhat adventurous) reading, Aquinas's arguments based upon the mode of intellectual cognition stand a reasonable chance of success.

The final chapter traces out some of the philosophical and theological implications of the human intellect's immateriality, particularly as they pertain to the afterlife. If the arguments of the previous chapters succeed, Aquinas is indeed able to establish that human souls persist after death in a disembodied state. I will argue that he thinks it can be shown that human souls will engage in certain types of intellectual activity after death, and thus count as immortal on at least one understanding of the term. Nevertheless, Thomas does not think that human souls are human beings or persons. We do not survive our deaths, even if our souls do. On Aquinas's view there can be a large temporal gap between a human's death and his or her resurrection on the last day. It is essential to Aquinas's view regarding the possibility of the resurrection, I argue, that our separated souls carry on with our acts of being during the period between death and rising again, even while we ourselves are no longer there to possess them. For Thomas, the possibility of human souls existing in a disembodied state crucially undergirds the possibility of God's raising us from the dead. This view was controversial in Aquinas's day and remains so. Aquinas's reason for holding it, I suggest, stems from his metaphysics of individuation, and likely would not sway any determined opponents of his position. Yet overall his stance on the human intellect's immateriality supports a philosophically interesting and theologically satisfying account of postmortem human existence.

Providing a sustained examination of Aquinas's claims regarding the human intellect's immateriality is the primary aim and organizing principle of this book. The central position that the intellect's immateriality occupies within Aquinas's philosophical psychology—and indeed within his thought as a whole—makes it an important topic to investigate. It also makes it impossible to examine without also engaging with many other aspects of Thomas's positions on physics, metaphysics, and psychology. In the opening section of this book alone, for instance, I will need to discuss Aquinas's celebrated views that being is not a genus, that a creature's essence is really distinct from its act of being, that matter individuates forms, that substances have just one substantial form, and so on. Each of these positions has been philosophically controversial from Aquinas's day forward. It is also controversial today how best to interpret many of them. I certainly will not be able to defend each of my interpretations against all possible alternatives, nor will I be able to defend each claim I discuss to the same degree of thoroughness.

Both the interpretations I offer and the arguments I employ to defend them rely in many ways on the excellent work of others, especially John Wippel, Robert Pasnau, Gyula Klima, Eleonore Stump, Anthony Kenny, Jeffrey Brower, and Brian Leftow, among active scholars, and Joseph Owens, Anton Pegis, and Herbert McCabe from earlier generations of commentators. I will indicate when this is the case. I will also indicate where the claims I am discussing or interpretations I am advancing are especially controversial.

Of course, it is my hope that in addition to relying on the work of others, this book makes original contributions in each of its chapters. These include the account of immateriality as a mode of being I offer in the first chapter, and the defense of Aquinas's inference from the human intellect's immateriality to the human soul's incorruptibility in chapter 3. They also include the analysis of the role final causality plays in Aquinas's cognitive theory in chapter 4, and, based on this analysis, the interpretation I present in chapter 5 of Thomas's argument for the human intellect's immateriality from its universal mode of cognition. One claim I stop short of defending in this book is that Aquinas offers us a mind-body theory superior to any others currently on offer, as some recent scholars have alleged. I doubt Thomas was in the business of constructing a mind-body theory, as this phrase is best understood. I do, however, attempt to situate Thomas's philosophical psychology in relation to contemporary physicalist, substance dualist, and emergentist mind-body theories in chapter 3. Philosophers interested in formulating a hylomorphic mind-body theory with roots in Aquinas's thought may find resources in these chapters.

I

FORMS AS LIMITING PRINCIPLES

Aquinas claims frequently—dozens, perhaps hundreds, of times—that the human intellect is immaterial. Yet in spite of its ubiquity throughout Thomas's corpus, the claim remains difficult to understand. Etymologically, "immateriality" obviously has something to do with matter, or rather the lack thereof. At first blush, it seems like "immaterial" should mean the state of lacking matter, or not being composed of matter, or something along these lines. Such superficial articulations of the notion tell us little, though. To understand Aquinas's claim concerning the human intellect, we need an account explaining what he thinks matter is, what *else* he thinks there is, and how he thinks that something else can lack matter. This chapter lays the foundation for such an account.

I begin by examining some of the ways in which Aquinas introduces the notion of matter, together with the corresponding notion of form, in his early work De principiis naturae. As we will see, however, the two most obvious ways to interpret his understanding of matter and form seem not to make provision for things existing immaterially. Aquinas points the way forward, I suggest in the second section, when he claims toward the end of De principiis that "being" (ens) is predicated not univocally, but analogically. Judging by the way that Aquinas unpacks this claim elsewhere, it turns out to mean that being is primarily divided into modes. After explaining in this chapter's third section how Aquinas thinks we recognize the primary divisions among modes of being, I turn in the fourth to why he identifies form or essence as the factor primarily responsible for producing these primary divisions by delimiting or determining an act of being (*esse*) in various ways. That Aquinas understands forms or essences in this way as limiting principles provides the key to understanding how they could be immaterial. In the fifth section, I scrutinize six primary divisions among modes of being that Aquinas recognizes. One is the division between material and immaterial modes of being. Hence, Aquinas's claim about the human intellect turns out to be primarily that it has its act of being in an immaterial mode. Importantly, the immaterial mode of the human intellect's act of being entails that the human soul itself has its act of being in a subsistent mode, which in turn serves Aquinas as a crucial premise in demonstrating the possibility of souls existing apart from bodies. The final section of this chapter considers two important objections against the way I have construed the intellect's immateriality and the soul's subsistence.

Form and Matter in *De principiis naturae*

De principiis is an early work, but because most of the Aristotelian philosophy of nature Aquinas outlines in it carries over throughout his career, it provides a helpful succinct introduction to the notion of matter in relation to a number of others, such as the act of being (*esse*), form, act and potency, substance and accident, generation and corruption, and privation. Here is how he presents the concept of matter in the opening passage of the work:

(1.1) Something can be [*potest esse*] though it is not [*non sit*], but something [else] is [*est*]. That which can be is said to be in potency [*esse potentia*]; that which is already is said to be in act [*esse actu*]. But the act of being is twofold [*duplex est esse*]: namely the essential or substantial act of being of a thing [*esse essentiale rei sive substantiale*], as for a man to be [*ut hominem esse*], and this is the act of being *simpliciter*. There is, however, another accidental act of being [*esse accidentale*], as for a man to be white [*ut hominem esse album*], and this is a qualified act of being [*esse aliquid*]. That which is in potency to both a substantial and an accidental act of being can be called matter, just as sperm and menstrual blood [is called the matter] of a human, and a human [is called the matter] of whiteness. But [matter] differs in this: matter which is in potency to a substantial act of being is called matter from which, [whereas that] which is in potency to an accidental act of being is called matter in which. Likewise, properly speaking, what is in potency to an accidental act of being is called a subject, but what is potency to a substantial act of being is called matter properly speaking.... Matter [properly speaking] differs from a subject since a subject is what does not have an act of being from what comes to it, but has a complete act of being on its own [*per se*],... while matter [properly speaking] has an act of being from that which comes to it, since it has an incomplete act of being on its own [*de se*].[1]

The infinitive of the Latin verb "to be," *esse*, appears twenty-two times in this passage. Often it clearly just means "to be" or "to exist," but Aquinas also often nominalizes it, as when he says in the second sentence that *esse* is *duplex* (twofold). Here Aquinas means by *esse* roughly "what a being [*ens*] does insofar as it is a being," in the same way that what a runner (*currens*) does insofar as it is a runner is to run (*currere*).[2] I translate *esse* as "act of being" in such cases to capture the term's active connotation, as well as to avoid confusing Aquinas's notion with the value of the existential quantifier, Fregean *wirklichkeit*, or whatever other notions of existence we may today have foremost in mind.[3] By claiming that *esse* is twofold Thomas is indicating that there are two fundamentally distinct ways to have an act of being. There is, first, what Aquinas calls "the essential or substantial being of a thing, as for a man to be": an act of being *simpliciter*. There is also, however, "accidental being, as for a man to be white." This is the act of being something (*esse aliquid*), or more clearly, the act of being in some qualified way. Bypassing for now further

---

1. *De principiis naturae* (hereafter, DPN) 1, in *Sancti Thomae Aquinatis Doctoris Angelici Opera omnia iussu impensaque Leonis XIII P.M. edita* (Rome: Commisio Leonina, 1882–) (hereafter, Leo.), 43:39.1–32.

2. See *Summa contra Gentiles* (hereafter, SCG) 1.98.2, *Sententia super Perihermeneias* (hereafter, In Peri) 1.5.18, and *Expositio libri De hebdomadibus* (hereafter, In DH) 2 for passages in which Aquinas explains the meaning of *esse* in reference to the act of running.

3. Anthony Kenny argues at book length against the coherence of Aquinas's notion of *esse* in *Aquinas on Being* (Oxford: Oxford University Press, 2002). Brian Davies in "Kenny on Aquinas on Being," *Modern Schoolman* 82, no. 2 (2005): 111–29, and Gyula Klima in "On Kenny on Aquinas on Being," *International Philosophical Quarterly* 44, no. 4 (2004): 567–80, defend Thomas against Kenny's criticisms. The literature on Aquinas's notion of *esse* is vast, but see Peter Geach, "Form and Existence," in *God and the Soul* (South Bend, Ind.: St. Augustine's Press, 1969), and Hermann Weidemann, "The Logic of Being in Thomas Aquinas," in *Thomas Aquinas: Contemporary Philosophical Perspectives*, ed. Brian Davies (Oxford: Oxford University Press, 2002), 77–96, for two important discussions of Aquinas's notion of existence in relation to Frege, and Etienne Gilson, *Being and Some Philosophers* (Toronto: PIMS, 1952), for a classic presentation of "existential Thomism."

details of the distinction between the two ways something can have an act of being, we can say that there are two fundamentally distinct kinds of beings (*entia*) corresponding to them, substances and accidents.

Matter, Aquinas says, is "that which is equally in potency to substantial and accidental acts of being." As there are two fundamentally distinct ways for something to have an act of being to which matter is in potency, there are also two fundamentally distinct types of matter. Aquinas calls the kind of matter that can receive a substantial act of being "matter from which," "matter properly speaking," or elsewhere "prime matter," and the kind in potency to an accidental act of being "matter in which" or "a subject."[4]

In the passage immediately following 1.1, Aquinas provides further details about the factors and processes by which matter, which has an act of being in potency, comes to receive an actual act of being:

(1.2) Whence, simply speaking, forms give an act of being [*esse*] to matter.... Just as everything which is in potency can be called matter, so everything by which something has an act of being, whether substantial or accidental, can be called form; just as a human who is white in potency is made white in act by whiteness, and sperm which is a human in potency is made a human in act by the soul. And since form produces an act of being in act, therefore form is called act. But what produces a substantial act of being in act is called a substantial form, and what produces an accidental act of being in act is called an accidental form. Since generation is a movement toward form, a twofold generation corresponds to the twofold nature of form: generation *simpliciter* corresponds to substantial form and generation *secundum quid* [corresponds to] accidental form.... And a twofold corruption corresponds to this twofold generation, namely *simpliciter* and *secundum quid*.... And since generation is a

---

4. To be clear, Aquinas would not regard sperm and menstrual blood as prime matter or "matter properly speaking," even though he speaks of them in passage 1.1 as the "matter from which" a human substance comes to be. Sperm and menstrual blood are the proximate, empirically-specifiable matter that combine to initiate the process of human generation, much like flour is the proximate, empirically-specifiable matter from which bread comes to be. Prime matter is not empirically specifiable, but survives a human's generation as her lowest-level material constituent. Similarly while in 1.1 Aquinas equates "matter in which" with the subject in potency to an accidental act of being, he uses the term differently elsewhere (see *Sententia super libros De generatione et corruptione* [hereafter, *In DGC*] 1.15.4/107) to refer to the empirically specifiable matter belonging to a substance: e.g., the water of a river, the wood of a fire, or the flesh and bone of an organism. See chapter 2, pp. 68–73, for more on the difference between prime matter and empirically-specifiable matter (at various levels).

certain change from not having an act of being or nonbeing into having one and being [*de non esse vel ente ad esse vel ens*],... generation is not produced from just any state of lacking an act of being, but from nonbeing which is being in potency: just as [when] a statue [is generated] from bronze the bronze is a statue in potency, not in act. Therefore for generation to happen three things are required: namely a being in potency, which is matter; and a state of not having an act of being in act, which is privation; and that by which [the matter] comes to be in act, namely form. Just as when a statue is made from bronze, the bronze which is in potency to the statue-shape is the matter, the lack of figure or disposition is called the privation and the shape by which it is called a statue is the form.[5]

Aquinas introduces here form and privation as the remaining two of the three "principles of nature" besides matter to which the title of his treatise refers.[6] Form is that which gives an act of being to matter. Corresponding again to the two fundamentally distinct ways something can have an act of being, there are two distinct kinds of forms: substantial forms by which matter properly speaking receives a substantial act of being, and accidental forms by which a subject receives an accidental act of being. A privation is the lack of form that gives matter its act of being in potency, and is replaced by form in the process of generation. In the reverse process of corruption, a form is lost and replaced by a privation.

Any form can be thought of as a privation and vice-versa. For instance, the redness of a surface could be thought of as a privation of greenness, and vice-versa. Furthermore, just as a surface in itself has no color, but is never without some color, so too matter in itself—matter "properly speaking" or "prime matter"—has neither form nor privation, but is never without them. Aquinas explains:

---

5. DPN 1 (Leo. 43:39–40.32–75).
6. Principles, according to Aquinas, are causal or explanatory factors; indeed the terms "principle" and "cause" are quasi-interchangeable. In the *De principiis* Aquinas explains that "principle" is only said of intrinsic causal or explanatory factors, but is used of the *per accidens* factor privation, whereas "cause" is said both of intrinsic and extrinsic factors, but only of those that are factors *per se*. A privation, according to Aquinas, is only a *per accidens* principle of nature, needed to dispose matter such that a change may occur in it, but does not remain constitutive of a natural entity after it has been generated. As Aquinas puts it, matter and form are principles of being (*esse*), but privation is only a principle of becoming (*fieri*): DPN 2 (Leo. 43:44.44–45); see also Sententia super Metaphysicam (hereafter, In Met) 5.1 and Sententia super Physicam (hereafter, In Phys) 1.13, 1.15, 2.5.

(1.3) Although matter does not have any form or privation in its nature,... nevertheless it is never denuded of form and privation, for it is sometimes under one form and sometimes under another. But it can never have an act of being *per se*, for since it does not have any form in its nature, it does not have an actual act of being (since there is no act of being in act except by a form), but has an act of being only in potency. Therefore whatever has an act of being in act cannot be called prime matter.[7]

Frequently Aquinas says that matter in itself is "pure potency."[8] Matter does not, and indeed could not—even by God's absolute power—exist in act by itself, because for what is wholly potential to be actual would involve an explicit contradiction.[9] Accordingly any matter that we might actually come across exists under some form or privation: "matter is never stripped of privation; for insofar as it is under one form, it has the privation of another, and conversely, as in fire there is the privation of the form of air."[10] When Aquinas writes, "only that matter which is understood without any form or privation, but which is subject to form and privation, is called prime matter, inasmuch as there is no other matter prior to it," the term "is understood" is important.[11] It indicates that prime matter does not in itself have any act of being except in potency, and can be thought of as if it did only by a sort of mental stripping away of every form and privation.[12]

---

7. DPN 2 (Leo. 43:41.109–19).
8. See John Wippel, *The Metaphysical Thought of Thomas Aquinas* (Washington, D.C.: The Catholic University of America Press, 2000), chap. 9, §2, for an extensive list of Aquinas's references to prime matter as *pura potentia*.
9. Aquinas argues for this conclusion in *Quaestiones quodlibetales* (hereafter, QQ) 3.1.1.
10. DPN 2 (Leo. 43:40.20–23).
11. Ibid., ll. 74–78.
12. See *Expositio super librum Boethii De trinitate* (hereafter, In DT) 4.2 for Aquinas's most detailed explanation of how prime matter can be understood by a sort of analogical reasoning. He claims to be following Aristotle, who says in *Physics* 1.7.191a9–12 that we understand prime matter as that which is related to all natural things as wood is related to a bed. The Thomistic doctrine of prime matter as pure potency is highly controversial. See Richard Cross, *The Physics of Duns Scotus* (Oxford: Oxford University Press, 1998), chap. 2, for a helpful presentation of John Duns Scotus's argumentation against matter as pure potency, and Jeffrey Brower, *Aquinas's Ontology of the Material World: Change, Hylomorphism and Material Objects* (Oxford: Oxford University Press, 2014), 30–33, for a defense of Aquinas's position. What Brower points out is that to say prime matter has no actuality through itself is not the same thing as to say it has no actuality whatsoever—that it simply is not real. This is a point other commentators have emphasized as well—see Wippel, *Metaphysical Thought of Thomas Aquinas*, 317, and Brian Leftow,

Now because matter is anything that can receive an act of being, and form is anything by which matter receives an act of being, one way of understanding form and matter is as the truthmaker and referent, respectively, of predications. Matter is any x about which it can be true to say "x is F" and form is whatever F-ness makes "x is F" actually true. The abstract counterpart to any concrete common term that can be predicated of a grammatical subject will be the name of a form. For instance, Aquinas says that whiteness is the form by which a man, who is a subject in potency to being or becoming white, actually is or becomes so. Aquinas's usual ways of characterizing the relation by which form makes matter actual are reception and inherence. Matter receives forms. Forms make matter actual by inhering in it. Klima has called the theory according to which simple predications are true in virtue of inherent forms the "inherence theory of predication." He writes that the theory "can easily be formulated in one sentence: a predicate is true of a thing if and only if the form signified by the predicate in the thing actually inheres in the thing, i.e., if this form, or property of the thing, actually exists."[13] So far as I know Aquinas never expressly states that this is his theory of predication, but Klima cites passages that certainly suggest it, such as the following: "since actuality, which the verb 'is' principally signifies, is generally speaking the actuality of every form, either the act of a substance or an accident, therefore when we want to signify that a certain form or act actually inheres in some subject, we signify it by the verb 'is,' either *simpliciter* or *secundum quid*."[14] Klima argues that this theory was not just Aquinas's, but was widely held in the Middle Ages.[15]

The Aristotelian illustration that Aquinas employs of the three principles of nature at work—the generation of a bronze statue in which the

---

"Souls Dipped in Dust," in *Soul, Body and Survival: Essays on the Metaphysics of Human Persons*, ed. Kevin Corcoran (Ithaca, N.Y.: Cornell University Press, 2001), 120–38, at 137.

13. Gyula Klima, "The Changing Role of *Entia Rationis* in Medieval Semantics and Ontology: A Comparative Study With a Reconstruction," *Synthese* 96, no. 1 (1993): 25–58, at 27; see also Klima's "The Semantic Principles underlying Saint Thomas Aquinas's Metaphysics of Being," *Medieval Philosophy and Theology* 5, no. 1 (1996): 87–141, at 106, and "Aquinas' Theory of the Copula and the Analogy of Being," *Logical Analysis and the History of Philosophy* 5 (2002): 159–76, at 161.

14. In Peri 1.5.22 (Leo. 1:28).

15. See also John Fox, "Truthmaker," *Australasian Journal of Philosophy* 65, no. 2 (1987): 188–207, for the claim that many medieval philosophers viewed forms as truthmakers, and chapter 2 for further discussion.

bronze as the matter, the initial lack of shape as the privation, and the statue-shape as the form—suggests another way of understanding form and matter. The bronze statue is a metaphysical composite of matter, the "stuff" it is composed of, and form is the matter's structure, configuration, or organization. While the statue's form is a static configuration, Stump points out that Aquinas typically conceives of form as dynamic:

It is easiest to approach [Aquinas's] theory of things by beginning with his views about things made out of matter. A macro-level material thing is matter organized or configured in some way, where the organization or configuration is dynamic rather than static. That is, the organization of the matter includes causal relations among the material components of the thing as well as static features such as shape and spatial location. This dynamic configuration or organization is what Aquinas calls "form." A thing has the properties it has, including its causal powers, in virtue of having the configuration it does; the proper operations and functions of a thing derive from its form.[16]

Insofar as they are dynamic principles responsible for organizing, configuring, or structuring material constituents into unified wholes, the forms of Aquinas's hylomorphic composites are something like the "lives" Peter van Inwagen invokes in his answer to what he calls "the special composition question."[17] Accounts like Aristotle's and Aquinas's that appeal in various ways to form and matter as ontological and explanatory principles seem to be increasing in popularity among contemporary metaphysicians. Kit Fine, Mark Johnston, David Oderberg, Kathrin Koslicki, Michael Rea, William Jaworski, Anna Marmodoro, and Robert Koons have all recently put forward views that they call (or that might reasonably be called) "hylomorphic."[18] Contemporary hylomorphists tend, however,

---

16. Eleonore Stump, *Aquinas* (London: Routledge, 2003), 36. I should note that Stump proposes this understanding of form only as it is found in "things made out of matter," and recognizes elsewhere that Aquinas thinks there are other things as well that are not made out of matter.

17. See Peter Van Inwagen, *Material Beings* (Ithaca, N.Y.: Cornell University Press, 1990), chap. 9. Aquinas, it should be noted, thinks of the life of a living thing as its act of being, often repeating that "the act of being of living things is their life"—*esse est vivere in viventibus*—a slogan he traces to *De anima* 2.4.415b13. Only in God's case would Aquinas equate form with life—see *Summa theologiae* (hereafter, ST) 1a.18.1–3.

18. Of the writers I just mentioned, only Oderberg professes interest in developing a view along Thomistic lines—see *Real Essentialism*, x. For reasons that should become clear in this chapter and those that follow, Aquinas's hylomorphism would count alongside

to treat matter as the stuff composing certain objects, and form as their structure, configuration, or organization.

It is easy enough to see how the view of matter and form as referent and truthmaker of predication and as stuff and structure might be combined into a unified account. Accepting that there must be truthmakers in virtue of which true predications are true is usually not taken to imply a commitment to any particular sort of entity playing the truthmaking role. In Aquinas's example, it seems plausible to say that the shape imposed on the bronze makes "the statue is" true. It seems plausible too that the form *whiteness* responsible for making "Socrates is white" true is some structure present in Socrates—perhaps a certain arrangement of pigment molecules in his cells. What is also clear, however, is that whether we understand matter and form as referent and truthmaker of predication, as stuff and structure, or in both of these ways, we still have no coherent means of parsing Aquinas's claim that the intellect is immaterial.

I mentioned an obvious difficulty with the "stuff and structure" view of matter and form in this book's introduction. If the intellect's immateriality means just that it is a structural feature of human beings, as opposed to a material feature, then there is an obvious sense in which we might call it immaterial. It is not matter. Instead, it is a form. Nevertheless, Aquinas thinks the immateriality of the intellect underwrites

---

Marmodoro's and Jaworski's as "staunch" as opposed to "faint-hearted" and unlike Fine's or Johnston's on the criteria Koons sets forth, given his commitment to a robust emergentism (see chapter 3) and a sparse ontology of fundamental substances and powers. See Koons, "Staunch vs. Faint-Hearted Hylomorphism: Toward an Aristotelian Account of Composition," Res Philosophica 91, no. 2 (2014): 151–77; Marmodoro, "Aristotle's Hylomorphism Without Reconditioning," Philosophical Inquiry 36, no. 1–2 (2013): 5–22; Jaworski, Structure and the Metaphysics of Mind: How Hylomorphism Solves the Mind-Body Problem (Oxford: Oxford University Press, 2016); Kit Fine, "Things and Their Parts," Midwest Studies in Philosophy 23 (1999): 61–74; and Mark Johnston, "Hylomorphism," The Journal of Philosophy 103, no. 12 (2006): 652–98. Insofar as Aquinas thinks of forms as dynamic (as opposed to merely static) principles, he could sympathize with those who characterize forms as operations (Marmodoro), processes (Koons), or activities (Jaworski). Nevertheless, he does not share these writers' aversion to thinking of forms as metaphysical parts of substances, and in that respect his view resembles Koslicki's—see The Structure of Objects (Oxford: Oxford University Press, 2008). Unlike Koslicki, however, Aquinas does not think of forms (apart from the divine nature) as perfectly simple, but rather as possessing "virtual" parts, namely the powers that flow from them (see chapter 2 for more on this notion). Oderberg is alone in arguing for the possibility of forms existing apart from matter (see Real Essentialism, section 10.5), although Koons thinks that his view is compatible with this possibility (see "Staunch vs. Faint-Hearted," 172n9).

the further claim that human souls are incorruptible, and capable of surviving in a disembodied postmortem state. As we see in passage 1.2, human souls are the substantial forms that structure some matter into an actual human being. But given our examples so far, structures appear to depend for their existence on having stuff to structure. The statue-shape cannot exist apart from the bronze. At times, when thinking of matter and form as stuff and structure, Aquinas himself seems to rule out the possibility of either existing without the other, as in this passage from the *De principiis*:

(1.4) Matter is also said to be the cause of a form, inasmuch as a form does not exist except in matter. Similarly, form is said to be the cause of matter, inasmuch as matter does not actually exist except through form. Matter and form are mutually related, as the second book of the *Physics* states. They are related to the composite as parts are to the whole and as the simple is to the complex.[19]

Because on the stuff-and-structure view of matter and form they are, as Aquinas says here, "mutually related," it is hard to see how they could possibly exist apart. On most of the contemporary accounts of hylomorphism I listed above, certainly, there cannot be forms existing without matter.

The immateriality of the intellect fares even worse on the "truthmaker and referent of predication" view of form and matter. According to the inherence theory of predication, at least as I sketched it above, if "the intellect is immaterial" is true, then it is true in virtue of some form, immateriality, inhering in some matter, namely the intellect.[20]

---

19. DPN 4 (Leo. 43:44.37–43).

20. To clarify, I am not proposing that the inherence theory of predication as Klima articulates it (or as Aquinas holds it) is committed to this result. Klima's formulation of the theory states just that forms make predictions true by inhering, and does not explicitly mention matter as recipient of inherent forms or referent of predications. Indeed, he explains that the inherence theory is not strictly speaking committed to forms making predications true by inhering in anything at all, but may do so by subsisting, as would be true in the case of "God is just" or "Gabriel is an angel" (see Klima, "Materiality of the Human Soul and Immateriality of the Human Intellect," 170). I will discuss Aquinas's distinction between the inherent and subsistent modes of being later in this chapter. Still, given that Aquinas says the verb "is" signifies the actual inherence of a form in a subject, and elsewhere in his *Perihermeneias* commentary that "a predicate is related to its subject as form to matter" (*In Peri* 1.8.11 [Leo. 1:38]), I think it reasonable to discuss the inherence theory the way I have done above.

But then, it would seem, the intellect turns out to be material after all. The problem leading to this incoherence is that on the inherence theory as I stated it, matter is the referent of *any* predication, leaving no way of speaking about anything lacking it. If the intellect were immaterial, it would be impossible for us to say so.

For reasons such as these, to make sense of what Aquinas meant by calling the intellect immaterial we must go beyond the conceptions of form and matter suggested by the opening chapter of the *De principiis*. To do so, the best place to begin is with the last chapter of the treatise, where Aquinas pronounces explicitly on an idea we have already seen in some of the passages, namely that there are multiple ways for something to have an act of being—an idea sometimes called "the analogy of being."

"Being" as Analogical

The notion that an act of being can be had in multiple different ways is present at least tacitly in the first two passages from the *De principiis*. In 1.1, Aquinas distinguished between substantial and accidental acts of being. In 1.2, Aquinas's view is that form, matter, and composite all share the same act of being, but have it in different ways: the statue itself has it as that which exists, the statue-shape has it as that by which the statue exists, and the bronze has it as that which is in potency to receiving it from the statue-shape. In the last chapter of the *De principiis* Aquinas further elaborates the notion that being is analogical:

(1.5) Certain things are the same [*idem*] numerically, like Socrates (when Socrates is being pointed at) and this man. Others are diverse numerically but the same specifically, like Socrates and Plato, who, although they are the same in human species, nevertheless differ numerically. Further, certain things are different specifically, but the same generically, like a human and a donkey, which are the same in the genus animal. Still others are diverse generically but the same only according to an analogy, like substance and quantity, which do not agree in any genus but are similar only analogically; for they are alike only in being. Being [*ens*] is not a genus, however, since it is predicated not univocally, but analogically.[21]

---

21. DPN 6 (Leo. 43:36.5–18).

Aquinas denies here that being is one in the numerical sense that I am one human being and you are another, or in which Parmenides might affirm "there is only one thing." Nor, however, is it one in the way that humanity is one kind of thing of which you and I are individual members, or that animality is one kind of thing of which humanity and asininity are subordinate kinds. Instead, being is one analogically. Aquinas says things which are the same analogically are the same "according to a proportion, a comparison, or agreement."

Analogy is primarily a semantic notion for Aquinas. When he talks about analogy, he typically talks about analogical predication, contrasting it with univocal and equivocal predication. In the last chapter of the *De principiis* Aquinas says that by claiming that beings are the same according to analogy, he means just that "being" is predicated analogically: "being ... is predicated analogically; and this is what we meant when we claimed that substance and quantity differ generically but are analogically the same."[22] He contrasts analogy with univocity and equivocity by comparing the ways in which a term corresponds to its *ratio*, or definition, and its objects. A predication is univocal "when something is predicated according to the same name and the same *ratio*, that is, definition, in the way that 'animal' is predicated of a man and a donkey."[23]

An equivocal predication is "when something is predicated of different things according to the same name but diverse *rationes*, as when 'dog' is said of a barking thing and a star."[24] An analogous predication, however, involves predicating some common term of different things "which have diverse *rationes* but that are related to some one thing."[25] The "one thing," or primary analogate, to which analogously common things are related can be some one end, some one activity or some one subject. For example, borrowing Aristotle's example, Aquinas notes that we predicate "health" of a healthy animal, a healthy urine sample, and healthy food. Although the term is predicated of urine as a sign of health, the animal as the subject of health, and the food as the cause of health, still "all of these *rationes* are attributed to one end, namely

22. DPN 6 (Leo. 43:47.57–62).
23. Ibid., ll. 21–24.
24. Ibid., ll. 27–30.
25. Ibid., ll. 33–35.

health."²⁶ Again, the term "medical" is said of the doctor who operates by the art of medicine, of the midwife who operates without the art of medicine and even of the instruments a doctor or a midwife might use in their operations, all by attribution to one sort of activity, in this case the art of medicine. On the other hand, Aquinas tells us:

(1.6) At other times, however, many things [are analogically the same] by attribution to one subject, as "being" [*ens*] is said of substance, quantity, quality, and the other categories. For it is not from entirely the same reason [*ratio*] that substance [is called] a being that quantity and the others [are called beings]. All the others are called beings inasmuch as they are attributed to substance, which is their subject. Therefore "being" is said first [*per prius*] of substance and only secondarily [*per posterius*] of the others. And therefore being is not the genus of substance and quantity, since no genus is predicated primarily and secondarily of its species, but ["being"] is predicated analogically.²⁷

So "being" is said of the substantial act of being as its primary analogate and of its other modes only secondarily. Just as urine and food are called healthy in different ways based on the different relationships they bear to a healthy animal, so too "being" is said of its *secundum quid* modes based on the different relationships they bear to the substantial act of being, that is, being *simpliciter*, which accords with what we saw in passage 1.1.

Aquinas's view that "being" is an analogical term was controversial in his day and remains so. What is usually called "ontological pluralism"—the view that there are different "ways of being"—has attracted some contemporary support, but remains a minority position.²⁸ So it is worth saying something about Aquinas's reasons for denying that being is a genus. Working in the Porphyrian tradition of Aristotelian logic, Aquinas holds that a genus is divided into species by the addition of a difference. For example, on the "Porphyrian Tree" the genus substance

---

26. Ibid., ll. 40–41; see *Metaphysics* 4.2.1003a33–b11.
27. DPN 6 (Leo. 43:46–47.42–60).
28. See Joshua Spencer, "Ways of Being," *Philosophical Compass* 7, no. 12 (2012): 910–18, for an introduction to contemporary ontological pluralism. Jason Turner and Kris McDaniel are its leading proponents; see Turner "Ontological Pluralism," *Journal of Philosophy* 107, no. 1 (2010): 5–34, and McDaniel, "A Return to the Analogy of Being," *Philosophy and Phenomenological Research* 81, no. 3 (2010): 688–717.

is divided into the species body and spirit by the differentiae quantified and unquantified, the genus body was held to be divided into the species living body (organism) and nonliving body by the differentiae animate (i.e., ensouled) and inanimate, and so on.[29] A difference added to a genus specifies it, or in other words, tells us the definition of some species: the answer to the question "what is it?" So the answer to the question "what is a body?" is "a material substance," and the answer to "what is a living thing?" is "an animate body." Aristotle used the convoluted phrase *to ti ên einai* to refer to what is signified by the answer to this "what is it?" type of question. Aquinas uses the equally convoluted *quod quid erat esse* or along with simpler terms like *essentia, quidditas, natura,* or *forma*.[30]

The reason why "being" cannot be the name of a genus is that a genus cannot be predicated of a difference, whereas "being" can be predicated of anything whatsoever. A genus cannot be predicated of a difference because if it were, then that difference would then fail to divide the genus into distinct species—it would fail to differentiate or specify. For example, if it could be said that "animate is a body," then saying that "an organism is an animate body," would do no more than to say "an organism is a body body," which is nonsense, and could in any case be said equally well of a nonliving thing. As Aquinas puts it, "a difference does not participate in a genus, [but] lies outside the essence of a genus."[31] On the other hand, being can be predicated of anything whatsoever that

---

29. See Porphyry, *Isagoge* 7–10 and 21–22 in Paul Vincent Spade, *Five Texts on the Mediaeval Problem of Universals* (Indianapolis, Ind.: Hackett, 1994), 2 and 4. Jonathan Barnes explains how the notion of Porphyry's tree originated in the Middle Ages in *Porphyry* (Oxford: Oxford University Press, 2003), 108–12. Note that Porphyry neither mentions what differentiates body from the other specific branch of the "tree" opposed to it under the genus substance, nor what this other species is named. Medieval philosophers would generally agree that spirit is opposed to body, but might disagree about the relevant differentiae. I have listed the differentiae of body and spirit as quantified and unquantified, rather than as material and immaterial, because, as I will explain near the end of the present chapter, some medievals denied that spirituality and materiality are mutually exclusive.

30. See *De ente et essentia* (hereafter, DEE) 1 for an explanation of the ways that *quod quid erat esse, essentia, forma, natura* and *quidditas* are related to one another. Bernard Lonergan, *Verbum: Word and Idea in Aquinas* (Notre Dame, Ind.: University of Notre Dame Press, 1967), 16–25, has a helpful discussion of the terminology Aquinas uses to render Aristotle's various terms signifying essence.

31. *In Met* 5.9.889 (Marietti 238).

is. Outside of being is nothing, and nothing cannot be a difference.[32] Hence being cannot be a genus.

It was a closely related line of reasoning, Aquinas believed, that persuaded the Eleatics to adopt monism. Through Aristotle, Aquinas was acquainted with Parmenides's and Melissus's rejection of multiplicity and change. Parmenides held, according to Aquinas, both that there is only one thing (that the only true thing one can say is "the one is") and that the one is immobile "since it would not have anything by which it would be moved, nor would there be anything outside of it by which it would be moved."[33] Aquinas says that Parmenides based his view on the following argument: "Besides being there is only non-being, and non-being is nothing. Therefore besides being there is nothing. But being is one. Therefore, besides the one there is nothing."[34] Aquinas agrees with Parmenides that being cannot be diversified like a genus is, by the addition of differences. But he also thinks it perfectly clear that Eleatic monism is false. Aquinas rehearses some of Aristotle's arguments against Parmenides's position and reasoning in his commentary on the *Physics*, but he concludes them with the summary statement: "against those who deny principles there can be no unqualified demonstration which proceeds from what is more known simply."[35] Here he is echoing Aristotle's remarks in *Metaphysics* IV about how to deal with those who reject the principle of noncontradiction. Evidently Aquinas regards the principle of bivalence and the falsity of Parmenidean monism as equally certain, and as certain in the same fundamental way. But this leaves him needing an answer to the following question: if being is neither a genus divided into species by the addition of differentiae, nor is numerically one, how is it diversified?

The short answer is that being is primarily diversified into various modes, which stand in relations of priority and posteriority to one another much like analogical terms do.[36] I take this to represent the core of

---

32. See ibid. and In Met 3.8.433, *Sententia super Posteriora analytica* (hereafter, In PA) 2.6–7, and DEE 2 for texts in which Aquinas elaborates Aristotle's arguments against being as a genus. For Aristotle, see Topics 4.1.122b20.
33. In Phys 1.6.2/37 (Leo. 2:19).
34. In Met 1.9.138 (Marietti 41).
35. In Phys 1.3.5/24 (Leo. 2:13).
36. See John Tomarchio, "Aquinas's Division of Being according to Modes of Existing,"

Aquinas's "doctrine" of the analogy of being. On closer inspection, however, the question itself turns out to be complex. One question is what distinct modes of being there turn out to be. Another question is how we manage to uncover whatever distinctions among modes of being there are. A further question is what explanatory factors are responsible for distinguishing being into these modes. I will not attempt an exhaustive survey of Aquinas's answer to the first question, although I will discuss six important divisions among modes of being that Aquinas recognizes. First, though, I will venture answers to the second and third questions raised here.

Identifying the Modes of Being

In response to the question about our ability to recognize accurately whatever divisions among modes of being there turn out to be, Aquinas's opinion is that we do so primarily by attending to the ways we talk. In his commentary on *Metaphysics* V, for example, immediately after dismissing the possibility that being is divided like a genus into species for the reason I outlined above, Aquinas writes:

(1.7) Being [*ens*] must then be narrowed down [*contrahatur*] to diverse genera on the basis of a different mode of predication, which flows from a different mode of being; for being is signified, i.e., something is signified to be, in just as many ways (or in as many senses) as we can make predications. And for this reason the classes into which being is first divided are called categories [*praedicamenta*], because they are distinguished by different ways of predicating.[37]

Aquinas is commenting here on the way we recognize and discuss the divisions of being, as opposed to the factors actually responsible for dividing it thus. We recognize these divisions by attending to the ways we make predications. How might this work? Aquinas continues:

(1.8) Therefore, since some predicates signify what (i.e., substance); some, of what kind; some, how much; and so on; there must be a mode of being corresponding to each type of predication. For example, when it is said that a man is an animal, "is" signifies substance; and when it is said that a man is white,

---

Review of Metaphysics 54, no. 3 (2001): 585–613, for analysis of Aquinas's division of being into its modes as an answer to Parmenides's problem.

37. *In Met* 5.9.890 (Marietti 238).

"is" signifies quality; and so on. For it should be noted that a predicate can be referred to a subject in three ways. This occurs in one way when the predicate states what the subject is, as when I say that Socrates is an animal; for Socrates is the thing which is an animal. And this predicate is said to signify first substance, i.e., a particular substance, of which all attributes are predicated. A predicate is referred to a subject in a second way when the predicate is taken as being in the subject, and this predicate is in the subject either ... absolutely and as something flowing from its matter, and then it is quantity; or as something flowing from its form, and then it is quality; or it is not present in the subject absolutely but with reference to something else, and then it is relation. A predicate is referred to a subject in a third way when the predicate is taken from something extrinsic to the subject...[38]

The ellipsis at the end of this passage represents the remainder of Aquinas's explanation of how different subject/predicate relations in sentences reveal nine distinct categories of accidents. A (probably) slightly earlier parallel treatment in the *Physics* commentary offers a somewhat different explanation of how to "derive" the ten Aristotelian categories by paying attention to the ways that we talk.[39] This suggests to me that the precise details of Aquinas's derivations are less important than the general strategy. Indeed, elsewhere in his *Metaphysics* commentary Aquinas appears to suggest that a similar approach—attending to various ways we call things "beings"—yields up a different, fourfold division among modes of being:

(1.9) Just as the above-mentioned terms have many senses, so also does the term "being." Yet every being is called such in relation to one first thing, and this first thing is not an end or an agent, as in the foregoing examples, but a subject. For some things are called beings, or are said to be, because they have being of themselves, as substances, which are called beings in the primary and proper sense. Others are called beings because they are affections or properties of substances, as the proper accidents of any substance. Others are called beings because they are processes toward substance, as generation and motion. And others are called beings because they are corruptions of substances; for corruption is the process toward non-being just as generation is the process toward substance. And since corruption terminates in priva-

38. Ibid., 5.9.890–92 (Marietti 238–39).
39. In Phys 3.5.15/322.

tion just as generation terminates in form, the very privations of substantial forms are fittingly called beings. Again, certain qualities or certain accidents are called beings because they are productive or generative principles of substances or of those things which are related to substance according to one of the foregoing relationships or any other relationship. And similarly the negations of those things which are related to substances, or even substance itself, are also called beings. Hence we say that non-being is non-being, and this would not be possible unless a negation possessed being in some way.[40]

The "above-mentioned terms" are "health" and "medical," the same examples of analogical terms we saw Aquinas employ in the *De principiis*. Just as attending to the way we call things healthy shows that health has one primary and at least two *secundum quid* modes, Aquinas claims here that we find at least four general modes of being. Primary among these is the substantial mode of being, being *simpliciter*, which Aquinas describes as "the one which is the most perfect, namely, what has in being in reality without any admixture of privation, and has firm and solid being inasmuch as it exists of itself."[41] Next there is the mode of being of accidents, which Aquinas says "admits of no admixture of non-being, yet is still an imperfect kind of being, because it does not exist of itself but in something else."[42] Finally, there are two modes of being that Aquinas says "exist only in the mind because the mind concerns itself with them as kinds of being while it affirms or denies something about them."[43] One of these, "which is the most imperfect," consists of negations and privations. The other, which "by reason of its imperfection comes close to [that of negations and privations]," consists of "motions toward or away from actuality, that is, generations and corruptions." The three *secundum quid* modes of being are related to its primary mode either by being in substance (as accidents are), by tending toward substances or accidents (as motions do) or by removing some substance, accident, or motion (as negations and privations do). More on what these modes of being involve below. For now, what is important to note in 1.9 is that Aquinas again seems to arrive at his fourfold list by focusing on

40. In Met 4.1.539 (Marietti 152).
41. Ibid., par. 543.
42. Ibid., par. 542.
43. Ibid., par. 540.

the various ways we call things "beings." It seems correct to say, as John Wippel puts it, that "as Thomas sees things, supreme and diverse modes of predication ... ultimately follow from and depend upon supreme and diverse modes of being. It is for this very reason that Thomas thinks we can discover these supreme modes of being by proceeding in the opposite direction, as it were, that is, by beginning with diversity in the mode of predication."[44]

Now, as Wippel hastens to note, we should not misunderstand Aquinas's reliance on language to uncover modes of being as supposing that we can simply read off kinds of beings from the structure of language. Indeed, this is essentially the error Thomas repeatedly criticizes Plato for making: supposing that because we talk or think about universals there must really exist universals, themselves by themselves, separated from the realm of particulars.[45] Certainly Aquinas would not agree that there is nothing more to ontological debate than linguistic analysis. Furthermore, as far as I can tell, he did not intend his "derivations" as any sort of rigorous proof that there are so many, and no more, modes of being. Instead, I think he would say that once we have grasped roughly what divisions of being there are by paying attention to the ways we discuss them, we will then be in a position to work towards a finer-toothed metaphysical analysis of the ways they are related to one another, and the factors responsible for producing them.[46] I turn next to this latter issue.

---

44. John Wippel, "Thomas Aquinas's Derivation of the Aristotelian Categories," *Journal of the History of Philosophy* 25, no. 1 (1987): 13–34, at 18. See also Paul Symington, "Thomas Aquinas on Establishing the Identity of Aristotle's Categories," in *Medieval Commentaries on Aristotle's Categories*, ed. Lloyd Newton (Leiden: Brill, 2008), 119–44, for another examination of Aquinas's "derivation" of the categories. William McMahon offers a broader look at the history of medieval *sufficientiae*—that is, passages like 1.8 that attempt to show the completeness of Aristotle's categorial scheme—in "The Medieval Sufficientiae: Attempts at a Definitive Division of the Categories," *Proceedings of the Society for Medieval Logic and Metaphysics* 2 (2002): 12–25. Herbert McCabe offers a compelling commonsense explanation of Aquinas's procedure in "Categories," in *Aquinas: A Collection of Critical Essays*, ed. Anthony Kenny (Garden City, N.J.: Anchor Books, 1969), 54–92. Many of Aquinas's successors rejected the notion that we can deduce general categories of being by paying attention to the ways we talk; see Giorgio Pini, "Scotus's Realist Conception of the Categories: His Legacy to Late Medieval Debates," *Vivarium* 43, no. 1 (2005): 63–110, for one example of such a view. Symington defends Aquinas's overall strategy at book length against criticisms like Scotus's in *On Determining What There Is: The Identity of Ontological Categories in Aquinas, Scotus and Lowe* (Frankfurt: Ontos Verlag, 2010).

45. See In Met 7.1.1252–55 for an extensive consideration of the ways abstract and concrete modes of signifying need not correspond to distinct abstract and concrete objects.

46. I suspect Aquinas would approve of John Heil's description of the way we make

Form as a Limiting Principle

For Aquinas, form is the factor primarily responsible for determining acts of being into various modes. Wippel proposes that we understand Aquinas's appeal to form in this regard as akin to the Eleatic Stranger's effort in Plato's *Sophist* to commit patricide against father Parmenides by showing how "that which is not" somehow is, insofar as "each part of the nature of the different that's set over against *that which is*."[47] Just as diversity among things in the *Sophist* stems ultimately from receiving "a share of the different," so too Aquinas appeals to a composition relation—in which an act of being is received into a form—as what fundamentally explains diversity among the ways things exist. As Wippel puts it, Aquinas regards form as a "principle of relative non-being" that limits or determines the act of being that it receives.[48] No single text I know of sets out this view in so many words, but we can come to a grasp of Thomas's thought on these matters by comparing a few different passages.

First, Wippel cites a question from Aquinas's late-1250s commentary on Boethius's *De trinitate* which reflects on the claim that "otherness is the principle of plurality" (*principium pluralitatis alteritas est*). Thomas agrees that it is, but offers the following as explanation of what Boethius's claim amounts to:

(1.10) It cannot be that one being is divided from another insofar as they are both beings, for nothing is divided from being except non-being. Whence one being is only divided from another insofar as within the one being the negation of the other being is included.... Hence it is clear that the primary reason or principle for plurality or division stems from negation and affirmation, so

---

progress in metaphysics: "We begin, as we must, with a common-sense conception of the universe that treats billiard balls as substances, property-bearers, and redness and sphericity as properties of billiard balls. In pursuing the idea of substances as bearers of properties, however, we come to recognize that the common-sense conception contains the seeds of its own revision, revision in light of empirical discovery, revision in light of what we determine to be the deep story about billiard balls." *The Universe as We Find It* (Oxford: Oxford University Press, 2012), 7.

47. See *Parmenides* 258e in Plato, *Complete Works*, ed. John Cooper (Indianapolis, Ind.: Hackett, 1997), 282, and Wippel, *Metaphysical Thought of Thomas Aquinas*, 189.

48. Wippel, *Metaphysical Thought*, chap. 6, §§3–4; see also Wippel's "Thomas Aquinas on the Distinction and Derivation of the Many from the One: A Dialectic between Being and Nonbeing," *Review of Metaphysics* 38, no. 3 (1985): 563–90.

that we must understand the order of the origin of plurality in the following way: first being and non-being are understood, from which the first divided beings are constituted, and through this [follows] their plurality. Whence just as unity is immediately found following upon being insofar as it is undivided, so too the plurality of the first simple beings is immediately found following upon the division of being and non-being. The notion of diversity, moreover, follows upon this plurality insofar as there remains in it the power of its cause, namely the opposition of being and non-being. For indeed one of many items is called diverse in comparison with another since it is not that.[49]

If we recall what Aquinas took to be the basic structure of Parmenides's argument against multiplicity, we can see that this is precisely the problem he is engaged with here. The Eleatic argument took the form of a dilemma. If there is more than one being—two beings, say—then the one being must differ from the other either insofar as they are beings or not. But one being cannot differ from another insofar as they are beings, for insofar as they are both beings they are identical. Nor can one being differ from another in any other way, for insofar as they are *not* beings they are nothing, and whatever is distinguished by nothing is identical as well. Here Aquinas's strategy is to grasp the second horn of this dilemma. Parmenides is right that one being cannot be divided from any other insofar as they are both beings. Instead, "divided beings" differ from one another because they are somehow composed of being and nonbeing. Within any one such "divided being" the negation of any other being must somehow be included; any such being must possess some principle of not-being any other. To be sure, however, whatever else we may say about this principle of nonbeing, it cannot be absolute nothingness whatsoever. Parmenides is surely correct that absolute nothingness cannot possibly differentiate one being from another. Instead, this differentiating factor is a principle of nonbeing only *relative* to anything else. In this passage Aquinas does not identify the principles of relative nonbeing fundamental to his explanation of multiplicity as forms; he simply argues that the root cause of multiplicity is some sort of composition between being and (relative) nonbeing.

It is instructive, then, to consider Aquinas's reply to Parmenides alongside another set of passages, in which Thomas argues that the act

---

49. In DT 4.1 (Leo. 50:120–21.96–100 and 122–31).

of being itself, absolute and unlimited, can only be one.[50] In the early treatise *De ente et essentia*, for example, Thomas explains this view as follows:

(1.11) If we posit some thing that is just the act of being alone, so that it is the act of being subsisting by itself, this act of being would not receive the addition of a difference since then it would not be just the act of being alone, but rather the act of being and in addition a certain form. Much less would it receive the addition of matter, since then it would not have a subsistent but a material act of being. Whence we must conclude that such a thing which is [identical to] its own act of being can only be one. Whence it is also necessary that in any other thing its act of being must differ from its quiddity or nature or form.[51]

Ignoring for now Aquinas's remark about matter and a material act of being, his main idea in the rest of the passage is that the factors which "add" the difference between one being and another are forms (which he says here we can also call quiddities or natures). It takes the "addition" of a form to an act of being to get many things. Hence an act of being subsisting just by itself can only be one. Aquinas's reasoning here does not require that there actually exist an act of being that subsists just by itself. His view is simply that *if* there existed such an absolute, unlimited act of being, there could only be one such. He does then quickly go on to argue in the *De ente* that such an act of being does in fact exist, namely, "the first cause, which is God."[52] So he holds that anything other than God himself—any creature—is composed of an act of being, on the one hand, and a form, nature, quiddity, or essence (to add one further term he uses), on the other.

Immediately after 1.11 in the *De ente* Aquinas makes clear that this goes even for the spiritual creatures that he usually calls angels or (here) intelligences: "it is necessary that in intelligences their act of being is in addition to their form, so it is said that an intelligence is both form and act of being."[53] Even though Aquinas is happy to call angels and

---

50. See SCG 1.42 and 2.52, ST 1a.11.3, and *Tractatus de substantiis separatis* (hereafter, TDSS) 8 for further passages arguing for this conclusion.
51. DEE 4 (Leo. 43:377.113–23).
52. Ibid., l. 146.
53. Ibid., ll. 123–26.

intelligences "simple substances" elsewhere, here he is acknowledging in them a certain sort of composition between their act of being and their form or essence, which limits or determines their act of being in some particular way.[54] An angel's form or essence is in potency, he says, with respect to the act of being that it receives from God, its creator. In fact an angel simply is a form or essence—Gabriellity, say—limiting or determining the act of being in a particular way.[55] Accordingly, we could regard an angelic essence as nonbeing both relative to God, the absolute unlimited act of being, and also relative to the act of being it receives from God.

Putting together what Aquinas says in 1.10 and 1.11, we can see that one fundamental conception of form in Thomas's thought is as a delimitation or determination of an act of being. To be sure, not every form must limit or determine an act of being by receiving it or being added to it in a composition relationship. There is one form, God, who is simply identical to the absolute, unlimited act of being itself. But Wippel is right to describe creaturely forms or essences as principles of relative nonbeing in at least three senses: relative to God, relative to the act of being they receive from him, and relative to one another. Aquinas notes in his *De trinitate* commentary that "one primary thing created might imitate [its creator] in a way in which a second [primary thing created] fails to, and might fall short in a way in which the second primary created thing succeeds in imitating [its creator], there can thus be found many first effects in any of which is found a negation both of its cause and of the other effect."[56] The idea is that because any given creaturely form

---

54. It is worth noting here that while Aquinas frequently speaks of "composition" between form or essence and act of being, some commentators read this as metaphor, denying that he thinks there is a real distinction between the two in creatures. See Brower, *Material World*, 17, and Francis Cunningham, *Essence vs. Existence in Thomism: A Mental vs. the "Real" Distinction?* (Lanham, Md.: University Press of America, 1988). Wippel, *Metaphysical Thought of Thomas Aquinas*, chap. 5, offers a literal interpretation of Aquinas's texts on composition between act of being and form or essence.

55. At least, this is the picture one garners from passages like *Scriptum super libros Sententiarum* (hereafter, *In Sent*) 2.3.1.1, DEE 4, QQ 9.4.1, SCG 2.50, ST 1a.50.2, and *Quaestio disputata de spiritualibus creaturis* (hereafter, QDSC) 1 in which Aquinas argues against hylomorphic composition in angels. QQ 2.2.2, dating probably from 1269 or 1270, complicates matters, because Thomas argues that there is a distinction between nature and *suppositum* in all creatures, including angels.

56. In DT 4.1 (Leo. 50:120.111–15).

or essence will delimit or determine the act of being in its own peculiar way, composition between act of being and form as relative nonbeing can explain both how creatures differ from their creator and how they differ from one another.

It is important to point out here that even if form plays the fundamental role for Aquinas explaining how being becomes divided, there remains a crucial respect in which form cannot be what accounts for the difference between one creature and another, namely, at the level of differences between individuals of the same kind. That is because Aquinas appeals to form or essence not only to explain how creatures differ from God and from one another, but also to explain kind-membership. An individual donkey is a member of its kind, donkeys, in virtue of possessing an asinine form or essence. He likewise accounts for same-kind-membership in terms of the co-possession of form or essence. Two donkeys, Blackie and Brownie, are members of the same donkey-kind in virtue of their possessing the same asinine form or essence. If these things are so, then Aquinas cannot very well appeal to asininity to explain how Blackie and Brownie differ from one another as individual members of donkey-kind. Instead, as is well-known, Aquinas appeals to matter as the factor responsible for distinguishing individuals of the same species. A typical formulation of his thesis that matter is the principle of individuation of forms is this: "things which agree in species but differ in number agree in form but are distinguished materially."[57] Accordingly, any creature that is, or can be, an individual member of a species is composed not just of a form or essence and an act of being, but also of its essence and the matter responsible for individuating it.

Anything lacking matter—such as God or an angel, on Aquinas's view—cannot be an individual member of a kind, but this does not mean that God or angels are themselves kinds as opposed to individuals.[58]

---

57. ST 1a.50.4 (Leo. 5:10).

58. In Thomas's terminology, the angel Gabriel is a *suppositum* or *subsistentia*, but is not a *res naturae*, because he does not "underlie some common nature, as, for example, an individual man is a thing of a human nature" (ST 1a.29.2 [Leo. 4:331]). The same is true of God. Aquinas is, at times, content to call simple substances like angels particulars or individuals. See, for instance, ST 1a.76.2 ad 3: "Separate intellects are subsistent substances, and consequently particulars" (Leo. 5:217) and *De unitate intellectus contra Averroeistas* (hereafter, DUI) 5: "separated substances, therefore, are individual and singular, but they are individuated not by matter but by the fact that it is not in their nature to exist in another and consequently to

I am not sure we have a good term today for entities that are neither individual members of a kind, nor are common to many such individuals. At any rate, according to Aquinas if there were no entities whose forms or essences were individuated by matter, there could be no creaturely kinds. Any creature would be diverse in kind from every other. Aquinas's certainty that there are in fact some creatures that belong to the same kind is one fundamental reason he has for thinking there must be some material entities.[59]

Returning to Wippel's phrase "principles of relative non-being," it turns out that for Aquinas there are in fact two such principles. Aquinas's primary explanation for the division of being into diverse modes appeals to forms or essences delimiting an act of being. But Thomas also appeals to matter-form composition to explain how some forms or essences are further determined at the individual level. Wippel cites a passage from Aquinas's *Tractatus de substantiis separatis* that nicely illustrates his two-tiered approach to the problem of Parmenides:

(1.12) If, when I say "non-being" I remove only the act of being in act, a form considered in itself is non-being, but rather participates in an act of being. If, however, [saying] "non-being" takes away not only the act of being in act but also the act or form through which something participates in an act of being, in that case matter is non-being, whereas a subsistent form is not non-being, but is an act which is a form that participates in the ultimate act, which is the act of being.[60]

---

be participated in by many" (Leo. 43:311.71–72). He is also willing to say that God is an individual. He thinks Boethius's definition of "person" as "an individual substance of a rational nature" is fittingly said of God (ST 1a.29.1 and 3), and explains that even though God is a pure self-subsisting form, he is individuated because he cannot be received into anything else (ST 1a.3.2 ad 3). But he cannot mean in these passages that angels or God are individual members of kinds, because he argues that there cannot be more than one angel of a given species (see QDSC 8, ST 1a.50.4), and that God is not contained in any genus whatsoever (ST 1a.3.5). Strictly speaking God is not even a substance, as Gilson explains in "*Quasi definitio substantiae*," in *St. Thomas Aquinas 1274–1974: Commemorative Studies*, ed. Armand Maurer et al. (Toronto: PIMS, 1974), 1:111–29.

59. His other fundamental reason stems from his analysis of change. There must be some material entities because things in the world change, and for things to change something (matter) must persist through the loss of one form and acquisition of another. See Wippel, *Metaphysical Thought of Thomas Aquinas*, 296–312, for a comparison of Aquinas's two reasons for positing matter-form composition, and Brower, *Material World* for an excellent examination and defense of Aquinas's reasoning based on the phenomenon of change.

60. TDSS 8 (Leo. 40:D55.236–44).

So, form is a principle of nonbeing relative to the act of being it receives and enters into composition with, whereas matter is nonbeing relative to the form through which it receives an act of being. I will say more about Aquinas's appeal to form to explain kind-membership and matter to explain individuation in the next chapter. For now, having garnered some understanding both of how Aquinas believes we discover the basic divisions among modes of being and of the factors responsible for dividing being into modes, we are now in a position to survey some of divisions among the modes of being Thomas thinks there are, including the division between materiality and immateriality.

Divisions among Modes of Being

We can demarcate most of these divisions fairly precisely by attending to the various ways beings are related to their acts of being, their form, and their matter. It will be useful, however, to begin with one division in being that Aquinas regards as mind-dependent.

Sometimes Aquinas refers to this as a division between real being (*esse reale*) and rational being (*esse rationis*). In the *De ente* he introduces it as follows:

(1.13) As the philosopher says in book five of the *Metaphysics* "being *per se*" is said in two ways: in one way as it is divided into ten genera, but in another way as it signifies the truth of propositions. The difference between these [two senses of "being *per se*"] is that in the second way anything can be called a being about which an affirmative proposition can be formed, even if this posits nothing in reality. In this way privations and negations are called beings, for we say that affirmation is the opposite of negation and that blindness is in the eye. But in the first way only that which posits something in reality can be called a being, whence in the first way blindness and things of this sort are not beings.[61]

If we recall the modes of being Aquinas mentioned in passage 1.9, he claimed that both privations and negations are beings. Here we get a more complete explanation how this is so. When we say "Homer is blind" or "Socrates is not a donkey," the "is" in both cases signifies simply that the propositions in question are true, not that something such

---

61. DEE 1 (Leo. 43:369.1–13).

as Homer's blindness or Socrates's non-asininity exists in reality. When we say "Socrates is sighted" or "Brownie is a donkey," in contrast, we are positing something in reality, namely Socrates's power of vision or Brownie's asininity. Aquinas holds that "is" in the first sense, which he states here "is divided into ten genera," *also* signifies the truth of a proposition. As Thomas puts it elsewhere:

(1.14) Whatever things are called beings in the first sense are beings in the second sense, for everything that has a natural act of being in things can be signified to exist through an affirmative proposition, as when it is said that color exists or a man exists. But not all things that are called beings in the second sense are beings in the first, since an affirmative proposition can be formed about a privation like blindness, as when it is said that blindness exists, even though blindness is not anything in the nature of things, but is rather the removal of something. And thus privations and negations are called beings in the second sense but not in the first.[62]

So "being" in the "ten genera" sense has a wider scope than "being" in the "truth of a proposition" sense, as the former includes the latter but not vice-versa. Call the former "real being" and the latter "rational being." That things like Homer's blindness exist in the second sense but not the first gives us one reason for thinking that Aquinas subscribes to a "sparse" rather than "abundant" theory of properties.[63] Contemporary metaphysicians sometimes think of abundant properties as "grounded in" the sparse properties which "cut nature at its joints."[64] Aquinas seems to hold something similar when it comes to real and rational being. Commenting on the same passage from Aristotle's *Metaphysics* that he mentions in 1.13, Thomas says that "the second [rational] sense of 'being' is related to the first [real sense of 'being'] as effect to cause, for because something is so in the nature of things, there follows the truth or falsity of a proposition, which the intellect signifies through this word

---

62. In Sent 2.34.1.1, in *Scriptum super libros Sententiarum*, ed. P. Mandonnet and M. F. Moos (Paris: P. Lethielleux, 1929–47) (hereafter, Mand./Moos), 2:872.

63. The sparse/abundant distinction stems from David Lewis, *On the Plurality of Worlds* (Oxford: Blackwell, 1986), chap. 1, §5.

64. See Jonathan Schaffer, "On What Grounds What," in *Metametaphysics: New Essays on the Foundations of Ontology*, ed. David Chalmers, David Manley, and Ryan Wasserman (Oxford: Oxford University Press, 2009), 347–83, at 375.

'is' which is the verbal copula."⁶⁵ So rational being is dependent partly upon the way things are in reality. It is also, however, mind-dependent, in the sense that without someone capable of judging certain statements to be true, there would be no beings of reason. To be sure, if Homer and everyone else able to note his blindness were suddenly struck incapable of forming judgments, it certainly would not be that Homer could suddenly see. But neither would Homer's blindness exist any longer, for no longer could the true proposition "Homer is blind" be formed, whereas Aquinas holds that "blindness exists in the second [rational] sense insofar as a certain proposition is true, in which it is said that something is blind."⁶⁶ As we will see in the following chapter, one important area where Aquinas invokes rational being is in discussing the ontological status of universals.

As for mind-independent divisions of being, one that we have encountered already is that between God's uncreated mode of being and the created mode of being possessed by everything else. As I explained above, Aquinas held that God alone is identical to the absolute, unlimited act of being itself, whereas any creature merely possesses an act of being that it receives, ultimately, from God as creator.⁶⁷

A second division between modes of real being we also encountered straightaway in passage 1.1 from the *De principiis* was between substantial being, which Aquinas characterized as being *simpliciter*, and accidental being, which he characterized as being *secundum quid*. At times, as in 1.13, Aquinas speaks as though all real beings are either substances or else fall into one of Aristotle's nine genera of accidents. Elsewhere, however, he will deny that this is the case. For one thing, Aquinas denies that God is strictly speaking a substance. He explains that the term "substance" applies only to "what has a quiddity to which it belongs not to have its act of being in something else," and claims that because nothing belongs to God's quiddity (i.e., essence) except the act of being itself, God is not a substance.⁶⁸ As God certainly is not in any category of ac-

---

65. *In Met* 5.9.896 (Marietti 239).
66. Ibid.
67. See *In Sent* 1.36.1.3 ad 2 and ST 1a.18.4 ad 3, where Aquinas explains that creatures have an uncreated act of being insofar as they exist as ideas in the mind of God, but a created act of being insofar as they exist in themselves.
68. Aquinas says that God has a substantial act of being, as opposed to an accidental

cident either, he is not in a genus at all.⁶⁹ A way of expressing Aquinas's thought on these matters would be to say that anything which *possesses* a substantial act of being is a substance, while God, who *is* his substantial act of being, is not. Hence Aquinas says that his description of substance as "what has a quiddity to which it belongs not to have its act of being in something else" is only a "quasi-definition." Complicating matters further, various other passages indicate that Thomas thinks a substantial act of being is something that can be had incompletely, namely by parts of a substance. Aquinas indicates that this is the case regarding body parts like hands or feet. He also holds that the substantial forms of material substances, such as the human soul, have a substantial act of being incompletely. To have a complete substantial act of being precludes being a part of something else.⁷⁰

A further class of real beings that lack either a substantial or an accidental act of being are those that Aquinas call beings *per accidens*, as opposed to beings *per se*. Thomas contrasts the substantial/accidental and *per se/per accidens* distinctions as follows:

(1.15) One being is so-called *secundum se* while another is so-called *secundum accidens*, but it should be known that this division of being is not the same as that division by which being is divided into substance and accident, which is clear since according to that last division being *secundum se* divides into the ten categories, of which nine are in genera of accidents. Therefore being is divided into substance and accident according to an absolute consideration, just as whiteness considered in itself is called an accident and man a substance. But

---

act of being, but denies that he is a substance. Whatever is in a genus like the category substance has its act of being in a way determined to that genus, but the divine act of being is not determined in any way. Everything that is in a genus, he says, has a quiddity that differs from its being. But God's quiddity is identical to the act of being itself. The definition of "substance," therefore, if it can be said to have one (Aquinas calls it a "quasi-definition" at In Sent 4.12.1.1.1 ad 2), is not just "being that is not in a subject," but rather "a thing having a quiddity to which it is given or belongs not to exist in something else" (In Sent 1.8.4.2 ad 2 [Mand./Moos 1:222–23]). God does not have his being in something else as his subject, but neither does he *have* a quiddity of the sort just described; his quiddity is just the act of being itself. So technically speaking, God is not a substance. See SCG 1.25 for further argumentation in support of the same claim. Aquinas is not always very careful about remembering this point. More often than not he will say that whatever has a substantial act of being is a substance. See Gilson, "Quasi Definitio," and Wippel, Metaphysical Themes, chap. 7, §3, for more on Aquinas's "quasi-definition" of substance and denial that God is a substance.

69. SCG 1.25, ST 1a.3.5, and *Compendium theologiae* (hereafter, CT) 12–13.
70. See In Sent 3.6.1.1.1 ad 1, ST 1a.29.1 ad 5, 75.2 ad 1, 75.4 ad 2.

being *secundum accidens* must be understood by combining an accident with a substance, and this combination is signified by the verb "is" when it is said "the man is white." Whence this whole "the man is white" is a being *per accidens*. Whence it is clear that the division of being *secundum se* and *secundum accidens* is based on the fact that one thing is predicated of another *per se* or *per accidens*, but the division of being into substance and accident is based on the fact that something is either a substance or accident in its very nature.[71]

Any attribution of being *per accidens* must involve an accident because if only predicates in the category of substance are involved, for instance in "a man is an animal," we are really just saying that a man exists, that is, we are predicating being *per se*. The way Aquinas describes *per accidens* being as "based on the fact that one thing is predicated of another" may sound similar to his characterization of rational being above as partly mind-dependent. In fact, however, he means simply that beings *per accidens* are always composed of a substance plus at least one accident, and that the names we give them typically involve predicating an accident of a substance. For instance, when we call someone a musician, we are predicating an accident—an ability to make music—of a certain human being. This person might have the ability to make music whether or not any minds were around to note the fact.[72] But it is true that most of the beings *per accidens* to which we give names like "musician" are those that are especially relevant to our interests. It may in many cases be a good question whether we are dealing with a *per se* or *per accidens* being. Artifacts such as the bronze statue in passage 1.2 would seem to represent one important instance of being *per accidens*, though just how to understand Aquinas on artifacts is controversial.[73] In any case, it is important

---

71. In Met 5.9.885 (Marietti 237–38).

72. The "musician" example is Aristotle's (see *Metaphysics* 5.7), but perhaps obscures the point at hand, as presumably if there is a person capable of making music, then there does indeed remain a mind capable of noting this fact. Perhaps "songbird" or "drafthorse" would be better illustrations.

73. Does Aquinas think that any artifacts are substances? Should he have thought so, given his criteria for substancehood? He frequently issues what appear to be blanket denials that any artifacts are substances, for example in DPN 1: "all artificial forms are accidental" (Leo. 43:40.79). But he also often refers to certain apparent artifacts, such as bread, as substances. A few important contributions to the literature surrounding these issues include Stump, *Aquinas*, 39–44, and "Substance and Artifact in Aquinas' Metaphysics," in *Knowledge and Reality*, ed. T. M. Crisp, M. Davidson, and D. Vander Laan (Dordrecht: Springer, 2006), 63–79; Brower, *Material World*, chap. 9, §4; Michael Rota, "Substance and Artifact in Thomas Aquinas," *History*

not to confuse the distinction between substantial and accidental modes with the distinction between *per se* and *per accidens* modes of being.

It is also important not to confuse the substantial/accidental division with a further distinction Aquinas draws between subsistent and inherent modes of being. While all substances do indeed have their act of being in a subsistent mode, it is not just substances that have this mode of being. In fact, Aquinas recognizes at least one miraculous case of accidents with a subsistent mode of being—namely, the accidents of consecrated eucharistic elements.[74] Nor do only accidents have an inherent mode of being, some substantial forms do as well. Aquinas frames the distinction between the subsistent and inherent modes of being in the following passage:

(1.16) This act of being [i.e., a real act of being, as opposed to a rational one] is attributed to something in two ways. In one way as to something that properly and truly possesses an act of being, or exists [*proprie et vere habet esse vel est*], and in this way it is attributed only to substances subsisting *per se*. ... But everything that does not subsist *per se*, but rather in another and with another, whether they are accidents or substantial forms or whichever parts, do not have an act of being in such a way that they truly exist, but an act of being is attributed to them in another way, that is, as that by which something exists [*quo aliquid est*], just as whiteness is said to exist not because it subsists in itself, but because by it something is white. An act of being is therefore properly and truly attributed only to a *per se* subsisting thing.[75]

The contrast is between the subsistent mode of being of something that "properly and truly" exists and the inherent mode of being of that *by which* a subsistent entity has one of its substantial or accidental acts of being. Because, as Aquinas claimed in 1.2, anything by which something has an act of being is a form, only forms have an inherent mode of being. Hence, even though Aquinas says in 1.16 that any parts (*quaelibet partes*) of something have an inherent mode of being, he typically treats body parts like hands and feet as subsistent rather than inherent.[76] Ac-

---

of Philosophy Quarterly 21, no. 3 (2004): 241–59; and Ben Page and Anna Marmadoro, "Aquinas on Forms, Substances and Artifacts," *Vivarium* 54, no. 1 (2016): 1–21.

74. See In Sent 4.12.1.1.1, ST 3a.77.1, SCG 4.65, QQ 7.4.3.
75. QQ 9.2.2 (Leo. 25.1:94.47–59).
76. ST 1a.75.2 ad 2.

cidental forms are the most obvious case of entities with an inherent mode of being; Aquinas points out in 1.16 that whiteness exists not in itself, but rather as that by which something else is white. He also notes, however, that the substantial forms of composite substances, despite having substantial acts of being, are for the most part inherent entities. Brownie the donkey's substantial form is that by which Brownie exists, rather than something existing in its own right. The substantial form of a simple substance like the angel Gabriel, in contrast, is subsistent because it simply *is* Gabriel, as opposed to inhering in prime matter as that *by which* Gabriel exists. We might roughly characterize the difference between the substantial/accidental distinction and the subsistent/inherent distinction by saying that the former is a distinction between existence full-stop versus existence as a qualification or modification of something, whereas the latter is a distinction between independent existence versus existence dependent on being *in* or *on* or *of* something else. This characterization is rough, however, insofar as most subsistent (and hence "independent") entities are still clearly dependent on other things for their continued existence. Hands and feet, which Aquinas supposes to have subsistent acts of being, are certainly in a clear sense dependent on the whole animals of which they are parts. Indeed, there is a clear sense in which nothing whatsoever with a created mode of being is independent of God; creatures depend on God both for their coming into existence in the first place, and for their preservation.[77]

So far we have surveyed five basic divisions Aquinas recognizes among modes of being:

(a) Between real and rational being.
(b) Between uncreated and created being.
(c) Between substantial and accidental being.
(d) Between *per se* and *per accidens* being.
(e) Between subsistent and inherent being.

We are now in a position to consider a final basic division, namely:

(f) Between immaterial and material being.

---

77. See *Quaestiones disputatae de potentia Dei* (hereafter, QDP) 3.1 and 5.1.

I said at the outset of this chapter that etymologically "immateriality" looks like it should refer to the state of lacking matter. And that is certainly what Thomas believes. But we are now in a better position to see what sorts of things might fit the description "lacking matter." Certainly matter itself does not. But neither, on Aquinas's view, do composite entities with matter as one of their constituent parts. Nor do forms that inhere in matter, such as the substantial forms of composite substances. Nor, finally, do forms that inhere in a matter-form composite, such as most accidental forms of composite substances. Hence, something may have a material mode of being either by being matter, being composed of matter, or inhering in matter. What is left? Forms, of various other sorts. God himself, who is the form or essence identical to the absolute, unlimited act of being itself, exists in an immaterial mode. So too do subsistent substantial forms or essences such as angels. Aquinas's view is that certain accidental forms exist in an immaterial mode as well, however, provided that they inhere in another form, rather than inhering in a substance composed of form and matter. As we will see in considerably further detail, this last situation is precisely what Aquinas takes to be the case with the human intellect: it is an accidental form inhering directly in the human soul, rather than in the human being as a whole. Consequently, the human intellect has its act of being in an immaterial mode. This is what Aquinas primarily means by asserting its immateriality.

Immaterial Intellect and Subsistent Soul

Recognizing that Aquinas's claim regarding the human intellect's immateriality is primarily a claim about the mode in which it has its act of being serves as an important first step towards clearing up some of the perplexing questions I mentioned in this book's introduction. To do so, it was important to move beyond the "referent-and-truthmaker" and "stuff-and-structure" views of matter and form, and appreciate Thomas's understanding of form as a principle delimiting the act of being into various analogously related modes. Yet having done so, we are some way from understanding how the human intellect's immaterial mode of being relates to its operating independently of any bodily organ or underwrites the possibility of human souls existing in a disembodied state. Furthermore, the referent-and-truthmaker and stuff-and-structure notions of matter and form from the *De principiis* surely *do* reflect something important about Thomas's understanding of the two hylomorphic principles. Hence, it will be important to clarify in the following chapter how form construed as a principle delimiting acts of being into various analogously related modes relates to form as truthmaker of a predication or form as structure of a hylomorphic composite. It will also be important to clarify what soul-body relations are involved in Aquinas's conception of the human intellect as immaterial.

Before turning to these tasks, however, I will conclude this chapter by noting an important implication of the human intellect's immaterial act of being, namely the human soul's subsistent act of being. As I noted above, for something to subsist in Aquinas's sense does not require that it be a complete substance. Hands and feet subsist, but are only parts of complete substances—the animals to whom they belong. Instead Aquinas characterizes subsistent beings as those which exist independently in their own right, as opposed to merely inhering in something else as that by which their inherent subject exists. For something to subsist, in Aquinas's mind, it suffices that it be itself the subject of inherent forms. Hands and feet meet this criterion in Thomas's estimation. So too does the human soul, due to the human intellect's immateriality. As just noted, Aquinas believes the human intellect is immaterial because it has as its immediate subject another form, the human soul. Accordingly the human soul has its own inherent forms, and exists as a subsistent entity in its own right.

Now to be sure Aquinas also holds that the human soul also exists as an inherent entity; on his view it is the substantial form by which the human being herself exists. Hence human souls are, to adopt Eleonore Stump's excellent phrase, "metaphysical amphibians."[78] Aquinas expresses this idea in several places by quoting Proclus's line from the *Liber de causis* about human souls existing somehow "on the horizon" between time and eternity.[79] Because of the way Aquinas understands subsistence and inherence, there is nothing obviously contradictory about

---

78. Stump, *Aquinas*, 17.
79. See *Expositio super librum De causis* (hereafter, *In DC*) 2 and *SCG* 3.61. Aquinas also often speaks of human souls existing "on the borderline" (*confinio*) between bodies and spiritual substances: see *Quaestio disputata de anima* (hereafter, *QDA*) 1, *ST* 1a.77.2, *SCG* 2.68, etc.

the notion of something possessing an act of being in both modes at once. Nevertheless, the notion has met resistance from several different quarters both in his day and in more recent scholarship. Consider two different styles of objection, one targeting Aquinas's conception of created forms subsisting without matter, the other attacking Aquinas's claim that human souls might *both* subsist and inhere at once.

First, Aquinas's notion that a form—the human soul—might itself be the immediate subject of a further form—the human intellect—was opposed by a prominent medieval view of the relationship between matter and form usually known today as "universal hylomorphism." Despite its name, the view was not that everything is composed of matter and form, but rather that every subsistent creature is. According to this view, matter is the principle of potentiality and form of actuality—across the board. Anything in potency to receiving a form must itself be a material subject, rather than a form alone. Hence human souls and angels, which are subject to the intellect, must be composed of matter and form. God is the only subsistent entity to lack hylomorphic composition, because he is not subject to receiving any forms, but is rather identical to all of his attributes. Bonaventure offers the following concise bit of reasoning for the human soul's hylomorphic composition: "Anything created that has its own proper operation has two diverse components, namely that which acts and that by which it acts, but the [human] soul considered in itself has its own proper operation [i.e., the operations of the intellect], so it seems that it cannot be form alone, since if it were pure form, then it would act itself by itself. Therefore it has some matter."[80]

Bonaventure argues for hylomorphic composition in angels in similar fashion. To be sure, the sort of matter Bonaventure thought human souls and angels possess is different than the sort possessed by ordinary material objects like the bronze statue from 1.2. It is "spiritual" as opposed to "corporeal" matter. Accordingly, it does not extend the objects to which it belongs with spatial dimensions, so that they remain empirically undetectable. It also is not in potency to receiving any other substantial forms, so that angels and human souls remain incapable of corruption by the replacement of their form with some other. Universal

80. Bonaventure, In Sent. 2.17.1.2, in Opera omnia, ed. Collegium S. Bonaventurae (Ad Aquas Claras: Ex Typographia Collegii S. Bonaventurae, 1882–1902), 2:414.

hylomorphism was defended chiefly by Franciscans in the thirteenth century, beginning most likely with Alexander of Hales, but including Roger Bacon, John Peckham, and Richard of Mediavilla, among others.[81] Its proximate source was unquestionably the eleventh-century Jewish philosopher Ibn Gabirol's (or Avicebron's) work *Fons vitae*, but its proponents often claimed that it derived from the teaching of both Augustine and Boethius.

Perhaps in part because of its supposedly impressive pedigree, Aquinas took universal hylomorphism seriously, and works hard to show how his own view can meet the concerns of its proponents.[82] He thinks there are good reasons for denying that human souls and angels alike have matter, based on their intellectual abilities. As I will consider these arguments at length in chapter 5, I will defer further discussion of them until then. There are further reasons for denying that human souls have matter.[83] But Aquinas is willing to concede that if we want to give the name "matter" to any principle of potentiality whatsoever, we can say that angels and human souls have matter in a sense, provided we keep in mind the difference between their "matter" and the prime matter of corporeal substances. He says:

(1.17) If any two things related to one another as potency to act are called matter and form, nothing keeps us from saying (since there is no power in words) that there is matter and form in spiritual substances. For it is necessary that there be two things in created spiritual substances, of which one is compared to the other like potency to act.[84]

---

81. For more on the history of universal hylomorphism see Odon Lottin, *Psychologie et morale aux XIIe et XIIIe siècles*, vol. 1 (Louvain: Duculot, 1942); James Weisheipl, "Albertus Magnus and Universal Hylomorphism," *Southwestern Journal of Philosophy* 10, no. 3 (1979): 239–60; Richard Dales, *The Problem of the Rational Soul in the Thirteenth Century* (Leiden: Brill, 2005); and Pasnau, "Form and Matter," in *Cambridge History of Medieval Philosophy*, ed. Pasnau (Cambridge: Cambridge University Press, 2010), 357–68. See also Nathan Jacobs, "Are Created Spirits Composed of Matter and Form: A Defense of Pneumatic Hylomorphism," *Philosophia Christi* 14, no. 1 (2012): 79–108, for an interesting contemporary defense of the view.

82. As Anthony Kenny puts it, "Aquinas rejected the theory that the soul was made of spiritual matter, but he did not treat the notion as a plain absurdity. He felt obliged to develop arguments against it, and went to some lengths to spell out the truths which the theory was a misguided attempt to express." *Aquinas on Mind* (London: Routledge, 1993), 139.

83. Aquinas argues, for instance, that if the soul were itself composed of form and matter it would be a complete entity in its own right, and could not serve as the form of a human being; see QDA 6.

84. QDSC 1 (Leo. 24.2:13.357–63).

Aquinas proceeds to recite a line of reasoning much like that found in passage 1.11, explaining why God, the first being, who is identical to the infinite act of being itself, can only be one, whereas anything else that exists must have its act of being received into something that contracts and limits it. Because a spiritual substance "is in potency in relation to its act of being," Aquinas writes, "there is in the spiritual substance a composition of potency and act, and accordingly of form and matter, provided that every potency be named matter, and every act form."[85] Hence, on one way of looking at things, Aquinas's disagreement with the universal hylomorphists is merely semantic. His preference is to say that in spiritual creatures it is the form, essence, nature, or quiddity that serves as the principle of potentiality limiting or determining an act of being, whereas Bonaventure wants to call this limiting principle spiritual matter.

Certainly Aquinas thinks there are reasons for preferring his way of speaking. That there is matter and form in spiritual creatures "is not properly said according to the common use of names."[86] He frequently cites his own Boethian precedent for speaking as he does: the distinction drawn in the Hebdomads between *esse* and *id quod est* (that which something is) in all beings other than God himself.[87] Aquinas thinks it makes sense to speak of a thing's form or essence as that *which* it is (*id quod est*), which stands nonetheless in potency to receiving an act of being (*esse*) from God. It does not make sense, on his view, to speak of matter as that *which* something is, given that matter only exists in potency.

What Aquinas really wants to make sure we keep in mind, however, are the differences between the principles of potency found in spiritual and corporeal creatures. Instead of attacking the notion of spiritual matter directly, Aquinas's discussions of universal hylomorphism often focus on showing that there cannot be "one matter"—one univocal principle of potency—for corporeal and spiritual substances alike. This is precisely the point we saw Aquinas making in passage 1.12, distinguishing between two different "principles of relative non-being." It was also something he and Bonaventure could in principle agree on. Unlike corporeal matter, the "spiritual matter" of human souls and angels does

85. Ibid. (Leo. 24.2:14.403–7).
86. Ibid., ll. 407–8.
87. See In DH 2, SCG 2.52, QDSC 1 ad 8.

not render them spatially extended, and furthermore cannot undergo the loss of a substantial form and its replacement by another. Because of these differences, substances with corporeal matter are in potency in further ways that spiritual substances are not. As Aquinas explains:

> (1.18) In composite things [i.e., substances with corporeal matter] a twofold act and potency must be considered. For first their matter is in potency with respect to their form, and form is its act, but also the nature composed of matter and form is in potency with respect to its act of being, inasmuch as it receives it. Therefore if the foundation of matter is removed and there remains a certain form of determinate nature subsisting in itself, not in matter, this will still be compared to its act of being as potency to act.... And in this way the nature of a spiritual substance which is not composed of matter and form is in potency with respect to its act of being, and thus in a spiritual substance there is composition of potency and act.[88]

As we saw, Aquinas concedes that we can call the potency and act found in human souls and angels matter and form if we so choose, though he thinks this an improper way of speaking. The important point, though, is that there is a "twofold" potency present in composite things that is not found in spiritual substances. Because their matter can undergo the loss of a substantial form and its replacement by another, composite substances are in potency to corruption, while human souls and angels are not. Furthermore, it is because their matter renders them spatially extended that composite substances are empirically detectable and individuated. Angels are neither. As for human souls, they are indeed empirically detectable and individuated, but this is because they are not just subsistent spiritual beings, but also inhere in corporeal matter as the substantial forms of human beings themselves. I will discuss these claims about individuation, empirical detectability, and incorruptibility further in the following two chapters.

A second style of objection pressed both by Aquinas's contemporaries and by more recent critics takes as its target Thomas's claim that human souls have a dual status as both subsistent entities in their own right and as inherent forms by which human beings themselves exist. Unlike Bonaventure, the "Latin Averroist" or "Radical Aristotelian"

---

88. QDSC 1 (Leo. 24.2:14.389–404).

Siger of Brabant was perfectly content with the idea of subsistent, immaterial forms. He also thought that forms of a different kind inhere in prime matter to compose bodily substances. He denied, however, that any single form could belong to both of these kinds. As he puts it:

> The soul has either the nature of a form of matter and the composite, or of a *per se* subsisting form. For the nature of a form is to be that according to which something else exists, just as the nature of composition is to be that according to which something is composed, and the nature of figure is to be that according to which something is configured; whence the nature of a form is something that is united to another; and the nature of composite or of a form freed from matter is to be something existing *per se* and separately, not sharing its existence with something else. From this it is argued thus. When the nature of something ceases, the thing itself is corrupted and no longer exists. But when a material form is separated from matter, its nature ceases, as it apparent from what we just said. No form is material, therefore, unless its separation from matter is its corruption. But the separation of the intellective soul from the body and matter is not its corruption. Therefore it is not united to matter.[89]

If Aquinas wants to say that human souls are forms inhering in matter and bringing about composite substance, that is fine, according to Siger. Similarly, it is fine for Aquinas to say that human souls exist *per se* apart from the body. What Aquinas cannot do is maintain both of these propositions at the same time. Forms that inhere in matter do so as part of their very nature, says Siger, so if a form that inheres in matter ceases to do so, it ceases to exist at all. But because it is equally part of the very nature of subsistent forms to be capable of existing apart from matter, no inherent form can also be subsistent.

More recently, Richard Cross has also argued against the human soul's subsistence along similar lines to Siger's. He cites Aquinas's occasional remarks that the human soul is the form of the body "according to its essence" as support for the claim that there could not be human souls subsisting apart from bodies.[90] If informing a body is essential to

---

89. Siger of Brabant, *Quaestiones de anima intellectiva* 3, in *Siger de Brabant et l'Averroisme Latin au XIIIme siecle*, ed. Pierre Mandonnet (Louvain: Institut Superieur de Philosophie de l'Universite, 1911), 2:151.

90. See Richard Cross, "Is Aquinas's Proof for the Indestructibility of the Soul Successful?," *British Journal for the History of Philosophy* 5, no. 1 (1992): 48–76. Cross cites just ST 1a.76.1

the human soul, then there cannot very well be souls existing without bodies.[91]

Yet Cross himself recognizes exactly what Aquinas's rejoinder to this style of objection is likely to be. When Thomas claims that a soul is "essentially" the form of a body, he is making a somewhat weaker claim than we might suppose. Several times Aquinas likens the soul's "essential" embodiment to the way it is essential for a light body (in Aristotelian physics) to rise up. Just as a helium balloon retains its "aptitude and inclination" to rise up even while tethered to a child's wrist, so too a human soul retains an aptitude and inclination to inform a human body even if it subsists in a disembodied state. Aquinas recognizes that to be disembodied is "unnatural" for a human soul, in the sense that an aptitude pertaining to its nature is going unfulfilled. But he does not think that there is anything strictly impossible about the human soul losing an inherent mode of being while retaining a subsistent one, or about the soul possessing its act of being in both modes at once while it informs the body.[92] Nor does he think weakening the soul's connection to the body as I have just described makes its embodiment merely accidental.[93]

Cross thinks this response of Aquinas's is "partially successful."[94] It succeeds in removing an obstacle to the very possibility of souls both in-

---

arg. 4 and ad 4, but Aquinas claims that the soul is united to the body according to its essence frequently: see *In Sent* 2.1.2.4 ad 4, *Quaestiones disputatae de veritate* (hereafter, QDV) 26.3, SCG 4.79.10, QDA 9 ad 11, etc.

91. Brian Leftow, for his part, is more optimistic about Aquinas's prospects for showing how the human soul might be both "a live immaterial particular" and something informing matter. In "Souls Dipped in Dust" he offers what he calls a "Platonic" way of doing this, by starting with the idea of souls as immaterial particulars, then showing how such things might also inform matter. In a second article, "Soul, Mind, and Brain," in *The Waning of Materialism*, ed. Robert Koons and George Bealer (Oxford: Oxford University Press, 2010), 395–415, he offers an "Aristotelian" way, by starting with souls as "configurational states" (a phrase he gets from Stump) and working toward the view that such states might be living things able to float free from their bearers. The reading of Aquinas I have offered, on which Thomas primarily thinks of forms as delimitations of an act of being, but also thinks such things can inform and structure matter, is more reminiscent of Leftow's "Platonic" approach, although I am not sure that "Platonic" is an appropriate label.

92. Aquinas's most extensive discussion of the soul's dual nature as form and *hoc aliquid* is QDA 1, which B. C. Bazan helpfully discusses in "The Human Soul: Form or Substance? Thomas Aquinas' Critique of Eclectic Aristotelianism," *Archives d'Histoire Doctrinale et Litteraire du Moyen Age* 64 (1997): 96–126. See ST 1a.76.1 ad 6 and 89.1 for Aquinas's comparison of separated souls to light bodies being held down.

93. QDA 1 ad 1.

94. Cross, "Indestructibility," 17–20.

hering in bodies and subsisting apart from them, but it does not provide any positive proof of the human soul's subsistence or "indestructibility." Cross also thinks it makes trouble for Aquinas in terms of explaining how souls are individuated. I will address the individuation of human souls further in the following chapter. As for their incorruptibility, I will examine Aquinas's arguments in chapters 3 and 5. Consider this, then, an initial rejoinder to Siger's and Cross's objection. A more thorough response will require further examination of the way Aquinas thinks human souls inform bodies, together along with his reasons for thinking them capable of subsisting on their own.

2

FORMS AS ESSENCES, STRUCTURES, TRUTHMAKERS, AND POWERS

Readers so far will have noticed that in discussing form as a limiting principle I treated the term as synonymous with essence, speaking at times of "forms or essences" interchangeably. In doing so, I follow Aquinas's own convention. At the beginning of the *De ente*, Aquinas explains how the terms essence, quiddity ("whatness"), nature, or form can all be used interchangeably, though differing in connotation. On the other hand, just a few sentences later in the same work we find Aquinas arguing that the essences of "natural substances" include both form and matter.[1] Clearly the form that is included in a thing's essence cannot be a form in the same sense Aquinas treats as co-referential with a thing's essence. And indeed this is precisely what we find Thomas explaining in his commentary on *Metaphysics* VII, where Aristotle discusses the parts of things and their lógoi, or formulae:

(2.1) Some say that the whole essence of a species is the form alone, so that the whole essence of a human is their soul. And because of this they say that

---

1. DEE 2: "the essence by which the thing is called a being is not just form or just matter, but both, although the form alone is in its own way the cause of an act of being of this sort" (Leo. 43:371.54–57). I will return to Aquinas's claim concerning "the form alone" later in this chapter. We saw evidence of the same view in passage 1.18, where Aquinas mentions "the nature composed of matter and form," that is, the form, nature, essence, or quiddity of a composite substance.

the form of the whole [forma totius], which is signified by the word "humanity," is the same in reality [secundum rem] as the form of the part [forma partis], which is signified by the word "soul," and that the two differ only according to reason [secundum rationem], for the form of the part is so-called because it perfects matter and makes it exist in act, but the form of the whole [is so-called] because through it the whole composite is located in a species. And for this reason they think that no material parts are posited in the definition indicating the species, but only the formal principles of the species. This seems to be the opinion of Averroes and certain of his followers. But this seems to be contrary to Aristotle's intention, for he says in book six above that natural things have sensible matter in their definition, and that they differ in this regard from mathematical things.... So sensible matter is part of the essence of natural substances, not only as regards individuals but also their species, for definitions are not given to individuals but to species. Whence there is another opinion that Avicenna follows, and according to this the form of the whole, which is the quiddity of a species, differs from the form of the part as whole [differs] from part; for the quiddity of a species is composed from matter and form, though not from this individual form and this individual matter. Rather an individual like Socrates or Callias is composed from these. And this is Aristotle's opinion in this chapter ... that it is impossible for there to be species of natural things without sensible matter, like a human without flesh and bone, and likewise for the others.[2]

Aquinas's terminology here—"form of the whole" versus "form of the part," "sensible matter" versus "individual matter" versus non-individual matter—can certainly confuse. But clarifying the relationship between the various principles Thomas discusses here provides a useful entry point both to clarifying the various metaphysical roles that Aquinas assigns to forms—limiting principles, truthmakers, structures, etc.—and to explaining how the souls of living things relate to their bodies. These are my chief aims in this chapter. Its ultimate goal is to provide readers an initial understanding of how Aquinas thinks certain parts of souls—psychological powers, such as the intellect—relate to the organic parts of living bodies.

At least four things are immediately worthy of note in passage 2.1. First, it is form in the "form of the whole" sense that Aquinas identifies

---

2. In Met 7.11.1467–69 (Marietti 358). See also In Phys 2.3.6/163 and 2.5.4/179.

with a composite substance's essence or quiddity, and which he says includes sensible matter, though not individual matter. Second, while forms in the "form of the whole" sense are responsible for placing individuals in their respective kinds, it is an individual's "form of the part" that "perfects" her matter such that it exists in act.[3] Third, the term "soul" signifies a form in the latter sense. Fourth, both forms and matter can be both individual and non-individual.

I will begin this chapter by considering in its first two sections the sense in which Aquinas thinks of forms and matter as individual versus non-individual: his views on what are often called the problems of universals and individuation. This is important not only to establish correctly Aquinas's understanding of the human soul as our substantial form, but also because Thomas's theories of universals and individuation loom large in debates concerning the argument for the human intellect's immateriality that I will consider in chapter 5. I then examine in the chapter's third section the relationships between forms of the whole, forms of the part, and souls, along with their corresponding types of matter. This will allow us to see more clearly in the fourth section how Aquinas thinks forms serve as truthmakers, and in the chapter's final section how the powers of composite substances serve as substructures of their bodies.

Universals

In the *De ente* immediately after arguing (much as he does in passage 2.1) that the essence of a hylomorphic composite includes both form and matter, Aquinas considers as a possible objection the individuating role matter plays vis-à-vis forms. Because matter is the principle of individuation, he says, "it might seem to follow that an essence that included both matter and form at the same time would be particular only, and not universal."[4] This would appear to pose a problem, he notes, given that definitions signify essences, yet only universals, not particulars, have definitions. The problem is merely apparent, however, as the sort of matter that individuates forms—designated matter (*materia signata*)—

---

3. More precisely speaking, this distinction between the functional roles played by forms of the whole versus forms of the part features in the Averroist view that Aquinas rejects in passage 2.1. I will discuss shortly the extent to which Thomas himself accepts it.

4. DEE 2 (Leo. 43:371.67–70).

is not included in a hylomorphic composite's essence, but rather only non-designated matter: "bone and flesh absolutely," as opposed to "this flesh, and these bones." Hence, Aquinas says, "the essence of man and the essence of Socrates differ only according to the designated and non-designated."[5] I will return to what Aquinas means by designated matter in the next section. First, however, in what sense does Aquinas think of essences as universals?

This is not easy to say. Difficulties stem partly from differences between the way medieval scholars framed debates about universals and the way we do today. They also stem from things Aquinas himself has to say on the topic, which can seem at times difficult to reconcile. Many of Aquinas's commitments make him sound like a realist regarding universals. As mentioned in the previous chapter, Aquinas appeals to form or essence to explain kind-membership. In 2.1 he seems to indicate that an individual is located in its species through its "form of the whole." But because multiple individual composite substances frequently belong to the same species, it seems that Aquinas must grant the possibility of multiple individuals sharing the same form in common. He frequently does refer to essences like "human" as "common natures."[6] Indeed, it is because essences are somehow common or non-individual in reality that he thinks their individuation must be explained. He claims that forms in themselves are "communicable," that is, "able to be received by many things."[7] All this makes Thomas's forms or essences sound very much like universals. And indeed we find Aquinas stating several times explicitly that "every form, in itself, is universal."[8]

On the other hand, Aquinas rejects in no uncertain terms what he takes to have been the Platonic view of universals. Plato, Aquinas thought, held that "because a species [such as humanity] is predicated of individuals [i.e., individual men], there must be a common human, who is human-in-himself, existing by himself, and who is a substance [*hoc aliquid*], i.e., something subsistent which can be pointed to and is

---

5. Ibid., ll. 85–87.
6. Joseph Owens lists a number of these references in "Common Nature: A Point of Comparison Between Thomistic and Scotistic Metaphysics," *Mediaeval Studies* 19, no. 1 (1957): 1–14, at 14n24.
7. *In Sent* 1.19.4.2 (Mand./Moos 1:483); see *In Sent* 1.4.1.1 and *In Peri* 1.10.6.
8. QDV 2.5 (Leo. 22.1/2:62.260); see also QDV 10.5 and QQ 8.1.3.

separate from sensible things."[9] Aquinas subjects this view to a barrage of Aristotelian objections in his *Metaphysics* commentary and elsewhere. He declares that "universals do not subsist outside the soul," and indeed that "universals do not have any existence whatsoever outside the soul."[10] Outside the soul (we would more likely say "outside the mind" today) there exists no human, for instance, that is common to many, but rather humanity is called a species only insofar as we consider it in certain of our intellectual operations.[11] Claims like this make Aquinas sound more like a nominalist than a realist.

To make sense of Aquinas's view, it is helpful first to recognize something of its Boethian and Avicennian background. Aquinas follows Avicenna in drawing a three-way distinction between natures (i.e., forms or essences) considered absolutely, natures as they exist in the soul, and natures as they exist in singular things. In the first of these ways, a nature is considered "according to its own proper notion" and hence "nothing is true of it except what pertains to it as such." Aquinas's example is humanity. Because its definition is "rational animal" only rationality and animality pertain to humanity when considered absolutely. Having a particular color, in contrast, falls outside the "proper notion" of humanity, and hence it would be false to ascribe whiteness or blackness to the nature considered this way. The same goes for universality and singularity. Avicenna had argued that "if [a nature like animality] were universal in itself ... no animal could possibly be singular; rather every animal would be universal."[12] On the other hand, "if animal from the fact that it is animal were singular, it would be impossible for there to be more than one singular, viz. the very singular to which animality is bound."[13] Aquinas takes over the same line of reasoning to argue that

---

9. *In Met* 7.14.1593 (Marietti 383).
10. SCG 2.75.8 (Leo. 13:474.27–28) and *In Sent* 2.17.2.2 ad 4 (Mand./Moos 2:433).
11. Strictly speaking, Aquinas insists that it is not humanity, the essence signified as a part, that is a species and hence a universal, but rather human, the essence signified as a whole, namely as including implicitly its designation by matter under particular dimensions—see DEE 3. But Aquinas also frequently refers to humanity as a species, and I will follow his usage.
12. Avicenna, *Logica* 3, in *Opera philosophica* (Venice, 1508), fol. 12a, trans. Martin Tweedale in *Basic Issues in Medieval Philosophy*, ed. Tweedale and Richard Bosley (Peterborough: Broadview, 2006), 371.
13. Ibid.

a nature considered absolutely is neither one nor many, neither in the mind nor in singular things and neither universal nor singular. Despite denying that natures considered absolutely are common to many things (as he does, for example, in passage 2.2 below), Aquinas follows standard medieval practice in calling them "common natures."[14]

Thomas follows Avicenna and Boethius alike in ascribing universality only to natures existing in the soul. Boethius had written that "species is to be regarded as nothing else than the thought gathered from the substantial likeness of individuals that are unlike in number."[15] As they exist in singular things, natures are themselves singular. They resemble what metaphysicians today call tropes, or abstract particulars.[16] As such, they are sensible, and we gain initial cognitive access to them with our senses. But the intellect "by divisions and abstractions and taking away from the things they exist in" is able to arrive at a "likeness gathered from the single things they exist in." For example, "from single men, dissimilar among themselves, the likeness of humanity is gathered," and this likeness "thought by the mind and gazed at truly" is the species, that is, the nature as a universal.[17] Avicenna, similarly, held that "the abstracted form" in the intellect "by one and the same definition pertains to many particulars" and that "in this respect it is universal."[18] As for the abstraction process, he explains that "you first represent the form ... in your imagination," then "if afterwards the intellect removes the accidents from its content, this very abstracted form will be acquired in [your] intellect."[19] Aquinas agrees that universality is a product of intellectual abstraction:

---

14. See Brower, "Aquinas on the Problem of Universals," *Philosophy and Phenomenological Research* 92, no. 3 (2016), 715–35, at 720n10, for a brief discussion of the origins of the term "common nature" in medieval philosophy.

15. Boethius, *Second Commentary on Porphyry's Isagoge*, par. 31, in Spade, *Five Texts*, 20–25, at 25.

16. Natures existing in singular things *resemble* contemporary tropes in their particularity and in that they belong to individual substances. But given the divergences between versions of trope theory on offer it would be misleading to suggest that Thomas embraces any of them fully.

17. Ibid., pars. 29–30.

18. Avicenna, *Metaphysics* 5.1, in *Liber de Philosophia Prima sive Scientia Divina V–X*, ed. S. Van Riet (Leiden: Brill, 1980), 237.

19. Ibid., 238.

(2.2) It cannot be said that the notion of universal belongs to a nature taken [absolutely], since unity and community pertain to the notion of a universal, but neither of these pertains to human nature according to its absolute consideration. For if community belonged to the understanding of a human being, then wherever humanity would be found, community would also be found. But this is false, since in Socrates no community is found, rather whatever is in him is individuated. It cannot be said that the notion of genus or species accrues to human nature according as it exists in individuals, because human nature is not found in individuals according to a unity such that it would be some one thing belonging to all, which the notion of a universal requires. So it remains that the notion of species accrues to human nature as it exists in the intellect. For human nature exists in the intellect abstracted from all individuating [conditions], and therefore it has a uniform relation to all individuals outside the soul, inasmuch as it is equally the similitude of all and leads to the cognition of all inasmuch as they are men. And since the nature has such a relationship to all individuals, the intellect forms the notion of species and attributes it to the nature.[20]

For now the precise mechanics of intellectual abstraction are unimportant, though I will have more to say about the process below, especially in chapter 5. At present what is important is that for Aquinas a universal is an essence *considered* insofar as it can be possessed by many distinct individuals. It is a being of reason in the sense I discussed in the previous chapter—it is true to say that "humanity is a universal" only in the truth-of-a-proposition sense dependent on a mental act of considering something a certain way.

Treating universals as beings of reason might again make Aquinas sound like a nominalist. So too might his declaration that natures considered in Avicenna's first way—that is, absolutely, or in themselves—do not exist. Thomas writes:

(2.3) Natures have a twofold act of being, one in singulars and another in the soul, and according to each certain accidents accrue to the aforesaid nature. And in singulars they have manifold acts of being according to the diversity of singulars, and nevertheless none of these acts of being is owed these natures according to the first consideration—namely the absolute one. For it is false to say that the essence of a human insofar as it is of this sort has an act of be-

---

20. DEE 3 (Leo. 43:374.73–99).

ing in this singular, since if having an act of being in this singular belonged to a human insofar as they are human, there could never be [humanity] beyond this singular. Similarly even if it belonged to a human insofar as they are human not be in this singular, [humanity] could never be in them.... Therefore it is clear that the nature of a human absolutely considered abstracts from any act of being whatsoever, though not in such a way as to exclude any of them.[21]

Some commentators have celebrated this move of Aquinas's—denying any act of being to natures absolutely considered, though in such a way as not to exclude any act of being attaching to them accidentally—as an important theoretical development that advanced Aquinas's view of universals beyond Avicenna's (and which later thinkers like Scotus failed to appreciate).[22]

Other readers of Aquinas express consternation on precisely this point. Nicholas Wolterstorff, for instance, asks how, if human nature = the nature of Socrates, and likewise human nature = the nature of Plato, Aquinas can deny that the nature of Socrates = the nature of Plato.[23] How can it be that there exists no nature common to Socrates and Plato alike? Even worse for Aquinas, as Paul Spade points out, is the fact that Thomas relies on natures considered absolutely to do real metaphysical work for him: the common nature "is supposed to ground the objectivity of knowledge; it is supposed to be the justification for the fact that we predicate the same term 'man' of Socrates and Plato without being arbitrary about it. These are not trivial theoretical tasks. And yet we are asked to entrust them to a complete non-entity!"[24] Spade charges Aquinas with violating what he calls "the Principle of Philosophical Fair Play."[25] It is certainly true that Aquinas relies on common natures to

---

21. Ibid., ll. 52–70.
22. See especially Owens, *Common Nature*, and Jorge Gracia, "Cutting the Gordian Knot of Ontology: Thomas's Solution to the Problem of Universals," in *Thomas Aquinas and His Legacy*, ed. D. Gallagher (Washington, D.C.: The Catholic University of America Press, 1994), 16–36.
23. Nicholas Wolterstorff, *On Universals: An Essay in Ontology* (Chicago: University of Chicago Press, 1970), 146.
24. Paul Spade, "Degrees of Being, Degrees of Goodness: Aquinas on Levels of Reality," in *Aquinas's Moral Theory: Essays in Honor of Norman Kretzmann*, ed. Eleonore Stump and Scott MacDonald (Ithaca, N.Y.: Cornell University Press, 1999), 254–76, at 270.
25. Ibid., "the idea is that if, in your philosophical thinking, you appeal to something to do a certain theoretical task for you, then it is only 'fair' to grant that something some kind of

perform the metaphysical work Spade highlights; we saw in 2.1 that it is through their form or essence that Socrates and Plato are both located in the human species and hence correctly called "human." Can Thomas's position evade Wolterstorff's and Spade's criticisms? Commentators have seemingly disagreed about Aquinas's best available response.

Spade himself thinks that "whether he likes it or not" Aquinas must grant some degree of being and unity to natures considered absolutely on pain of outright incoherence, and thus that "his metaphysical commitments are much closer to Duns Scotus's than has generally been thought."[26] Sandra Edwards agrees, claiming that "Aquinas turns out to be almost as strong a realist as Duns Scotus," and indeed that "Duns Scotus can perhaps be seen as offering a solution to some of the difficulties that remain unresolved in Aquinas."[27]

Brian Leftow, in contrast, thinks Aquinas is a trope nominalist. Wolterstorff is mistaken, Leftow claims, in thinking that Aquinas would equate the nature of Socrates with human nature *simpliciter*.[28] For Aquinas, rather, the nature of Socrates = Socrates's human nature, which is an instance of human nature individualized by Socrates's designated matter. Similarly the nature of Plato ≠ human nature *simpliciter*, but rather Plato's human nature. Hence Socrates's human nature ≠ Plato's human nature, even though Socrates and Plato are both human. When Aquinas states that "a nature in itself is common" he does not mean that there exists a certain unified thing, human nature. Instead, what Aquinas means is that a certain sort of relation—the "same-species-as" relation—supervenes upon Socrates's human nature, Plato's human nature, and all the other human natures there are as its bases.[29] Socrates's human nature, Plato's, and all others are tropes, individualized by inhering in designated matter. Similarly, Socrates's height and Plato's are tropes for Aquinas, individualized by inhering in their substantial subjects. But if Socrates's height is 5'1" and Plato comes to be 5'1" as well,

---

'ontological status' in your theory. After all, if it is not even there, it can hardly do any serious work, solve any philosophical problems for you. In short, the basic idea is *no pay, no work*."

26. Ibid., 273.

27. Sandra Edwards, "The Realism of Aquinas," in *Thomas Aquinas: Contemporary Philosophical Perspectives*, ed. Brian Davies (Oxford: Oxford University Press, 2002), 97–116, at 97 and 112.

28. Brian Leftow, "Aquinas on Attributes," *Medieval Philosophy and Theology* 11, no. 1 (2003): 1–41, at 23.

29. Note that this is an "internal relation."

a relation—equality—immediately supervenes, with the two heights as its base. So too when Aquinas says that "a nature in itself is common" he means simply that each nature-trope "is intrinsically apt to subvene a same-species-relation."[30]

It may be that despite the apparent disagreement between Spade and Edwards on the one hand and Leftow on the other, their respective suggestions on Aquinas's behalf are in fact compatible with one another. Jeffrey Brower argues that when Aquinas denies unity and existence to natures considered absolutely he is denying only that they are numerically one, or that they exist in the way individuals do.[31] Just because natures in themselves lack the sort of unity we would associate with an individual member of a kind, or, for that matter, with a Platonic universal, does not mean that they lack unity altogether. Indeed, the fact that Thomistic natures are only "derivatively individual"—deriving their individuality *from* their inherence in designated matter—means that they have a sort of internal sameness.[32] Two human nature tropes do not differ at all from one another in virtue of their internal, intrinsic features. They are distinct individuals only in virtue of inhering in different designated matter. Brower agrees with Leftow that Aquinas is a kind of trope nominalist, with individual humanities subvening same-species relations. In that respect he resembles other medieval nominalists like William of Ockham. But whereas Ockham regards the numerical distinctness of natures from one another as primitive, Aquinas thinks it is analyzable in terms of its dependence on natures inhering in designated matter. Because Thomas thinks the numerical distinctness of natures from one another is derivative, he countenances a peculiar sort of trope—derivatively distinct individuals—not typically recognized in disputes about universals. He then analyzes the sameness of natures in terms of the lack of intrinsic differences between numerically distinct nature-tropes. Thomas's view is also, Brower thinks, not too different from Scotus's.

I think Brower is correct that for Aquinas, forms (of the whole), essences, or natures are only derivatively distinct individuals. That is, any

---

30. QDP 9.2 ad 1 (Marietti 71) and Leftow, "Aquinas on Attributes," 40.
31. Brower, "Aquinas on the Problem of Universals."
32. Ibid., 729.

really existing nature exists as an individual, numerically distinct from any other nature of its kind. On the other hand, because the numerical distinction between two natures of the same kind depends on the designated matter in which the natures are found, they are only derivatively distinct from one another. As Brower has it, they are "internally the same." Or to put it another way, they are intrinsically non-individual. That Thomas thinks of forms this way will play a significant role in his argumentation for the intellect's immateriality that I consider in chapter 5.

Is it a defensible view? Contemporary hylomorphists are divided on whether to regard forms as universals.[33] Arguably Aquinas's position inherits some of realism's strengths. It is able to ground the truth of statements about same-kind-membership or resemblance in terms of intrinsically non-individual natures, instead of taking these as primitive. By appealing to such natures, it also grounds our knowledge of facts about genera and species with whose instances we may have only limited acquaintance. Arguably too it provides these advantages over standard forms of trope nominalism without inheriting realism's central liability, namely the existence of universals as really existing shared entities. It does incur the cost, however, of countenancing derivatively individual tropes—a class of entities that might strike some as bizarre. Furthermore, because Thomas's natures are intrinsically non-individual, something must explain their individuation and numerical distinctness from one another. I turn next to Aquinas's analysis of what does this individuating work.

Individuation

I mentioned in the previous section that what explains the individuation of forms Thomas calls "designated matter," but precisely what he means by this term has long been controversial among his interpreters.[34] It cannot be just any matter that individuates forms. Prime mat-

---

33. Kathrin Koslicki prefers to view forms as universals in *The Structure of Objects* (Oxford: Oxford University Press, 2008), 257–58; William Jaworski argues for trope nominalism in *Structure and the Metaphysics of Mind*, chap. 3. Michael Rea prefers a neutral view in "Hylomorphism Reconditioned," *Philosophical Perspectives* 25, no. 1 (2011): 341–58.

34. Linda Peterson, "Cardinal Cajetan and Giles of Rome," and Maurice Beuchot, "Chrysostum Javellus and Francis Sylvester Ferrara," both in *Individuation in Scholasticism, the*

ter, for instance, is on Aquinas's view "pure potency," and accordingly is "numerically one in all things ... since it lacks the dispositions that would bring about numerical difference."³⁵ Aquinas consistently holds that designated matter is matter "under" (*sub*) quantitative dimensions, but changes the terminology with which he refers to these dimensions throughout his career. In *De ente* he says they are determinate (*determinatis*), but also calls them simply terminate (*terminatae*), and elsewhere even indeterminate (*indeterminatae*).³⁶ It is not hard to see why Aquinas might prefer indeterminate dimensions to determinate ones, given that a substance's dimensions seem to change consistently throughout its career.³⁷ Some commentators deal with these terminological difficulties by referring to designated matter as a "chunk of matter."³⁸ This may be a helpful heuristic, but leaves vague what "chunk" is under discussion. In the case of living substances it certainly cannot be any particular set of empirically-identifiable material constituents (such as a particular grouping of elemental material) because, as Aquinas recognized, such constituents cycle in and out constantly to maintain homeostasis.³⁹ It

---

Later Middle-Ages and the Counter-Reformation, 1150–1650, ed. Jorge Gracia (Buffalo: State University of New York Press, 1994), 431–56 and 457–74, provide a portrait of disagreements on how to interpret Aquinas on the principle of individuation amongst sixteenth-century Thomists. Thomas de Vio Cajetan and Crisostum Javellus represent one interpretation with thirteenth-century roots in Giles of Rome, while Sylvester Ferrara defends a different interpretation traceable back to the fifteenth-century Thomist John Capreolus.

35. DPN 2 (Leo. 43:41.98–108). For a different view on prime matter's role in individuation see Jeffrey Brower, "Matter, Form and Individuation" in *The Oxford Handbook of Aquinas*, ed. Brian Davies and Eleonore Stump (Oxford: Oxford University Press, 2012), 83–103.

36. See for *determinatis* DEE 2, along with QDV 8.6 ad 5 and *Sententia super De anima* (hereafter, In DA) 2.12.377; for *terminatae* see In Sent 3.1.2.5 ad 1 and QQ 9.6 ad 2; for *indeterminatae* see esp. In DT 4.2. For discussion of how to understand this varied terminology see Wippel, *Metaphysical Thought of Thomas Aquinas*, chap. 9, §4, and Joseph Owens, "Thomas Aquinas: Dimensive Quantity as Individuating Principle," *Mediaeval Studies* 50, no. 1 (1988): 279–310.

37. This is exactly how Aquinas explains his preference for indeterminate dimensions in In DT 4.2. For a detailed examination of the extensive treatment of individuation in Aquinas's *De trinitate* commentary see Kevin White, "Individuation in Aquinas's *Super Boetium De Trinitate*, Q. 4," *American Catholic Philosophical Quarterly* 69, no. 4 (1995): 543–56.

38. See Stump, *Aquinas*, 47; Anthony Kenny, *Aquinas on Mind* (New York: Routledge, 2003), 138, and Gyula Klima's notes to his translation of DEE in *Medieval Philosophy: Essential Readings with Commentary*, ed. Klima, Fritz Alhoff, and Anand Jayprakash Vaidya (Malden, Mass.: Blackwell, 2007), 237n18.

39. Aquinas adopts the metaphors of a city, whose population comes and goes, and a fire, into which new bits of wood are constantly thrown and which consumes the old ones, to illustrate the relationship between a living thing and the particular material constituents it has at any given time; see In Sent 2.30.2.1 ad 4, ST 1a.119.1 ad 5, QQ 8.3 ad 2, In DGC 1.15.4/107.

may well be that Aquinas changed his mind, even repeatedly, about how best to describe the matter responsible for individuation. By my lights, though, at least one plausible interpretation of his position would single out the dimensions a substance starts out with as the ones that do the individuating work.[40] In virtue of starting out in this matter *here* and *now* as opposed to some other matter elsewhere or at some other point in time a substantial form is rendered sufficiently unique that it is able to preserve its bearer's individual identity even as the individual substance gains and loses matter and changes its dimensions over time.

To appreciate why this is a plausible interpretation of Aquinas's view, it is helpful to understand Aquinas's motivations for identifying designated matter as the principle of individuation in the first place.[41] It is easy enough to see why Thomas would hold that quantitative dimensions play a role in differentiating numerically distinct individuals. Such dimensions determine something's position or location, and positions or locations are primitively diverse from one another. On the other hand, Aquinas could not straightforwardly accept Boethius's suggestion in *De trinitate* that quantitative dimensions are responsible for individuation just by themselves. Quantities are accidents, and hence possess only a qualified, *secundum quid* mode of being as modifications of some substance. But if quantities, in order to exist, must exist as quantities *of* some individual substance or other, then apparently they cannot be what explains the substance's individuality.[42] Aquinas acknowledges that accidents are dependent on substances for their individuation.[43] He insists that it is a component of material substances themselves—

---

40. Robert Pasnau suggests a view along these lines in *Thomas Aquinas on Human Nature* (Cambridge: Cambridge University Press, 2002), 391–92.

41. Among Aquinas's motivations was certainly the fact that Aristotle several times indicates that matter is responsible for individuation: see *Metaphysics* 7.8.1034a5–8. As far as I can tell, there is no consensus among contemporary Aristotle scholars about whether he took matter to be the principle of individuation; compare A. C. Lloyd, "Aristotle's Principle of Individuation," *Mind* 79, no. 316 (1970): 519–29, who thinks that matter is Aristotle's principle of individuation with William Charlton, "Aristotle and the Principle of Individuation," *Phronesis* 17, no. 3 (1972): 239–49, who rejects this view.

42. Abelard was first responsible for pressing this line of objection against allowing accidents to do individuating work; see for discussion Peter King, "The Problem of Individuation in the Middle Ages," *Theoria* 66, no. 2 (2000): 159–84, and Jorge Gracia, "The Legacy of the Early Middle Ages," in *Individuation in Scholasticism*, ed. Gracia, 21–38, at 32–34.

43. ST 1a.29.1.

their matter—that individuates them, even though matter only does so insofar as it is positioned or located according to certain quantitative dimensions. Matter, he says, is the primary principle of individuation, but dimensions are a secondary principle of individuation.[44] Because matter is indivisible without them, no two things lacking dimensions are distinct from one another as individuals within a species.

Some of Aquinas's readers have questioned the coherence of his position, suggesting that his appeal to designated matter ends up illicitly relying on accidental features to perform individuating work.[45] In response to this worry, Thomas's defenders have sometimes distinguished between different orders of priority. It is true that quantities, as accidents, are dependent on their substantial subjects for their existence, yet the substances themselves depend for their individuation on the quantitative dimensions to which their matter is subject. Because substances and their quantitative dimensions are mutually interdependent according to different orders of explanatory priority, Aquinas's view involves no vicious circularity.[46]

Keeping this idea of different explanatory orders in mind, here is a fuller account of how material substances are individuated. As we saw in passages 1.1 and 1.2 from *De principiis*, substances depend for their existence on a substantial form giving an act of being in act to prime matter, which in itself exists only in potency. Yet because Aquinas thinks forms are only derivatively distinct individuals, they depend in turn for their individuation on reception in matter, which in turn comes in distinct "chunks" on account of the distinct quantitative dimensions to which it is subject. Again, these dimensions belong not to prime matter in itself, which lacks all forms whatsoever. But as we saw Aquinas claiming in 1.8, quantity "flows from" matter. By this I take him to mean that any prime matter actualized by a substantial form immediately becomes designated by quantity, which he says at one point is the first in order of

---

44. *In Sent* 4.12.1.1.3 ad 3.
45. This is essentially Scotus's criticism in *Ord.* 2.3.1.4.
46. This is essentially how Thomas of Sutton defends Aquinas's view against Scotistic criticism in his *Quodlibet* 1.21, ed. Michael Schmaus (Munich: Bayerischen Akademie, 1969), 139–51; see for discussion Gyula Klima, "Thomas of Sutton on Individuation," *Proceedings of the Society for Medieval Logic and Metaphysics* 5 (2006): 70–78. John Wippel articulates a similar defense of Aquinas's view in *Metaphysical Thought of Thomas Aquinas*, 364–65.

accidents to "supervene" upon a substance.⁴⁷ Upon reception into matter of this sort, substantial forms are rendered unique individual tropes. They are thereupon able to preserve a substance's individual identity even as its matter changes constantly over time with regards both to its quantitative dimensions and to its empirically-identifiable material constituents. Hence while matter along with its quantitative dimensions jointly explains a substance's individual identity at first, its substantial form assumes the explanatory role of preserving its individual identity diachronically. Furthermore, Thomas maintains that substantial forms retain their individuality even if they should subsequently become detached from matter. As he puts it (citing Avicenna), "the individuation and multiplication of souls depends on the body for its beginning, but not for its end."⁴⁸ I take it this is the response Aquinas would offer to the worry we saw Cross raise at the end of the previous chapter regarding the individuation of human souls.

Considered the way I have just described it, Aquinas's position on individuation shares similarities with the "origins essentialism" that Saul Kripke and others have defended.⁴⁹ Just as Kripke thinks his particular lectern could not have originated from any other block of wood than the one it did, so too Aquinas thinks an individual material substance could not have originated from matter under different quantitative dimensions. Frequently he speaks of the dimensions conferring individuality in temporal terms as well as spatial ones, characterizing individuality in terms of existing as *this* thing *here* and *now*.⁵⁰ This is notably the case when he speaks of the intellectual abstraction required to produce universal concepts as a matter of removing natures from their individuating, here-and-now conditions. I will assume that Aquinas has in mind both spatial and temporal dimensions when it comes to individuation.

It is important to remember that the account of individuation I have presented in this section applies only to composite substances. It cer-

---

47. In DT 5.3 (Leo. 50:148.189).
48. DEE 5 (Leo. 43.379.68–71).
49. See Saul Kripke, *Naming and Necessity* (Cambridge, Mass.: Harvard University Press, 1972), 113–15; Jeffrey Brower and Susan Brower Toland agree with this comparison between Aquinas and Kripke in "Aquinas on Mental Representation: Concepts and Intentionality," *The Philosophical Review* 117, no. 2 (2008): 193–243, at 214–15n36.
50. See, e.g., SCG 1.65.8; ST 1a.57.2 and 110.1, 1a.2ae.6.6; QDV 2.6 ad 1 and 8.11; and In DT 4.2.

tainly would not apply, for Thomas, to God, who is an utterly unique particular because he is the only form or essence identical to the absolute unlimited act of being. It does not apply to spiritual substances such as angels either. As I noted in the previous section, Aquinas prefers to deny that angels possess matter at all, and certainly denies that they have the kind of matter that gives rise to quantitative dimensions. Accordingly, while angels are certainly particulars as opposed to universals, they are distinct from one another as distinct forms or essences, not as individuals of the same kind.

In fact, it is far from clear that Aquinas means for his appeal to designated matter as principle of individuation to cover all composite substances. It may be limited to sublunary substances subject to generation and corruption, as opposed to the celestial bodies, which Aquinas supposed to be incorruptible. Aquinas insists that heavenly bodies possess different matter than corruptible substances do.[51] It is spatially extended, unlike the nonmaterial principle of potency in spiritual substances. But it cannot undergo the loss of a substantial form and its replacement by another. Scholars have disagreed about how to interpret Aquinas on the distinction between celestial and corporeal matter. It may be that he acknowledges a primitive distinction between kinds of prime matter for celestial and sublunary substances.[52] Another possibility is that he is simply pointing out a difference between the ways that celestial and sublunary substantial forms operate on prime matter that is, in itself, one through lack of any forms to differentiate it.[53] However this may be, Aquinas remarks at various points that the forms of celestial bodies "use up" all the matter of the kind available to them when they first come into existence.[54] Accordingly, each celestial body is one of a kind, not because they lack matter to individuate them (as in the case of angels),

---

51. See SCG 2.16, ST 1a.66.2, In Phys 7.8.8/937, QDA 7, etc.

52. This is Jeffrey Brower's take on Aquinas's position, at least by the time Thomas wrote *Summa theologiae*; see *Material World*, chap. 9, §1; Joseph Bobik thinks the celestial bodies do not have prime matter at all on Aquinas's view—see *Aquinas on Matter and Form and the Elements* (Notre Dame, Ind.: University of Notre Dame Press, 1998), 2000.

53. Stephen Baldner thinks this is the view Aquinas arrived at toward the end of his career; see "Thomas Aquinas on Celestial Matter," *The Thomist* 68, no. 3 (2004): 431–67, along with TDSS 8 and *Sententia super libros De caelo et mundo* (hereafter, In DCM) 1.6 for the main texts in support of Baldner's interpretation.

54. See ST 1a.119.1, SCG 2.93.6, In Phys 6.3.9/774, In Peri 1.10.5.

but because once one is created, there is no suitable matter left over for there to be any others of their kind.[55] One significant ramification of Aquinas's view on the individuation of celestial bodies will come to light in this book's concluding chapter.

For now, having seen in this section and the preceding one how Aquinas thinks there can be both individual and non-individual form and matter, I turn now to a further set of questions involving the various kinds of form and matter we have encountered so far. What is the relationship between the different kinds of form: forms of the part, forms of the whole, essences, structures, and souls? And how are these different kinds of form related to prime matter, designated matter, non-designated matter, sensible matter, and bodies? I will address these questions in the following section.

Form of the Whole, Form of the Part, and Soul

Passage 2.1 raises some perplexing questions. Here are two. First, Aquinas indicates that a composite substance's form of the part and form of the whole must be really distinct from one another. Yet each must surely count as a substantial form. And it is one of Aquinas's best-known metaphysical positions that a given substance has just one substantial form. This seems like an inconsistent set of claims. Second, Aquinas says that a form of the part perfects the matter of a composite substance such that it exists in act. It seems like he has prime matter in mind. Yet he also suggests that what corresponds with forms of the part in the case of natural things is sensible matter, such as flesh and bone in the case of human beings. Surely flesh and bone cannot be prime matter, however. So do our souls join with prime matter, sensible matter, or what? In this section I will show how Aquinas might answer these perplexing questions in turn, before concluding with a look at some of the different ways Aquinas assigns identity-determining and unifying roles to substantial forms.

Before addressing the first apparent difficulty, it will be helpful to begin by reviewing Aquinas's basic reason for insisting on one substantial

---

55. I owe the suggestion that Aquinas recognized different individuating conditions for celestial bodies than he did for sublunary material entities to Giorgio Pini, "The Individuation of Angels from Bonaventure to Duns Scotus," in *A Companion to Angels in Medieval Philosophy*, ed. Tobias Hoffman (Leiden: Brill, 2012), 79–116, at 92–93.

form per substance: the thesis usually called "the unicity of substantial forms." Aquinas asserts and defends the unicity thesis numerous times in different contexts.[56] To name just one, in arguing that there cannot be just one matter for angels and corporeal substances alike, Aquinas attacks a position he attributes to Avicebron, on which an undifferentiated "universal matter" is perfected by a layered succession of substantial forms.[57] First a form of substancehood makes matter into actually existing stuff, then a form of corporeity turns it into bodily stuff, then further successive substantial forms yield a bodily substance of some specific kind. Aquinas's basic reason for opposing a view like this is that he appeals to substantial form to explain the numerical unity of substances. In fact, he can see no other way to secure genuine substantial unity. For Thomas, a substance counts as numerically one if and only if it has one substantial form. Accordingly, something assembled from multiple substantial forms could not be numerically one—it would be a being *per accidens* of the sort described in chapter 1 (pp. 35–36).

It might seem, however, that this is precisely the position to which passage 2.1 commits Aquinas. Both forms of the part and forms of the whole alike must surely count as substantial forms. Yet Aquinas rejects Averroes's position, that the two "differ only according to reason," and instead recommends Avicenna's view, on which they differ "as whole differs from part." The way to escape the seeming inconsistency here, I think, is to read Aquinas in 2.1 as marking a distinction between two different senses in which individual composite substances have forms. First, each has a form in the sense of essence, nature, or quiddity, which as we saw in the previous chapter Aquinas understands as a principle delimiting or determining an act of being in some specific way.[58] Aquinas

---

56. See Wippel, *Metaphysical Thought of Thomas Aquinas*, 333–51, for discussion of many of these contexts.

57. In DGC 1.10.8/80; see also In DA 2.1.225, QQ 11.5, QDSC 1 ad 9, QDSC 3, TDSS 6. Aquinas associates Avicebron chiefly with the universal hylomorphism I discussed in chapter 1, and appears to think it goes hand in hand with a pluralistic view about substantial forms. It is not completely obvious to me that the two views are in any way mutually entailing, but they did tend to be held in tandem—see Paul Spade, "Binarium Famosissimum," in *The Stanford Encyclopedia of Philosophy* (2008), ed. Edward Zalta, available at plato.stanford.edu/entries/binarium/, and D. A. Callus, "The Origins of the Problem of the Unity of Form," *The Thomist* 24, no. 2 (1961): 257–85.

58. See Armand Maurer, "Form and Essence in the Philosophy of St. Thomas," *Mediaeval*

calls a substance's essence, nature, or quiddity its form of the whole. It includes every non-accidental feature of the individual minus those responsible for and stemming from its individuality. Second, part of the substance's essence, nature, or quiddity is a form in the sense of an overarching dynamic structure, responsible for configuring or organizing matter in some specific way. Aquinas calls the substance's overarching structure its form of the part. Keeping in mind the distinction between these two senses of "form," we can reconcile the seemingly inconsistent set of claims from the previous paragraph as follows. Even though Aquinas insists on a real distinction between form of the whole and form of the part, he is not claiming that there are two distinct substantial forms of the same type, each belonging to a particular composite substance. He is simply claiming that structure is only part of a composite substance's nature, essence, quiddity, or "form of the whole." The other part is what gets structured, namely, the substance's matter. Thomas's position on the unicity of substantial forms is that a given individual substance has just one nature, quiddity, or essence—one form of the whole—however many "substantial predicates" may be true of it at a given time. That is, Socrates has just one form of the whole in virtue of which he is at once a human, rational, an animal, an organism, a body, and a substance. Part of this form of the whole is Socrates's overarching structure: his "form of the part." Here again, Aquinas holds that a given individual substance has just one such overarching structure, however many substructures it may have. I will say more about why Aquinas insists on just one form of each type at the end of this section, and more about "overarching" versus "sub-" structures near the end of this chapter.

Before moving on to the second perplexing question, one explanatory note is in order about the way I have proposed answering the first. Aquinas's suggestion in passage 2.1 that there can be both individual and non-individual form and matter appears to be true only of the form and matter that are included in an individual composite substance's form of the whole or essence. Essences themselves, in contrast, are in a sense only non-individual, while their corresponding matter is only

---

Studies 13, no. 1 (1951): 165–76, for an account of forms or essences in Aquinas's thought as determinations or specifications of acts of being.

individual. This follows from Aquinas's views on universals and individuation that I surveyed above. Thomas's claims about natures are best understood as applying to essences or forms of the whole.[59] Hence when he speaks about common natures, he means primarily that the essences of composite substances are intrinsically non-individual. They are only derivatively distinct from one another, depending for their individuation on designated matter. As a result, Aquinas often denies that individual composite substances are identical to their essences: "Socrates is not his humanity," he will say.[60] Only if we understand the essence as implicitly including the designation of its matter can we predicate it of individuals, which is what we do when we say "Socrates is a human."[61] Accordingly, essences or forms of the whole are in a sense only non-individual, and their corresponding matter is only individual, that is, designated. Forms of the part, in contrast, can be either individual or non-individual depending on whether we are thinking of them as part of a composite substance's essence—in which case they are "common" or intrinsically non-individual—or as part of the composite substance herself, in which case they are individual.[62] Hence we can think of Socrates himself as

---

59. In DEE, for instance, Aquinas's claims about matter as the principle of individuation are immediately preceded by his argument that the essences of composite substances contain matter and form, while his discussion of universals begins: "having seen what the term 'essence' signifies with respect to composite substances, it must be seen how it is related to the notions of genus, species and difference" (DEE 3 [Leo. 43.374.1–4]). In both cases it is clear that he is discussing the individuation and universality of forms of the whole—those that include both form (of the part) and matter.

60. DEE 1, SCG 1.21.4, QDP 9.1, In Met 7.11.1521 and 1535, In DA 3.8.706.

61. In DEE 2 and SCG 4.81.10 Aquinas explains that the term *humanitas* not only signifies a human's form of the part, but also signifies it "as a part" (*ut partem*), that is, in a way that precludes designation by matter. The term *homo*, in contrast, signifies a human's form of the part "as a whole" (*ut totum*), that is, as implicitly including its designation by matter under determinate dimensions. For several helpful discussions of Aquinas's views on essences as individual and non-individual see Joshua Hochschild, "Form, Essence, Soul: Distinguishing Principles of Thomistic Metaphysics," in *Distinctions of Being: Philosophical Approaches to Reality*, ed. Nikolaj Zunic (Washington, D.C.: American Maritain Association Publications, 2013), 21–35, and "Kenny and Aquinas on Individual Essences," *Proceeding of the Society for Medieval Logic and Metaphysics* 6 (2006): 45–56, along with Gabriele Galluzzo, "Aquinas on Common Nature and Universals," *Recherches de Théologie et Philosophie Médiévales* 71, no. 1 (2004): 131–71, at 135–37.

62. See ST 1a.85.1 ad 2, where Aquinas distinguishes between common matter and designated matter, claiming that the former, but not the latter, is included in the essence of composite substances. See also 1a.29.2 ad 3 (Leo. 4.330): "in things composed of matter and form, the essence signifies not only the form, nor only the matter, but what is composed of matter and the common form, as the principles of the species."

composed of form and matter in two different ways. On the one hand, Socrates is his form of the whole or essence plus the quantitative dimensions responsible for designating the matter included in it. On the other hand, Socrates is his form of the part or structure plus the matter, designated by quantitative dimensions, in which it inheres. Either way of looking at Socrates's composition is correct, depending on which type of substantial form we are focused on.[63]

But what of Socrates's composition from soul plus flesh and bones, turning to the second perplexing question? Typically, as in passage 2.1, Aquinas identifies the soul as a living thing's form of the part or overarching structure, as opposed to its form of the whole or essence.[64] Our question, however, was how to think of the matter corresponding to souls. In passages 1.2 and 1.3 from *De principiis*, what corresponds to a composite substance's overarching structure is prime matter, which in itself exists only in potency. When Aquinas says in 2.1 that a form of the part "perfects matter and makes it exist in act," it seems like he has prime matter in mind. But he goes on to say that individual humans are composed of form plus sensible matter, such as flesh and bones. So which is it? Both, I think, in different senses. In fact, there are at least three different senses in which Aquinas habitually speaks of living composite substances as composed of soul plus matter of some sort.

First, and fundamentally, Thomas does indeed think that what corresponds to a composite substance's overarching structure must be prime matter, in pure potency. If a composite substance's matter were not pure potency, then any forms coming to inhere in it would not give it an act of being *simpliciter*, that is, a substantial act of being, but rather would cause it to be in some qualified way. In other words, they would be accidental forms, and the resulting composite would be a being *per accidens* rather than a substance. As Thomas puts it at one point:

---

63. This is Gyula Klima's point in reminding us that "there is more than one way to slice a cake" in his "Man = Body + Soul: Aquinas's Arithmetic of Human Nature," in Davies, *Aquinas: Contemporary Philosophical Perspectives*, 257–74.
64. See *In Sent* 2.3.1.1: "in things composed of matter and form the nature of the thing, which is called its quiddity or essence, results from the conjunction of form with matter, as human [results from] the conjunction of the soul and the body." See also *In Sent* 3.2.1.3.3 ad 1, *QQ* 2.2.1 ad 1, *In Met* 5.5.822, *In Met* 5.10.902.

(2.4) If prime matter had in itself some form proper to it then it would be something in act, and so when any other form was introduced into it, it would not simply be matter by itself, but would be this or that being, and thus it would be a case of generation *secundum quid* and not *simpliciter*. Whence all those positing the primary subject to be some body, such as air or water, held that generation is the same as alteration. But it is clear from this argument what our understanding of prime matter must be taken to be, since it is related to all forms and privations just as an alterable subject [is related] to contrary qualities.[65]

Aquinas's reasoning in 2.4 presupposes, of course, that there can only be one substantial form per substance. That is why any additional forms coming to matter already existing in act can only be accidental. This reasoning applies to any composite substances whatsoever, including living bodies, whose substantial form is a soul. Hence in a fundamental sense Aquinas holds that a human being like Socrates is composed of his soul plus prime matter.

In a second sense, however, Aquinas speaks just as often of humans like Socrates as composed of their soul plus their body. An organism's body is not prime matter. Instead, the division between soul and body is between the part of the living thing that gives it life and the part that simply occupies three-dimensional space. As Aquinas explains in one important passage from *De ente*:

(2.5) The term "body" can be taken in different ways. For that which has such a nature that three dimensions can be designated in it is called a body, insofar as it is in the genus substance; and indeed these three designated dimensions themselves are body, insofar as it is in the genus quantity. It happens in things, however, that what has one perfection may also acquire some further perfection.... Beyond the perfection of having such a form that three dimensions can be designated in it, there can be joined to it another perfection, such as life or something of that sort. Accordingly, the term "body" can mean a certain thing that has such a form from which designability in three dimensions follows with precision (namely, that no further perfection follows from that form, and if something further is added it will lie beyond the meaning of "body" taken in that way). And in this way a body will be an integral and material part of an animal, since the soul will lie beyond what is signified by the

65. In Met 8.1.1689 (Marietti 404).

term "body" and will supervene on such a body such that from the two (namely soul and body) an animal is constituted, just as from its parts. The term "body" can also be taken in such a way that it means a certain thing having such a form from which three dimensions can be designated in it (whatever form that might be) whether or not some further perfection may come from it as well. And in this way body will be the genus of animal, since nothing is contained in [the meaning of] "animal" that is not implicitly contained in "body." For the soul is none other than that form through which three dimensions can be designated in a thing; and therefore when it is said that a body is that which has such a form from which three dimensions can be designated in it, the form understood was whichever: whether animality, or stoniness or any whichever other. And so the form of an animal is contained implicitly in the form of a body, since body is its genus.[66]

An organism is a body in the sense that it is, itself, a substance with "such a nature that three dimensions can be designated in it." That is, it is a corporeal substance, something having corporeity as its essence, nature, or form of the whole. This sense of "body" does not exclude a body's having what Aquinas calls "further perfections" such as life, sense-perception, or rationality. Indeed, a human being is a body that possesses all of these further perfections. The term "body" is also sometimes used in an "exclusive" sense, however, to mean "what has such a form from which designability in three dimensions follows with precision (namely, that no further perfection follows from that form, and if something further is added it will lie beyond the meaning of 'body' taken in that way)." In this sense, a body is just the three-dimensional part of a living thing, as opposed to the part responsible for its vital operations, etc. This other "animating" part of the living thing is its soul. Comparing the soul/body division with the division between form of the

---

66. DEE 2 (Leo. 43.371.109–50). Aquinas goes on to explain that the distinction between body and soul as he construes it here can also be drawn between the animal and rational parts that compose us: "and such is the relation between animal and man as well, for if 'animal' names a certain whole thing which has such a perfection that it is able to sense and move through a principle existing within itself with precision from any other perfection, then whichever other further perfection supervenes on it will be related to the animal as a part, rather than being implicitly contained in the meaning of the term, and so animal will not be a genus. But it is a genus if it signifies a certain thing from whose form sense and motion occur, whatever that form be, whether it be a sensible soul alone or sensible and rational alike" (ibid., ll. 151–63).

part and prime matter, it is clear that the latter is more fundamental, as any composite substance is composed in the latter way, while only organisms are composed of soul plus body. It is true that in a sense no composite substance is just a body. That is, any substance with "such a nature that three dimensions can be designated in it" must also possess further perfections that characterize it as a body of such-and-such a sort. Only in the case of living things, however, do we tend to mark a division between the three-dimensional part of a composite substance (its body) and the part responsible for its further perfections (its soul).

This brings us to a third way of marking the contrast between a living thing's soul and its material component. Just as no composite substance is just a body, but is always a body of such-and-such a sort, so too no composite substance's three-dimensional part (i.e., its body, as discussed in the previous paragraph) is just three-dimensional. This is, roughly, the point Aquinas is trying to make by claiming in passage 2.1 that Averroes's view—on which form of the part and form of the whole are really the same—collapses the distinction between physics and mathematics that Aristotle draws in *Physics* 2.2 and *Metaphysics* 6.1 with the example of snubness versus concavity. A mathematical entity like concavity is simply curvature in stuff of any sort. Physical entities, however, cannot be understood without specifying some particular sort of matter: a nose, in the case of snubness. Because it typically requires some empirical research to discover what particular sort of matter a given physical entity depends on, Aquinas says that physical essences include sensible matter. In contrast, mathematical essences include only "intelligible matter": matter we can understand without doing any empirical research.[67] I will return to the significance of this point, as well as the sort of empirical research required to understand certain physical entities, in chapter 3. At any rate, when Aquinas says that Socrates is composed of soul plus flesh and bones, he is drawing attention to the fact that the matter of any composite substance is not just designated by quantitative dimensions, but is also configured in various different

---

67. See *In DT* 5.3 and *In Phys* 2.3, where Aquinas explains that because quantity is the first sort of accident that "supervenes on" matter before any others, we can think of material objects just in terms their quantitative dimensions, without any qualitative features—that is how mathematicians regard their objects.

empirically discoverable ways. Of course, to speak of matter as configured in different ways means we are no longer speaking of prime matter. Indeed, to speak of certain sorts of sensible matter, such as flesh and bone, implies the presence of soul in prime matter. Aquinas embraces Aristotle's so-called homonymy principle: upon the departure of soul flesh and bone no longer remain, rather the flesh and bone of a corpse are so-called only equivocally.[68] They are dependent for their identity on the whole to which they belong.

From what we have seen so far, it is clear that Aquinas thinks we can carve composite substances like human beings along various different mereological joints depending on what theoretical roles we are interested in emphasizing. In passage 2.1 Aquinas appears to associate the role of determining what kind a given substance belongs to with forms of the whole, and with forms of the part the role of perfecting matter such that it exists in act. In 2.5 he apparently associates one such "perfecting" role in particular with souls, namely that of animating or giving life.[69] Caution is in order, however, lest we wrongly suppose that the forms in question are really distinct items of the same type, or that they perform their roles independently of one another. Indeed, on closer inspection, passage 2.1 appears to associate a sharp distinction between the functional roles just mentioned with the Averroist view Thomas goes on to reject.

Consider the claim that a composite substance's essence is what locates it in its given kind. Certainly Aquinas is willing to say this elsewhere: "the word 'essence' must signify something ... through which diverse beings are located in their genera and species, as, for example, humanity is the essence of man, and so with other things."[70] Yet within the essence it is the form of the part that does the important identity-determining work, because matter on its own, or prime matter, is pure potentiality, and not actually anything at all. It takes some structuring or "perfecting" by a form of the part for matter to exist in act as flesh, bones, or anything else. Perhaps for this reason, Aquinas often simply

---

68. Aristotle, *De anima* 2.1.412b20, and Aquinas, In DA 2.2.239; see SCG 2.72.3, 4.32.6; ST 1a.76.8; and QDA 10.

69. See also ST 1a.75.1; Aquinas takes for granted that "soul" means "the first principle of life in things that live."

70. DEE 1 (Leo. 43.369.22–26); see QQ 9.2.1 ad 1, In Met 7.9.1467.

says it is form that locates substances in their genera and species, leaving ambiguous whether he means form of the whole or of the part.⁷¹

As for the "perfecting" work done by a form of the part (or soul, in the case of a living thing), we might view this as a unifying role. A substance's overarching structure unifies its material components into a single composite whole synchronically, and maintains its unity diachronically even as it cycles bits of matter in and out throughout its career.⁷² In addition, however, because a form of the whole confers on a substance identity at both the specific level and at various generic levels, essences or natures could be viewed as playing a unifying role with respect to the determinable and determinate components of a thing's definition.⁷³ *Pace* Avicebron, it is one and the same form of the whole in Socrates that makes him at once a human, a rational thing, an animal, an organism, a body, a substance, etc. Hence his form of the whole could be seen as bringing together these different aspects of his identity and as playing a unifying role alongside his form of the part.

I will say more about the unifying role that forms play later in this chapter, and more about their identity-determining roles in chapter 6, particularly as regards the diachronic identity of composite substances. Beyond this point, I will use the term "substantial form" to mean form of the part, and use "essence," "nature," or "quiddity" for forms of the whole. Having examined various senses in which Aquinas thinks of forms as essences and structures, I now turn to the sense in which they serve as truthmakers of predications.

Forms as Truthmakers

The notion that forms are truthmakers emerges naturally enough from comments such as we saw Aquinas making in 1.2: "everything by which something has an act of being, whether substantial or accidental, can be called form; just as a human who is white in potency is made white in

---

71. See SCG 3.7.7 and 4.81.7 and QDA 15.
72. See the passages cited in note 39.
73. See Marmodoro, "Aristotle's Hylomorphism without Reconditioning," 19–21, for a helpful discussion of the ways Aristotle's forms play this role. Nonetheless, as noted both in Maurer, "Form and Essence," and Wippel, *Metaphysical Thought of Thomas Aquinas*, 329–31, it seems likely that Averroes better captures Aristotle's own view in the *Metaphysics* by claiming that the essences of composite substances comprise their forms alone, rather than form and matter together.

act by whiteness." Because Aquinas appears to identify whiteness here as the feature in virtue of which "the human is white" is true, and also appears to be making a general claim about forms, it might appear that whatever F-ness makes a predication of the form "x is F" actually true will be a form. Matter might then appear to have a corresponding role as referent; it is any x about which "x is F" can be true. I noted one reason for thinking this view must at least be nuanced in chapter 1. I will not try to say anything exhaustive about Aquinas's account of truthmakers here, but I will propose five points of clarification drawing on what we have seen so far.[74]

First, while substances composed of form and matter do indeed serve as the referents of predications, certain forms themselves are the referents of predications as well, whereas matter in itself (prime matter) is only ever the referent of predication in a derivative way. Passage 1.1 makes it obvious how Aquinas thinks of substances as the referents of accidental predications: they serve as the subjects of inherent accidental forms. Prime matter is the subject of inherent substantial forms, but Aquinas insists that a predication like "Socrates is a human" is not about prime matter, but rather about Socrates. Indeed, the view that all predications are ultimately about matter is a fair approximation of Aquinas's take on Avicebron's universal hylomorphism, introduced in the previous chapter. Both Avicebron and the ancient naturalists, Aquinas thinks, make "all things one" in the sense that all predications ultimately ascribe features to a homogenous material substratum. Such a view "destroys the foundations of natural philosophy by removing true generation and corruptions from things" and also "destroys the true nature of prime matter" by turning it into a being in actuality, as opposed to something completely in potency.[75] The view Aquinas prefers when it comes to predication about composite substances is similar to the "thick particularism" David Armstrong prefers over "thin particular-

---

74. Aquinas certainly seems to endorse something like the slogan "truth supervenes on being," which is often invoked in contemporary discussions of truthmaking; in In Met 5.9.896 (Marietti 239), Thomas writes: "from the fact that something exists in the nature of things truth and falsity in a proposition follow."

75. TDSS 6 (Leo. 40.D50.69–72, 77–79). While in TDSS Aquinas groups Plato with Aristotle as a believer in prime matter as pure potency, elsewhere he appears to associate Plato with the view that matter becomes one thing or another by participating in various transcendent Ideas; see QDA 11.

ism" in that it ascribes attributes to something complex, as opposed to a "bare particular."[76] The same is not true when it comes to statements about God or simple substances, but here the referent of the predication is not matter, but rather a subsistent form.[77]

Second, while Aquinas would agree that a form serves as the truthmaker for any predication that has one, there is an important sense in which they do not perform this role on their own in the case of predications about composite substances. I take it that part of Aquinas's reason for insisting that a composite substance's essence includes both its substantial form (of the part) and matter is to highlight the fact that matter also plays a role in making statements about such substances true, in addition to form. A passage from Aquinas's *Metaphysics* commentary sheds light on Thomas's view:

(2.6) In composite substances the composition itself of form with matter ... or also the composition of subject and accident, should be regarded as the foundation and cause of a truth about composition, which the intellect forms within itself and expresses by an utterance. For when I say "Socrates is a man" the truth of this enunciation is caused by the composition of human form with individual matter, through which Socrates is this man; and when I say "the man is white" the cause of its truth is the composition of whiteness with its subject, and similarly in other cases.[78]

In both substantial and accidental predications about composite substances Aquinas assigns a truthmaking role to matter as well as form, whether the matter in question is the prime matter corresponding to a substantial form or the substantial subject corresponding to an accidental form.[79] More properly speaking, it is the actual inherence of a form in matter that makes statements about composite substances true.

---

76. See D. M. Armstrong, *Universals: An Opinionated Introduction* (Boulder, Colo.: Westview, 1989), 94–96, and Brower, *Material World*, chap. 6, §§3–4, for discussion.

77. Of course we are able to say true things about prime matter; what is their truthmaker? Brower, *Material World*, 145–47, proposes that Aquinas countenances cases of "basic characterization" in which a subject "can be characterized as an F and yet there is no further explanation for such characterization." Predications about God are one such case, and predications about prime matter are another.

78. In Met 9.11.1898 (Marietti 456).

79. See Ross Inman, "Essential Dependence, Truthmaking and Mereology: Then and Now," in *Metaphysics: Aristotelian, Scholastic, Analytic*, ed. Lukas Novak, Daniel D. Novotny, Prokop Sousedik, and David Svoboda (Frankfurt: Ontos Verlag, 2012), 73–90, at 84–86.

Third, however, Aquinas also clearly believes that not all statements with truthmakers are true in virtue of forms inhering in matter; some are true in virtue of forms subsisting by themselves. This is obviously true of any statements about God. It is true of substantial predications about simple substances such as angels. It is true in the peculiar case of the miraculously subsisting accidents of the eucharistic host.

Fourth, as Timothy Pawl argues, Aquinas is not a "truthmaker maximalist."[80] Thomas does not believe that all truths have truthmakers, but rather only those about beings. As Pawl explains, this restriction implies that truths about the past and future lack truthmakers.[81] So too with truths about nonbeings in the sense discussed in the previous chapter. Certainly predications such as "Homer was blind" or "unicorns do not exist" are true, but they are not true in virtue of any forms like blindness or unicorneity. Instead, Aquinas traces the truth of such predications to intellectual activity on our part.[82] This is not to say that truths about nonbeing are untethered from reality. We saw in chapter 1 that Aquinas thinks that rational being—being that "signifies the truth of propositions"—is related to real being "as effect to cause." Pawl explains helpfully that statements like those just listed are true in virtue of their complements—"Homer can see" or "there are unicorns"—*lacking* truthmakers, rather than in virtue of possessing truthmakers themselves. I mentioned in chapter 1 that Aquinas's distinction between real and rational being is one reason for supposing he would endorse a sparse, rather than abundant conception of properties; not every predicate has a substantial or accidental form corresponding to it.

Fifth and finally, a further reason for drawing the same conclusion about how Aquinas would conceive of properties (i.e., that they are sparse) stems from the fact that one and the same form can serve as

---

80. See Tim Pawl, *A Thomistic Account of Truthmakers for Modal Truths* (PhD diss., St. Louis University, 2008), and "A Thomistic Truthmaker Principle," *Acta Philosophica* 25, no. 1 (2016): 45–64.

81. As Pawl puts it, "truths about the past and future require truthmakers at the times that they were about, but they don't require currently existing truthmakers at any time that they are true" (*Thomistic Account*, 103).

82. See ST 1a.16.7 ad 4, cited in Pawl, *Thomistic Account*, 118–19. See also Gloria Wasserman, "Thomas Aquinas on Truths about Non-Beings," *Proceedings of the American Catholic Philosophical Association* 80 (2006): 101–13.

truthmaker for many different predicates. This is true in several different ways.

For one thing, Aquinas thinks that one substantial form can serve as truthmaker for many different substantial predications. We saw how Aquinas opposes Avicebron's view on which a succession of distinct substantial forms belonging to a human being perfect her first as a substance, then as a body, then as living, sensitive, rational, etc. Occasionally Aquinas also associates the view that substances have multiple substantial forms with Plato, for whom (Thomas thought) Socrates is a body, a human, an animal, rational, etc., by participating in distinct "separate forms" or "Ideas" of corporeity, humanity, rationality, animality, etc.[83] Aquinas, for his part, holds that "we must not admit diversity in things of nature according to the diverse notions or logical intentions which follow our mode of understanding, since reason can apprehend one and the same thing in diverse ways."[84] In other words, just because "Socrates is a body" and "Socrates is a human" are diverse predications does not mean that Socrates's corporeity and humanity are diverse in reality. As noted above, Thomas insists on the unicity of substantial forms against many of his contemporaries because he assigns them the role of unifying a substance into something numerically one.

Aquinas also believes that one and the same accidental form may serve as truthmaker for multiple predicates. This is certainly true when it comes to the powers of created substances, which Aquinas frequently treats as "multi-track" in the sense that they are dispositions for various different types of activity.[85] For instance, Aquinas thinks humans are able both to retain a storehouse of past sense experiences, recall these experiences to mind, and to manipulate them into various combinations, through one and the same "imaginative" power.[86]

---

83. See QDA 11 and ST 1a.76.3.

84. ST 1a.76.3 ad 4 (Leo. 5:221).

85. Gilbert Ryle introduces the "single-" versus "multi-track" discussion in *The Concept of Mind* (New York: Barnes and Noble, 1949), chap. 2, §7; E. J. Lowe is a recent defender of single-track powers while John Heil and George Molnar think powers can be multi-track.

86. ST 1a.78.4. More controversially, some commentators suggest that while passages like 1.8 may seem to commit Aquinas to accidents in nine irreducibly distinct categories, Thomas is able in fact to dispense with real beings in all but a few categories (quality, quantity, and possibly action/passion) by treating accidents of these privileged kinds as truthmakers for

One way that Aquinas might have further reduced his ontology, however, and did not, is indeed important for the way I understand his view: his refusal to identify souls (or indeed substantial forms in general) with their powers. In the following section I will explain how Aquinas thinks our substantial forms, the overarching structures of composite substances, are related to powers as the substructures of organic bodily parts, along with the lower-level structures of non-organic bodily parts. This will provide an initial framework for understanding how psychological powers operate through bodily organs, on which the following chapter will build.

---

predications involving the others. See Robert Pasnau, *Metaphysical Themes 1274–1671* (Oxford: Oxford University Press, 2011), chap. 12, esp. §3; Brower, *Material World*, chap. 9, §3; Joseph Owens, *An Elementary Christian Metaphysics* (Houston, Tex.: Center for Thomistic Studies, 1963), chap. 14, and Wippel, "Aquinas's Derivation" and *Metaphysical Thought of Thomas Aquinas*, 225–28. Certainly an "ontological reduction" program of this sort was prominently at work in the thought of many later medieval scholastics like William of Ockham—see Gyula Klima, "Ockham's Semantics and the Ontology of the Categories," in *The Cambridge Companion to Ockham*, ed. Paul Spade (Cambridge: Cambridge University Press, 1999), 118–42. They found apparent Aristotelian license for the procedure in *Physics* 3, which claims that "just as . . . the steep ascent and the steep descent are one—for these are one and the same, although their definitions are not one . . . so it is with the mover and the moved" (*Physics* 3.3.202a17–20). Aristotle appears here to identity the action of the mover with the passion of what is moved. Perhaps all the six categories listed after relation might similarly be identified with entities in the first three categories related to one another in various ways. Aquinas does say in the last sentence of passage 1.8 that when it comes to the last six categories, "the predicate is taken from something extrinsic to the subject" and in *In Phys* 3.5.15/322 he calls entities in these categories "extrinsic accidents." Perhaps he means that having an accident in one of these categories does not involve any real item actually inhering in a subject beyond entities in quality and quantity related to one another in various ways. See Robert Pasnau, "Response to Arlig and Symington," in *Metaphysical Themes: Medieval and Modern*, ed. Gyula Klima and Alexander Hall (Newcastle-upon-Tyne: Cambridge Scholars Publishing, 2014), 57–74, at 65–71, for an exposition of this view. As for relations, Aquinas certainly thought they were founded on nonrelational items in the categories of quality, quantity, and action/passion, but what this implies about their reducibility or otherwise to these nonrelational items is a vexed question; discussions of Aquinas's views on relations include Mark Henninger, *Relations: Medieval Theories: 1250–1325* (Oxford: Oxford University Press, 1989), and Jeffrey Brower, "Medieval Theories of Relations" in *The Stanford Encyclopedia of Philosophy* (2015), ed. Edward Zalta, available at plato.stanford.edu/archives/win2015/entries/relations-medieval/. For my purposes not very much rides on whether action and passion are one and the same accidental form—a motion—that inheres jointly in the moved and what is moved, or whether action and passion are two accidents in irreducibly distinct categories that are jointly comprised by one entity, a motion. The same is true regarding the reducibility or otherwise of relations to their bases.

Powers as Substructures

For many of Aquinas's contemporaries, the view that a substance's powers are neither really distinct from its substantial form(s), nor from one another, enjoyed both Augustinian support and independent argumentative grounds.[87] It might sound odd to suggest that an animal's power of reproduction is really the same as its powers of sight or hearing. But the oddness could be mitigated by recognizing multiple substantial forms in a given composite substance. The "vegetative soul" responsible for reproduction need not be the same as the "sensitive soul" responsible for sight and hearing. Furthermore, the apparent differences between sight and hearing themselves could be accounted for by recognizing a substantial form of corporeity, distinct from the soul (or souls), that molds distinct bodily instruments through which what is really one and the same power (of sensation, say) can nonetheless exercise distinct operations (of sight versus hearing, say). Both the number of substantial forms and the mechanism for carving out some measure of distinction between different powers varied from one scholastic to another. But the great majority of medieval thinkers other than Aquinas, his teacher Albert the Great, and a few others agreed in rejecting what Roger Bacon calls "the damnable vulgar opinion of Paris," namely that the soul's powers are accidental forms, really distinct from it and from one another.[88] In short, they agreed that just one or a few substantial forms, together with some bodily involvement, serve as truthmaker for any and all predications about a substance's abilities. Aquinas, in contrast, believed additional items in some category of accident are needed. These he calls powers.

---

87. The way Augustine describes the "trinity" of memory, understanding, and will as "not three substances, but one substance" in *De trinitate* 10.11.18 was very influential. One influential line of reasoning in favor of identifying a substance's powers with its substantial form stems from Henry of Ghent's *Quodlibet* 3.14: if powers are *not* identical to substantial forms, then what causes them? Either a further power or a substantial form. If the former, the question is repeated *ad infinitum*. If the latter, then why not say that the substantial form itself is the true source of the substance's ability to carry out the relevant action or passion? See my "Faculties of the Soul and Some Medieval Mind-Body Problems," *The Thomist* 75, no. 4 (2011): 585–636, at 605–10, for further discussion of Henry's reasoning.

88. Roger Bacon, *Communia naturalium* 4.3.5, in *Opera hactenus inedita Rogeri Baconi*, ed. Robert Steele (Oxford: Oxford University Press, 1909–40), 3:296.

For Thomas, powers are accidents in the category of quality.[89] They are *propria*, or "necessary accidents," in that they "flow" naturally from the essence of a given substance as their "root" or "source," such that the substance cannot naturally speaking lack its normal complement of powers unless through some injury or impediment to its development.[90] He sometimes speaks of powers as "virtual parts" of the substantial form, drawing the term from Boethius's *De divisione naturae*, but this should not be taken to imply that by adding together a bunch of virtual parts, one gets a substantial form.[91] Rather, as mentioned, Aquinas uses the term "flowing" to describe the relationship between substantial forms and powers.[92] He deploys a variety of different arguments in support of the view that powers are really distinct from substantial forms. Some of them seem to me more persuasive than others. As most have been amply discussed by other commentators, I will focus here on two he brings up rather briefly regarding the powers of living things (and humans in particular).[93] They are especially worth considering because of what they reveal about the significance and ramifications of his view.

First, when it comes to the powers of humans in particular, Aquinas notes that some of them are material, inhering in the composite of soul and body, while our intellectual powers (as explained in the previous

---

89. ST 1a.77.1 ad 5.

90. Ibid. Aquinas sometimes says that someone can lack a certain power but retain it "in its root" (*in radice*)—see 1a2ae.85.2 ad 3, In Sent 3.33.1.4 ad 4, QDA 19 ad 2.

91. See ST 1a.76.8 and QDSC 4; for more on potential or virtual wholes and parts see Andrew Arlig, "Medieval Mereology," in *The Stanford Encyclopedia of Philosophy* (2015), ed. Edward Zalta, available at plato.stanford.edu/entries/mereology-medieval/.

92. In Sent 1.3.4.2, ST 1a.77.6, QDV 25.6 ad 1, QDA 19. He inherits the "flowing" language from Albert the Great. In speaking of the souls powers as its parts Aquinas thinks he is simply following Aristotle's usage in *De anima*; see In DA 2.5.279. As far as the sort of causal relation "flowing" involves, Aquinas says the soul is the final cause, "in a way" the efficient cause, and in some cases (i.e., those of intellect and will) the material cause of its powers. See Matthew Walz, "What Is a Power of the Soul? Aquinas's Answer," *Sapientia* 60, no. 218 (2005): 319–48, at 332–47, and John Wippel, *The Metaphysical Thought of Godfrey of Fontaines* (Washington, D.C.: The Catholic University of America Press, 1981), chap. 4, for discussion.

93. See my "Faculties of the Soul"; Walz, "What Is a Power?"; Pasnau, *Aquinas on Human Nature*, chap. 5, §2; Wippel, *Metaphysical Thought of Thomas Aquinas*, chap. 8, §§3–4; and Peter King, "The Inner Cathedral: Mental Architecture in High Scholasticism," *Vivarium* 46, no. 3 (2008): 253–74. Two classic studies of the relationship between souls and their powers are Lottin, *Psychologie et morale*, and Pius Künzle, *Das Verhältnis der Seele zu Ihren Potenzen* (Freiburg: Universitätsverlag, 1956).

chapter) are immaterial, inhering in the soul alone.[94] Based on this observation Aquinas argues as follows:

(2.7) Some have posited that the soul's powers are nothing but its essence, so that one and the same essence of the soul, according as it is the principle of a sensitive operation is called the [power of] sense, while according as it is the principle of the intellectual operation it is called the [power of] intellect, and so on for the rest.... But this position is entirely impossible ... because of differences between the powers, of which some are acts of certain parts of the body, as is the case with the powers of the sensitive and nutritive parts, while other powers are not acts of any part of the body, like intellect and will; which could not be the case if the powers of the soul were the same as its essence.[95]

Aquinas's reasoning is that one and the same soul cannot be identical to powers with the opposed attributes of materiality, on the one hand, and immateriality on the other. Hence the powers must be really distinct from the soul itself and from one another. Whatever one makes of this argument, the distinction between the human soul and its powers is certainly important when it comes to explaining, in response to the sort of objection we saw Siger and Cross pressing, near the end of chapter 1, how our soul is able to possess at the same time both an inherent and a subsistent act of being. The first objection that Aquinas considers makes a point similar to Siger's, drawing on the authority of Aristotle: "it seems that the intellective principle is not united to the body as its form, for the philosopher says in DA 3.4 that the intellect is separate, and is not the act of any body, so it is not united to the body as its form."[96] Thomas's response is to acknowledge that while the soul is "separate"—that is, possesses a subsistent act of being—"according to its intellective power," nevertheless it is in matter—that is, possesses an inherent act of being—inasmuch as "the soul itself to which this [intellective] power belongs is the form of the body."[97] This response hinges on there being a distinction between the intellective power it-

---

94. QDSC 11 and ST 1a.77.5.
95. QDSC 11 (Leo. 24.2:118.190–200 and 220–27).
96. ST 1a.76.1 arg. 1 (Leo. 5:208).
97. Ibid.; see Pasnau's helpful discussion of this passage in *Aquinas on Human Nature*, chap. 5, §4.

self and "intellective principle," namely the soul to which the intellective power belongs, and from which it "flows" as its source or root.[98]

A second argument Thomas offers for distinguishing the powers of living things from their souls and from one another is equally instructive to consider. It is based on the idea that such powers are often located in different parts of the body:

(2.8) Since a perfection and what is perfected are proportioned to one another, it is necessary that what is perfected by diverse proportions should receive diverse perfections. But the diverse organs of an animate body are [perfected by] diverse proportions in the mixture. Therefore they are perfected in diverse ways by the soul. Not according to their act of being, however, since the soul, which is the substantial form of the body, gives just one act of being to the whole body. Therefore it is necessary that they are perfected in diverse ways as regards the perfections following on this act of being, according to which they have diverse operations. But these perfections, which are principles of the soul's operations, we call powers. So it is necessary that the powers of the soul are diverse from its essence, namely as emanating from it.[99]

Aquinas's reasoning here relies first on the observation that living things exercise different operations through different parts of the body. As we saw, there is a sense in which the opponents of Thomas's view could agree: distinct operations pertain to distinct bodily parts simply because the latter serve the soul in distinct instrumental roles. What Aquinas points out, however, is that distinct bodily parts get to be the way they are because they are perfected by certain "proportions," that is, by certain forms or structures. Now according to its essence the soul is equally distributed throughout the body, to which it gives a single act of being. In fact, to play the unifying and identity-determining roles I sketched above Aquinas thinks souls according to their essences must

---

98. It is instructive to contrast Aquinas's position here with that of John Buridan, who agreed that the human soul is our only substantial form but identified the soul with its powers (see Buridan's QDA 2.5). Buridan struggles to explain how one and the same soul could both inhere in the body and subsist on its own. He ends up acknowledging this as something we must accept by faith but cannot understand. See my "Faculties of the Soul," 624–31, and Jack Zupko, "How Are Souls Related to Bodies? A Study of John Buridan," *Review of Metaphysics* 46, no. 3 (1993): 575–601, at 598–99.

99. In Sent 1.3.4.2 sc 3 (Mand./Moos 1:115–16).

be fully present in every bodily part.[100] After all, every part of a human body is fully human. Robert Pasnau uses Henry More's helpful term "holenmerous" for this way of being present as a whole in each part of something else.[101] According to Aquinas and many other medievals, it is the way God is present in creation.[102] Thomas says it is because of the way substantial forms bestow identity not just on a whole composite substance but on each of its parts as well that Aristotle maintains the homonymy principle: that body parts like hands or flesh are only equivocally so-called upon the soul's withdrawal.[103] If the soul is uniformly present throughout the body according to its essence, however, then the "diverse proportions" that structure different bodily parts in different ways to carry out different operations cannot be identical to the soul's essence or to one another. Hence Aquinas's view that they are accidental forms "flowing" or "emanating" from the soul itself.[104]

If the substantial forms are overarching structures responsible in various ways for the unity and identity of the composite substances to which they belong, I think it makes sense in many cases to regard powers as substructures responsible for configuring the body such that it is capable of carrying out or contributing to certain operations. Aquinas's comments on Aristotle's claim that "if the eye were an animal, sight would be its soul," provide helpful insight into his view. Aquinas writes that "sight is the substantial form of the eye, and the eye is the matter of sight just as the organic body is the matter of the soul."[105] Of course, the eye is not an animal but part of one, and the power of sight is not a substantial form but an accident. Thomas suggests that Aristotle is try-

---

100. ST 1a.76.8, QDSC 4, QDA 10; see Anton Pegis, *St. Thomas and the Problem of the Soul in the Thirteenth Century* (Toronto: PIMS, 1934), 141–47, for a helpful discussion of these texts.

101. Pasnau, *Metaphysical Themes*, chap. 16, pars. 4–6.

102. See ST 1a.8.4 (Leo. 4:89): "however many places there are, it is necessary that God is in every one of them, not as a part [of him], but as his very self."

103. ST 1a.76.8 and QDA 10.

104. To be sure, Aquinas's critics might respond that the body *does* just happen to be structured in certain ways. In that case I think Thomas might still argue for what I have called his distinction thesis by appealing to the explanatory roles powers are supposed to play, and the necessity of localization to explain how they play these roles. See my "Aquinas vs. Buridan on the Substance and Powers of the Soul," in *Questions on the Soul by John Buridan and Others: A Companion to Buridan's Philosophy of Mind*, ed. Gyula Klima (Cham: Springer, 2017), 77–94.

105. In DA 2.2.239; De Anima 2.1.412b17.

ing to explain soul-body relations through examples involving accidental forms because these are "nearer to our senses" than are substantial forms. Referring back to this passage later in his *De anima* commentary, Thomas offers the following clarification:

(2.9) A sense organ like the eye is the same in subject with that power [i.e., the sense of sight], but has a different act of being since power and body are different in definition. For the power is as it were the form of the organ, as was said above. And therefore he says that a magnitude, that is, a corporeal organ, receives a sensation because it is what receives a sense power, just as matter receives form. But the definition of the magnitude and of the sensitive power or sense are not the same, but the sense is a certain ratio, that is, a proportion or form and power of the magnitude.[106]

I take it that when Aquinas says a sense power and its corporeal organ are the same in subject but differ in terms of their act of being, he is contrasting the organ's subsistent mode of being with the power's inherent mode—a point he makes more explicit elsewhere.[107] What is especially noteworthy here, however, is Thomas's insistence that sense powers are related to their bodily organs as their forms or structures.

Now certainly not all powers are substructures related to bodily organs in this way. This must be true for at least three reasons. First, not all substances with powers have bodies at all. Aquinas thinks angelic powers are accidental forms flowing from their essences much as ours do from our souls.[108] If it makes sense to think of angelic essences as structures, then we might regard their powers as substructures, but these substructures would not be responsible for configuring bodily organs.[109] Second, certain composite substances have powers but do not exercise them through bodily organs. This is certainly true of celestial bodies.[110] It is also true of the "lowest-level" composite substances—

---

106. *In DA* 2.24.555; see ibid., 2.2.7/241: "the eye is something composed from the pupil as its matter and sight as its form."
107. *In Sent* 3.15.2.1.2 (Mand./Moos 3:485): "powers of this sort are not subsistent, but are the forms of bodily organs."
108. *ST* 1a.54.3.
109. Stump thinks it makes sense to speak of even God and angels as organized or configured on Aquinas's view: "for Aquinas, to be is to be configured" (Aquinas, 37).
110. Aquinas would deny that the sun, for instance, exercises its power of lighting things up through any bodily organ—see *ST* 1a.70.3. The sole material constituent of celestial bodies like the sun is a fundamental stuff Aquinas calls "the fifth body" (see *In DCM* 1.3–5). As I

what Aquinas calls elements—and it is probably true of certain other nonliving substances such as stones and metals as well.[111] It might still make sense to regard the powers of non-organic composite substances like these as substructures, as they are still accidents really distinct from their substantial forms. But they would not necessarily correspond to any part of these composite substances identifiable on its own in the way organs are. Finally, within organisms themselves Aquinas recognizes multiple levels of composition, not all of which are organic, and accordingly also multiple levels of powers as substructures, not all of which correspond to bodily organs. Let me further unpack this last set of claims.

The language of "levels of composition" is not Aquinas's own, but Thomas following Aristotle does often speak of degrees of proximity and remoteness in causation, including in the material causes of certain composite substances. Where Aristotle says that "we must state the proximate causes," Aquinas comments:

(2.10) Cognition of a given thing through its first causes is only imperfect and universal, but through its proximate causes perfect cognition of a thing can be had, just as if someone should ask about the material causes of a human

---

mentioned earlier in this chapter, it may be that this celestial stuff is an irreducibly distinct kind of prime matter from that of sublunary bodies. Aquinas calls it "the fifth body," however, to indicate that it is not one of the four elements he recognizes (following Empedocles and Aristotle) as the "lowest-level" material constituents of all sublunary bodies: air, water, fire, and earth.

111. I say "probably" here because it is hard to know what nonliving substances Aquinas thinks there are. He often speaks of stones or metals as though they were substances. But as I discussed in chapter 1, Thomas distinguishes between *per se* and *per accidens* modes of being, and associates the latter with artifacts like statues. Such artifacts are the result of combining one or more substances with at least one accident; they are not simply substances in their own right. He also apparently thinks there are nonartifact beings *per accidens* as well as manmade ones. That is, through nature or by chance certain units come about that are not substances but rather combinations of substances with one or more accidents. He often speaks of a heap of stones as an example of such a being *per accidens*. Presumably he would say the same about other arbitrary sums of nonliving stuff. As Pasnau explains (*Aquinas on Human Nature*, 85–88), however, Aquinas thinks there are *minima* of natural bodies—minimum amounts that cannot be divided any further without being destroyed and changed into something else. Aquinas clearly believes there are *minima* of elements (see *Sententia super De sensu et sensato* [hereafter, In DSS] 7/8.9, 14/15.5, 17/18.15); perhaps he believes the same about nonliving mixed bodies such as stones or metals. I will say more about Aquinas's criteria for the emergence of genuine substances as opposed to such accidental unities as heaps in chapter 3. See for further discussion Christopher Brown, "Aquinas on the Individuation of Non-Living Substances," *Proceedings of the American Catholic Philosophical Association* 75 (2001): 237–54.

being fire or earth should not be assigned as his causes, since these are the common matter of all generable and corruptible things, but rather his proper matter should be assigned, such as flesh and bone and things of this sort.[112]

Aquinas's point is certainly not to deny that fire and earth enter into the composition of human beings in any way whatsoever. But much as Thomas insisted in 2.1 that matter could not be left out of a composite substance's definition, so too he is insisting here that a complete understanding of a living thing's matter must encompass all of its various levels.

In animals Thomas recognizes at least four such levels. First, for reasons I discussed earlier in this chapter, Aquinas thinks that prime matter must ultimately underlie their substantial forms. Prime matter in itself is not sensible, but animals have at least three levels of sensible matter. The elements fire, water, air, and earth are the lowest level of composite substances. Aquinas's list of elements comes from Empedocles via Aristotle, but less important than what items appear on the list is the theoretical role they share: they are simply whatever things in the natural world cannot be explained in terms of any lower-level sensible matter.[113] Aquinas thinks that the elements combine to form mixed bodies, some of which (such as stones or metals) may exist on their own, but others of which must exist as a further layer of sensible matter in living things: flesh, bone, blood, nerves, marrow, and fat are all examples Aquinas mentions.[114] Aquinas regards them as homoeomerous, in the sense that their powers and other accidental features are distributed uniformly throughout. Any given quantitative part exactly resembles any other of the same size, except in terms of location. We would probably call them tissues today. They themselves combine in turn to form anhomoeomerous parts such as bodily organs, which Aquinas treats as the highest level of sensible matter present in organisms.

Aquinas offers a helpful explanation of the latter two levels of composition in organisms when he unpacks Aristotle's definition of soul in De anima as "the first grade of actuality of a natural body having life in potency," namely, "a body which is organized":

---

112. In Met 8.4.1738 (Marietti 415); Metaphysics 8.4.1044b1.
113. Aquinas defines elements in DPN 3, In Met 5.4.795–98, In Phys 1.1.5.
114. See In Met 3.8.423, 5.4.800, 7.17.1674; In DGC 1.1.10; In Sent 4.44.1.1.3.

(2.11) Since [Aristotle] said that the soul is the act of a physical body having life in potency, he also says that any such body is organic, and he says that an organic body is one with a diversity of organs. For diversity of organs is necessary for supporting life in a body because of the diverse operations of the soul. For the soul, since it is the most perfect form among the forms of corporeal things, is a principle of diverse operations; and therefore it requires a diversity of organs in what it perfects. But the forms of inanimate things because of their imperfection are principles of fewer operations, whence they do not require a diversity of organs in what they perfect. Among souls, furthermore, the souls of plants are less perfect, whence in plants there is less a diversity of organs than in animals. And therefore to show that every body capable of supporting life is organic, he pursues an argument based on plants in which there is a lesser diversity of organs. And this is why he says that the parts of plants are diverse organs. But the parts of plants are thoroughly simple, that is, homoeomerous, for they do not exhibit the same diversity as in the parts of animals. For the foot of an animal is composed from diverse parts, namely from flesh, nerve, bone, and things of this sort. But the organic parts of plants do not exhibit such a diversity of parts from which they are composed. But that the parts of plants are organic is clear since diverse parts are oriented toward diverse operations, just as a leaf is a covering for the shell or fruit-bearing part, that is, that part in which the fruit is born, but the shell or fruit-bearing part is a covering for the fruit, while the roots in plants are proportionate to the mouths of animals, since each brings in food.[115]

There are several things worth noting in this passage. First, Aquinas draws the contrast between tissues and organs not just in terms of the former being homoeomerous and the latter anhomoeomerous, but also in terms of the theoretical roles they play. Organs are oriented toward certain "systems-level" life-preserving tasks, while the latter perform what we might regard as "subtasks." Aquinas offers several lists of such systems-level tasks, drawing chiefly from Aristotle. His example in 2.11 probably is not ideal, but he appears to think of feet as organs of the systems-level task of locomotion, composed of flesh, nerve, bone, etc., each with their own specific roles in making locomotion possible. Occasionally Aquinas assigns the elements themselves their own subtasks

---

115. In DA 2.1.230–32 (Leo. 45:71–72.322–57); De anima 2.1.412b4.

within systems-level vital operations such as nutrition.[116] Second, as feet do not seem to make locomotion possible just by themselves, Aquinas evidently does not think that a single organ must be capable of performing a systems-level task on its own, without the contributions of other organic parts. Organs are simply the highest-level parts oriented toward systems-level tasks he discusses. Third, Aquinas thinks we should not expect the levels of composition to look the same in all living things. Plants are simpler than animals, and hence are able to carry out all of their vital operations with homoeomerous organic parts.

I am not sure if Aquinas would continue to say that plants have only homoeomeous parts if he were writing today. He might alter his account of the levels of composition in organisms in certain other ways as well. For instance, he might recognize organ-systems, rather than organs, as the highest-level sensible matter in organisms. He might identify subatomic particles of some sort as elements rather than the Empedoclean four. He would likely recognize further layers of sensible matter capable of existing apart from living things beyond just the elements: chemical compounds of various sorts, for instance. He would certainly recognize cells as a basic unit of composition in living things.

Many aspects of his account would remain unchanged, however. He would continue to say that something must play the theoretical role he assigns to the Empedoclean elements.[117] He would retain the notion of certain systems-level tasks as fundamental to the lives of organisms. He would continue to hold that levels of organization need not look the same in all living things, but might vary on a species-by-species basis.

Most important, perhaps, he would retain the notion of powers as accidental forms, flowing from substantial forms as their root or source, and describable at least in the case of certain composite substances as substructures responsible for configuring their bodies in certain ways. As we saw, a composite substance's body can be understood simply as the part extended in spatial dimensions, as opposed to the part that "perfects" its three-dimensional bulk such that the substance, as a

---

116. For instance, the subtask of fire in nutrition is to cook food so that it can be digested; see In DA 2.8.331.

117. As for what might play this role, see Bobik, *Aquinas on Matter and Form*, 245–87, and Pasnau, *Aquinas on Human Nature*, 87.

whole, can do whatever it does. It may be that Aquinas thinks some composite substances are able to exercise their powers through relatively simple bodies, with solely spatial or quantitative parts, such as a top half and bottom half. When it comes to organisms such as ourselves, however, this is clearly not the case. Rather, our bodies have an array of other parts as well at various levels: elements, tissues, organs, etc. Each of these parts has an accidental form—a power—as its structure. All of the powers of living things, from systems-level tasks right down to the lowest-level subtasks, can be understood as substructures responsible for configuring their bodies in certain ways—with one crucial exception. Intellectual powers are not the structures of any bodily organs (or organ-systems, or suborganic parts, for that matter). In that sense they are incorporeal powers. Aquinas concludes his comments on De anima 2.1 with the following:

(2.12) Since it was shown that the soul is the act of the whole body, and its parts are acts of the body's parts, [and since] moreover an act and form is not separated from that of which it is an act and form, it is clear that the soul cannot be separated from the body, either as a whole or with regard to any of its parts, if it should happen that the soul in some way has parts. For it is clear that some parts of the soul are acts of certain parts of the body, just as when it was said that vision is the act of the eye. But according to certain parts nothing prohibits the soul from being separated, since certain parts of the soul are acts of no part of the body, as will be proved below by what is said about the intellect.[118]

As we have seen, Aquinas thinks souls do indeed have (virtual) parts, in the sense that they have powers flowing from the souls themselves as their source. Most of these powers, as he says here, correspond to parts of the body as their acts or forms, and cannot exist without the body parts they structure or configure. The intellect, however, does not correspond to any bodily part in this way. As the last sentence of the quotation indicates, Thomas takes this fact to license a further inference to the possibility of souls existing in a separated or disembodied state. In the following chapter I will investigate further how and why Aquinas takes this to be so.

---

118. In DA 2.2.242 (Leo. 45.1:76.141–53).

3

FROM INCORPOREALITY TO INCORRUPTIBILITY

So far we have seen that, for Aquinas, claiming that the human intellect is immaterial means primarily that it has its act of being in an immaterial mode. We have also seen that Aquinas thinks of the human intellect as a power of the soul—an accidental form "flowing from" and "rooted in" the human soul—which, however, inheres in the soul itself directly as its subject, rather than in the human composed of soul and body as a whole. Finally, we have seen that while most of the psychological powers of living things are, for Aquinas, substructures responsible for configuring body parts at various levels into organs capable of carrying out or contributing to one or more systems-level operation, the human intellect is not related in this way to any bodily organ or organ-system. In this sense it is an "incorporeal power." Often Aquinas expresses this last idea by saying that the operations of intellectual powers are "not shared with the body," nor "carried out through any corporeal organ."[1] They are incorporeal operations. But locutions like these leave it unclear how intellectual powers and operations are related to body parts, states, and processes. The connection must surely be an intimate one. We have seen that Aquinas thinks that the intellective principle (the human soul) is the form of the human body. He also acknowledges that brain dam-

---

1. "Not shared with the body": In Sent 2.19.1.1, ST 1a.75.2, CT 1.84, etc. "Not carried out through any corporeal organ": QQ 10.3.2, ST 1a.75.2, In DA 1.2.19, etc.

age impedes intellectual operations, as I will explain further. Yet the connection cannot be *too* intimate, because the fact that intellectual operations are incorporeal factors importantly in Aquinas's reasoning for supposing that there can be human souls without bodies, that is, separated souls.

In this chapter my aim is to present one way of understanding Aquinas's claims concerning the incorporeality of intellectual powers and operations, and to show how, if true, they do indeed license his inference to the human soul's separability. I will go on, in the next two chapters, to examine the truth of Aquinas's claims about the intellect's incorporeality.

One factor making my aim in this chapter difficult to achieve is that while Aquinas frequently acknowledges that Aristotle thought the human soul is separable from the body, and agrees with him, Thomas never mounts a discrete argument in which this is his explicitly-stated conclusion.[2] He argues in various places that separated souls are capable of understanding (and various related operations).[3] These arguments turn out, though, to consist of explanations of how God is able to assist human souls such that they are capable of understanding (etc.) in separation from bodies even though they lack senses or various other powers that cooperate with their intellectual operations while they are attached to bodies. They presuppose the existence of separated human souls, rather than attempting to show that such separation is possible in the first place. Aquinas also argues that human souls are subsistent and incorruptible.[4] Conversely he argues that the souls of other living things (such as brute animals), are not subsistent, and hence are corruptible.[5] In chapter 1 we saw roughly what Aquinas means by subsistence, and

---

2. Aquinas takes Aristotle to affirm or presuppose the human soul's ability to exist in separation from the body in numerous passages: De anima 1.4.408b18, 2.1.413a4–7, 2.2.413b25–29, 3.4–5; Metaphysics 12.3.1070a25–27; Nicomachean Ethics 10.7.1177b27–35, etc. Interpreters of Aristotle have, of course, been long divided as to the proper understanding of these passages, especially the cryptic remarks in De anima 3.5 about *nous poiētikos* as *chōristos* (separate), *athanaton* (deathless), and *aidion* (everlasting). See Fred Miller, "Aristotle on the Separability of Mind," in *The Oxford Handbook of Aristotle*, ed. Christopher Shields (Oxford: Oxford University Press, 2012), 306–39, for one helpful introduction to contemporary positions in the debate.

3. See In Sent 3.31.2.4 and 4.50.1.1, QQ 3.9.1, QDV 19.1, QDA 15, ST 1a.89.1.

4. See In Sent 2.19.1.1, SCG 2.79–81, QQ 10.3.2, ST 1a.75.2 and 6, QDA 14, CT 1.84, In DA 1.2.16–22.

5. See SCG 2.82 and ST 1a.75.3.

why he links the human soul's subsistence with its possession of inherent intellectual powers. The human soul's incorruptibility presumably has something to do with its capacity for being destroyed or ceasing to exist, but exactly what, and how it relates to the soul's subsistence, is hard to pin down. This may be partly because Aquinas shifted strategies for demonstrating the human soul's incorruptibility in the middle of his career.

I will begin this chapter by examining some of Aquinas's attempts to prove the human soul's incorruptibility, and arguing that at root each of them relies on a similar core argumentative strategy to show that human souls can exist in separation from bodies. One premise in this core argument is a claim that the human intellect is in some way incorporeal. I then, in the second section, consider various interpretations of this incorporeality claim and single out one of them as getting at the root of Aquinas's meaning. Roughly, Thomas means that intellectual operations cannot be explained in bodily terms.

The following three sections defend this interpretation both *as* an interpretation of Thomas, and as philosophically plausible. In the third section of the chapter I examine Aquinas's physics to show why he is committed to its objects being explicable in bodily terms, despite embracing a robust emergentism and antireductivism. I also explain why he thinks our inability to explain intellectual operations in such terms entails their ontological independence and separability from the body. The fourth section argues that both physicalists and substance dualists alike should agree with Aquinas that psychological powers are ontologically dependent on the body if, and only if, their operations are explicable in bodily terms. The fifth argues that Aquinas's fellow emergentists should also embrace this conclusion. I conclude in the last section by contrasting Aquinas's strategy for demonstrating the possibility of separated souls with one sort of reasoning often employed by substance dualists like René Descartes. By the end of the chapter readers should not only have a clear sense of how Aquinas ties the possibility of disembodied human souls to the immateriality and incorporeality of our intellectual operations, but also of how his philosophical psychology relates to contemporary versions of physicalism, substance dualism, and emergentism in the philosophy of mind.

Aquinas's Arguments for the Human Soul's Incorruptibility

Aquinas argues for the human soul's incorruptibility in at least six different passages, spanning his career from his *Sentences* commentary to his unfinished *Compendium theologiae*. Lawrence Dewan and Joseph Owens both examine an apparent shift in Aquinas's argumentative strategy that they think can be observed between *Quodlibet* 10.3.2 (ca. 1258) and his treatment of the subject in *Summa contra Gentiles* (ca. 1261).[6] They are correct, I think, that Aquinas begins in *SCG* to supplement the sort of argument he uses early on with a different strand of reasoning. The later arguments also seem to defend a stronger sort of incorruptibility than what Aquinas tried to prove earlier on. As far as I can tell, however, the later arguments continue to rely on the earlier strategy at their crux, and continue to defend just the *possibility* of souls existing in separation from bodies.

Consider first Aquinas's argument in *Quodlibet* 10.3.2, from the "early period." The question is "whether the rational soul is incorruptible according to its own substance." Aquinas thinks it is:

(3.1) If it were corrupted, this would happen to it either *per se* or *per accidens*. But to be corrupted *per se* cannot happen except to things composed of matter and form and having contrariety, which could not happen unless [the rational soul] were an element or a thing made from elements, as was held by the ancient philosophers whose positions are refuted in *De anima* book one. To be corrupted *per accidens* could not happen either unless we suppose that [the rational soul] does not have an act of being *per se*, but only has an act of being in something else, as is true of all material forms, which do not properly have a subsistent act of being, but belong *per se* to the composite substances of which they are parts, and thus are corrupted *per accidens* when their composites are corrupted. But this cannot be said about the rational soul, for it is impossible for anything lacking an act of being *per se* to operate *per se*, whence also those other forms do not operate, but rather the composite through the forms. But

---

6. Both likewise think the *De immortalitate animae* edited by L. A. Kennedy represents Aquinas in a period of transition between these two argumentative strategies. See Joseph Owens, "Aquinas on the Inseparability of the Soul from Existence," *New Scholasticism* 61, no. 3 (1987): 249–70; Laurence Dewan, *Form and Being: Studies in Thomistic Metaphysics* (Washington, D.C.: The Catholic University of America Press, 2006), chap. 10.

the rational soul has a *per se* operation that it exercises through the mediation of no corporeal organ, namely understanding, as the philosopher proves in *De anima* book three.[7]

Aquinas goes on to recite Aristotle's argument from *De anima* 3.4.429a13–29, which I examine in chapter 5.[8] As far as the reasoning in passage 3.1 goes, it divides into strands showing that the human soul cannot be corrupted *per se*, then that it cannot be corrupted *per accidens* (by the corruption of something else). I will examine these in turn.

The first turns out not to be particularly impressive. Both "generation" and "corruption" are technical terms Aquinas takes over from Aristotle that refer to a specific sort of change through which substances naturally come into or pass out of existence.[9] For this sort of change to happen, Aquinas thinks, substances must be composed of (prime) matter and form, as something (the matter) must survive throughout the change, in which one form is lost and another comes about. Furthermore, to be generable or corruptible a substance must either be one of the four elements, or be composed from elemental matter, as opposed to the matter of heavenly bodies, which Aquinas calls "the fifth body."[10] As noted in chapter 2 (p. 63), it is somewhat unclear whether Aquinas regards this fifth body as a primitively distinct type of prime matter or a type of proximate matter. Elements can be corrupted and transformed into other elements, according to Aquinas, because from their essence flow certain powers—heating, cooling, drying, moistening, and motion up or down—that have contraries. What is cold can be heated, what is wet can be dried, and if enough heating and drying happens to a wet, cold element like water, it will be transformed into a different element altogether, such as fire.[11] As a result, substances composed of elements

---

7. QQ 10.3.2 (Leo. 25.2:132.55–75).
8. *De anima* 3.4.429a13–29.
9. In passage 1.2 Aquinas says that generation *simpliciter* refers to the coming about of substances, while generation *secundum quid* refers to the coming about of accidents. Elsewhere, however, as at In Phys 5.3, Thomas distinguishes between generation and corruption, on the one hand, which involve the coming about or cessation of substances, and motions, on the other hand, which involve coming about or ceasing to be in accidental categories.
10. See In DCM 1.4–5.
11. ST 1a.49.1 and *Sententia super Meteora* (hereafter, In Meteor) 1.3–4. We do not get the full account of elemental transformations because Aquinas did not comment on the second book of DGC.

are corruptible as well. In contrast, whatever powers heavenly bodies have are not subject to contraries in this way, so such bodies cannot be corrupted. Aquinas's claim that the rational soul cannot be corrupted *per se*, then, follows straightforwardly from the fact that it is a form, as opposed to something composed of form and (elemental) matter. As only hylomorphic composites—indeed, only sublunary hylomorphic composites—can be corrupted *per se*, the rational soul cannot be.[12] But then, neither can any form be corrupted this way. Even the most ephemeral accidental form is immune to *per se* corruption. That certainly is not to say that such forms cannot be destroyed, just that they cannot be corrupted *per se*. Hence the fact by itself that human souls cannot be corrupted *per se* is not terribly significant.

The way most souls are corruptible, Aquinas believes, is *per accidens*, when the living bodies they inform are (*per se*) corrupted. Aquinas says in 3.1 that this is what happens to all "material forms," by which I take it he means those with only a material act of being. Such forms, he sometimes says, are "immersed in," or "totally circumscribed by" the material body, in the sense that all of their powers are exercised through it or its parts.[13] In contrast, the rational soul has a power that it exercises on its own, without the mediation of any bodily organ. Aquinas reckons that if this is so, then it has an act of being on its own. At least, its act of being is independent of the body's, such that it cannot be corrupted *per accidens* by the body's corruption.

As Owens notes, in arguing this way Aquinas is mainly following Aristotle's lead. Here is how Thomas understands Aristotle's dialectic:

(3.2) If there turns out to be some passion or operation proper to the soul, then it will turn out that the soul can be separated from the body, since whatever has an operation *per se*, also has an act of being and subsistence *per se*. If, however, there is no operation or passion proper to the soul, by the same reasoning it will turn out that the soul will be inseparable from the body.[14]

---

12. See Frederick Wilhelmsen, "A Note on Contraries and the Incorruptibility of the Human Soul in St. Thomas Aquinas," *American Catholic Philosophical Quarterly* 67, no. 3 (1993): 333–38.
13. See ST 1a.76.1 ad 4, QDA 1 and 2 ad 12, QDSC 2, SCG 2.68.12.
14. Aquinas, In DA 1.2.21 (Leo. 45.1:10.89–93), commenting on *De anima* 1.1.403a2–12.

By "proper to the soul" I take it Aquinas means "not shared with the body" and "not carried out through a bodily organ." Aquinas agrees with Aristotle that if souls are able to act or to be acted upon by themselves, apart from the body, then they must also be capable of existing by themselves apart from the body as the subjects of such incorporeal powers and operations.[15]

Now turning to the "later period" of Aquinas's thought on the soul's incorruptibility, it may seem that a new, stronger line of reasoning emerges. In the *Summa theologiae*, for example, Aquinas first rules out the possibility of the human soul's being corrupted *per accidens* for the same reason we have just seen.[16] Because they have an operation that is not shared with the body or carried out through any bodily organ, human souls are subsistent, and what subsists apart from something else cannot be destroyed by the destruction of that other thing. When it comes to the soul's corruption *per se*, in contrast, Aquinas argues against this possibility as follows:

(3.3) This is entirely impossible not only for the human soul, but for anything subsistent that is just a form. For it is clear that what belongs to a thing by itself is inseparable from it, but an act of being belongs to a form (which is an act) by itself. Whence matter acquires an act of being in act by acquiring a form, while corruption takes place in it through its form being separated from it. Now it is impossible for a form to be separated from itself, whence it is impossible that a form should cease to exist.[17]

I confess that I find this reasoning, versions of which also appear in various other passages, somewhat obscure.[18] It makes it appear as though it is absolutely impossible for souls to cease to exist. But this cannot be correct. Because souls are created forms, they are not identical to their act of being, and hence depend on God for their sustained existence. By withholding this sustenance God is just as capable of annihilating souls as anything else. Aquinas recognizes this. The second objection he con-

---

15. See In DA 3.7.699. See Phil Corkum, "Aristotle on Ontological Dependence," *Phronesis* 53, no. 1 (2008): 65–92, at 88–90, for a discussion of Aristotle's reasoning concerning the separability of *nous*.
16. ST 1a.75.6 (Leo. 5:204).
17. Ibid.
18. See QDA 14, SCG 2.55 and 2.79, CT 1.74, In DC 26.

siders in the *Summa theologiae* against the soul's incorruptibility points out that "whatever is [created] out of nothing can be returned to nothingness," and Aquinas's reply implicitly concedes that this is so.[19] Still, Aquinas says in his response, "a thing is said to be corruptible because there is in it some potency for nonexistence." Owens thinks Thomas is trying to show that there is no "intrinsic possibility for [a subsistent form] to lose existence."[20] In other words, the possibility that human souls should cease to exist is due entirely to their dependence on God, not on some tendency within the souls themselves to fall apart.[21] As far as I can tell, however, the reason why Thomas thinks souls lack this tendency to fall apart is simply that, because they are forms, they lack matter of the right sort. I am not sure that the "later" arguments actually aim at a stronger conclusion than those of the "earlier period."[22] In both periods, the real work is accomplished by demonstrating that souls are not corruptible *per accidens* by the corruption of the body.

Sometimes commentators gloss "incorruptibility" as "indestructibility." This is somewhat misleading both in that it obscures the technical Aristotelian sense in which Aquinas understands "corruption," and in that strictly speaking God could destroy souls just as easily as any other creature. The root of Aquinas's reasoning throughout his career regarding the incorruptibility of human souls, I submit, is that because our souls

---

19. ST 1a.75.6 arg. 2 and ad 2 (Leo. 5:203–4); Aquinas maintains that God could annihilate any creature there is (QDP 5.3) but that it would not be fitting for God to annihilate any creature, and hence that he will not ever actually do so (QDP 5.4 and QQ 4.3.1).

20. Commenting on In DC 26 Owens writes that "a thing's matter is made actual by the form, while through that same form the thing has existence in actuality. As long as the form is exercising its actuality the thing continues to exist. There is no way of separating the actual functioning of the form and the thing's continuance in existence. But where it is the actuality of matter, the form requires the matter to sustain it. Accordingly loss of the matter means loss of the actuality, and in consequence loss of existence for the material thing. Where on the other hand the form is subsistent in itself, there is no matter to be lost. So there is no intrinsic possibility for it to lose existence" ("Aquinas on the Inseparability," 259).

21. I take it the parallel is with creation: just as there was not something sitting around with a potency to be created, because creation was *ex nihilo*, depending simply on the will of God, so too the soul has no potency for destruction that is not dependent on the will of God.

22. I agree with Dewan and Owens that Aquinas introduces a new argumentative strategy starting in SCG that is not present in earlier discussions of incorruptibility at In Sent 2.9.1.1 and QQ 10.3.2, but I am not sure how much this further line of argument ultimately contributes to Thomas's defense of the soul's ability to exist apart from bodies. See also Pasnau, *Aquinas on Human Nature*, 48–52, and chap. 12, §1, for further discussion of Aquinas's reasoning for the soul's incorruptibility.

operate in some sense independently of the body, they are capable of existing independently of the body—in other words, it is possible that they may exist in a separated state. Of course it remains an open question so far what Aquinas means by saying that human souls have a power or operation proper to themselves apart from the body, much less how he might show this to be the case. I turn next to the interpretation of this claim.

Operating Independently of Corporeal Organs

From what we have seen in the preceding section it should be clear that a charitable interpretation of Aquinas's notion that our intellectual powers and operations are independent of the body and its organs must be strong enough to show how or why this idea might plausibly underwrite the possibility of human souls existing independently of bodies, at least in Thomas's estimation. Here I will examine four interpretations that fail to meet these criteria, either because they obviously could not support an inference to the separability of human souls, or because they attribute to Aquinas claims he would clearly reject. I will then introduce what I take to be the most promising interpretation of his claims concerning the human intellect's incorporeality, although my defense of this interpretation will extend through the next three sections as well.

An initial suggestion as to what the human intellect's "operating independently of any bodily organ" might mean is this: when I carry out an intellectual operation there occur no predictably corresponding physiological states or processes. In contrast, operations that do depend on bodily organs are always accompanied by certain predictably corresponding physiological states or processes (just as, for example, the operation of breathing is always accompanied by certain predictably corresponding physiological processes in the lungs).

This straightforward initial suggestion cannot be an accurate interpretation of what Aquinas means by claiming that the intellectual operations are incorporeal. This is clear because Thomas believes that for every intellectual operation you or I ever undergo, there do indeed predictably correspond certain physiological states or processes, including certain brain states.[23] He thinks our brain states typically have

---

23. I use term the "states" here instead of "processes" because it is not clear that Aquinas believes that dynamic processes take place in the brain in the same way we might think of

a profound impact on our ability to carry out intellectual operations. The immaturity of a child's brain impedes his ability to think well, as does drunkenness or other sorts of damage.[24] Indeed if the brain is injured, Aquinas says, our soul "cannot directly understand either itself or anything else."[25] Hence Aquinas would reject the suggestion that no predictably corresponding physiological state or processes accompany our intellectual operations.

On the other hand, the reason why Aquinas holds that intellectual operations typically correspond predictably with brain states is that he believes our abilities to think, understand, reason, etc., are intimately tied to our senses. I will have more to say about the intimate ties between the intellect and sense operations of various sorts in the following chapters. Aquinas thinks, though, that so long as our souls are embodied, every one of our intellectual operations depends on a particular sort of sense operation that he calls imagination or (following Aristotle) *phantasia*. Unlike the intellect, furthermore, Thomas thinks the power of imagination/*phantasia* does indeed operate through a corporeal organ: the brain, specifically its anterior ventricle.[26] Hence, immediately before passage 3.2 Aquinas explains that:

(3.4) The operation of the intellect is in one way proper to the soul, but in a certain way belongs to the composite [of soul and body]. For it must be known that some operations or passions of the soul depend on bodies both as their instrument and as their object, just as seeing depends on a body as its object (since color, which is the object of sight, is in a body) and also as its instrument (since vision, although it is done by the soul, nonetheless cannot be

---

events like synapse growth or neuron firing as processes. For that matter, it is not clear that he believes any sort of processes such as these take place in any cognitive organs. See chapter 4 for further discussion. Even if Aquinas does not believe that processes take place in the brain, he does believe that it must be in a certain state for cognition to occur, and that damage can disrupt this state.

24. See QDV 18.8, In DT 6.2 arg. 6, In Sent 2.20.2.2, ST 1a.84.7.
25. QDSC 2 ad 7 (Leo. 24.2:31.397–99).
26. Following Galen, Avicenna, and the Salerno school of medicine, Aquinas assigns the so-called interior senses to different parts of the brain (see ST 1a.78.4, In Sent 2.20.2.2, QDV 15.1). See Simon Kemp and Garth Fletcher, "The Medieval Theory of the Interior Senses," in *American Journal of Psychology* 106, no. 4 (1993): 559–76; Mark Jordan, "Medicine and Natural Philosophy in Aquinas," in *Thomas von Aquin*, ed. Albert Zimmerman, Miscellanea Medievalia 19 (Berlin: De Gruyter, 1988), 233–46, and Anthony Lisska, *Aquinas's Theory of Perception: An Analytic Reconstruction* (Oxford: Oxford University Press, 2016), 214–18.

carried out except through the organ of sight, namely the pupil, which is its instrument, so that seeing does not belong just to the soul but to the body as well). There is also a certain operation that depends on the body not as its instrument but just as its object. For the intellectual operation is not carried out through a corporeal organ, but depends on a corporeal object, since as the Philosopher says in the third book of this work, phantasms are related to the intellect like colors are to sight.... Moreover, since there cannot be phantasms without a body, it seems that understanding cannot happen without a body, though only as its object, not as its instrument.[27]

Phantasms are (roughly speaking) the conscious experiences that normally accompany any acts of sensation.[28] Here Aquinas claims that just as seeing a certain color depends on there being a colored body to see, so too intellectual operations regarding color depend on accompanying conscious experiences of color.[29] Thomas frequently brings up the latter dependence claim as a potential objection against the view that human souls are incorruptible.[30] In reply Aquinas usually points out that God will assist separated souls supernaturally, and refers us to his discussions of how God will do so. I will consider in chapter 6 whether this response is satisfactory. What passage 3.4 makes clear, however, is that even though in this life intellectual operations are always accompanied by certain physiological states, their relationship to these states is not one of instrumentation. Hence, it would be perfectly correct to say that by calling intellectual powers and operations incorporeal, Aquinas means that they do not use any bodily organs as their instruments. But this leaves us still needing to know what exactly it means for the soul to use organic parts of the body as instruments for many of its operations, though not those of the intellect.

---

27. In DA 1.2.19 (Leo. 45.1:9.48–69).

28. Stump writes that "for Aquinas, phantasia is the cognitive power that makes things appear to us or that gives us access to the sensory data taken in by the senses; or, as we would put it, phantasia is the power that produces the conscious experience which is a component of ordinary sensing" (Aquinas, 259).

29. It is important to note that we may entertain the phantasms that normally accompany a given act of sensation without this act itself taking place, as for instance when I "hear" the opening chord and arpeggio of Schubert's *Trout* Quintet "in my head" even while in a perfectly quiet room. Hence, the fact that intellectual operations depend on accompanying conscious experiences of certain objects does not entail that the objects themselves be present.

30. In Sent 2.19.1.1 arg. 6, SCG 2.80.6, QQ 10.3.2 arg. 1, ST 1a.75.6 arg. 3, QDA 14 arg. 14, etc.

Two further interpretations of this claim might be drawn from philosophers influenced by Wittgenstein, such as Peter Hacker and Anthony Kenny, who also often deny that human intellectual activities use a bodily organ.[31] They mean this in at least two senses. First, there is not a particular part of our body that we must move around voluntarily to help us accomplish intellectual tasks as we do with our eyes and ears in our operations of seeing and hearing. Second, intellectual activities are arguably ascribable only to the whole human, as opposed to any particular part of her. To say that someone thinks with her brain, for instance, is to commit what Kenny calls "the homunculus fallacy" or Hacker "the mereological fallacy," that is, the mistake of ascribing "psychological predicates" to mere parts of a human.[32] Hacker quotes Wittgenstein's line approvingly: "Only of a human being and what resembles (behaves like) a living human being can one say; it has sensations; it sees, is blind; hears, is deaf; is conscious or unconscious."[33] Hence, one interpretation of Aquinas's claim concerning the human intellect's incorporeality might be there is no particular bodily organ it moves around voluntarily

---

31. Anthony Kenny, *The Metaphysics of Mind* (Oxford: Oxford University Press, 1989), and P. M. S. Hacker, *The Intellectual Powers: A Study of Human Nature* (Oxford: Wiley Blackwell, 2013).

32. Kenny, "The Homunculus Fallacy," in *Interpretations of Life and Mind*, ed. M. Grene (London: Routledge, 1971), 65–83, and Hacker, *Intellectual Powers*, 287.

It is worth noting here that Aristotelians like Aquinas would understand the phrase "psychological predicates" differently than Kenny or Hacker do. Hacker, writing with the neuroscientist Maxwell Bennett, says by "psychological predicates" they mean such states as believing, reasoning, knowing, thinking, posing questions, seeking answers, remembering, sense-perception, feeling pain or pleasure, and so on: "those that have been invoked by neuroscientists, psychologists, and cognitive scientists in their endeavors to explain human capacities and their exercise." M. R. Bennett and P. M. S. Hacker, *Philosophical Foundations of Neuroscience* (Oxford: Blackwell, 2003), 73–74. But for Aristotle and Aquinas eating, digesting, and reproducing are psychological predicates as well, in the sense that they are operations of living things, and hence operations of soul. Furthermore, while Aristotle and Aquinas ascribe the full range of psychological predicates—from eating, digesting, and reproducing all the way up to thinking, understanding, reasoning, etc.—to human beings alone, at least some predicates from this range are ascribable to any living thing, including to many that resemble human beings very little. Any living body must minimally be capable of feeding itself and reproducing. There are also nonbodily living beings such as God and angels that are capable of understanding and willing. Aquinas and Aristotle think we can ascribe psychological predicates (in their sense of "psychological") to things like mushrooms and God that do not "behave like" human beings (or anything at all). I will say more in this section shortly about how Aquinas thinks we can handle the "multiple realizability" of psychological predicates.

33. Hacker, *Intellectual Powers*, 288, and Ludwig Wittgenstein, *Philosophical Investigations*, trans. G. E. M. Anscombe (Oxford: Blackwell, 2001), par. 281.

in carrying out its operations. And another interpretation might be that intellectual operations are ascribable only to the whole human, and not to any of her body's parts.

As regards the latter interpretation, it is worth pointing out that even though Aquinas frequently speaks of parts of humans carrying out psychological operations, he is not obviously guilty of the homunculus/mereological fallacy in any problematic way. Hacker (writing with the neuroscientist Maxwell Bennett) thinks neuroscientists often fall into the fallacy, but that Aristotle did not, as evidenced by what Jonathan Barnes calls his "celebrated Rylean passage" in *De anima* 1.4: "to say that it is the soul which is angry is as inexact as it would be to say that it is the soul that weaves webs or builds houses. It is doubtless better to avoid saying that the soul pities or learns or thinks and rather to say that it is the man who does this with his soul."[34] But if Aristotle avoids the homunculus/mereological fallacy, then Aquinas does as well. Certainly Thomas is willing to speak of souls doing things or having things done to them, but then so is Aristotle. Aquinas brings up the "Rylean passage" in several places as a potential objection against the human soul's subsistence or ability to operate apart from the body.[35] The soul cannot be subsistent, the objection runs, for what is subsistent operates, but according to the Aristotelian passage, the soul does not. Aquinas's response is that there is no trouble in ascribing operations to subsistent parts of other things provided we understand what we are saying. An eye or hand, he says, is a subsistent entity in the sense that it may be the subject of various accidents, including operations. Nevertheless, because they are not substances in their own right but only parts of substances, there is also a sense in which hands and eyes do not operate *per se*. Instead, Aquinas writes:

(3.5) The operation of [a substance's] parts is through each part attributed to the whole. For we say that man sees with the eye, and feels with the hand.... We may therefore say that the soul understands just as the eye sees, but it is more correct to say that a human understands with his soul.[36]

---

34. *De anima* 1.4.408b12–15. See Bennett and Hacker, *Philosophical Foundations of Neuroscience*, 15, and chap. 3, §1, along with Jonathan Barnes, "Aristotle's Concept of Mind," *Proceedings of the Aristotelian Society* 72, no. 1 (1972): 101–14, at 103.

35. See *In Sent* 4.50.1.1 arg. 2, ST 1a.75.2 arg. 2, QDA 15 arg. 1, QDV 19.1 arg. 1.

36. ST 1a.75.2 ad 2 (Leo. 5.197).

Thomas's argument is that even though the intellectual operations of the human soul have it as their subject, giving it a subsistent act of being, nevertheless as long as it retains its inherent act of being as that by which a human herself exists, it remains a mere part of a substance, and its operations should properly speaking be attributed to the whole human. It is no more troublesome, in principle, to speak of the intellective soul as the subject of its operations than to speak of the batter grasping a bat with his hand.

With this in mind, Aquinas could agree with Kenny and Hacker that there is no particular part of our body we must move about like a tool to help us accomplish intellectual tasks like we do with our eyes and ears when we see and hear. As 3.5 shows, he also agrees in a sense that a human's intellectual activities are ascribable to her as a whole, though they are also in another sense ascribable to some of her parts: her soul and her intellectual power. Certainly he would agree that there is no particular body part through which she carries them out.

Nevertheless, for intellectual operations to lack a bodily organ in either of the ways that Kenny and Hacker spell out is clearly insufficient to underwrite the separability of human souls. In the midst of arguing that the brain is neither the organ, agent, nor locus of human thinking, Hacker agrees that "we would not be able to think but for the normal functioning of our brain," although he points out that the same is true of walking, which no one says we do with our brains as opposed to our legs.[37] Kenny thinks the brain is probably the "vehicle" for our mental abilities, that is, "the physical ingredient or structure in virtue of which the possessor of an ability possesses the ability and is able to exercise it."[38] If our souls cannot think without the normal functioning of the brain, or depend on it as the vehicle of their intellectual operations, then such operations cannot support the possibility of souls existing in separation from bodies. Hence, neither version of intellectual incorporeality suggested by Kenny or Hacker can adequately represent what Aquinas means by denying that the human intellect uses a bodily organ.

Here is a fourth possible interpretation of what Thomas means by claiming that intellectual operations lack a bodily organ: intellectual

---

37. Hacker, *Intellectual Powers*, 399.
38. Kenny, *Metaphysics of Mind*, 72.

operations are not identical to any given bodily states or processes. In contrast, on this interpretation, non-intellectual vital operations are indeed identical to certain bodily states or processes. If we understand the identity claims this interpretation mentions in terms of type-identity, there are at least two reasons why it cannot be correct.

To begin with, Aquinas thinks vital operations are "multiply realizable" at least in the sense that the same type of operation can take place in organisms with significantly different organic structures from our own, or indeed without any organic structures at all.[39] Generally speaking I think the way Aquinas would handle the multiple realizability of psychological powers and operations is by appealing to the analogical kinds we saw him mention in 1.5, from *De principiis*. That he must do so with respect to certain psychological phenomena is clear from the fact that he attributes them both to God and to creatures, something he thinks we can only do when speaking analogically.[40] Aquinas is typically able to muster a rationale for his willingness to predicate a term of one thing but not another: to predicate "love" of God, say, but not "anger."[41] In the following chapter I will consider the difficult case of his willingness to predicate "cognitive" of animals but not the "media" of cognition.[42] At any rate, because Aquinas thinks vital operations are in

---

39. Consider passage 2.11, in which the roots of plants are equivalent to the mouths of plants. See also *In DA* 2.19.480, where Aquinas explains why our sense of smell is so weak compared to that of other animals and discusses "hard-eyed" animals like locusts and certain kinds of fish.

40. This is an idea that John O'Callaghan defends in "Aquinas, Cognitive Theory, and Analogy: A Propos of Robert Pasnau's *Theories of Cognition in the Later Middle Ages*," *American Catholic Philosophical Quarterly* 76, no. 3 (2002): 451–82.

41. See ST 1a.20.1 ad 2 and SCG 1.89–91.

42. Some caution is in order here lest we suppose that when Aquinas offers formal accounts of psychological powers like anger as the desire for revenge, or nutrition as a living thing's power to preserve itself "in being and due quantity," he is thinking of anger or nutrition as higher-order kinds the way some functionalists do. Stump seems to make this mistake when she likens Aquinas's cognitive theory to Richard Boyd's functionalism in *Aquinas*, 213–16. For one thing, Aquinas thinks that such formal accounts do not provide complete definitions of anger or nutrition on their own, but need to be supplemented with a material account specifying the bodily parts, states, and processes involved in such powers or operations. For another thing, because Aquinas thinks that everything that exists extramentally is individual, it seems likely that he would regard higher-order, functional phenomena as mere beings of reason, the same way he thinks of all universals. Kevin Sharpe points out another reason that Stump is wrong to liken Aquinas's philosophical psychology to Boyd's in "Thomas Aquinas and Nonreductive Physicalism," *Proceedings of the American Catholic Philosophical Association* 79 (2005): 217–28, namely that Aquinas would reject the view that all mental states are

some sense multiply realizable, he cannot believe they are type-identical to any particular bodily state or process.

A further reason for reaching the same conclusion stems from the fact that Aquinas endorses a sort of externalism about psychological states, such that no interior processes within the body are sufficient to determine their identity. In general, as I will explain in further detail in the following section, Thomas considers psychology to be a branch of physics or natural science, and thinks that natural scientific definitions make appeal to four different explanatory factors: the material, formal, efficient, and final causes.[43] Because the last two of these are frequently external to the organism in which psychological powers reside and operations occurs, there is a sense in which Aquinas is an externalist about such phenomena. As Aquinas sees it, powers must be understood in terms of their operations, while operations are understood in part in terms of their objects: their efficient causes, in the case of passive powers to be acted upon in certain ways, or their final causes, in the case of active powers to act in certain ways.[44] To cite one example, we saw in 3.4 that color is the object of visual operations. Aquinas thinks of senses as passive powers, and that color is the efficient cause of vision. Accordingly, any interior events that are *not* caused by colors would not count as vision for Thomas (even if they were phenomenally indistinguishable from vision-events).

The case is similar with the passion of anger, which Aquinas discusses shortly after 3.2.[45] To become angry is also a passive power on Thomas's view. Formally speaking, Aquinas thinks of anger as a sort of desire, which has corresponding to it the physiological process of blood heating up around the heart as its material cause. But it is not just any sort of desire; it is a desire for revenge. As Aquinas unpacks this in various places it means that anger must be brought about by the perception of a slight or injury as its efficient cause, and that it is oriented toward some sort of vengeance-directed activity as its final cause.[46] If

---

"implemented in" bodily states. Intellectual states are not "implemented in" bodily states in that they use no bodily organs as their instruments.

43. See In DSS pr./1, In DA 1.2.23–30, DPN 3–5, In Phys 2.5, In Met 1.4.70.
44. See In DA 2.6.205 and ST 1a.78.1.
45. In DA 1.2.22–24.
46. See 1a2ae.46–48 and QDM 12.

any of these explanatory factors is missing, the resulting state will not be anger. For instance, Aquinas notes, if my body is inflamed such that the blood around my heart is boiling, I may act like one who is angry without any provocation or real desire for revenge.[47] In such a state, I might perhaps be said to be irritable or cranky, but I am not angry.[48] Similarly, if I am very sleepy I may perceive an insult without desiring revenge, and then I will not be angry either.[49] Or else, as Aquinas points out elsewhere, even if God or an angel manifests the sort of activity symptomatic of desiring revenge, they are not literally angry, for getting angry requires a body.[50] In each case one of the causes necessary for the presence of anger has not been met. Whatever state we might be in, it is not anger. Because Aquinas denies that interior states or processes—such as physiological states or processes in bodily organs—are sufficient to determine the identity of psychological powers or operations, he would also deny that such powers or operations are identical to any given physiological goings-on.[51] This is equally true, furthermore, whether we have type- or token-identity in mind.

Now Aquinas would agree that all non-intellectual powers and operations of the soul *include* physiological states and/or processes in bodily organs as their material causes.[52] For example, we saw in chapter 2 that,

---

47. In DA 1.2.22.
48. What would be lacking here is the perception of an insult that would bring about a desire for revenge. Aquinas argues that appetite always follows apprehension. It is only animals that have sensitive powers that have appetitive powers: see In DA 2.5.288 and ST 1a.78.2.
49. As Robert Bolton notes in "Perception Naturalized in Aristotle's De anima," in *Metaphysics, Soul, and Ethics in Ancient Thought: Themes from the Work of Richard Sorabji*, ed. Ricardo Salles (Oxford: Oxford University Press, 2005), 209–44, at 214.
50. See ST 1a.20.1 ad 2 and 1a.59.4.
51. I will not push too far for similarities between Aquinas's externalism about psychological operations and the mental content externalism of Tyler Burge and Hilary Putnam, though it seems likely to me that there are interesting parallels. For opposed views on externalism versus internalism about mental content in Aquinas's thought see Brower and Brower Toland, "Aquinas on Mental Representation," 235–37, and Gyula Klima, "Semantic Content in Aquinas and Ockham," in *Linguistic Content: New Essays on the History of Philosophy of Language*, ed. Margaret Cameron and Robert Stainton (Oxford: Oxford University Press, 2015), 121–35.
52. Consider Brian Leftow's interpretation of what it means for a power to operate "with" a bodily organ: "B is an organ for A's G-ing iff (a) A is an animal; (b) B is a proper part of A's body; (c) A can G; (d) G-ing is a use of a power sited in B; (e) A's G-ing is or includes B's being in a particular state or process, and so pairs 1:1 with B's coming to be in this state or process; and (f) if B is a cognitive organ, B fully embodies or encodes received forms (the media and/or content of cognition)." From "Soul, Mind and Brain," in *The Waning of Materialism: New Essays*, ed. Robert Koons and George Bealer (Oxford: Oxford University Press, 2009), 395–415,

for Thomas, "the eye is the matter of sight," and in passage 3.4 that the pupil is vision's organ. Hence, as he sees it, certain physiological states in the pupil of the eye are the material causes of visual operations.[53] Or else, as we just saw, the material cause of anger is the boiling of the blood around the heart. When it comes to intellectual operations, in contrast, Aquinas could agree that because they rely on no body parts, states, or processes as their instruments, they do not include such physiological phenomena as their material causes. This is certainly an important part of what he means by saying that the human intellect operates independently of any bodily organ. Furthermore, unlike some of the previous interpretations I have canvassed in this section so far, it seems that if Aquinas could establish that the human intellect lacks a bodily organ in this way, he might indeed have the premise he needs to establish the separability of human souls from bodies. If intellectual acts are not causally linked to any matter, then it seems possible they might exist without it.

Nevertheless, as I explained above, because of the way our intellects rely on *phantasia*/imagination, Aquinas thinks that certain physiological states and/or processes in the brain accompany every intellectual act any human ever undertakes. On the face of it, it is difficult to see what sort of argument might show that these bodily states or processes are material causes merely for the objects of our intellectual operations, that is, for our phantasms, as opposed to being material causes for our intellectual acts themselves.

To solve this problem, what I think we ought to acknowledge is that Aquinas's claims about causation are in part claims about explanation.[54] When Thomas claims that intellectual powers and operations

---

at 407–8. An incorporeal power, then, on Leftow's interpretation, would be one that fails to meet one of criteria (a)–(f). When it comes to Leftow's (e), I think Aquinas would deny that *any* psychological operation is (identical to) a bodily part coming to be in some particular physiological state or process. But I think Thomas would agree that the operations of corporeal powers *include* certain bodily states and/or processes as their material causes.

53. See *In DSS* 2–4/3–5 for discussion of what states the eye and its pupil must be in for vision to occur. An example: the pupil must contain liquid water so that light can enter it, for which reason it is surrounded by fatty tissue in the white of the eye, which prevents freezing (*In DSS* 3/4.7). See chapter 4 for discussion of whether Aquinas believes that certain dynamic physiological processes as well as static states must accompany visual operations.

54. I take it this is a familiar point to make about Aristotelian causes—see Nathanael Stein, "Causation and Explanation in Aristotle," *Philosophy Compass* 6, no. 10 (2011): 699–707,

are proper to the soul alone, depend on no bodily organ or instrument, and have no material cause, he is in part making a claim about how they can be explained. More precisely, he is making a claim about how they *cannot* be explained. The claim is that intellectual powers cannot be explained as structures responsible for coordinating certain bodily parts, states, and processes. Their operations cannot be explained in terms of coordination between these parts, states, and processes, in response to certain efficient causal inputs, and resulting in certain teleological outputs. In contrast, powers and operations that are shared with the body depend on bodily organs or instruments, have material causes, and can indeed be explained in the ways just mentioned. They have bodily "vehicles," to use Kenny's term.

In general, on the interpretation I am proposing, Aquinas subscribes to this biconditional for psychological powers: a psychological power depends ontologically on the body if and only if its operations can be explained in terms of coordinated bodily parts, states, and processes, together with the relevant efficient causal inputs and teleological outputs. I will call this biconditional OD/E (for Ontological Dependence/Explanation) in what follows.

Four things are worth noting about OD/E. First, it is restricted to psychological powers and their ontological dependence on the body. It may be that Aquinas would accept something stronger than OD/E, ranging over all physical powers, or even all physical objects. But I will focus on the more limited claim. Second, while the claim is partly that psychological powers are ontologically dependent on the body just in case they have bodily parts, states, and processes as their material causes, OD/E includes all four causes. Claiming that the bodily parts, states, and processes in question must be properly coordinated takes into account the role of formal causation—structure, configuration, or organization. And OD/E makes specific mention of the efficient and final causes of the psychological powers it ranges over. Third, what OD/E expresses in terms of explanation could be put just as well in terms of real definition, at least for Aquinas. Indeed Thomas is more likely to speak in scientific

---

and Christopher Shields, *Aristotle* (London: Routledge, 2007), chap. 2—but it is often enough made about Aquinas as well: see Shields and Robert Pasnau, *The Philosophy of Aquinas* (Boulder, Colo.: Westview, 2004), chap. 2.

contexts of assigning definitions to various phenomena than of explaining them. But because for contemporary readers the notion of definition is more likely to connote assigning lexical meaning to words than specifying a thing's essence, I will typically speak in terms of explanation. See, however, the fifth section of this chapter for more on the notion of real definition in relation to ontological dependence.

Finally, the claim is that psychological powers are ontologically dependent on the body just in case they are explicable in the terms OD/E mentions *at all*—either completely or in part. Aquinas would, I think, claim that all the psychological powers of most organisms are completely explicable in terms of OD/E's four-causal schema. But this may not be true of human powers due to the intimate ties between our corporeal powers and our incorporeal intellectual powers. Nevertheless, even if it is only possible to give a partial explanation of the way our sense powers (for instance) operate in bodily terms, so long as their operations are explicable in these terms at all OD/E claims that they are ontologically dependent on the body.

Astute readers may observe at this point that given Aquinas's claims in 3.4 about the involvement of phantasms in intellectual operations as their objects, one might easily suppose that Thomas's account of the intellect's functioning does indeed involve the body, and thus that it should count as corporeal based upon OD/E. After all, Aquinas thinks our imaginative abilities depend on the brain, so if Thomas's explanation of intellectual operations involves phantasms, it would seemingly involve the brain as well. Briefly, my response to this potential difficulty is that according to OD/E, psychological powers depend on the body just in case they themselves are explicable in bodily terms. Hence, even if it should happen that some of the causal inputs giving rise to our intellectual operations include body-dependent psychological states, it would not necessarily follow that these operations themselves are body-dependent. Analogously, just because Aquinas thinks that colors are the efficient causes of visual operations, and hence partly explain how these operations occur, it does not follow that he would deny the possibility of sighted beings existing in a colorless world.[55] The reason

55. Admittedly, it is odd to consider the possibility of sighted beings in a colorless world. Jaworski (*Structure and the Metaphysics of Mind*, 162) suggests an example that is perhaps easier

Aquinas thinks vision is body-dependent, rather, is that its operations themselves can indeed be explained partly in terms of coordinated states (and perhaps processes) in the eye, in response to the causal input that colors provide. I will have more to say about the intellect's dependence on phantasms as a potential problem for Aquinas's account in chapter 6.

Aquinas's argumentative burden in demonstrating the human intellect's immateriality, then, is to show that purported explanations of intellectual operations in terms of bodily parts, states, and processes coordinating with certain inputs and teleological outputs do not and cannot succeed, even as partial explanations. I will examine his attempts to heft this burden in chapter 5. First, however, what evidence is there that Aquinas himself subscribes to the biconditional I have just proposed? And why suppose it is correct? I will answer these questions in the three sections that follow, beginning with a look at how and why explanation and ontological dependence are interrelated in Aquinas's physics.

Ontological Dependence and Explanation I: Aquinas's Physics

As far as I know, Aquinas never explicitly avows anything like the OD/E biconditional that I just described. The ways he understands physics as a science and psychology as a subset of physics, however, show that he endorses something like it. Or so I will argue in this section. I will begin with an overview of Aquinas's physics and the way psychology fits within it. I will then explain why even though Thomas's physics and psychology are committed to a robust emergentism—and accordingly reject reductivism in at least one clear sense—there are nevertheless

---

to grasp: the power to throw a baseball is not ontologically dependent on the existence of baseballs even if its operations are partially explicable in terms of baseballs. It is, however, a body-dependent power because it can be explained in terms of coordinated bodily parts, states, and processes, together with the relevant causal inputs and outputs (which include, obviously, baseballs). In any case, as I will explain further in chapter 6, Aristotle's analogy between colors and sight, phantasms and intellect, is imperfect for various reasons. Phantasms do not act upon the agent intellect as colors do upon vision; that is one reason why Aquinas thinks there must be an agent intellect (see ST 1a.79.2–3). Phantasms also are not the ultimate objects of intellectual cognition, as colors are of sight. Rather they are simply one causal intermediary through which the intellect arrives at its ultimate object, namely an essence, nature, or quiddity.

clear senses in which Thomas thinks that physical entities *qua* physical are exhaustively decomposable into their lowest-level material constituents, ontologically speaking, and in which physical entities supervene upon and are necessitated by these material constituents. Furthermore, importantly, there is a clear sense in which Aquinas's physics is indeed committed to reductivism, albeit (obviously) of a different sort than he rejects: he is committed to emergent physical entities being explicable in terms of the material constituents on which they depend ontologically, together with certain efficient causal inputs and teleological outputs. This is certainly true in the case of most psychological powers, which are both ontologically dependent on bodily parts, states, and processes as their matter and explicable in terms of these material constituents. Hence the ways Aquinas understands physics and psychology together commit him to something like the OD/E biconditional.

Following Aristotle, Thomas characterizes physics both as the science of being that is subject to motion (*ens mobile*), and also of being that is separable from matter neither in fact nor in account.[56] In his *De trinitate* commentary Aquinas explains why he links matter and motion as follows:

(3.6) Since every motion is measured by time, and the primary motion is local motion (since without it there exists no other motion), it is necessary that a thing is mobile inasmuch as it exists here and now. But this happens to a mobile thing insofar as it is individuated by matter existing under determinate dimensions.[57]

The idea is straightforward. While local motion from point A to point B is just one of the kinds of motion Aquinas recognizes, he follows Aristotle in regarding it as primary, in the sense that without it no other motion can occur.[58] Any beings capable of local motion, however, must have definite quantitative dimensions, limiting them to a particu-

---

56. In Phys 1.1 and 2.4, In Met 6.1–2, In DT 5.1–4.
57. In DT 5.2 (Leo. 50:143.87–94).
58. See In Phys 5.2 and 8.14. As mentioned in note 9, in his Aristotelian commentaries Aquinas tends to reserve the terms "generation" and "corruption" for the gain and loss of substantial form respectively, and introduces several distinct types of accidental change in the categories of quality, quantity, and location. These kinds of change are motions strictly speaking, as Aquinas claims in In Phys 5.3. Thus "motion" is broader in its application than "local motion," but narrower than "change."

lar place and time, such that at some subsequent time they may occupy some different position. And because it is by having designated matter, according to Aquinas, that composite substances have quantitative dimensions, only such substances are capable of motion. Accordingly, physics, which is the study of mobile being, is also the study of what depends for its being on matter: either of substances that have matter as one of their constituent parts, or of their motions or capacities for motion. Any entities that do not depend upon matter in this way are not among the objects of physics but of metaphysics, about which I will say more in this chapter's final section.[59]

We continue to think of physics as having to do with matter and motion, of course, but Aquinas's physics reflects his multi-leveled understanding of how things in the world are put together, introduced in the last section of chapter 2. This can be seen in the way Thomas thinks that Aristotle's physical works are organized. The *Physics* itself Aquinas takes to be a general work dealing with "those things which are consequent on mobile being in common"—that is, what is true of mobile being insofar as it is mobile.[60] *De caelo* focuses on mobile being according to its local motion, including the circular motions of the heavens and the rectilinear motions of the elements. Its subject matter corresponds most closely to that of contemporary physics. The rest of the works deal with various other motions to which both elements and mixed bodies in the sublunary realm are subject. *De generatione et corruptione* is devoted to motions that all sublunary substances share in common, namely generation and corruption; *Meteora* discusses changes of the elements; and the pseudo-Aristotelian *De mineralibus* considers changes proper to nonliving mixed bodies.

The psychological works consider changes proper to living bodies. They are themselves divided in a similar fashion. The *De anima* is a general work, analogous to the *Physics*, establishing the criteria for studying living things by considering the soul in itself. There is an intermediate tier of works which consider "what belongs to soul according to a con-

---

59. Does this mean that simple substances and God are incapable of motion? Yes, strictly speaking. When Aquinas discusses angelic motion in ST 1a.53, In DT 5.4 arg. 3, and elsewhere he is always careful to note that he is predicating motion of angels only in a qualified sense of the term. God, of course, is everywhere (ST 1a.8).

60. In Phys 1.1.4 (Leo. 2:4).

cretion or application to body, but in general."⁶¹ Then there is a range of works that consider how "all this applies to individual species of animals and plants, determining what is proper to each species."⁶² The intermediate tier of psychological works contains some that deal with "what pertains to a living thing insofar as it is living," that is, works like *De vita et morte*, *De iuventate et senectute*, and *De longitudine et brevitate vitae*.⁶³ These would also include the *De nutritione* if there existed such a work, Aquinas says, because taking in nutrition is something that all living organisms share in common. Other works pertain to parts of the soul that only certain living things possess. There are works devoted to animal motion, such as the *De motu animalium*, "in which there is a determination about the parts of animals adapted for movement."⁶⁴ There are also works devoted to the cognitive powers that Aquinas calls exterior and interior senses.

Hence Aquinas's physics encompasses most of what we would consider natural science. It ranges from physics and astronomy (the *De caelo*) to chemistry, meteorology, geology (the *De generatione* and *Meteora*), and biology (the psychological works), including not just the physiology and anatomy of individual organisms, but also ethology and ecology.⁶⁵ Aquinas's natural scientific corpus is nowhere near as extensive

---

61. In DSS pr./1.5 (Leo. 45.2:4.43–44).
62. Ibid., ll. 51–54. Aquinas's focus is primarily on the first tier of psychological inquiry in both in his lengthy commentary on Aristotle's *De anima*, his *Disputed Question on the Soul*, and the treatise on human nature from the *Summa theologiae*. In the latter work he gives what might be construed as a reason for this: "the theologian considers the nature of man in relation to the soul, but not in relation to the body, except insofar as the body has a relation to the soul. Hence the first object of our consideration will be the soul" (prologue to ST 1a.75–89 [Leo. 5:194]). Aquinas, as a theologian, is principally interested in human beings out of the rest of living things, and principally in the part of human beings that is subject to the capacities that distinguish them from other organisms and enable them to communicate with God. Of course, Aquinas found time to discuss other living things as well, and to undertake several forays into the second tier of psychological inquiry, considering "what belongs to soul according to a concretion or application to body, but in general." But unlike Albert the Great, he did not do original work or thinking of his own in this area, and was mostly content to parrot Aristotle, Avicenna, and others. In ST, Aquinas says that as a theologian, he is interested in other states of the soul than intellect and will just as "preambles to the intellect" (ST 1a.78 pr.).
63. In DSS pr./1.5 (Leo. 45.2:5.85–86).
64. Ibid. (Leo. 45.2:6.100–101).
65. Given the sort of externalism regarding psychological activities that I discussed in the previous section, the study of psychology for Aquinas would ultimately include investigations of group behavior and environmental considerations.

as that of his teacher Albert, whose massive *De animalibus* and *De plantis* revived briefly Aristotle's zoological research program as an active area of study.[66] Nor did Thomas undertake his own original research. In psychology Aquinas focuses mainly on the first tier of inquiry just mentioned, sorting through various philosophical puzzles arising from the formal consideration of living things and their activities, as opposed to working toward a "concretion or application" of these considerations to living bodies, either in general or specifically.[67]

Aquinas's physics is committed to an emergentism that is robust in that it posits not only emergent accidental features but also emergent substances and substantial forms. As we saw in chapter 2 (p. 86), the elements are the lowest-level physical entities. Underlying their substantial forms is just prime matter. Accordingly, at the lowest level of Aquinas's physics is a theory about how the elements come about from one another, due to certain changes in their basic qualities (heat, coolness, etc.).[68] The next level of Aquinas's physics, however, includes a theory about how the elements combine to form mixtures, which are emergent substances. Aquinas speaks of their forms being "educed from the power of matter," by which he means in part that various changes (heating, cooling, etc.) transpiring in the mixed body's elemental constituents set the stage for a new substantial form to "supervene," as Thomas sometimes says.[69] We would call this emergence. Metaphysically speaking, Aquinas holds the controversial view that any materials composing an emergent substance must lose the substantial forms they had before becoming parts of that substance, and exist in it only "potentially" or "virtually."[70] Beyond this, Aquinas leaves his criteria for emergence

---

66. See Michael Tkacz, "Albert the Great and the Revival of Aristotle's Zoological Research Program," *Vivarium* 45, no. 1 (2007): 30–68, for discussion.

67. A good example is the way Aquinas discusses puzzles related to growth in In DGC 1.11–16.

68. See In Meteor 1.3–4.

69. QDP 4.1 ad 13, In Met 5.5.819 and 7.7.1430, ST 1a.118.2 ad 2.

70. See *De mixtione elementorum*, In Sent 2.12.1.4, QQ 1.4.1 ad 3, ST 1a.76.4 ad 4, QDP 5.7, In Met 7.13.1588 and 7.16.1633–36. Aquinas's commitment to the merely virtual presence of elements in mixed bodies is conceptually tied to his unicity thesis regarding substantial forms (see chapter 2), which was highly controversial in his day. Interestingly, however, many of Aquinas's contemporaries who rejected his unicity thesis accepted that the elements composing mixtures lose their substantial forms—for two accounts of Duns Scotus's position see Thomas Ward, *John Duns Scotus on Parts, Wholes and Hylomorphism* (Leiden: Brill, 2014), chap. 8,

largely tacit, but there is reason for thinking he would accept the widely held idea that emergence happens when qualitatively distinct causal powers appear.[71] That is, a new substance emerges when a substantial form is "educed" from which causal powers flow that cannot be understood simply as a quantitative aggregate of powers possessed by things at lower-levels.[72] The emergent causal powers themselves are accidents, and hence metaphysically dependent on the substances in which they inhere and the substantial forms from which they flow. But to figure out what substances and substantial forms there are Aquinas thinks we rely on observing their powers at work.[73] Hence the presence of quali-

---

and Cross, *The Physics of Duns Scotus*, chap. 4, §5. Contemporary hylomorphic accounts such as Jaworski's and Koons's however tend to accept that substances can enter into the composition of other substances without ceasing to exist. Jaworski argues against what he takes to be a Thomistic view regarding the presence of elements in mixed bodies in *Structure and the Metaphysics of Mind*, chap. 6, §5. For more on Aquinas's own view see Christopher Decaen, "Elemental Virtual Presence in St. Thomas," *The Thomist* 64 (2000): 271–300; Stephen Baldner, "St. Albert the Great and St. Thomas on the Presence of Elements in a Compound," *Sapientia* 54 (1999): 41–57, and Christopher Brown, *Aquinas and the Ship of Theseus: Solving Puzzles about Material Objects* (London: Continuum, 2005), chap. 4.

71. See Cynthia MacDonald and Graham MacDonald, "Emergence and Downward Causation," in *Emergence in Mind*, ed. Cynthia MacDonald and Graham MacDonald (Oxford: Oxford University Press, 2010), 139–68.

72. See William Wimsatt, "Emergence as Non-Aggregativity and the Biases of Reductionisms," *Foundations of Science* 5, no. 3 (2000): 269–97. On what it means for substantial forms to be "educed" from pre-existing matter see *In Met* 7.7.1430 and Leftow, "Souls Dipped in Dust," 120–21.

73. Thomas frequently claims that we apprehend what substances there are on the basis of their accidents, and in particular on the basis of their proper accidents, of which their active and passive powers are the most important example. At the beginning of *De anima* Aristotle raises as a methodological question whether it is better to start by considering souls in general, or by considering the powers of particular souls, and inferring from these capacities whatever conclusions we might reach about souls themselves. Commenting on this passage Aquinas writes: "because the essential principles of things are unknown to us we must use accidental differences in designating essential differences.... It is through these accidental differences, consequently, that we reach cognition of essential characteristics" (*In DA* 1.1.15 [Leo. 45.1:7.254–60]). Later in his commentary (*In DA* 2.6), Aquinas elaborates on the methodological procedure he takes Aristotle to have followed. To know about souls we need to know about living things' vital capacities, and to know about these capacities, we need to know about the vital operations they enable organisms to carry out. To know about these operations, in turn, it is helpful to know about the aims at which activities are directed, or about the factors that act on organisms in the case of passive operations. That is why Aquinas spends so much time, in the case of nutrition, discussing food, which he takes to be one of the factors involved in bringing the process about (see *In DA* 2.9.333). The methodological principle he is describing here applies not just to living things, but to substances and their substantial forms in general. In the *De ente*, for instance, he states regarding sensible things in general that their "essential differences in themselves are unknown. They are, therefore, signified through accidental

tatively distinct powers is a sign that an emergent substance is present.

Aquinas sometimes discusses what seems like a weaker form of emergentism, on which what emerges are "complexions" or "harmonies" resulting from elements combining in certain proportions.[74] He attributes a view like this to Empedocles, Galen, and a few others. Its details are somewhat obscure, but Aquinas seems to think of proportions as a sort of accidental form modulating the qualities present in the elements, making them hotter, colder, wetter, drier, etc. On this view the soul and other psychological phenomena are "given off" by modulating the elements in ways like these, somewhat as harmonies are given off by arrangements of sounds. Aquinas considers this view insufficient for several reasons. At root, he thinks such "emergence" is compatible with a sort of reductivism that he is keen to reject.

What sort of reductivism? On Ernest Nagel's influential understanding of reduction, it is a relation between the theoretic statements of different sciences, in which the descriptive and explanatory statements of the reduced science can in principle be derived from statements in the reducing science *via* a set of identity statements linking items in the reduced and reducing sciences.[75] Aquinas nowhere discusses reduction in these terms, of course. But the weak emergentism of Empedocles and others resembles it, in that it treats emergent entities as mere beings *per accidens*, and hence as nothing "over and above" their elemental constituents possessing accidental forms of certain sorts. Aquinas thinks that complexions and harmonies are epiphenomal, so in principle all

---

differences which arise from essential ones, just as a cause is signified by its effect" (DEE 5 [Leo. 43:379.76–80]). Aquinas's stock examples of such "accidental differences" were capacities for certain sorts of vital operation, such as the ability to laugh, which "flow from" the soul itself as I explained in chapter 2, and thus are indicative of its nature. Elsewhere, however, he makes the same point with regard to nonliving things like fire: "since substantial differences are unknown to us ... it is sometimes necessary to use accidental differences in their place, as, for example, we may say that fire is a simple, hot, and dry body; for proper accidents are the effects of substantial forms, and make them known" (ST 1a.29.1 ad 3 [Leo. 4:328]). Again, the point here is that we recognize fire as a substance, and as the sort of substance it is, based on its distinctive abilities to heat and to dry. It is important to keep in mind that even though Aquinas's criteria for emergence involve epistemological considerations, it is nevertheless an ontological doctrine.

74. See In DA 1.9, QDA 1, SCG 2.62–64.
75. Ernest Nagel, *The Structure of Science: Problems in the Logic of Scientific Explanation* (New York: Harcourt, 1961). See Jaworski, *Structure and the Metaphysics of Mind*, chap. 11, §3, for a helpful account of Nagel-style reduction as it relates to physicalism.

the descriptive and explanatory roles we assign to them could be played by the elements and their powers.[76] These latter serve as truthmakers for all our emergent-entity statements in this weak sense of emergence.

Aquinas would probably be willing to treat some entities that his physics discusses as "reducible" in this way to their lowest-level constituents. His *Meteora* commentary discusses phenomena such as rainfall, for example, and Thomas might consider a rainstorm a large-scale being *per accidens*, merely weakly emergent in the Empedoclean sense.[77] It is "nothing over and above" its elemental constituents, in the sense that it is just a bunch of water moving about together. Its ability to drench a field is just an aggregate of water's wetness. All the descriptive and explanatory roles we assign to the storm could in principle be played by water and its powers, which serve as the truthmakers for our rainstorm statements.[78]

In contrast, Aquinas clearly rejects this sort of reductive approach when it comes to genuinely emergent entities such as living things. For Thomas, genuinely emergent entities are more than the sum of their parts ontologically speaking, and also cannot be understood in terms of their components without also understanding the way those components are structured, configured, or organized. His antireductivist stance is on display in his comments on *De anima* 2.4, where Thomas understands Aristotle to refute two different erroneous opinions concerning nutrition and growth. The first, Empedocles's view, ascribes downward growth in living things to the heavy, earthy elements present in them, and upward growth to their light, fiery elements. The second view ascribes both nutrition and growth to the presence of fire, which seems in a way to feed itself and to grow. Empedocles's view, however, misunderstands what counts as up and down for a living thing by trying to understand them just in terms of their elemental constituents:

---

76. See SCG 2.63.4 and 64.2 and In DA 1.9.134.
77. In Meteor 1.14.
78. As far as I know, Aquinas never in his *Meteors* commentary comes out and says that any of the phenomena he is dealing with are *entia per accidens*. That this is what he believes is, however, implicit in his claim that the subject of the treatise is "the species of changes that affect the elements" (In Meteor 1.1.2 [Leo. 3:326]). Aquinas believes that what he is discussing when he talks about meteorological phenomena are the elements *with respect to* certain changes that affect them.

(3.7) Up and down and other differences of position (like in front of and behind or right and left) are in certain things distinguished according to nature, but in other things just according to their position relative to us. For in certain things there are determinate parts which are naturally principles of certain motions, and in those things the aforementioned differences of position are distinguished according to nature. For example, in the universe heavy things are naturally borne to the middle and light things to its outskirts, whence in the universe up and down are naturally distinguished, and the place where light things are borne is called up and that to which heavy things are naturally borne is called down or the middle. In living and mortal things too up and down are determined according to the motions of growth and decrease, for that part whence living things receive food is called up and down is the opposite part through which superfluities are emitted.[79]

Just as it would be a mistake to suppose that up and down in the universe as a whole switch when we stand on our heads, so too it would be a mistake to suppose that up and down in a living thing can be understood in terms of the positions of the elements in the cosmos. Similarly, while fire appears to feed and grow, it does not truly exhibit the limited patterned growth characteristic of living things. Hence it does not truly feed either. Instead, Thomas writes:

(3.8) When combustible material is added to a lit fire a new fire is generated in that combustible material, but not in such a way that the added combustible [material] results in the conservation of the fire previously lit in other material. Rather, if some wood is freshly lit the burning of some other wood previously lit is not preserved through this lighting. For the whole fire which results from the grouping together of many flames is not one *simpliciter*, but seems to be one by aggregation, just as a heap of rocks is one, and because of such a unity, there is a certain resemblance to nutrition.[80]

This passage provides a good indication of the way Aquinas thinks about emergence as opposed to reduction in general. While a conflagration has the power to incinerate me, and a rockpile to squash me, these powers are mere aggregates of fire's ability to heat and stone's heaviness, as opposed to the qualitatively distinct powers characteristic of genuine emergence. Accordingly, Aquinas is willing to think of conflagrations

---

79. In DA 2.8.325 (Leo. 45.1:99–100.32–50).
80. Ibid., 2.8.325 (Leo. 45.1:104.137–39).

or rockpiles as mere beings *per accidens*. In contrast, Thomas does not think we can understand a living thing's ability to preserve itself "in being and due quantity" in merely aggregative terms. In that sense he is a committed antireductivist about emergent entities and their powers.

Nevertheless, as Aquinas notes in an interesting aside in his *De anima* commentary, there is "something of the truth" in the view that fire is involved in nutrition.[81] Food must be cooked, and this is indeed done by fire. Hence fire is involved in a certain way in nutrition and growth, as a secondary and instrumental agent. This brief comment about nutrition and fire prompts three important comments about Aquinas's stance on emergence and antireductionism.

First, there is a sense in which the entities populating Aquinas's physics are indeed exhaustively decomposable into their lowest-level material constituents, ontologically speaking. That is, higher-level material parts such as tissues and organs (and things that have them) are always ultimately composed of elements as their lowest-level empirically specifiable constituents. The elements, in turn, have only prime matter as a material constituent. Hence emergent entities can in a sense be exhaustively "broken down" into their elemental constituents, ontologically speaking, while the latter cannot in a sense be broken down at all, except by being transformed into some other element.

Second, there are also senses in which physical entities supervene on and are necessitated by their lowest-level material constituents. Because Aquinas denies that emergent higher-level phenomena can be described or explained entirely in terms of the elements and their characteristics, he follows Aristotle in denying that emergent entities are necessitated by their material components in one way. Commenting on the *Physics*, Thomas writes:

(3.9) [Aristotle] says that some think the generation of all natural things happens due to the absolute necessity of matter, as if someone were to say that the wall or the house is such from the necessity of matter, because heavy things are borne downwards but light things upwards, and because of this heavy and hard stones remain in the foundation, while lighter earth is lifted up above, as is clear in walls made of earthen bricks, and the wood that is the lightest is placed highest, namely in the roof. Likewise they supposed that the

81. Ibid., 2.8.331 (Leo. 45.1:101.137).

dispositions of natural things come to be such as they are from the necessity of matter, as if it were said that a human has feet below and hands above because of the heaviness or lightness of his humors.[82]

Aquinas's antireductivism commits him to rejecting "absolute" material necessitation of this sort, as should be clear from the case of nutrition just discussed. Nevertheless, like Aristotle Aquinas thinks that matter does impose necessity in a different, "conditional" way. Just as a pile of stones, bricks, and wood is not a house, a bunch of elements is not a human, but *if* there is to be a house, *then* there must be stone, brick, and wood, and *if* there is to be a human, *then* there must be hands and feet, and likewise there must be various elements. Aquinas denies that any higher-level physical changes happen without changes in the "primary qualities" of the elements, which he regards as "the cause of generation and corruption and alteration in all other bodies."[83] For a physical substance to acquire a quality like health, flavor, or odor requires changes in its elemental constituents, even though such qualities are emergent.[84] The same holds for all of its activities and powers, and indeed for the generation or corruption of the substance itself. In this conditional way emergent entities are indeed necessitated by their lowest-level material constituents. As for supervenience, when Aquinas uses *supervenire* and its cognates he means something different than we do today.[85] But I think he could agree that duplicate worlds in terms of their elements and elemental features would be physical duplicates *simpliciter*. Part of the reason for this, though, is that one important feature characterizing any of Aquinas's elements is whether or not it has been caught up into the composition of an emergent substance or one of its parts such that it exists not in act, but virtually.[86]

Finally, and most importantly for our purposes, Aquinas's antireductivism as described above is compatible with reductions of a different sort. In fact, his physics requires them. It is the science of what depends

---

82. In Phys 2.15.3/271 (Leo. 2:98).
83. In DGC pr. 2 (Leo. 3:262).
84. See In Sent 1.17.2.2, In Phys 7.5.2/914, In DGC 1.13.4/94, QDV 13.4.
85. Consider passage 2.5: Aquinas apparently means nothing more by "will supervene on" than "will accrue to."
86. My thoughts on necessitation and supervenience in this paragraph owe much to chap. 9 of Jaworski, *Structure and the Metaphysics of Mind*.

on matter not just in fact but also in account. It contrasts with metaphysics, the objects of which do not depend on matter at all, and also with mathematics, which studies objects that depend on matter only for their being but not for their being understood: things like numbers and shapes. Recall Aquinas's insistence in 2.1 from the previous chapter that the essences of composite substances include both form and common sensible matter. As I explained, Thomas has in mind Aristotle's distinction between things like snubness and concavity. We cannot understand the former apart from its material subject, namely a nose, whereas the latter is curvature in any old surface. In fact, on closer inspection, the objects of mathematics turn out in a certain sense to depend on matter for being understood as well. Concavity can be understood apart from a nose, but not apart from some surface or other. As Aquinas puts it, mathematical objects include intelligible matter, but not sensible matter.[87] Hence in both cases Aquinas links ontological dependence on matter with matter factoring into our explanations. By insisting that physical objects include sensible matter, furthermore, Aquinas is indicating the necessity of employing a certain sort of reductive explanatory strategy in physics, namely the strategy of understanding complex physical phenomena by breaking them down into their component parts, states, and processes. Consider the example of humanity including flesh and bone. Aquinas's claim is that we cannot understand what it is to be a human without understanding the various bodily parts through which we exercise our characteristically human functions. Singling out flesh and bone is a shorthand for the full range of anhomoeomerous and homoeomerous parts we need to execute our full range of functions, from our organs all the way down to our elemental constituents. Here the contrast with mathematics is clear. In his *Metaphysics* Aristotle argues against the "younger Socrates's" view that animals can be understood in the same way as circles, that is, without reference to any particular matter or material parts. This is not so, Aquinas agrees, rather: "such parts as are necessary to complete an operation proper to the species are parts of the species, both such as are formal parts and such as are material parts."[88]

87. See In DT 5.3 and In Met 7.11.1520–21.
88. In Met 7.11.1519 (Marietti 368).

Aquinas's comment regarding the role of fire in nutrition helpfully illustrates this point. When Thomas says that food must be cooked, he clearly does not mean that we cannot eat raw carrots or apples. Instead he is referring to the "natural heat" that he thinks animals have in their stomachs, and which he thinks serves them as an instrument in breaking food down into useable and unusable components. Aquinas's entire analysis of the nutritive power's operations includes the way animals take in food, digest it, distribute its useable components throughout the body, and expel unusable components.[89] He assigns organic body parts to each of these subprocesses, and in the case of digestion he thinks fire serves as a sub-organic part contributing to one of nutrition's subprocesses. Today, of course, we would add many further steps to the reductive analysis of nutrition that Aquinas provides. As Aquinas's comparison of plants and animals in 2.11 suggests, there may be different local levels of composition at work in the operations of different organisms. Generally speaking, however, 2.11 indicates that our complete analysis of an animal's activities would include descriptions of states or processes in anhomoeomerous parts, their homoeomerous constituents, and the elements that compose these in turn. Because the animal as a whole is simply a body whose substantial form gives rise to the abilities to engage in these activities, we cannot understand animals like human beings apart from the flesh, bone, and other parts at various levels through which we do what we do.

The reductive explanatory strategy we see at work in Aquinas's account of nutrition shares similarities with what contemporary philosophers sometimes call functional analysis or mechanistic explanation.[90]

---

89. See In DA 2.7.326 for the mouth as the organ through which animals take food in; QDP 5.10 arg. 9, In DSS 13/14.15, and In Meteor 2.2 for the stomach as the organ in which animals receive food and break it down; QDP 5.10 arg. 9, ST 1a2ae.17.9 ad 2, and De motu cordis (hereafter, DMC) for the heart, blood, and veins; and In Meteor 2.6–7 for the excretory functions of the skin, bladder, and intestines. As regards the circulatory functions, I am not sure that Aquinas understood how the heart circulated oxygen and nutrients by pumping blood throughout the body. He does link the movement of the heart to the pulsing of blood in the veins (in DMC) and links the stomach and veins to the distribution of food (in QDP). But from what I understand, it was not until the anatomical explorations of Vesalius and Harvey that circulation was properly understood. Still, Aquinas seems to have the basic contours of the digestive and circulatory systems correct.

90. See Robert Cummins, "Functional Analysis," *Journal of Philosophy* 72, no. 20 (1975): 741–65; Peter Machamer, Lindley Darden, and Carl Craver, "Thinking about Mechanisms,"

These explanatory strategies also involve breaking complex phenomena down into the organized component processes, states, or entities that they comprise. While they are sometimes regarded as reductive strategies, neither presupposes anything like the Nagel-style intertheoretic reduction discussed above.[91] In fact, because they tend to deny that higher-level phenomena can be understood as aggregates of anything at lower levels, they are compatible with the sort of emergentism Aquinas's physics also presupposes. Nor do functional analysis and mechanistic explanation suppose that the levels of organization will be uniform across the physical world. Like Aquinas, their proponents would agree that the parts, states, and processes involved in plant and animal nutrition might differ. There is no reason to suppose that everything will have the same levels of organization except, perhaps, at the lowest levels.

Aquinas's physical explanations extend beyond functional analysis or mechanistic explanation in that they focus not just on internal parts, states, and processes, but also on the efficient causal inputs and teleological outputs of physical phenomena, as we saw toward the end of the last section. Hence, as we saw, he insists that a complete explanation of visual perception must include not just a description of the structure of the eye and its subparts (e.g., the fatty tissue in the white of the eye, or the water contained in the pupil), but also discussion of colors as the efficient causes of vision.[92] I will have more to say about Aquinas's formal account of visual perception and its final cause in the following chapter. Likewise, a complete explanation of anger must include

---

Philosophy of Science 67, no. 1 (2000): 1–25; Carl Craver and Gualtiero Piccinini, "Integrating Psychology and Neuroscience: Functional Analyses as Mechanism Sketches," *Synthese* 183, no. 3 (2011): 283–311.

91. William Bechtel writes that "the theory reduction model ... is much stronger than what scientists generally have in mind when they speak of reduction. For many scientists, research is reductionistic if it appeals to lower-level components of a system to explain why it behaves as it does under specified conditions. This sense of reduction is captured in ... accounts of mechanistic explanation.... Reductions achieved through mechanistic explanations are ... compatible with a robust sense of autonomy for psychology and other special sciences." From "Reducing Psychology While Maintaining its Autonomy Via Mechanistic Explanations," in *The Matter of the Mind: Philosophical Essays on Psychology, Neuroscience and Reduction*, ed. M. Schouton and Huib Looren de Jong (Malden, Mass.: Blackwell, 2007), 172–98, at 173–74.

92. See *In DA* 2.14 for more on color as the object of sight, and 2.15 for discussion of the roles light and air/water play as environmental factors enabling visual perception to occur.

not just its form (a desire for revenge) and matter (heated blood around the heart) but also its efficient cause (a perceived injury) and final cause (vengeance-directed activity). The case of nutrition is similar; Aquinas thinks that a complete explanation must include discussion of food, the object of nutrition, and also of nutrition's end, namely preserving living things in "existence and due quantity."[93] Even Aquinas's discussions of nonliving phenomena exhibit the same pattern. Rainfall, for instance, is local motion downward (formal cause) in liquid water arranged into droplets (material cause) produced by condensation from water vapor, that has in turn been produced by the heating effects of the sun (efficient cause), for the sake of nourishing living things here on earth (final cause).[94]

It sounds odd to talk about the final cause of rainfall. This might cause us to wonder whether Aquinas really thinks we can use the same kind of explanatory strategy throughout the physical domain, and whether, if he does, this will present problems in light of contemporary scientific methods. Functional analysis and mechanistic explanation figure prominently in sciences like biology and psychology, but not in lower-level sciences like physics and chemistry. Does Aquinas's insistence that physical entities depend on matter for their being understood commit him to employing these explanatory strategies across the board? If so, is this commitment problematic? I think the answers to these questions are, respectively, "not quite, but nearly so" and "not obviously."

Aquinas clearly does not expect to be able to employ any sort of reductive explanatory strategy at the very lowest physical level, namely that of the elements. These are physical entities and hence in a sense depend on matter for their being understood, but epistemological limitations prevent us from saying anything informative about the sort of matter they depend on. We cannot understand them by breaking them down into their component parts, states, and processes.[95]

---

93. ST 1a.78.2.
94. See In Meteor 1.14 and In Phys 2.12 for these details.
95. Aquinas does think it possible to give an account of the way elements are generated from one another (see In Meteor 1.3–4), but this account trades solely on the qualities the elements possess (heat, cold, etc.) along with their spatial locations. It does not attempt to analyze elemental transformations in terms of states or processes in parts of the elements.

When it comes to understanding emergent phenomena, however, I think Aquinas does expect that we will be able employ across the board something akin to the reductive strategy we saw at work in the case of nutrition. While Aquinas offers a fairly detailed account of the ways living bodies are generated, develop the powers they have, and exercise these powers, he has much less to say about emergence from the level of physics to chemistry (or in Aquinas's terms from the elements to nonliving mixed bodies) beyond highly abstract descriptions in the *De mixtione elementorum* and elsewhere.[96] In one interesting *opusculum*, however, Aquinas discusses "certain natural actions that appear in certain natural bodies of which the principles clearly cannot be understood" (*manifeste apprehendi non possunt*).[97] He means actions like magnets attracting iron or sapphires stopping bleeding. The powers to perform these activities are emergent; Aquinas says they "transcend the power and activity of the elements."[98] Yet he thinks we cannot, in some sense, explain them. Curiously, this is exactly what he appears to do in the course of the *opusculum*. He begins with what looks at first like a conflicting set of claims:

(3.10) We see indeed that bodies composed out of elements follow the motions of the elements dominant in them. For instance a rock moves downwards due to the property of the earth dominant in it, and metals also have the power of cooling due to the property of water. Therefore any actions or motions whatsoever of bodies composed out of elements are due to the properties and powers of the elements from which such bodies are composed, and so actions and motions of this sort have a clear origin, concerning which there arises no doubt. Yet there are certain [actions and motions] of bodies of this sort which cannot be caused by the powers of the elements, namely magnets attracting iron or certain medicines purging certain humors in determinate parts of the body. Therefore it is necessary that actions of this sort be reduced to some higher principles.[99]

It is puzzling to see Aquinas claiming, on the one hand, that all the powers of sublunary substances can be traced somehow to the elements they

---

96. For Aquinas's account of generation see QDP 3.9 ad 9, SCG 2.89.8–9, ST 1a.118.
97. *De operationibus occultis* (Leo. 43:183.3).
98. Ibid., 185.228.
99. Ibid., 183.5–22.

comprise, yet on the other hand that some of their powers cannot be caused by the powers of the elements, but must be traced to "higher principles." The puzzlement clears up, however, once we realize what these higher principles turn out to be. They are the heavenly bodies, whose causal influence Aquinas thinks is pervasive throughout the sublunary order. This influence is entirely natural, Aquinas is at pains to stress. It merely operates as a sort of environmental factor partially responsible for bringing about new emergent substances, the possibility of which could not be explained by the elements just by themselves. When it comes to the actions and motions of these substances themselves, however, Aquinas's claim that they are "due to the properties and powers of the elements" from which they are composed holds good—again, not in the sense that emergent powers like magnetism can be understood as a mere aggregate of elemental powers. Rather, we ought in principle to be able to see how such powers are traceable to the elements composing their bearers, suitably structured, and with environmental influences (such as the influence of heavenly bodies) taken into account.[100]

Stump offers a very helpful illustration of the way Aquinas might approach the emergence of chemical substances.[101] Water has various emergent powers—a strong surface tension, the ability to act as a solvent, etc.—that result from bonds between its hydrogen atoms, which are possible in turn because of the way water molecules as a whole are structured. Water's emergent properties cannot be understood as aggregates of the properties of hydrogen or oxygen atoms taken in isolation. Yet they are traceable, in some sense, to the atoms that compose water molecules, once these atoms are suitably structured.

With an illustration like this in mind I think we can see how Aquinas's reductive approach to understanding physical substances might coexist with his emergentism across the natural world, without recent scientific developments posing obviously insurmountable difficulties. The way we explain lower-level emergent phenomena in terms of their component parts, states, and processes may not exactly resemble the

---

100. See Pasnau, *Aquinas on Human Nature*, chap. 2, §3, for more on the way Aquinas thinks the heavenly bodies are involved in bodily operations, such as those of the senses.
101. Eleonore Stump, "Emergence, Causal Powers and Aristotelianism in Metaphysics," in *Powers and Capacities in Philosophy: The New Aristotelianism*, ed. John Greco and Ruth Groff (London: Routledge, 2013), 48–68, at 54–62.

sorts of descriptions and explanations Aquinas offers for psychological powers like vision, anger, or nutrition. They may not count as cases of functional analysis or mechanistic explanation. Perhaps if he were writing today Thomas would say that phenomena like magnetism are better handled by means of a "deductive-nomological" explanatory strategy, emphasizing general laws and theories rather than functional analysis or mechanistic explanation. But such approaches might still count as broadly reductive if they appeal to an emergent substance's components, and ways that they are structured.

Aquinas's physics would probably look somewhat different in light of contemporary scientific discoveries and methodologies. I doubt he would continue to assign final causes to phenomena like rainfall. He might replace appeals to influence of heavenly bodies with different environmental considerations, or in the case of living things, with evolutionary considerations.

In the case of psychological operations, however, Aquinas would continue to insist upon the OD/E biconditional I proposed at the end of the previous section. He would continue to treat them as emergent phenomena that cannot be understood solely in terms of their lowest-level components. He would also continue to insist that if they are truly emergent physical phenomena, and hence ontologically dependent on sensible matter, then they must be explicable in terms of this matter, together with certain efficient causal inputs and teleological outputs. In the case of psychological powers, the sensible matter in question will be some combination of bodily parts, states, and processes. As we have seen in the cases of nutrition, anger, and visual perception, Aquinas does indeed believe that they can be explained in terms of states or processes in organs of the body, along with subparts, substates, or subprocesses, all the way down to the contributions of elements like fire and water. Of course, it bears repeating, claiming that such phenomena can be understood in these terms does not imply that they are "reducible" to the elements in the way Empedocles thought they were. The role of form is crucial to Aquinas's physics and psychology alike. Yet in the case of a power like nutrition, Aquinas would say that we can successfully explain its operations in terms of bodily parts, states, and processes provided we attend to the ways they are structured, organized, or configured, together with the efficient causal inputs that bring them about and the final causes for the sake of which they are done. If it could be demonstrated that certain psychological operations cannot be explained this way, in contrast, this would continue to serve for Aquinas as evidence that these operations are not dependent on matter or bodies at all. This, I take it, is exactly what he thinks is the situation when it comes to the operations of our intellectual powers. Should anyone else be convinced by reasoning of this sort? I will argue in the following section that physicalists and substance dualists alike implicitly accept something like OD/E.

Ontological Dependence and Explanation II: Physicalism and Substance Dualism

While it is probably straightforwardly correct to say that physicalists think that everything is physical, there is no uncontroversial way to interpret "everything" or "is physical" in the central physicalist claim. Jaworski argues that an adequate definition of physicalism ought to be both strong enough to rule out the possibility of nonphysical entities and weak enough to accommodate disagreements among physicalists such as what to say about Hempel's dilemma, whether to embrace eliminativism, reductivism, or nonreductivism, etc.[102] I think he is right about this, and I will rely in what follows on the definition he proposes to meet these criteria: "*Physicalism*: everything can be exhaustively described and explained by the most empirically adequate theories in current or future physics."[103] One advantage of this definition is that many substance dualists could accept it too, provided we insert "except minds" between "everything" and "can." I am not sure there is any less controversy about what substance dualism holds than about the definition of physicalism. But René Descartes is usually considered a paradigmatic substance dualist. And I think Descartes could agree that apart from mental phenomena, the rest of what there is can be exhaustively described and explained by physics. Because of this broad agreement between physicalists (understood one way) and substance dualists (of a Cartesian sort), I am able to address both groups together in this section with a single argument.

102. Jaworski, *Structure and the Metaphysics of Mind*, chap. 11, §§1–2.
103. Ibid., 224.

Briefly, the reason I think physicalists and substance dualists alike should accept the OD/E biconditional is this. Both groups agree that the physical world is exhaustively describable and explicable by physics. But physical explanations are given (roughly) in terms of bodily parts, states, and processes. So both groups can agree that the physical world is exhaustively describable and explicable (roughly) in terms of bodily parts, states, and processes. For physicalists, the physical world is all there is, so physicalists will agree that psychological operations depend on bodies if and only if they can be explained in terms of bodily parts, states, and processes. For substance dualists psychological operations do not depend on bodies at all. But if they did, they would be physical entities, and would be explicable in the same way everything physical is. Hence both physicalists and substance dualists should accept the OD/E biconditional. Several explanatory notes are in order regarding this argument.

First, why suppose that physical explanations are given in terms of bodily parts, states, and processes, even roughly speaking? It might be objected that this description does not accurately capture how physicists describe and explain things. It is true that the sort of bodily parts, states, and processes I have in mind are chiefly those of organisms. Aquinas thought that bodies must be spatially extended, so subatomic particles probably would not count. But I see no reason in principle why the meaning of "bodily parts, states, and processes" could not be broadened or updated to include physical particles as bodies or body parts, spin or charge as states, or wave-function collapse as a process.

Second, Cartesian substance dualists would disagree with Aquinas about what count as psychological phenomena.[104] Aquinas counts any powers or operations proper to living things. Descartes counts just conscious experiences. So Descartes would say that some of the phenomena that Aquinas considers to be psychological are indeed explicable in terms of bodily parts, states, and processes, and that others are not. But Descartes would agree, I think, that if some phenomenon is explicable in a bodily way, then it depends on the body, and likewise that if it does not depend on bodies, then it is not explicable in bodily terms either.

Third, eliminative physicalists think that there are no psychologi-

104. See note 32.

cal phenomena strictly speaking. Hence they will deny that psychological phenomena can be explained in any way whatsoever, just as they will deny that intelligences, *elan vital*, or phlogiston can be explained. None of these things are real. But if there were psychological phenomena, then they would be both exhaustively describable and explicable by physics (just like everything else) and ontologically dependent on the physical (because they are wholly physical, just like everything else).

The most serious opposition I would foresee arising against my argument in this section would be from nonreductive physicalists of various sorts. These might agree that everything is ontologically dependent on the physical, but deny that everything can be described and explained at the physical level, or indeed in terms of bodily parts, states, and processes. Consider for instance Donald Davidson's anomalous monism, which is sometimes considered a sort of nonreductive physicalism. Davidson thinks the psychological supervenes on the physical, and hence is ontologically dependent on it.[105] Yet he also denies that there are any psychophysical laws linking psychological and physical phenomena. Accordingly, he would deny that the former can be explained in terms of the latter (or, for that matter, in terms of bodily parts, states, and processes). Hence it seems that Davidson would also reject the mutual entailment I have proposed between dependence on the body and explicability in bodily terms.

I think Aquinas would agree with Davidson that we should reject the existence of psychophysical laws linking the sorts of psychological phenomena he has in mind—that is, rational phenomena—with physical phenomena, or indeed with bodily phenomena in general. That is, however, because he would take rational phenomena to involve the intellect, and would deny that the intellect is explicable in bodily terms. But what about Davidson's idea that rational phenomena—though inexplicable in physical terms—nonetheless depend ontologically on physical phenomena? My response to this idea depends on how Davidson means for it to be understood. Is Davidson committed to physicalism in the sense set down above, or not?

It might initially appear that he must reject physicalism under-

---

[105]. Donald Davidson, "Mental Events," in his *Essays on Actions and Events* (Oxford: Oxford University Press, 2001), 207–25, at 214.

stood as the thesis that everything can be exhaustively described and explained by physics, because of the anomalous character of the mental. Yet Jaworski argues this is not so, provided Davidson (and other nonreductive physicalists like him) distinguish between two different senses of explanation, one "objective," the other "subjective" or "interest-relative."[106] Christopher Shields unpacks this distinction with a helpful illustration:

> At one stage scientists wondered why malaria spread so rapidly in tropical areas. An explanation was proposed to the effect that warmer water in temperate zones is hospitable to spores carrying the disease. Such spores might then be carried through rivers and other water ways, which would explain why outbreaks of the disease tended to be concentrated near bodies of water. Eventually, this suggestion was shown to be false when it was demonstrated that certain sorts of mosquitoes are the primary transmitters. How should we think about the initial proposal regarding spores in the drinking water? We may say either: (i) our initial explanation was supplanted by a superior explanation; or (ii) spores in the drinking water never really explained the spread of malaria at all, not least because there never were any such spores. The first way of speaking treats explanations as *interest-relative* or as somehow *subjective*, such that something's qualifying as an explanation simply consists in its satisfying a curiosity. The second approach to explanation, Aristotle's preferred, treats explanation as *objective*, such that x explains y just in case (i) x and y are states of affairs in the world, and (ii) states of affairs of the x-type *cause* states of affairs of the y-type.[107]

The point of the illustration is not that the spore-explanation turned out to be false, but to bring out the question whether it counts as an explanation in the first place. With this distinction between subjective and objective explanations in hand, Davidson might say that while physicalism is true in the sense that everything can be given an exhaustive objective description and explanation by physics, nevertheless physics cannot provide a subjective description and explanation of rational phenomena due to the nature of our explanatory interests. This is one way of understanding Davidson's commitment to physicalism, on the one hand, and the anomalousness of the mental, on the other.

---

106. Jaworski, *Structure and the Metaphysics of Mind*, 231–37.
107. Shields, *Aristotle*, 40.

If it accurately reflects Davidson's own views, then my response on Aquinas's behalf would be as follows. Thomas follows Aristotle in preferring an objective approach to explanation. When he claims that intellectual operations cannot be explained in terms of bodily parts, states, and processes, he means this in an objective sense, and likewise when he claims that psychological operations dependent on the body can be explained in these terms. Hence, he might say, Davidson's view is entirely consistent with mutual entailment between dependence on the body and objective explicability in bodily terms, even if mental phenomena are subjectively inexplicable in physical terms.

I am not certain that Davidson's view is best understood in terms of a distinction between subjective and objective explanations. It may be, instead, that Davidson would reject physicalism understood in the sense I set down above altogether. Davidson mentions "supervenience" in discussing the anomalousness of the mental, and it might be that he would accept a weaker formulation of physicalism, such as Daniel Stoljar's "Supervenience Physicalism": "Physicalism is true at a possible world w iff any world which is a physical duplicate of w is a duplicate of w simpliciter."[108] Stoljar thinks supervenience physicalism entails sort of necessitation physicalism, namely that "Physicalism is true at [a possible world] w if and only if for every property F instantiated at w there is some physical property G instantiated at w such that F is necessitated by G."[109] Foregoing these modal notions, Davidson might also focus on constitution, claiming with Lynne Rudder Baker that "according to any materialist, every concrete particular is made up entirely of microphysical items."[110] Rudder Baker claims that constitution is not identity, and thinks of her view as a sort of nonreductive physicalism.

It is not clear that any of these theses are strong enough to uphold the central physicalist claim that everything is physical. Supervenience and necessitation relations between physical phenomena and others, for example, are compatible with forms of emergentism, epiphenomenal-

---

108. Daniel Stoljar, "Physicalism," in *The Stanford Encyclopedia of Philosophy* (2015), ed. Edward Zalta, available at plato.stanford.edu/entries/physicalism/.
109. Daniel Stoljar, *Physicalism* (London: Routledge, 2010), 112.
110. Lynne Rudder Baker, "Non-Reductive Materialism," in *The Oxford Handbook of Philosophy of Mind*, ed. Brian McGlaughlin, Ansgar Beckermann, and Sven Walter (Oxford: Oxford University Press, 2009), 109–27, at 110.

ism, and even substance dualism (Leibnizian parallelism, for instance) that physicalists would probably wish to reject.[111] I will not try to persuade physicalists against defining their view in terms compatible with these possibilities.

Instead, at this point I will switch tacks. If physicalism is not in fact a thesis about the descriptive and explanatory power of physics, but rather some weaker claim about supervenience, necessitation, or composition, then my main argument in this section will not persuade physicalists to adopt the biconditional I have proposed regarding ontological dependence on bodies and explanation in bodily terms. We saw in the previous section, however, that Aquinas's physics models a framework on which emergent phenomena are exhaustively decomposable ontologically speaking into their lowest-level components, which impose on them a certain sort of necessity, and on which they supervene. Hence Aquinas could agree, in a broad sense, that Stoljar's and Rudder Baker's formulations of physicalism aptly characterize his physical world. If that means his brand of emergentism might aptly be considered a sort of nonreductive physicalism, so be it. In the following section, however, I aim to show that emergentists in general are tacitly committed to something like the OD/E biconditional.

Ontological Dependence and Explanation III: Emergentism

It is even more difficult to give a generally acceptable account of emergentism than of physicalism or substance dualism. Jaegwon Kim notes that "those discussing emergence, even face to face, more often than not talk past each other. Sometimes one gets the impression that the only thing that the participants share is the word 'emergence.'"[112] There are many competing taxonomies of the concept, drawing different versions of distinctions between "weak" versus "strong" emergence, "on-

---

111. See Jaworski, *Structure and the Metaphysics of Mind*, 196–97.

112. Jaegwon Kim, "Emergence: Core Ideas and Issues," *Synthese* 151, no. 3 (2006): 547–59, at 548. He continues: "The intuitive associations this word evokes in us do not add up to a concept robust enough to do any useful work, or even to serve as helpful constraints on a theoretical account or construction of the concept. 'Emergence' is very much a term of philosophical trade; it can pretty much mean whatever you want it to mean, the only condition being that you had better be reasonably clear about what you mean, and that your concept turns out to be something interesting and theoretically useful."

tological" versus "epistemological" emergence, and so forth. So that my argument in this section has a target, however, I will begin by listing four assumptions that I think most emergentists could accept, albeit in varying degrees of strength. Aquinas could accept robust versions of all of them. I will then argue in two different ways that anyone making these assumptions should agree with the biconditional I proposed on Aquinas's behalf above.

An initial assumption about emergent entities: they are "systems-level" phenomena. That is, they are higher-level entities resulting in some way or other from lower-level entities standing in certain relations to one another. Furthermore, they are neither identical to, nor possessed by, any of the lower-level entities taken just by themselves apart from their relations to other lower-level entities. This formulation is neutral as to whether there are any emergent substances or merely emergent properties. I take it to be compatible with the "weak emergentism" of Galen and Empedocles, on which harmonies or complexions are emergent properties possessed not by any corresponding emergent substances, but rather by lower-level entities standing in certain relations of proportion to one another.[113]

Second, the sort of relations in question can be aptly characterized as structural, configurational, or organizational: that is, as the sort of relation typically associated with forms on the hylomorphic model suggested by Aristotle's bronze statue illustration. I am not proposing that all emergentists are hylomorphists, but I am proposing that emergent phenomena (whether substances or accidents) result from lower-level entities being structured, organized, or configured in certain sorts of ways. This proposal finds frequent, if not ubiquitous, support in the ways that emergentists describe their views. Brian McGlaughlin writes that for the British Emergentists of the nineteenth and early-twentieth centuries,

---

113. This assumption may already be too strong to reflect accurately the views of certain "weak emergentists," like Mark Bedau, for whom emergent phenomena not only lack irreducible causal powers, but are also derivable in principle from a full knowledge of micro-level facts. See Bedau, "Weak Emergence," in *Philosophical Perspectives*, vol. 11: *Mind, Causation and World*, ed. James Tomberlin (Malden, Mass.: Blackwell, 1997), 375–99. But given that Bedau thinks that emergent phenomena (such as psychological powers) are explicable in principle by the lower-level phenomena they comprise, it seems unlikely he would disagree with the biconditional I am defending in this section anyway.

emergent powers emerge from certain types of structures: "the property of having a certain type of structure will thus endow a special science kind with emergent causal powers."[114] Timothy O'Connor and Hong Yu Wong think that emergent properties appear only "in physical systems achieving some specific threshold of organized complexity."[115] William Wimsatt states that the "emergence of a system property relative to the properties of the parts of that system indicates its dependence on their mode of organization."[116] William Hasker that says emergent properties "manifest themselves when the appropriate material constituents are placed in special, highly complex relationships," but "are not observable in simpler configurations."[117] And so forth.

Third, emergent phenomena enjoy some manner of autonomy from entities at lower-levels. Sometimes emergentists express this autonomy in epistemological terms, by saying that emergent phenomena could not be predicated by or deduced from even an exhaustive examination of items at lower levels. Sometimes they put it in expressly ontological terms, claiming that emergent phenomena exhibit causal powers distinct from any possessed by lower-level entities, and hence are capable of "top-down" causation. Whatever the manner of autonomy that emergent phenomena enjoy, emergentists frequently characterize them as irreducible to anything at lower levels. This need not imply that they possess an ontological status "over and above" the lower-level items they comprise if "irreducibility" is construed in some epistemological way.

Fourth, emergentists agree with Rudder Baker broadly speaking that everything is composed entirely of microphysical items, ontologically speaking.[118] I say "broadly speaking," because some emergentists may

---

114. Brian McGlaughlin, "The Rise and Fall of British Emergentism," in *Emergence or Reduction? Essays on the Prospects of Nonreductive Physcialism*, ed. Ansgar Beckermann, Hans Flohr, and Jaegwon Kim (Berlin: De Gruyter, 1992), 45–93, at 51.

115. Timothy O'Connor and Hong Yu Wong, "The Metaphysics of Emergence," *Nous* 39, no. 4 (2005): 658–78, at 664.

116. Wimsatt, "Emergence as Non-Aggregativity," 271.

117. William Hasker, *The Emergent Self* (Ithaca, N.Y.: Cornell University Press, 1999), 189–90.

118. McGlaughlin, for instance, describes the British Emergentists as holding that "there is a hierarchy of levels of organizational complexity of material particles that includes, in ascending order, the strictly physical, the chemical, the biological and the psychological level. There are certain kinds of material substances specific to each level, and the kinds of each

count properties as constituents of their bearers alongside microphysical items. With that caveat and a few others in mind, we have seen that Aquinas can accept this emergentist commitment at least when it comes to strictly physical entities.

In fact, I think that Aquinas's robust emergentism about the physical world could take on board most of the other suggestions just mentioned as well. Thomas thinks there are emergent substances, and that their emergence is due to their possessing emergent substantial forms, on account of which they also possess emergent powers and operations. Hence, emergent properties are systems-level phenomena, existing due to structure, organization, or configuration among lower-level entities. They enjoy autonomy from anything at the lower level in both respects I mentioned. They are qualitatively distinct, and thus cannot be explained solely as aggregates of lower-level entities. They are also causally efficacious. I am not assuming that all emergentists will follow Aquinas in all of these respects, however.

Understood in terms of the four commitments I have just mentioned, emergentists clearly will not be persuaded by the line of reasoning in the previous section. I relied there on the physicalist commitment to everything being exhaustively describable and explicable in physical terms. But because emergent entities are supposed to enjoy autonomy from those at lower levels, emergentists reject this physicalist commitment, even while maintaining that everything is composed of physical items and ontologically dependent upon them. To see one reason that emergentists should nonetheless still link the ontological dependence of certain emergent phenomena—psychological powers—with their explicability in terms of coordination between bodily parts, states, and processes (along with the relevant efficient causal inputs and teleological outputs), it will be helpful to begin by considering claims about ontological dependence more generally.

The most obvious way to understand claims of the form "X is ontologically dependent on Y" is in a "modal/existential" way: "it is impossible for X to exist without Y existing." Emergentists who think that psychological powers depend ontologically on the body would most

---

level are wholly composed of kinds of lower-levels, ultimately of kinds of elementary material particles" ("Rise and Fall," 50).

likely agree that such powers cannot exist without the body. They are "essentially embodied," as Jaworski puts it, for example.[119]

As many philosophers have pointed out in recent years, however, there is reason to believe that the modal/existential construal of ontological dependence only captures part of what is meant by many such claims.[120] It is impossible for Socrates to exist without the singleton set containing only Socrates existing. He cannot exist without having a color and gender. Supposing that numbers are necessary objects, it is impossible for Socrates to exist without the number eight existing. It does not seem as though Socrates depends ontologically on the set, the number eight, or having a color or gender. It is impossible for water to exist without H_2O existing, but it seems at least odd to say that water depends ontologically on H_2O.

Instead, it seems as though "H_2O" is a compressed formula expressing water's essence; it tells us what water is. Various philosophers have argued that the sense of many ontological dependence claims can better be captured in terms of essence than in the modal/existential way. Koslicki, for instance, building on a suggestion of Fine's, proposes that an entity X ontologically depends on entity (or entities) Y just in case Y is a constituent (or are constituents) in X's real definition, where "real definition" must be understood in a narrower sense than "list of all necessary properties," but rather means something like "formula expressing an essence."[121] On this understanding, it makes perfectly good sense to say that water is ontologically dependent on hydrogen and oxygen atoms, as these are constituents in its real definition. Because neither

---

119. Jaworski, *Structure and the Metaphysics of Mind*, chap. 8, §3. An exception to this would seem to be Hasker, who despite criticizing versions of dualism for failing to account for the dependence of the mind on the brain, goes on to suggest that there might be able to exist disembodied selves, as a sort of "emergent soul-field" (*The Emergent Self*, 232–33).

120. Kit Fine, "Ontological Dependence," *Proceedings of the Aristotelian Society* 95, no. 3 (1995): 269–90; E. J. Lowe, *The Possibility of Metaphysics* (Oxford: Clarendon, 1998), chap. 6; Brad Schnieder, "A Certain Kind of Trinity: Dependence, Substance, Explanation," *Philosophical Studies* 129, no. 2 (2006): 393–419; Kathrin Koslicki, "Ontological Dependence: An Opinionated Survey," in *Varieties of Dependence: Ontological Dependence, Grounding, Supervenience, Response-Dependence*, ed. Benjamin Schnieder, Miguel Hoeltje, and Alex Steinberg (Munich: Philosophia Verlag, 2013), 31–64, and Koslicki, "Varieties of Ontological Dependence" in *Metaphysical Grounding: Understanding the Structure of Reality*, ed. Fabrice Correia and Benjamin Schnieder (Cambridge: Cambridge University Press, 2012), 186–213.

121. Koslicki, "Varieties of Ontological Dependence," 196–201.

Socrates's singleton set nor the number eight are constituents in Socrates's real definition, he is not ontologically dependent upon them.

Now consider a case where a psychological power clearly depends ontologically on the body: nutrition. It is certainly true that there cannot be nutrition without there being bodies. But on Koslicki's proposal what better captures the sense of ontological dependence relevant here is that various bodily parts, states, processes, etc., are part of nutrition's real definition.

Could it be that certain psychological powers have body-involving real definitions without being explicable in terms of bodily parts, states, processes, etc.? It seems not. Certainly not all real definitions seem to explain what they define, in any obvious sense. H_2O does not seem in any obvious way to be an explanation of water, nor rational animality an explanation of humanity. But the real definitions of powers do seem to explain what they define.[122] Water is a solvent, with the power to dissolve things like salt. What is it to dissolve salt? A real definition of water's solvency might say something about how the dipolar structure of water molecules enables them to bond with the oppositely charged ions of salt molecules, thus pulling apart their lattice structure. It would explain how it is that water dissolves salt. I take it that something similar is true of all real definitions of powers. Now it certainly might happen that certain bodily factors are part of a power's real definition without our knowing it. At one point we did not know that water was H_2O, despite this being water's real definition, nor that dissolution had anything to do with polarity. But that is just to say that we did not know the real definition of water or dissolution.

Summarizing what we have seen so far, if a power X is ontologically

---

122. Ansgar Beckermann helpfully explains the difference between terms like "water" and those like "solvency"; the former "work rather like names" and "apply to kinds of things the nature of which has to be revealed by science," while the latter "admit of an analysis" and "apply on the basis of associated characteristic features." When it comes to the former terms, we do not expect our definitions to explain what they define; water just is H_2O and that is all there is to it. When it comes to the latter sort of terms, we naturally want to know *why* water is a solvent, and to answer that sort of question we need an explanation: "it's because of thus and such about the structure of water molecules, which allows them to ... etc." See Beckermann, "What Is Property Physicalism?," in *The Oxford Handbook of Philosophy of Mind*, ed. Brian McGlaughlin, Ansgar Beckermann, and Sven Walter (Oxford: Oxford University Press, 2009), 152–72, at 167–69.

dependent on some bodily feature Y, then Y is part of X's real definition. But for some Y to be part of a power X's real definition is for it to be involved in the explanation of how X operates. Hence if a power X is ontologically dependent on a bodily feature Y, then X's operation is explicable in terms of Y.[123] Can we then infer with Aquinas that if some operation is not explicable in terms of bodily features, then its corresponding power is not ontologically dependent on the body?

Not without further ado, apparently, for as I noted earlier, explanations can be both partial and complete, and the reasoning in the previous paragraph is open to ambiguity on this score. Consider the involvement of fire in nutrition (on Aquinas's account). Arguably fire is part of the real definition of nutrition, for Aquinas, but he also thinks that talking about fire alone leaves us far short of understanding how nutrition works. Failure to explain nutrition (completely) in terms of fire would not show us that there could be nutrition without fire.

Suppose, however, that by stipulation "bodily feature Y" was an ensemble including all of the body's organic parts, and all of their subparts, down to the lowest level. Suppose it included even parts we might not yet know about. And suppose the ensemble included also the ways these parts, with their associated states and processes, coordinate to bring about the operation in question, together with any relevant environmental inputs and teleological outputs. Suppose now that a detailed account like this turned out not to provide a complete explanation of how a given power operates. Should the emergentist then conclude that the power is independent of the body?

I think she should, for I cannot see what other explanatory factors the emergentist might cite as "missing ingredients" that would render

---

123. Some of the literature on ontological dependence suggests that it is even more directly linked to explanation, and in an even broader range of cases, than I have suggested here. See Schnieder, "A Certain Kind of Trinity," and Fabrice Correia, *Existential Dependence and Cognate Notions* (Munich: Philosophia Verlag, 2005), chap. 5. Koslicki writes: "As a number of writers have noted, it is plausible to think that dependence and explanation are related in something like the following way: an explanation, when successful, captures or represents (e.g., by means of an argument or an answer to a 'why'-question) an underlying real world relation of dependence of some sort which obtains among the phenomena cited in the explanation in question" ("Varieties of Ontological Dependence," 212–13 and n27). She notes that if this suggestion is correct, the notion of explanation in question cannot be subjective (in the sense I explained in the previous section), but rather must be something more like the Aristotelian notion of causation.

our putative explanation complete. For emergentists, because everything is composed entirely of microphysical items, everything is in some sense bodily. To be sure, emergent phenomena enjoy autonomy of some sort from anything at lower levels. But given that emergentists appeal to some sort of structuring, organizing, or configuring relation to explain how higher-level phenomena emerge, it seems as though they must locate explanatory power either in lower-level phenomena by themselves, or in those phenomena *together with* ways they are structured, organized, or configured. Hence supposing that our putative explanation takes into account not only all of the body's parts, but also structural, environmental, and teleological factors, I am not sure what else emergentists might cite to render it complete. Call a putative explanation of the sort I have been discussing a "complete bodily profile." In summary, I think emergentists should accept something like the following line of reasoning:

(1) If a power X is ontologically dependent on some bodily feature Y, then Y is part of X's real definition.
(2) If Y is part of X's real definition, then it either completely explains how X operates or is part of a complete bodily profile that does.
(3) So if a power X is ontologically dependent on some bodily feature Y, then either Y completely explains how X operates or is part of a complete bodily profile that does.

Hence if we suppose that:

(4) Even a complete bodily profile cannot explain how X operates, then, given that Y is just a stand-in for any bodily feature or features whatsoever, we would be licensed to conclude that:
(5) X is not ontologically dependent on the body.

There, then, is one argument showing why emergentists should accept a link between psychological powers depending ontologically on the body and being explicable in bodily terms. While the argument from (1)–(5) is not one that I find Aquinas stating explicitly, I think it accurately reflects views that he holds. We saw in the previous section that Aquinas thinks the objects of his physics are ontologically dependent on matter partly because he thinks that matter is included in their essence, and hence also in their real definitions. We also saw that he thinks that the real definitions of powers like anger and nutrition explain how these powers operate. Aquinas sometimes addresses questions about metaphysical possibility or impossibility *via* the notions of essence and real definition. God cannot make a rational horse, for instance, because lacking reason belongs to the definition of a horse.[124] I think he would say that in similar fashion even God could not bring about a case of disembodied nutrition or anger because these powers include bodily parts, states, and processes in their definitions.[125]

Now emergentists could certainly reject the reasoning from Koslicki, Fine, and the rest that I relied on to establish a link between ontological dependence and essence or real definitions. They might insist that ontological dependence be understood in solely modal/existential terms. In that case, we might switch to a second argumentative strategy, and ask what reasons such emergentists have for thinking that all psychological powers are ontologically dependent on the body. I doubt that there are good reasons for maintaining this sort of dependence claim that do not boil down to the idea that psychological powers can be explained in bodily terms. Yet there ought to be some good reason for making sweeping claims about ontological dependence. Hence emergentists end up committed to something like Aquinas's biconditional. To explain this second line of reasoning further, it may help to focus on a concrete case.

Consider again, then, Davidson's anomalous monism, on which reasons are causally efficacious entities that are ontologically dependent on physical events but that cannot be explained in physical terms. Jaegwon Kim has repeatedly criticized Davidson's position for involving overdetermination.[126] An emergentist who wanted to defend something like Davidson's view might sidestep Kim's arguments by alleging causal pluralism; reasons are a *sui generis* kind of cause that represent part of the complete explanation of behavior, while physical causes represent

---

124. ST 1a2ae.67.3 and QQ 9.1. See ST 3a.77.1 ad 2, where Aquinas addresses the supposed impossibility of the eucharistic host's accidents remaining without a subject by calling into question the definitions of substance and accident that the objection presupposes.

125. Hence when Aquinas denies in ST 1a.75.3 and SCG 2.82 that brute animal souls are subsistent or immortal, I take it he would say that even God could not bring it about that there should be dog souls in heaven.

126. See the essays collected in Jaegwon Kim, *Supervenience and Mind* (Cambridge: Cambridge University Press, 1993), especially chaps. 10, 11, 14, and 17.

another part. Jaworski adapts terminology from Fred Dretske to express this difference: physiological events like nerve firing are "triggering causes" of animal behavior, explaining why the behavior occurred *then*, but reasons are "structuring causes" (or "rationalizing causes," as Jaworski prefers), explaining why *that* behavior occurred then.[127]

Aquinas might well agree with this response to Kim, as far as it goes, but would want to know why reasons are supposed to be ontologically dependent on physical events. Reasons are, presumably, things like beliefs and desires. When it comes to at least some of the latter, Aquinas would agree that they are ontologically dependent on the body—anger, for instance. But Aquinas holds this view about anger because he thinks its real definition includes heated blood around the heart, which he holds in turn because he thinks heated blood partially explains how living things get angry (in conjunction with certain efficient causal inputs and teleological outputs). Thomas would agree, of course, that lower-level parts, states, and processes cannot explain emergent phenomena just by themselves. But he thinks they can indeed do so once we have also made clear how they are structured or organized, together with whatever efficient and final causal factors turn out to be relevant.

Dretske is committed to the project of "naturalizing the mind," of showing how there can be "reasons in a world of causes," or of "baking a mental cake using physical yeast and flour," as he variously puts it.[128] He would broadly speaking agree that reasons are not only ontologically dependent on the physical, but also their presence in the world can be explained ultimately in terms of coordination between our physical parts, social and environmental stimuli, and teleological outputs. I will return to Dretske's "teleosemantic" account of mental content in the following section. Suppose, though, that an emergentist wishes to reject the view that reasons can be explained in anything like the way Dretske believes, yet to maintain that all psychological operations nonetheless depend ontologically on the body. What sorts of reasons might they give?

One answer might be that all psychological operations can be empir-

---

127. Jaworski, *Structure and the Metaphysics of Mind*, chap. 13, §3, and Fred Dretske, *Explaining Behavior: Reasons in a World of Causes* (Cambridge, Mass.: MIT Press, 1988), 42–43.

128. See Dretske, *Explaining Behavior*, along with *Naturalizing the Mind* (Cambridge, Mass.: MIT Press, 1995) and *Knowledge and the Flow of Information* (Cambridge: Cambridge University Press, 1981), xi.

ically observed to correlate with physiological occurrences. As we have seen, however, Aquinas addresses these correlations in the case of intellectual operations by appealing to the role that phantasia/imagination plays in supplying the intellect its objects.

A second answer might appeal to inductive generalization. Jaworski suggests that because many psychological powers are obviously ontologically dependent on the body, and in fact are the products of evolution, it is likely that all psychological powers are this way.[129] A proponent of this sort of argument must tread carefully, however. Why is it so obvious that many psychological powers are ontologically dependent on the body? If the answer is "because they can obviously be explained in bodily terms," then this line of reasoning tacitly endorses Aquinas's view that ontological dependence is related to explanation. Appealing to the role that evolutionary factors play in bringing about many of the powers of living things sounds very much like suggesting that these powers can be explained in evolutionary terms—either when it comes to their initial appearance on the world stage, or when it comes to how they operate (as in Dretske's teleosemantics), or in both of these ways. Perhaps this is precisely what Jaworski believes. In that case, however, perhaps Jaworski agrees with Aquinas after all that psychological powers are ontologically dependent on the body just in case they can be explained in (broadly speaking) bodily terms.[130]

---

129. Jaworski, *Structure and the Metaphysics of Mind*, 170.

130. It sometimes looks as though Jaworski wants to deny that reasons can be explained in any sort of bodily terms. He agrees that emergent powers and operations are necessitated by and supervenient upon lower-level phenomena, but thinks that "one of the most common misunderstandings about the nature of necessitation and supervenience relations is that they entail some type of explanatory condition" (*Structure and the Metaphysics of Mind*, 196). He denies that emergent phenomena are determined by anything at lower levels. Determination conjoins necessitation with explanation. And Jaworski holds that while "the higher-level activities of a structured whole might covary in all metaphysically possible worlds with certain lower-level material conditions," nonetheless "those lower-level conditions do not explain why the structured whole engages in the higher-level activities it does, at least not in the way exponents of lower-level determination envision" (ibid., 205–6). Jaworski thinks that hylomorphists can safely reject the question often put to other emergentists, namely how emergent phenomena are generated by things at lower levels: "according to hylomorphists, higher-level phenomena are ways in which lower-level occurrences are structured, and structures in general are not generated or produced by the things they structure" (ibid., 277). It might make sense to ask an emergentist of Empedocles's or Galen's ilk how harmonies or complexions are given off by elements proportioned in certain ways, but Jaworski thinks that hylomorphic powers and operations are not "given off" by lower entities at all. Claims like

A last refuge to which emergentists committed to the essential embodiment of psychological powers might retreat is to insist that such psychological powers are ontologically dependent on the body in a brute, metaphysically primitive way. But such an insistence might prove theoretically costly indeed. If a brute, metaphysically primitive relation of ontological dependence holds in this case, then why not in many others? Might it turn out that I am ontologically dependent on all sorts of surprising entities without my knowing it, or even being able to know it? A theory that countenanced such a possibility faces some obvious liabilities.

I have presented two lines of reasoning for thinking that emergentists are committed to something like Aquinas's claim that psychological powers are ontologically dependent on the body just in case they can be explained in bodily terms. The first involved the idea that ontological dependence claims involve claims about essences or real definitions, together with the idea that to give a real definition of a power is in part to explain how its operations occur. The second was inductive: emergentists have no other good reasons for thinking that psychological powers are ontologically dependent on the body unless they can be explained in (broadly) bodily terms, but they should not make such ontological dependence claims without some good reason. Of course emergentists might have reasons at their disposal that I have not canvassed. But I am not sure what they would be.

Many emergentists will probably need no convincing that psychological powers are ontologically dependent on the body just in case their

---

this make it seem like Jaworski rejects the notion that emergent powers can be explained at all, much less in terms of coordination between bodily powers, parts and structures. This appearance may be misleading, however. Jaworski's discussion of emergence goes on to allow the legitimacy of asking how certain structures come to exist in the universe. He tentatively suggests that just as we may come to understand the physical conditions responsible for the emergence of life, we may also ultimately come to understand how consciousness works. Conscious experiences, he says, are "composed of the coordinated manifestation of the powers of something's parts and surrounding materials" (ibid., 279). But then, if we can explain the coordination between powers of parts, surrounding materials, etc., that yields the conscious experience, have we not explained the experience itself? Jaworski agrees that while lower-level determination is false in the sense described in the previous paragraph, lower-level entities do explain higher-level behavior in the Aristotelian sense of "conditional necessity" that I discussed above (ibid., 206). Hence, perhaps he agrees with Aquinas after all that psychological powers are ontologically dependent on the body just in case they can be explained in (broadly speaking) bodily terms.

operations can be explained in bodily terms. Many will simply maintain, I imagine, that all psychological operations can (either in principle, or already) be explained in terms of coordination between bodily parts, states, and processes, together with relevant efficient causal and teleological factors. Again, I will examine Aquinas's efforts at showing this not to be the case in chapter 5. So far, I have focused on arguing that emergentists, physicalists, and substance dualists alike ought to accept that if Aquinas can show that intellectual operations escape explanation in bodily terms, then they are ontologically independent from the body. As I explained at the beginning of this chapter, this is precisely the claim that Thomas relies on to prove the incorruptibility of human souls.

The Human Intellect as an Object of Metaphysics

Aquinas does not think that the human intellect is an emergent power, and because of this he does not think that human souls are "educed from the potencies of matter" like other substantial forms either. God creates them at some point in the process of embryonic development.[131] While the human soul is an object of physics insofar as it is joined to the body, it is an object of metaphysics insofar as it possesses an immaterial power and operation. I will explain in this section why considering the human intellect as an object of metaphysics might raise a potential worry, and how Aquinas might respond. I will conclude by noting some differences between the way Aquinas arrives at conclusions regarding our intellects and souls and the way philosophers influenced by Descartes often do so.

As we saw earlier in this chapter, Aquinas regards psychology in general as a branch of physics. In his *De anima* commentary he explains why:

(3.11) Consideration of the soul pertains to the natural philosopher ... [because] operations and passions of the soul are operations and passions of the body, ... but every passion, when it is defined, must have in its definition that to which it belongs. For the subject always comes into the definition of

---

131. Aquinas notes that Aristotle thought this succession took about forty days for male offspring and about ninety for females; see In Sent 3.3.5.2 and Aristotle, *Historia animalium* 7.4.583b2–30.

a passion. So if these sorts of passions belong not to soul alone but also to the body, then the body must necessarily be put into their definition. But everything in which there is a body or matter pertains to natural philosophy. Therefore these sorts of passions also pertain to natural philosophy. But who considers passions also considers their subject. And so it also belongs to the physicist to consider soul; either every soul, simply, or else those that are attached to the body.[132]

By this point in his commentary, Aquinas has already claimed that the intellect operates independently of any bodily instrument, and consequently that human souls are separable from the body as well. The implication seems to be that physics might not consider such psychological operations and passions as are not also operations and passions of the body, nor such souls as are not attached to bodies.

Two further passages provide clearer indication that Thomas thinks human psychology pertains to physics only up to a certain point:

(3.12) Therefore the endpoint of what natural science considers is with forms that are indeed separated in a certain way, but nevertheless have an act of being in matter. And rational souls are forms of this sort, which are indeed separated according to the intellective power, which is not the act of any bodily organ ... but are in matter inasmuch as they give an act of being to such a natural body.... Hence the consideration of the natural [scientist] extends to the rational soul ... but how forms totally separated from matter might exist, and what they are, or even how *this* form, namely the rational soul, might exist this way according as it is separable and capable of existing without the body, and what it is according to its separable essence—to determine any of this pertains to first philosophy.[133]

(3.13) Among the powers [of the soul], intellect is the actuality of no part of a body, as is proved in book 3 of the *De anima*, and so it cannot be considered by a concretion or application to a body or to any bodily organ, for its greatest concretion is in soul and its highest abstraction is in separate substances. This is why Aristotle did not write, in addition to the *De anima*, a book *De intellectu et intelligibile*, but if he had done so, it would not pertain to natural science, but rather metaphysics, to which consideration of separate substances belongs. But all the other parts of soul are actualities of parts of a body, and so there

---

132. In DA 1.2.23 (Leo. 45.1:11.139–58).
133. In Phys 2.4.10/175 (Leo. 2:66).

can be a special consideration of them by application to a body or bodily organs beyond the consideration made of them in the De anima.[134]

The first passage, from Aquinas's Physics commentary, indicates that the consideration of human souls belongs to natural philosophy insofar as they have their acts of being in an inherent mode. Insofar as they have immaterial operations, however, and hence also possess a subsistent mode of being, their study belongs to metaphysics.[135] The second passage, from Aquinas's commentary on the De sensu et sensato, explains why we find no treatise on the intellect or its objects among Aristotle's psychological works. Aristotle discusses intellect in the De anima, according to Aquinas, because it is indeed a vital power of human organisms, and the De anima is devoted to dealing with souls and their powers at a general, abstract level. But there could not be a treatise on the intellect occupying the "intermediate tier" of psychological investigation—the tier that considers psychological powers in terms of their "concretion or application" to bodies or bodily organs—because it employs no bodily organ in its operation.

So Aquinas thinks it pertains to metaphysics to study human souls insofar as they have immaterial intellectual powers and operations. Like all theoretical sciences, metaphysics involves abstraction.[136] Unlike physics and mathematics, however, Aquinas thinks that metaphysics involves a characteristic sort of abstractive judgment that he calls *separatio*.[137] He characterizes it as a negative judgment to the effect that

---

134. In DSS pr./1.4 (Leo. 45.2:5.68–83).

135. Aquinas's further discussion of Physics 2.2 in DUI 1 corroborates the reading I am suggesting. Aquinas writes: "A further question might be asked: if intellect does not understand without a phantasm, then how will the soul have an intellectual operation after being separated from the body? Someone asking this should know, however, that it does not pertain to natural [philosophy] to answer that question. Whence Aristotle, speaking about the soul in Physics 2 says 'however, how [the soul] is situated and what it is like when it is separated it is the business of First Philosophy to determine'" (Leo. 43:299.681–89).

136. See esp. In DT 5.3 for a detailed description of the different ways this is true of physics, mathematics, and metaphysics.

137. Aquinas uses the term *separatio* to describe an abstractive judgment only a few times: most notably at In DT 5.3 and ST 1a.85.1 ad 1. However, there is evidence from Aquinas's redactions of the DT question showing that he reworked it several times with the specific aim of emphasizing the role of *separatio*. See Louis Geiger, "Abstraction et séparation d'après S. Thomas. In De trinitate q. 5, a. 3," Revue des sciences philosophiques et theologiques 31 (1947): 3–40; Armand Maurer's introduction to St. Thomas Aquinas, The Division and Methods of the Sciences: Questions V and VI of His Commentary on the De trinitate of Boethius Translated with Introduction and

some subject-matter does not depend on matter for its existence. Accompanying this negative judgment about ontological dependence on matter, furthermore, is a negative assessment of our epistemological prospects when it comes to the objects of metaphysics. As Mark Jordan puts it, "[the] denial of the claim that all being is material is attended by a denial of [our] own capacity to proceed to final knowledge of the immaterial. There are, then, two quite different senses in which *separatio* is a 'negative' judgment."[138] Aquinas often repeats Aristotle's adage that when it comes to such matters we are like bats in the daytime.[139] The reason both say this is because they are committed to all knowledge beginning with the senses, and indeed to the continued involvement of the senses even in rarefied intellectual activities, which depend on *phantasia* or imagination for their objects.[140] Because God, angels, and the other objects of metaphysics are immaterial, they cannot be sensed, so we cannot rely on phantasms when we think about them in the same way we can when we do physics. The proper objects of our intellect, Aquinas frequently says, are material natures, quiddities, or essences.[141] We are not very well suited for metaphysics.[142]

If this is true, and the study of our own nature insofar as we are intellectual pertains to metaphysics, does this mean Aquinas thinks we are not very well suited for understanding ourselves? That might seem like a surprising result, and potentially worrisome, if not obviously

---

Notes (Toronto: PIMS, 1963), and Mark Jordan, *Ordering Wisdom: The Hierarchy of Philosophical Discourses in Aquinas* (Notre Dame, Ind.: University of Notre Dame Press, 1986), chap. 5, §2.

138. Jordan, *Ordering Wisdom*, 163. See also Wippel, "Metaphysics and *Separatio* According to Thomas Aquinas," *Review of Metaphysics* 31, no. 3 (1979): 431–70.

139. See *Metaphysics* 2.1.993b10.

140. Aquinas claims that all knowledge begins in the senses with considerable frequency; see ST 1a.1.9, 12.12, 17.1, 84.6; QDV 1.10, 1.11, 10.2 arg. 5; In Phys 2.1.8/148 and 2.4.6/171; In Met 7.16, etc. He claims that intellectual operations (at least in this life) always rely on phantasms frequently as well: In DA 3.12 and ST 1a.84.7, etc. This is true even when it comes to thinking about God or angels: In DT 6.2.

141. ST 1a.84.7, 84.8, 85.5 ad 3.

142. At least this is true in comparison with physics, as Aquinas points out in In DT 6.1 (Leo. 50:159–60.164–72, 194–96): "natural science preserves in its processes the proper mode of the rational soul in two ways. First, insofar as just as the rational soul receives from sensible things, which are better-known to us, cognition of the intelligible things that are better-known according to nature, so natural science proceeds from things that are better-known to us and less-known according to nature.... Because of this natural science out of all the others is most in conformity with the human intellect." See also In DC 1 and *Sententia super libri Ethicorum* (hereafter, In NE) 6.7.

false. Some scholars have suggested that it is precisely what Thomas did think, however. Pasnau, for instance, compares Aquinas's position on self-knowledge to Colin McGinn's pessimistic "mysterianism."[143] I am not sure that we are in such bad shape as this for two reasons. First, when it comes to understanding ourselves, unlike God or angels, we are aided by the fact that our intellects are presently embodied. We can learn about our intellects through the ways they depend on bodies both for their objects and for their expression.[144] Second, our intellectual operations, because they are incorporeal, are self-reflexive in ways that no operations explicable in bodily terms can be. I will return to this point in the third section of chapter 5; it stands at the core of one way Aquinas thinks he can demonstrate the human intellect's immateriality. The self-reflexive character of intellectual operations plausibly enables certain research strategies for self-understanding, such as phenomenology, that we could not employ in the case of other metaphysical objects.

It is important to recognize, however, that Aquinas's intellectual self-reflexivity is not the same as Cartesian introspection. Furthermore,

---

143. Pasnau, *Aquinas on Human Nature*, 354–55; Colin McGinn, "Can We Solve the Mind-Body Problem?," *Mind* 98, no. 391 (1989): 349–66.

144. Kenny has argued in a series of papers since the late 1960s that Aquinas fails to emphasize the connection adequately, and consequently leaves himself without a good answer to a question "what makes my thoughts my thoughts?" See Kenny, "Intellect and Imagination in Aquinas," in *Aquinas: A Collection of Critical Essays* (ed. Kenny); *Aquinas on Mind*, 122–25; "Body, Soul and Intellect in Aquinas," in his *Essays on the Aristotelian Tradition* (Oxford: Oxford University Press, 2000), 76–91; and "Intentionality: Aquinas and Wittgenstein," in *Aquinas: Contemporary Philosophical Perspectives* (ed. Davies), 243–56. Kenny reasons that because, for Aquinas, intellect deals with universal generalizations, there is nothing about the *content* of my thoughts that would distinguish them from yours. This leaves Aquinas without any effective response to the proposal of his Averroist contemporaries that there is just one intellect, connected periodically to different humans through their phantasms. What Aquinas needed to say, Kenny argues, was that what makes my thoughts my thoughts is that they are the ones that are expressed by my body (or *would be* expressed by my body, were they to be expressed). He writes that "we must add Wittgenstein to Aquinas if we are to save Aquinas from falling despite himself into the arms of Averroes" ("Body, Soul and Intellect," 90). Putting to one side the issue of whether Aquinas, without Wittgenstein, is in such bad shape as Kenny suggests when it comes to the unicity of the intellect, other commentators on Aquinas—McCabe, Davies, and Geach among them—have supposed that Aquinas *does* in fact emphasize a tight connection to thinking and talking. McCabe, for instance, writes that "although Aquinas frequently and cheerfully speaks of understanding as, metaphorically, seeing, in fact he thinks of understanding not on the model of a sensation, sight, but on the model of an activity, talking. You can best understand him by beginning with the idea that solitary thinking is a kind of talking to yourself." McCabe, *On Aquinas*, ed. Brian Davies (London: Continuum, 2008), 20.

while some sort of inward-looking activity is evidently central to Descartes's strategy for proving that he is really distinct from his body, it plays only a peripheral role in the structure of Aquinas's arguments for the intellect's immateriality or the human soul's incorruptibility. Descartes establishes *a priori* that his own essence consists in thinking, his body's essence consists in extension, and reasons that whenever we can clearly and distinctly conceive of two essences not including one another, their possessors can exist apart from one another, at least by God's power. Aquinas's arguments for the intellect's immateriality, in contrast, hinge on observations we could garner simply by observing linguistic behavior, as opposed to *a priori* reflection on our own essences. We will see what some of these observations are in chapter 5, when I consider Thomas's efforts to show that we cannot account for the phenomena they highlight, even in principle, by means of explanations couched in terms of coordination between bodily parts, states, and processes (even together with various efficient causal inputs and teleological outputs). If these efforts succeed, then based on the reasoning I have discussed in this chapter Aquinas can argue for the possibility of human souls existing in separation from their bodies as follows:

(SS1) A psychological power depends ontologically on the body if and only if its operations can be explained in terms of coordinated bodily parts, states, and processes, together with the relevant efficient causal inputs and teleological outputs (OD/E).

(SS2) Intellectual operations cannot be explained in this way.

(SS3) Intellectual operations are not ontologically dependent on the body.

(SS4) If human souls, the subject of intellectual operations, can operate independently of the body, then they must themselves be capable of existing apart from the body.

(SS5) Human souls can exist in a disembodied state.

I have argued in this chapter that reasoning along these lines represents the core of Aquinas's strategy for moving from the immateriality of intellectual operations, along with the incorporeality it implies, to the incorruptibility of human souls. I have focused so far on defending OD/E—

premise SS1 in the argument above—as one that physicalists, substance dualists, and emergentists alike should accept. I doubt that physicalism, substance dualism, or emergentism exhaust the range of mind-body theories that philosophers might hold, but my hope is that arguments like those I have presented here might be adapted to address other possible views as well. I turn in the next two chapters to Aquinas's defense of premise SS2, beginning with an account of his theory of cognition.

4

AQUINAS'S THEORY OF COGNITION

The arguments that Aquinas uses to demonstrate the immateriality of the intellect hinge on the way it operates. Each has the form: the intellect can do X, but doing X cannot be explained in bodily terms. In the previous chapter we saw why Aquinas supposes—with good reasons—that if a power's operations are inexplicable in bodily terms, they are not ontologically dependent on the body either. Hence the human souls that are subject to intellectual operations are capable of existing in a disembodied state. The next chapter will examine some of the ways Aquinas tries to show that intellectual operations are inexplicable in bodily terms. The aim of the present chapter is to provide an account of Aquinas's theories of cognition in general, and of intellectual cognition in particular, that undergird his arguments for the human intellect's immateriality.

Aquinas's cognitive psychology is complex, and there already exists a sizeable literature devoted to understanding it. Hence my treatment here must necessarily be selective. In the first section, I will begin by reviewing five well-known items of terminology Aquinas frequently uses to describe cognition. I will also describe what I take to be a helpful interpretative strategy for understanding this terminology, namely that Aquinas thinks of cognition as a sort of information processing. The next section focuses on a question specific to sense cognition, namely whether Aquinas in fact thinks it is explicable in bodily terms; I argue that he does. The third section draws an analogy between Aquinas's cognitive theory and contemporary teleofunctional and teleosemantic theories of mind, with the aim of showing how Thomas can respond to an objection. The charge is that pretty well anything can satisfy the abstract criteria Aquinas's theory sets down for cognition, so that it entails pan-cognitivism. I will call this the Liberalism Objection because it charges that Aquinas's theory doles out cognition too liberally to things that obviously lack it. Aquinas is able to avoid this objection, I argue, because of the teleological roles he assigns to cognitive states. Importantly, however, Aquinas understands the teleology of sense cognition and intellectual cognition differently. In the final section I focus on this and several other differences between sense and intellectual cognition, and conclude by considering whether these differences render the latter an "unanalyzable primitive" or mysterious in some problematic way.

Aquinas's Terminology for Cognition

The terminology Aquinas uses in discussions of cognition stems mostly from Aristotle, but also in several important cases from Aristotle's Greek and Arabic commentators. I will canvas five important items of terminology here, all of which appear frequently in Aquinas's corpus. I will then explain one promising strategy for interpreting them.

First, following Aristotle, Aquinas frequently treats cognition as a sort of change in which the cognizer comes to possess the form of what it cognizes. That is, cognizers become formally identical with what they cognize. This is true of both sense and intellect; Aquinas says frequently that "the intellect in act and what is understood in act are one, just as the sense in act and what is sensed in act [are one]."[1] Sometimes Thomas likens cognition to the natural process of heating. Just as something heats up by receiving the form of heat, so too something cognizes by receiving the form of what is cognized.[2] Of course, however, cognition cannot resemble heating in all respects. It may be that in order to feel heat my skin must literally get hot, but my intellect need not literally heat up to think about heat, nor (fortunately) do I become a literal donkey when I cognize donkeys. Perhaps for this reason, Aquinas characterizes cognition in one much-discussed passage as a change in which the

---

1. SCG 2.59.13 (Leo. 13:415); see also SCG 1.51.6 and 2.74.2, and ST 1a.14.2 and 1a.87.1 ad 3.
2. ST 1a.56.1, In Sent 4.49.2.1 arg 8, QDP 9.5, QDSC 2.

cognizer comes to possess the form of what it cognizes *in addition to* or *alongside* its own forms:

(4.1) Cognizers are distinguished from non-cognizers in that non-cognizers have only their own form whereas a cognizer is apt to possess the form of something else in addition [to its own form], for the *species* of what is cognized exists in the cognizer. Whence it is clear that the nature of a non-cognitive thing is more restricted and limited, whereas the nature of cognitive things has a greater amplitude and extension. On this account the Philosopher says in DA 3 that "the soul is in a way all things." The contraction of a form, however, is through matter, whence it was said above that forms, according as they are more immaterial, approach more a certain infinitude. It is clear, therefore, that the immateriality of a certain thing is the reason why it is a cognizer, and according to its mode of immateriality corresponds its mode of cognition. Whence in DA 2 it is said that plants do not cognize because of their materiality, while a sense cognizes since it receives *species* without matter and the intellect cognizes still more because it is separated from matter and unmixed, as is said in DA 3.[3]

Aquinas acknowledges here that his initial claim about how cognizers are distinguished from non-cognizers stems from Aristotle's well-known dictum that *nous* becomes what it thinks, and thus that the thinking soul "is in a way all things."[4] So he is still claiming that cognition involves formal identity between cognizer and what is cognized. Here, however, Aquinas also notes that while non-cognizers have only their own forms, cognizers have the forms of other things in addition to or alongside their own. This may be a way of indicating that cognizers need not literally exemplify the forms they receive in order to cognize.[5]

That this is indeed what Aquinas has in mind is made clearer in several other passages where he invokes the notion of *species*—a second important bit of terminology he uses to discuss cognition. I will leave the term untranslated, as it appears in 4.1, to indicate the difference be-

---

3. ST 1a.14.1 (Leo. 4.166), see *De anima* 2.12.424a32, 3.5.430a17–19, 3.8.431b21.
4. See *De anima* 3.4.429a15–17. See also *De anima* 2.5.417b2–5 for Aristotle's mention of changes that do not involve any loss of form on the part of their subject as the kind relevant in perception, and *In DA* 2.11.369 for Aquinas's acceptance of this notion.
5. John O'Callaghan suggests this interpretation of ST 1a14.1 in *Thomist Realism and the Linguistic Turn: Toward a More Perfect Form of Existence* (Notre Dame, Ind.: University of Notre Dame Press, 2003), 229.

tween cognitive species and the logical species subordinate to genera. The use of the term *species* in medieval discussions of cognition and related subjects has a complex background, and I will not try to trace the antecedents to Aquinas's own usage.[6] For Thomas, there are *species* in the senses, in the intellect, and in cognitive media. In this passage he discusses all three:

(4.2) In a given case of vision a threefold medium can be considered: one is the medium under which [*sub quo*] [something] is seen, another is that by which [*quo*] [something] is seen (namely, the *species* of the thing seen), and a third is that from which [*a quo*] the cognition of the thing seen is received. Thus, for example, in bodily vision the medium under which [something] is seen is light, by which something is visible in act and vision is perfected such that it can see, but the medium by which [something] is seen is the *species* of the sensible thing existing in the eye, which, as the form of the one seeing inasmuch as they are seeing, is the principle of the visual operation. Moreover, the medium from which cognition of the thing seen is received is like a mirror from which the *species* of something visible like a stone might sometimes come to be in the eye, rather than immediately from the stone itself. And these three are found in intellectual vision too, since the corporeal light corresponds to the light of the agent intellect as the medium under which the intellect sees, while the visible *species* corresponds to the intelligible *species*, by which the possible intellect comes to understand in act, and the medium from which cognition of what is seen is taken, like from a mirror, is comparable to the effects from which we arrive at cognition of the cause.[7]

Sensible *species*, as Aquinas describes them here, are forms that sense-cognizers receive in virtue of which they are able to sense. To see a stone I must receive a stony *species* in my eye, the organ of visual cognition. To reach my eye, however, Aquinas thinks the stony *species* must pass through certain intermediaries. At the least, it must be present in the air between the stone and my eye, that is, in what he calls here in 4.2 "the

---

6. Leon Spruit writes that "Thomas puts forward, for the first time in the Middle Ages, a theory of mental representation that is sufficiently complex and complete to bear scrutiny of its own. In this respect, Thomas's theory eclipses all its (possible) sources." Species Intelligibilis: *From Perception to Knowledge* (Leiden: Brill, 1994), 156–57. Spruit nevertheless lists Aristotle, Augustine, Averroes, Alexander of Hales, Peter of Spain, and Albert the Great as possible sources for Thomas's theory of intelligible *species* (ibid., 157n216).

7. QDV 18.1 ad 1 (Leo. 22.2:532.227–49).

medium from which" cognition is received.⁸ As he notes, sometimes things like mirrors serve as media from which we receive cognition too. Parallel ingredients are necessary for intellectual cognition. Intelligible *species* are the formal principles by which intellectual operations occur. The "effects" from which we arrive at an intellectual grasp of whatever it is we are cognizing are, I take it, the phantasms on which human intellectual cognition depends. The role that light plays in making colors actually visible to us is analogous to the agent intellect's role in rendering the objects represented by these phantasms actually intelligible to us.⁹ I will say more about the agent intellect's abstractive activity in chapter 5. For now, however, note that in passage 4.1 Aquinas apparently wants us to understand the sort of formal identity that cognition involves in terms of *species* possession. A cognizer must become formally identical to what it cognizes only in the sense that it must possess a *species* of its object. The case of the mirror shows that *species* in cognitive media may at times literally exemplify the very characteristics they enable us to cognize. When I see a rock's redness reflected in a mirror, the mirror literally exemplifies redness. On the other hand, the mirror does not literally become a rock, and this seems to be Aquinas's point in the passage: cognitive formal identity need not involve cognizers literally exemplifying the characteristics they cognize. As Thomas explains elsewhere, it was the mistaken view of ancients like Empedocles that the soul literally needed to be made of earth to cognize earth, of fire to cognize fire, etc., whereas when Aristotle says that cognizers become formally identical to the objects they cognize he means just that they receive *species* of these objects.¹⁰ Air need not literally become red when it contains a *species* of redness, nor the eye when it receives red sensible *species*, nor the intellect when it receives redness as an intelligible *species*. It seems likely, then, that Aquinas's claims about formal identity from above should be un-

---

8. Aquinas thinks there is a medium for each sense modality, and that sense cognition always occurs through a medium (*In DA* 2.23.542). See *In DA* 2.14.404 for a discussion of the medium of vision, 2.17.451 for sound, 2.20.491 for smell, 2.21.505 for taste, and 2.22–23 for an extended discussion of the medium of touch.

9. See Therese Scarpelli Cory, "Rethinking Abstractionism: Aquinas's Intellectual Light and Some Arabic Sources," *Journal of the History of Philosophy* 53, no. 4 (2015): 607–46, for an illuminating discussion of the parallel between light's role in visual cognition and the abstractive activity of the agent intellect.

10. *In DA* 1.12 and 3.13.789 and *ST* 1a.85.2.

derstood this way too: a cognizer that receives the form of something else in addition to its own forms need not literally exemplify the additional form in question.

A third important idea involved in Aquinas's discussions of cognition, also on display in 4.1, is that cognition involves receiving forms in an immaterial way. In fact, it seems that there are two different ideas present here. One is the notion that because designated matter "contracts" forms when it individuates them, the sort of universal cognition characteristic of the intellect requires that intelligible *species* and indeed the intellect itself be immaterial. I will examine this line of reasoning along with its sources closely in the fourth and fifth sections of chapter 5. Another idea present in 4.1, however, as the passage itself indicates, is Aristotle's claim in *De anima* that sense cognition involves receiving a thing's form without receiving its matter.[11] Aquinas's gloss on the passage is worth quoting at length:

(4.3) Sense is receptive of *species* without matter, just as wax receives the sign of the ring without iron or gold. But this might seem to be common to every receiver, for every receiver receives something from an agent insofar as it is an agent. But the agent acts through its own form, and not through its matter, so every patient receives form without matter. And this is also apparent to sense, for air does not receive matter from the agent fire, but its form. So it does not seem like being receptive of *species* without matter is something proper to sense alone. It must be said, therefore, that although it is true that every patient receives a form from the agent, nevertheless there is a difference in the mode of receiving. For sometimes the form that the thing affected receives from its agent has the same mode of being in the thing affected and in the agent. This happens when the thing affected has the same disposition for the form that the agent has.... In [such a] case, form is not received without matter.... And it is in this manner that air is affected by fire, and so too for anything else affected naturally. Sometimes, on the other hand, a form is received in the thing affected according to a mode of being different from the agent's, because the material disposition of the thing affected for receiving

---

11. *De anima* 2.12.424a18–24. Martin Tweedale, "Origins of the Medieval Theory that Sensation is an Immaterial Reception of a Form," *Philosophical Topics* 20, no. 2 (1992): 215–31, explains how Albert, Averroes, and Themistius served as sources for Aquinas's own interpretation of this passage, which Tweedale considers both un-Aristotelian and conceptually confused.

is not like the agent's material disposition. In that case a form is received in the thing affected without matter, insofar as the thing affected is made like the agent with respect to form and not matter. And this is how sense receives form without matter. For the form has a different manner of being in the sense and in the sense object: for in the sense object it has natural being [*esse naturale*], whereas in the sense it has intentional and spiritual being [*esse intentionale et spirituale*]. And [Aristotle] posits a fitting example involving a signet and wax. For the wax is not disposed to the image in the same way as the iron or gold was. And therefore he adds that the wax receives the sign, that is the golden or brazen image or figure, but not inasmuch as it is gold or bronze. For the wax is assimilated to the golden signet as regards the image, not as regards the disposition of the gold. And similarly a sense is affected by something sensible having a color or moisture (that is, a taste) or sound, but not inasmuch as it is called a certain one of those, that is, it is not affected by a colored stone inasmuch as it is stone, nor by sweet honey inasmuch as it is honey, since in the sense there does not result the same disposition to the form that is in those subjects, but it is affected by them inasmuch as they are of this sort, either inasmuch as they are colored or tasty or according to their notion [*secundum rationem*], that is according to their form. For a sense is assimilated to something sensible according to its form, but not according to the disposition of its matter.[12]

Aquinas's discussion of the example Aristotle offers to illustrate the notion of receiving forms without matter may make it look as though sense-cognizers do indeed literally exemplify the characteristics they cognize. A wax blob does not turn into gold when it receives the signet's impression, but it does literally take on the signet's shape. So too, Aquinas might appear to say here, a visual cognizer does not turn into stone when viewing a red rock, but does literally exemplify redness. On the other hand, in the beginning of the passage Aquinas acknowledges explicitly the contrast between non-cognitive cases of form reception, such as air being heated up by fire, and cognitive cases such as those involving the senses. While it is true that air receives the form of heat from fire when it is heated up, it receives the form according to the same mode of being it has in the fire itself, whereas the senses receive forms according to a different mode of being than they have in the objects cog-

---

12. In DA 2.24.551–54 (Leo. 45.1.168–69.15–75).

nized. The most obvious way to read this is that while the air receiving heat becomes literally hot just as the fire that heats it is literally hot, a cognizer need not literally exemplify the characteristics it cognizes.

This interpretation is confirmed by Thomas's discussions elsewhere of a fourth important bit of terminology he employs to describe cognition, namely the "intentional" or "spiritual" mode of being that he mentions in 4.3 as distinctive of cognitive form reception. This terminology is not Aristotelian, but rather stems from Aquinas's reading of Avicenna and Averroes.[13] Thomas contrasts the intentional or spiritual mode in which cognizers receive forms with the "natural" mode of being the forms have in objects of cognition. Here is one oft-cited passage in which Aquinas wields this distinction, again in a discussion of the senses:

(4.4) Change comes in two kinds, one natural and the other spiritual. Natural change happens when the form that causes the change is received into the thing changed according to its natural being [*esse naturale*] as happens when heat is received into a thing that is heated. Spiritual change, in contrast, happens when the form that causes the change is received into the thing changed according to its spiritual being [*esse spirituale*], as happens when the form of color is received into the pupil of the eye, which does not, as a result, become colored. A spiritual change is required for a sense operation to take place, through which the intention [*intentio*] of a sensible form comes to be in a sense organ. Otherwise, if natural change alone sufficed for a sense operation to take place, any natural body would sense whenever it was altered.[14]

In this passage Thomas makes it quite clear that seeing some color need not involve the cognizer (in this case, the pupil of the eye) literally exem-

---

13. See Jörg Alejandro Tellkamp, "Aquinas on Intentions in the Medium and in the Mind," *Proceedings of the American Catholic Philosophical Association* 80 (2006): 275–89, for a discussion of how Aquinas combines the *intentiones* Avicenna discusses in his *De anima* with the spiritual being Averroes invokes in his *Long Commentary on the De anima* to arrive at the notion of "intentional or spiritual being" as we see in passage 4.3. Miles Burnyeat, however, reminds us that "on occasion, knowledge of the previous history of a term may be a hindrance as much as a help to understanding. Origins, to repeat, are less important than the way Aquinas uses 'intentional' and 'spiritual' to elucidate the Aristotelian text he is commenting on. They pick out the very same thing as Aristotle expresses by 'form without matter.'" From "Aquinas on Spiritual Change in Perception," in *Ancient and Medieval Theories of Intentionality*, ed. Dominik Perler (Dordrecht: Springer, 2001), 129–54, at 141.

14. ST 1a.78.3 (Leo. 5:254); see In Sent 4.44.2.1.3 ad 2 and In Met 1.1.6.

plifying it, because cognizers receive forms only according to a spiritual or intentional mode of being. I take it, then, that is how we should also understand Aquinas's claims about the notion of receiving forms without matter in 4.3 as well.

The links that Aquinas establishes between immateriality, spirituality, and intentionality might give the appearance that he agrees with Franz Brentano's famous thesis that intentionality pertains exclusively to nonphysical phenomena. Yet claims Thomas makes elsewhere should give us pause. Consider two passages:

(4.5) One angel knows another by means of the *species* of the [other angel] existing in its intellect, which differs from the angel whose similitude it is not in terms of material versus immaterial being, but in terms of natural versus intentional being. For the angel is a subsisting form in its natural being, but not as far as its *species* which is in the intellect of the other angel is concerned, rather it has there just an intelligible being [*esse intelligibile*]. Likewise also the form of a color on the wall has natural being, whereas when it is being conveyed in a medium it has just intentional being.[15]

(4.6) Color is in a colored body as a quality complete in its natural being, but it is in the medium incompletely, according to a certain intentional being. Otherwise it would be impossible for white and black to be seen through the same medium. For whiteness and blackness cannot both exist at the same time in the same thing inasmuch as they are forms complete in their natural being, but according to the aforementioned incomplete being they are indeed in the same thing.[16]

In the first passage Aquinas's point is that when one angel cognizes another, the cognized angel possesses his form in a natural way, while the cognizing angel receives it in an intentional way. Both angels are, of course, spiritual creatures, and hence have their acts of being in an immaterial mode. But Aquinas's distinction between natural and spiritual

---

15. ST 1a.56.2 ad 3 (Leo. 5:65). Sometimes instead of *esse naturale* Aquinas uses the terms *esse reale* or *esse materiale* to contrast with *esse intentionale* or *esse spirituale*—see In Sent 2.17.2.1 and QDA 2. Somewhat confusingly, then, Aquinas would say that the cognized angel's essence exists both with *esse immateriale* (insofar as the angel is a subsistent form) and with *esse materiale* (in the sense equivalent to *esse naturale*, that stands in contrast to *esse intentionale* or *esse spirituale*). Clearly, much care is needed on the reader's part to navigate these different modes of being.

16. In DSS 4/5.4 (Leo. 45.2:28.46–54).

or intentional modes of being in discussions of cognition apparently need not track the ontological distinction between material and immaterial modes of being. That "intentional" need not mean "nonphysical" is confirmed by the way both passages attribute an intentional mode of being to *species* in cognitive media like air. Surely air is physical stuff, yet Aquinas thinks it perfectly capable of possessing forms in a spiritual or intentional way insofar as it serves as a medium for cognition. Of course, clarifying that "spiritual" or "intentional" do not mean "nonphysical" when they are involved in discussions of cognition does not by itself yield any firm grasp of what the terms do mean.

Before turning to one possible account of their meaning, however, 4.5 contains a fifth important term that Aquinas often uses to discuss cognition: "similitude." The intelligible *species* by which the first, cognizing angel cognizes the second, cognized angel is the second angel's similitude. The same is true of *species* in general: they are similitudes of the objects they enable us to cognize. Aquinas often uses both terms at once, speaking of a *species et similitudo* or *species vel similitudo*. Above I mentioned that in 4.1 and elsewhere Aquinas seemingly wants us to understand the formal identity of cognizer and what is cognized in terms of *species* possession. Given the link between *species* and similitude, it is not surprising that we should find him analyzing cognitive formal identity in terms of similitude as well.[17] Some commentators think there is no more to Aquinas's notion that cognizer and what is cognized are formally identical than can be spelled out in terms of similitude.[18] This may well be true. Still, it is important to note that cognitive similitude, just like cognitive formal identity, must be similitude of a peculiar sort. My eye does not literally become red when I look at a red apple, but no more does it come to resemble redness. Aquinas knows this, of course, and accordingly distinguishes between "natural similitude" and a special sort of "representational similitude"; only the latter need be involved in cases of cognition.[19] In other words, cognizers are formally identical to the characteristics they cognize insofar as they possess *species*

---

17. See ST 1a.76.2 ad 4, 78.1, 88.1 ad 2; In DA 1.4.43; SCG 1.53.

18. For example, Claude Panaccio, "Aquinas on Intellectual Representation," in *Ancient and Medieval Theories of Intentionality*, ed. Dominik Perler (Dordrecht: Springer, 2001), 185–202.

19. See In Sent 4.49.2.1 ad 7, SCG 4.26.7, ST 1a.44.3 ad 1, QDV 2.3 ad 9, 2.5 ad 5, 8.1.

resembling these characteristics, but *species* resemble their objects insofar as they represent them. Commentators often speak of sensible and intelligible *species* as mental representations, with some justification, though this should not necessarily be taken to imply that Aquinas holds a representationalist theory of cognition as opposed to some sort of realism.[20] The question, however, is what makes *species* represent certain objects? To answer this question, commentators sometimes retreat back to the notion of formal identity with which we began. Claude Panaccio, for instance, thinks that similitude is the basic notion that Aquinas's theory of cognition hinges on, not formal identity.[21] Yet to elucidate the notion of representational similitude he suggests it involves some sort of abstract isomorphism. What is isomorphism except sameness of form?[22]

So far I have surveyed five items of terminology that Aquinas uses in various interlocking ways when he discusses cognition: formal identity, *species*, receiving forms without matter, intentional or spiritual being, and similitude. Instead of pursuing further any of the many disputes among commentators about how to understand the relationships between these notions, let me turn at this point to what I consider a promising strategy for interpreting all of them.

Stump, Klima, and many others have proposed that the key to understanding Aquinas's terminology of cognition is the notion of information processing.[23] Cognizers become formally identical to what they cognize in the same sense that maps become formally identical

---

20. See QDV 3.1 ad 2 and 8.1, in which Aquinas speaks of *species* as representations. Panaccio, "Aquinas on Intellectual Representation," and Robert Pasnau, *Theories of Cognition in the Later Middle Ages* (Cambridge: Cambridge University Press, 1997), chaps. 5–6, argue that Aquinas is indeed best thought of as a representationalist, while O'Callaghan, *Thomist Realism and the Linguistic Turn* strenuously resists this suggestion.

21. Panaccio, "Aquinas on Intellectual Representations," 197.

22. See Stephen Pimentel, "Formal Identity as Isomorphism in Thomistic Philosophy of Mind," *Proceedings of the American Catholic Philosophical Association* 80 (2007): 115–26.

23. Stump, *Aquinas*, 252; Gyula Klima, "Tradition and Innovation in Medieval Theories of Mental Representation," in *Mental Representation*, ed. Gyula Klima and Alexander Hall, Proceedings of the Society for Medieval Logic and Metaphysics 4 (Newcastle-upon-Tyne: Cambridge Scholars Press, 2011), 7–17; see Gerard Casey, "Immateriality and Intentionality," in *At the Heart of the Real*, ed. F. O'Rourke (Dublin: Irish Academic Press, 1992), 97–112; Pimentel, "Formal Identity as Isomorphism"; Robert Pasnau and Christopher Shields, *The Philosophy of Aquinas* (Boulder, Colo.: Westview, 2003), 176; and Peter King, "Medieval Intentionality and Pseudo-Intentionality," *Quaestio* 10 (2010): 25–44.

to cities or compact discs become formally identical to songs written on them.[24] That is, they do so by encoding information about cities or songs. They receive forms without matter in the same way as a map encodes information about a city's subway grid without itself being made of steel and concrete. The subway's form exists in natural being in the steel and concrete of the city, but exists in an intentional or spiritual way on the page. Of course, for the subway's form to be received intentionally or spiritually on the map requires certain concomitant natural changes. The page must literally exemplify certain colors in order to encode information about the subway's various lines. Likewise, when I write a song on a compact disc I am bringing about certain natural changes, namely a pattern of tiny pits on its surface, but I am also bringing about a spiritual change insofar as I am encoding information about some music by means of these pits. These natural and spiritual changes clearly are not independent processes that just happen to be correlated with one another.[25] Rather their relationship is arguably one of hylomorphic union. The writing on the compact disc or the map is a *species* of the song or city insofar as it resembles them in representational way. Panaccio says these cases illustrate the sort of abstract isomorphism that representational similitude involves. Receiving information about some characteristic clearly does not require literally exemplifying it, just as Aquinas denies that cognizers must literally become whatever they cognize. Hence it appears that all five items of Thomas's cognitive ter-

---

24. The map is Stump's example and the compact disc Klima's; Casey, "Immateriality and Intentionality," 111, also offers the recording of a song as an example of intentional form reception, although his example involves a vinyl record.

25. D. W. Hamlyn, *Sensation and Perception* (New York: Humanities Press, 1961), apparently misunderstands Aquinas's theory of sense cognition in just this way—by supposing that acts of sense perception consist of two really distinct changes: a natural change in a sense organ and a spiritual change in the sensitive soul. He writes: "[Aquinas] views sense-perception primarily as a form of change in which the sense-organ is altered. But this cannot be all that is involved, for along with the physical change there goes the reception of a sensible form without the matter. The latter Aquinas takes to be not something that happens to the sense-organ, but something that happens to the faculty of the soul or mind. It is, in his words a spiritual change" (ibid., 46). Sheldon Cohen, "St. Thomas Aquinas on the Immaterial Reception of Sensible Forms," *The Philosophical Review* 91, no. 2 (1982): 193–209, argues persuasively against this interpretation of Aquinas and appears to have convinced most subsequent commentators. John Haldane, nevertheless, disagrees, claiming that there is equal evidence to be found in support of both Hamlyn's and Cohen's views in Aquinas and thus that it is ultimately incoherent. "Aquinas on Sense Perception," *Philosophical Review* 92, no. 2 (1983): 233–39.

minology that I surveyed in this section can be plausibly interpreted in terms of information processing. I will assume from this point forward that some interpretation along these lines is broadly speaking correct. Even if this is true, Aquinas's theory of cognition faces some clear difficulties. I will address three in the following sections of this chapter.

The "Immateriality" of Sense Cognition

We saw in passage 4.1 that Aquinas thinks that cognition of any sort requires some kind of immateriality on the part of what does the cognizing, and in 4.3 that sense cognition requires receiving forms without matter. We also saw, to be sure, why passages like 4.5 and 4.6 should give us pause before equating the immaterial, spiritual, or intentional being that Aquinas thinks is involved in cognition with nonphysicality, ontologically speaking. Yet some commentators think there is ample evidence that Aquinas regarded sense cognition as immaterial in a way somehow opposed to their physicality. In this section I will consider two lines of argument that challenge my interpretation of Aquinas's argument for the human soul's incorruptibility by claiming that Thomas takes sense cognition to be somehow nonphysical. The two objections differ, nonetheless, as to the way in which they claim that Aquinas regards the senses as nonphysical.

As we saw in the previous chapter, "physical" can mean many things. Aquinas's emergentism commits him to denying that even such humble phenomena as the nutritive power's operations are physical in one sense. They cannot be "reduced" to their lowest-level material constituents in that they exist "over and above" these constituents ontologically speaking, and cannot be exhaustively described and explained in terms of these constituents and their powers. Nevertheless, Aquinas does believe that investigating the power of nutrition is a job for physics, in his sense of the term. The nutritive power can be described and explained by examining how coordination between certain bodily parts, states, and processes, together with certain efficient-causal inputs and teleological outputs, bring about its activities. In that sense it is physical indeed. Call the sort of reductive physicalism Aquinas rejects about emergent entities R-physicalism, and the sort of physicalism he accepts about them T-physicalism.

The first objection I will consider in this section argues that Aquinas rejects T-physicalism about the senses. If true, this would pose a serious problem for my interpretation of Aquinas's argument for the human soul's incorruptibility from the previous chapter. An assumption I made there is that T-physicalism is true of all psychological powers other than intellectual ones. Otherwise, given the OD/E biconditional, it would turn out that these other psychological powers too are capable of operating independent of the body—something Aquinas takes to be exclusively true of human intellectual capacities.

The second objection accepts that Thomas regards sense cognition as T-physical, but argues that Aquinas's understanding of the senses is nevertheless obviously unacceptable from the standpoint of contemporary science. So unacceptable, in fact, as to vitiate Aquinas's argument for the human soul's incorruptibility altogether.

I will argue here that neither of these objections succeeds, starting with the first. Paul Hoffmann is sometimes taken to have advanced the first style of objection. In fact, he did not, and it will be helpful to consider the reasons for this first, before turning to the way John Knasas does indeed advance it.[26] Hoffmann's chief aim is to show that Aquinas thinks sense cognition is only partly physical, but is also partly nonphysical. His interpretation is meant to serve as a corrective to Sheldon Cohen's claim that sense cognition is always a physical event; Hoffmann thinks this is only partly true.[27] His reasoning is based on the many passages in which Aquinas argues for a gradation among the forms of composite substances: first those of the elements, then those of nonliving mixed bodies such as minerals, then of plants, animals, and finally human beings whose souls, as noted in chapter 1, exist "on the borderline between corporeal and incorporeal things."[28] Hoffman interprets these passages to mean that corporeality and materiality come in degrees for Aquinas. Only the elements are wholly corporeal and material;

---

26. See Paul Hoffman, "St. Thomas Aquinas on the Halfway State of Sensible Being," *Philosophical Review* 99, no. 1 (1990): 73–92, and "Aquinas on Spiritual Change," *Oxford Studies in Medieval Philosophy* 2 (2015): 98–103; John Knasas, "Aquinas on the Cognitive Soul: Physics, Metaphysics or Both?" *American Catholic Philosophical Quarterly* 77, no. 4 (1998): 501–27.

27. See Cohen, "Aquinas on the Immaterial Reception."

28. Representative passages include SCG 2.68, QDA 1 and 9, QDP 3.11, DEE, ST 1a.47.2, QDSC 2.

all other composite substances are partly corporeal and partly incorporeal, partly material and partly immaterial.

Hoffmann is quite right that Aquinas sometimes speaks this way. At one point Thomas says that the forms of the elements are "the lowest forms" and "are wholly material, and totally immersed in matter," whereas "above these are found the forms of mixed bodies" which (the passage implies) are *not* wholly material and totally immersed in matter.[29] On the other hand, just a few lines later in the same passage, Thomas also says that all the forms of composite substances other than the human soul and its intellectual powers are "totally immersed in matter."[30] These claims seem inconsistent.

I think Aquinas's meaning can be understood perfectly well, however, in terms of the emergentism I discussed in the previous chapter, together with the "information processing" interpretation of cognition proposed by Stump and Klima. The forms of any mixed bodies are not immersed in matter insofar as they are emergent substances, with powers qualitatively distinct from those of their elemental constituents. Furthermore, there are degrees of emergence. Vital powers such as nutrition are higher-grade emergent powers than those of nonliving mixed bodies insofar as living things are self-movers. Sense powers represent an even higher grade of emergence insofar as they are cognitive, and hence "receive forms without matter," that is, in an "intentional or spiritual way." As we saw above, however, we can plausibly interpret these items of cognitive terminology as referring simply to information processing. If so, then just as we might explain how information gets encoded on a compact disc using something like functional analysis or mechanistic explanation, so too might we explain how sense operations work. Indeed, all non-intellectual powers *are* indeed immersed in matter insofar as their operations are emergent, and hence can be explained "reductively," in the special sense of "reduction" I likened in the third section of the previous chapter (pp. 122–23) to functional analysis or mechanistic explanation. Only intellectual powers, which are not emergent but directly created, cannot be explained this way.

Such, at least, is the interpretation of Aquinas that I favor. Sense

---

29. SCG 2.68.8 (Leo. 13:441).
30. Ibid., par. 12.

powers are indeed immaterial and incorporeal both in the sense that they are high-grade emergent powers, and in the sense that their operations involve information processing. But they are material and corporeal in that they are T-physical, and can be explained in a way similar to other items populating Aquinas's physical world. As far as I can tell, Hoffmann could wholly agree with this interpretation, insofar as it takes on board Thomas's references to degrees of corporeality and materiality, explaining them in terms of degrees of emergence. If I am understanding him correctly, then Hoffmann does not really advance the first objection I mentioned above.

John Knasas does, however; that sense powers are T-physical on Aquinas's understanding is something he is keen to deny. In the previous chapter's final section we saw how Aquinas thinks that to investigate the human intellect pertains primarily to metaphysics, as opposed to physics. Knasas thinks this is true of any cognitive powers as such. He collects many potential items of evidence for this view, the strongest of which appeals to a passage in which Aquinas distinguishes the sort of motion involved in sense cognition from the sort discussed in Aristotle's *Physics*:

(4.7) Something that senses is neither acted on nor altered by what is sensed in a proper sense of "being acted on" and "alteration," namely [in the sense] which [involves passage] from one contrary to another. And since the motion which is in corporeal things, about which it was determined in the book *Physics*, is from one contrary to another, it is clear that to sense, if we call it a motion, is a different species of motion from that about which it was determined in the book *Physics*. For that motion is the act of a thing existing in potency, since while receding from one contrary, as long as it is moved it does not attain the other contrary which is the end of motion, but rather it is in potency. And since everything in potency, as such, is imperfect, therefore that motion is an act of the imperfect [*actus imperfecti*]. But the motion [of the senses] is an act of the perfect [*actus perfecti*], for a sense operation has already been put in act by its *species*. For to sense only happens to a sense power insofar as it exists in act, and therefore that motion is simply different from physical motion. And motion of this sort is properly called an operation: for instance, to sense and understand and will.[31]

31. In DA 3.12.765–66 (Leo. 45.1:230.14–34).

This passage does indeed, on the face of it, seem to indicate that the sort of motion involved in sense cognition, insofar as it can be called motion at all, is not the sort of motion studied by physics as Thomas understands it, and hence is not T-physical. Knasas adds to his case by referring to a passage from Aquinas's *De trinitate* commentary in which Thomas explains why studying angels is a job for metaphysics, despite the fact that angels are subject to motion insofar as they make choices.[32] To choose, Thomas says, is a motion only in the improper sense of "motion" called operation. Knasas reckons that because sense cognition is also an operation, according to 4.7, studying the senses is a job for metaphysics too.

What distinction exactly is Aquinas drawing here between operations and physical motions? Passage 4.7 is commenting on an Aristotelian text, the main point of which is that acts of sense cognition are not instances of *kinêsis* but of *energeia*.[33] This is an important and much-discussed distinction for Aristotle, and Aquinas comments on several of the passages in which he draws it.[34] More revealing than any of these comments for our purposes, however, is that Aquinas frequently invokes the distinction between operations, as the "act of the perfect," and motions, as the "act of the imperfect."[35] He links it to his own distinction between immanent and transient actions.[36] And despite what some commentators have claimed, Thomas typically limits immanent actions to cases involving cognition: will, intellect, and sense.[37] Aquinas frequently refers back to 4.7 when he wants to draw the immanent/transient distinction.[38] This might appear to bolster Knasas's contention that sense, along with intellectual operations, is non-T-Physical.

Still, I think there are good reasons for doubting that this is true, at least in any sense that would threaten my reasoning from the previous chapter. For one thing, Thomas sometimes offers as an example of an "act of the perfect" the perfectly physical activity of shining (lu-

32. In DT 5.4 ad 3.
33. *De anima* 3.7.431a5–7.
34. See In Met 9.5 and J. L. Ackrill, "Aristotle's Distinction between *Energeia* and *Kinesis*," in *New Essays on Plato and Aristotle*, ed. R. Bambrough (London: Routledge, 1965), 121–41.
35. See Bernard Lonergan, *Verbum*, 101–11, for references and discussion.
36. See ST 1a.14.2 ad 2 and 18.3 ad 1.
37. See Marie George, "On the Meaning of 'Immanent Activity' according to Aquinas," *The Thomist* 78, no. 4 (2014): 537–55.
38. See In Sent 1.40.1.1 ad 1 and ST 1a.58.1 ad 1, 1a2ae.31.2 ad 1.

cere), which "remains in the agent itself as its own perfection, and... is properly called an operation."[39] In addition, and more importantly, upon inspecting more closely within the *De anima* commentary itself the way Aquinas understands the distinction he draws in 4.7, it is not clear that he means anything more than that sense cognition, like intellect and will, involves intentional or spiritual change, as opposed to natural change. Aristotle had debated the issue of the soul's motion in *De anima* 1.4, arguing that it is moved only according to an improper sense of the term.[40] Aquinas's commentary distinguishes between three different ways this is true:

(4.8) Motion is found in three different ways in the operations of the soul, for in some it is found properly, in others less properly, and in still others least properly. For motion is found properly in the operations of the vegetable soul and in the sensitive appetite. In the operation of the vegetable soul motion properly speaking is indeed involved ... and likewise in the sensitive appetite motion properly is found both according to alteration and to local motion, for in desiring a certain thing a man is immediately moved and altered either to anger (as in the desire for revenge) or to joy (as in the desire for pleasure), likewise as a result the blood around the heart is also moved to the exterior parts of the body, and the man himself [moves] from place to place as a result of what he desires. Less properly, motion is found in the operations of the sensitive soul, for in these there is no motion according to natural being, but only according to spiritual being, as in clear in sight, whose operation is not according to natural being but according to spiritual being, since it happens through sensible *species* being received into the eye according to spiritual being. But nevertheless there remains something of mutability insofar as the subject of visual power is a body.... Least properly, however, and only metaphorically, motion is found in the intellect, for in the operation of the intellect there is no change according to natural being ... nor a subject that is changed spiritually, as in the sensible [soul]. But there is in this case an operation, which in a certain way is called motion, inasmuch as from understanding in potency there comes about understanding in act. Yet its operation differs from motion since its operation is the act of the perfect, while motion is the act of the imperfect.[41]

39. QDV 8.6 (Leo. 22.2:238.108–11); see In Sent 2.11.2.1.
40. See Christopher Shields, "Aristotle on Action: The Peculiar Motion of Aristotelian Souls," *Aristotelian Society Supplementary Volume* 81, no. 1 (2007): 139–61.
41. In DA 1.10.157–60 (Leo. 45.1:50–51.169–210). See also In DA 2.12.382, which gives a

Certainly Aquinas groups sense cognition with intellect here insofar as neither involves natural changes but only spiritual or intentional ones. Yet as we saw above, it cannot immediately be assumed that spiritual or intentional change involves anything non-T-physical. Air and water undergo spiritual changes when they become cognitive media. In any case, Aquinas also groups sense cognition with vegetative operations and sense appetite in 4.8 inasmuch as all depend ontologically upon motions (whether natural or spiritual) in bodily organs. This is something that he is at pains to stress elsewhere, too; following closely the discussion of spiritual/intentional versus natural being in passage 4.3 is passage 2.9, in which Aquinas describes sense powers as the forms of corporeal organs. The sentence immediately preceding passage 2.9 reads:

(4.9) Since it was said that sense is receptive of *species* without matter, which is true of intellect as well, someone might think that sense is not a power in a body (as is true of the intellect), and therefore to exclude this possibility he assigns to [sense] an organ, claiming that primary sensitive [subject], namely the primary sense organ, is that in which a power of this sort is located, namely one receptive of *species* without matter.[42]

As Stump notes, this seems explicitly intended to ward off the misunderstanding that the senses, like the intellect, operate independently of the body, and hence might be understood without analyzing the coordinated bodily phenomena its operations involve.[43] Aquinas is claiming, I take it, that sense cognition must be explained using the same tactics characteristic of emergent T-physical phenomena in general. Knasas is surely right that it falls to metaphysics to investigate the sort of activity Aquinas discusses in 4.7 in many cases. But I doubt that Aquinas regards the senses as non-T-physical in any way that might throw into question his endorsement of the OD/E biconditional from the previous chapter.

Turning, then, to the second objection mentioned at the beginning of this section, a succinct way of expressing it is this: even if sense cognition involves bodily parts and states, Aquinas thinks it involves no

---

similar impression that the peculiar kind of motion involved in sense perception means that it involves not natural changes but rather taking on *species* or similititudes.

42. In DA 2.24.555 (Leo. 45.1:169–70.77–85).
43. Stump, *Aquinas*, 254.

bodily processes—and this is a grave problem for him. Miles Burnyeat argues that for Aristotle, no physiological states underlie sense operations as matter to form.[44] He thinks the same is even more obviously the case for Aquinas.[45] Furthermore, Burnyeat claims, because we today are clearly committed to sense cognition being explicable at least partly in terms of physiology, "all we can do with the Aristotelian philosophy of mind and its theory of perception as the receiving of sensible forms without matter is what the seventeenth century did: junk it."[46] If Burnyeat is correct that Aquinas's theory of cognition must be junked, then Thomas's arguments for the human intellect's immateriality must be junked as well, dependent as they are on the contours of this theory being at least broadly acceptable. I will argue, however, that while Burnyeat's claim about the absence of physiology from Aquinas's cognitive theory is considerably more plausible than most commentators have acknowledged, he overstates the extent to which this harms the theory overall. It reflects a gap in Aquinas's understanding that could be plugged in light of contemporary science, not one that threatens to sink the ship of his philosophical psychology altogether.

I think it should be admitted that the case for Burnyeat's "spiritualism" about Aquinas's senses is much stronger than many commentators have acknowledged. Stump, Klima, Pasnau, Kenny, Cohen, and various others all agree that Aquinas's spiritual changes are accompanied by some sort of underlying physiological occurrence.[47] The evidence they cite for this view consists largely of statements that sense powers are the acts of bodily organs, and hence never occur apart from changes in the body.[48] A frequently-cited passage can be found in the *Summa theologiae*:

---

44. Miles Burnyeat, "Is an Aristotelian Philosophy of Mind Still Credible? A Draft," in *Essays on Aristotle's De anima*, ed. Martha Nussbaum and Amelie Oksenberg Rorty (Oxford: Oxford University Press, 1992), 15–26.

45. Burnyeat, "Aquinas on 'Spiritual Change' in Perception," in *Ancient and Medieval Theories of Intentionality*, ed. Dominik Perler (Dordrecht: Springer, 2001), 129–54.

46. Burnyeat, "Still Credible?," 26.

47. See Stump, *Aquinas*, 253; Klima, "Aquinas on the Materiality," 175; Pasnau, *Aquinas on Human Nature*, 59, and *Theories of Cognition*, chap. 1, §2; Kenny, *Aquinas on Mind*, 34; Cohen, "Aquinas on the Immaterial Reception." See also Stephen Brock, *The Philosophy of Saint Thomas Aquinas* (Eugene, Ore.: Cascade Books, 2015), 72–74; Lisska, *Aquinas's Theory of Perception*, 109; Pimentel, "Formal Identity as Isomorphism," 119.

48. See passages 2.9 and 2.11, as well as *In DA* 2.12.377, *In Phys* 7.4.910, QDV 2.5 ad 2, ST 1a2ae.22.2 ad 3, CT 1.52, etc.

"to sense and the resulting operations of the sensitive soul clearly occur along with a certain change in the body, just as in seeing the pupil is changed through the *species* of color, and is apparent in the other cases."[49] Interestingly, Burnyeat thinks that this passage actually provides good evidence for his view. He agrees that sense cognition involves a change in the body. But as we saw in passage 4.4, Aquinas does not think that the pupil literally instantiates redness when it sees red. I know of no commentators on Thomas who question this.[50] What bodily change transpires then? Burnyeat thinks it is just a matter of the sense organ receiving a *species*, a form without matter, spiritually or intentionally, and hence encoding information about some sensible characteristic, of which the cognizer thereby becomes aware. There is no corresponding physiological change. He grants that sense cognition is T-physical. Yet he believes that Aquinas's physics differs radically from our own.

Burnyeat runs through Aquinas's discussions of the five external senses in order to show that none of the changes Thomas does connect with their operations underlies them as matter to form. He refers to several passages in which Aquinas "ranks" the senses in terms of their spirituality.[51] Sight, Aquinas says repeatedly, is the most spiritual sense because it involves no natural changes whatsoever. Hearing involves natural changes in its medium: disturbances in the air or water through which sounds are transmitted. Smell is accompanied by natural changes in the objects we smell, which give off a sort of smoky exhalation. Taste and touch do in fact involve natural changes in certain bodily organs, the skin or tongue. But these are not in fact the organs of taste and touch. Rather they are media between the objects of these senses and their organs, which are themselves located deep within the body.[52]

---

49. ST 1a.75.3 (Leo. 5:199–200).

50. The same is not true among Aristotle scholars: Richard Sorabji has argued for years that Aristotle thinks the eye-jelly literally becomes red when I perceive a red object, and Stephen Everson, John Sisko, and others agree. See Sorabji, "Intentionality and Physiological Processes," in *Essays on Aristotle's De anima*, ed. Nussbaum and Rorty, 195–225; Stephen Everson, *Aristotle on Perception* (Oxford: Oxford University Press, 1996); John Sisko, "Material Alternation and Cognitive Capacity in Aristotle's 'De Anima,'" *Phronesis* 41, no. 2 (1996): 138–57.

51. In DA 2.14.417–18, In Met 1.1.6, ST 1a.78.3, QDA 13.

52. As Burnyeat notes, Aquinas agrees with Aristotle that a sense object placed directly in contact with the organ cannot be sensed; see In DA 2.20.496. Thomas explains where the organs of taste and touch are located in In DSS 4/5.16.

Hence none of the natural changes Aquinas discusses in relation to the senses are physiological processes underlying their operations. Perhaps this should not surprise us given 4.8, in which Thomas contrasts the way blood moving around the heart underlies emotions like anger or joy with the way no such motions correspond with sense cognition.

Can it really be true that Aquinas never mentions physiological changes to sense organs corresponding directly with their reception of sensible *species*? The commentators are not forthcoming with examples, although there might be a few oblique references here and there.[53] But direct textual support for this reading is thin.

Let me conclude this section, then, by explaining why even if Burnyeat is correct about the absence of physiological processes in Aquinas's account of sensation, it need not be junked. Doubtless Aquinas is quite mistaken if he believes that sense cognition can be explained simply in terms of coordination between static parts and states of sense organs, together with efficient causal inputs from sense-objects and certain teleological outputs (about the latter of which I will say more shortly). Certain dynamic physiological processes are a necessary part of the story as well. But I see no reason that Aquinas's theory of sense cognition could not be revised to accommodate this fact. As noted earlier (pp. 71–73 and 110–28), he believed that investigating the sensible matter underlying physical phenomena is a matter of empirical inquiry. He recites many

---

53. For example, in *Sententia super libri De memoria et reminiscentia* 8/5, Aquinas writes "those people are most greatly disturbed ... by reminiscence in whom there is abundant moisture around the place where the sense organs are located, namely around the brain and heart, since moisture that has been set in motion is not easily put to rest until the thing that is sought occurs and the movement involved in the search proceeds directly to its end point. This does not contradict what was said above, namely that this happens most in the melancholy, who are dry by nature, since it happens in them by a violent impression" (Leo. 45.2:132.88–99). The mentions of moisture sloshing around or of violent impressions certainly give the appearance of physiological processes accompanying (in this case) reminiscence. I owe this example to Victor Caston, "The Spirit and the Letter: Aristotle on Perception," in *Metaphysics, Soul and Ethics: Themes From the Work of Richard Sorabji*, ed. Ricardo Salles (Oxford: Oxford University Press, 2004), 245–320, at 292.

Of course, to maintain that physiological processes do indeed accompany the sense operations will require interpreting in a particular way Aquinas's frequent denials that natural changes accompany them: Thomas means only that sense organs do not literally come to instantiate the characteristics they receive, not that no physiological occurrences whatsoever are involved. This does indeed seem to be the way many of Aquinas's commentators read him. See Pasnau, *Theories of Cognition*, 41, for an example of such an interpretation.

conclusions derived from inquiry of this sort even when it comes to the maximally "spiritual" sense power of vision: anatomical details about the eye and its connection to the brain, and details regarding the conditions necessary for colors to be born through media like air and water such that they reach the eye and other centers of visual information processing.[54] Suppose it were demonstrated to him that what happens inwardly when we see colors is not simply that light passes through the pupil to the principle of sight, but rather that certain other parts of the eye—rod and cone photoreceptor cells—undergo a natural change called hyperpolarization. In that case I think Aquinas could simply say, "Ah, I see, so visual cognition includes natural changes analogous to the way the blood around my heart heats up when I get angry." He could incorporate these physiological changes as part of the explanation of how forms are received without matter, spiritually or intentionally, as *species* or similitudes encoding information about sense-objects. With this empirical updating, his theory itself can avoid the junkyard.

Part of what drives Burnyeat's pessimism about Aristotle and Aquinas is that he thinks they do not consider it necessary to offer any explanation why certain phenomena are cognitive and others are not. Aquinas thinks there are *species* in cognitive media such as air and water, present in them spiritually or intentionally, not naturally, that are representational likenesses of the forms they enable us to cognize—colors, or sounds, or whatever else.[55] Presumably they are also formally identical to the forms they enable us to cognize. Hence they fit many of the abstract descriptions offered by Aquinas's theory of cognition. Why then

---

54. The pupil of the eye has water in it, with some passages behind it leading to the brain, and fatty tissue around it to keep the water from freezing. Light must actualize the transparent medium between a colored object and the eye such that colors spiritually present in it are received into the pupil. The light must also reach pass through the pupil to the principle of sight for vision to take place, as evidenced by cases where the passages between eye and brain are damaged in battle, preventing light from penetrating the interior of the head. See In DSS 4/5.7 and In DA 2.14–15 together with ST 1a.67 and In Sent 2.13 for further details on the nature of light.

55. Aquinas speaks of *species* received in cognitive media spiritually, as opposed to in a "natural mode," in In DA 2.14.418 and In Sent 2.13.1.3. In In DA 2.14.420 he says *species in medio* have *esse intentionale* (again, as opposed to *naturale*) and at par. 425 he refers to forms impressing their *similitudines* on the medium. Pasnau cites various other passages in which Aquinas discusses *species* in cognitive media in Theories of Cognition, 39n15 and 87.

are they not themselves cognitive? Burnyeat thinks Aquinas's response is contained in this brief passage:

(4.10) What is it to smell, if not to be affected by a smell? To smell is for something to be affected by a smell such that it senses the smell. Air is not affected such that it senses, though, because it does not have a sensitive power, though it is affected such that it is sensible, namely inasmuch as it is a medium for sense.[56]

The passage comes right after Aquinas, following Aristotle, has conceded that air and water can be made to stink, and so are affected by smells. Why do they not cognize these smells? Burnyeat says of 4.10: "What a very simple answer! I have the power of perception, the air around me does not. A modern reader could be forgiven for thinking it no answer at all. But within the framework of Aristotelian physics it is complete and conclusive."[57] For Burnyeat, this illustrates just how foreign Aristotle and Aquinas's understanding of the physical world is from our own, and why it must be discarded. I agree it would be quite shocking to modern sensibilities if Aquinas's only answer to the question that 4.10 poses were as Burnyeat describes it. Maybe shocking enough for the junkyard to threaten. But I think Aquinas has considerably more to say about why air, water, etc., do not cognize than Burnyeat recognizes, as I will discuss in the following section.[58]

The "Liberalism Objection" and Aquinas's Teleofunctional Cognizers

In this section I will discuss Aquinas's response to what I called above the Liberalism Objection to his theory of cognition: that it doles out cognitive states too liberally to entities that obviously lack them. In brief, my suggestion will be that Aquinas can respond to this objection by ap-

---

56. In DA 2.24.563 (Leo. 45.1:171.189–95).
57. Burnyeat, "Aquinas on Spiritual Change," 150.
58. Indeed Aquinas seems to have something more to say just a few lines before passage 4.10 in In DA 2.24.557 where he traces plants' inability to sense to their lack of the "proportion" or "midpoint" between tangible qualities which the organ of touch requires. Without this, he says, nothing can sense. This may be an additional bit of evidence in favor of an interpretation on which Aquinas did indeed acknowledge certain physiological changes corresponding with sense operations, as Caston, "Spirit and Letter," 310–16, argues at length.

peal to the teleological role cognition plays in the lives of cognizers. In this respect, then, his theory of cognition resembles contemporary teleofunctionalism in the philosophy of mind, and teleosemantic accounts of mental content. I will first explain more thoroughly what objection Aquinas faces, then how I think he might respond to it.

Pasnau draws a different moral than does Burnyeat from the fact that cognitive media satisfy many of Aquinas's abstract criteria for cognition, namely that Thomas thinks air, water, etc., are indeed themselves low-level cognizers. Pasnau writes: "We seem then to be left with a contradiction: everything that receives intentionally existing forms is cognitive; but air and water receive intentionally existing forms; therefore air and water are cognitive."[59] He goes on to suggest that while "it is obviously not plausible to accept the conclusion outright," nonetheless we should consider the possibility that Aquinas thought air and water "are (from a theoretical perspective) participating in the same sort of operations as are the properly cognitive faculties of sense and intellect."[60] He notes that Thomas at one point speaks of air and water as perceptive of color.[61]

While Pasnau does not think it necessarily represents a serious mark against Aquinas's theory of cognition that air and water should turn out to possess the "same capacity" for cognition as living things have, John O'Callaghan has argued that this would be a damaging concession indeed.[62] He argues that because just about anything could serve as a medium for cognition of some kind or other, attributing to cognitive media the same capacity as more sophisticated cognizers possess opens the floodgates to pan-cognitivism.[63] O'Callaghan's own view is that "cog-

---

59. Pasnau, *Theories of Cognition*, 50.
60. Ibid.
61. In DA 3.1.570.
62. O'Callaghan, "Aquinas, Cognitive Theory and Analogy." Pasnau notes that William of Ockham agreed with O'Callaghan on this score, and criticized Aquinas's view accordingly; see *Theories of Cognition*, 33. Peter King also criticizes Aquinas for failing to see that on his view, representation is a fairly universal feature; see his "Rethinking Representation in the Middle Ages: A Vade-Mecum to Mediaeval Theories of Mental Representation," in *Representation and Objects of Thought in Medieval Philosophy*, ed. Henrik Lagerlund (Aldershot: Ashgate, 2005). Martin Tweedale sees this as a serious problem with Aquinas's view as well, in "Origins of the Medieval Theory," 218.
63. O'Callaghan, "Aquinas," 470–71. Given the tight connection Aquinas recognizes between cognition and life, O'Callaghan thinks Pasnau's interpretation opens the gates to panpsychism as well.

nition" functions as an analogous term for Aquinas, with its extension "limited by need."[64] Aquinas *could* call air and water cognitive, just as he is willing to grant that they possess *species* in an intentional and spiritual way as representational likenesses of forms in the world, but "there would be no point in doing so."[65] There is some textual evidence for thinking that Aquinas regarded "cognition" as extended in analogous senses to God, angels, humans, and nonhuman animals, though not to plants or nonliving things.[66] Still, as Pasnau has pointed out, a problem with O'Callaghan's suggestion is that merely claiming that "cognition" has various analogously related senses tells us nothing about the phenomenon itself, or why some things—like God or brook trout—should count as cognitive while others—like air and water—do not.[67] To "avoid the deluge of pan-cognitivism," O'Callaghan says, we must rely "upon a prior judgment as to which kinds of beings will count as cognitive and which will not."[68] But upon what do we base this judgment? If the criteria I discussed in the first section of this chapter do not suffice for cognition, what other conditions must be met to count as cognitive? We have already seen Burnyeat's take on Aquinas's "answer" to this question: Thomas provides us no answer at all. A better way forward, I propose, parallels the way some functionalists responded to their own version of the Liberalism Objection.

By "teleofunctionalism" I have in mind theories that add to classical machine-state functionalism a requirement that mental states must play a teleological role in the lives of organisms. Ned Block argued that the criteria Hilary Putnam and other early functionalists gave for something

---

64. Ibid., 482.
65. Ibid., 481.
66. In Sent 4.49.3.1 qc 2 ad 3, in *Sancti Thomae Aquinatis Opera omnia* t. 7/2: *Commentum in quartum librum Sententiarum magistri Petri Lombardi* (Parma: Petrus Fiaccadoris, 1858) (hereafter, Parma), 7.2:1215: "Things that are common according to one notion to us and to brute animals do not pertain to the intellective part, but something is common to us and to brute animals not according to the same notion which pertains to the intellect in us, just as cognition, and other things of that sort, which are extended according to a certain community of analogy to God and to brute animals, and even up to plants, as life, and even up to rocks, as being, as is clear from Dionysius's *On the Divine Names*. And it's according to this [sort of analogical community] that spiritual delight has something in common with the pleasures of brute animals."
67. Robert Pasnau, "What Is Cognition? A Reply to Some Critics," *American Catholic Philosophical Quarterly* 76, no. 3 (2002): 483–90, at 487.
68. O'Callaghan, "Aquinas, Cognitive Theory and Analogy," 480.

to count as a mental state were so abstract as to rule in many systems that clearly seem not to enjoy mental lives.[69] So classical machine-state functionalism faces a liberalism objection as well. William Lycan and others responded by limiting mental states to organisms, and insisting that they must be capable of playing some role in the lives of their possessors.[70]

In a parallel development Fred Dretske, Ruth Millikan, and others also appeal to teleology to construct naturalistic theories of mental content.[71] Dretske's early effort at such a theory was purely information-theoretic.[72] And certainly information encoding of a sort happens in nature. Think of the cases given to illustrate Gricean "natural meaning": red spots on one's visage *mean* measles or smoke *means* fire.[73]

But Dretske came to see that any systems capable of genuine mental representation must also be capable of misrepresentation, and that Gricean natural meanings cannot misrepresent. Red spots cannot *misinform* us about the presence of measles. They cannot *mean* measles when there are none. Gricean natural meaning is just a matter of regular (frequently causal) covariation. Red spots mean measles because they are regularly caused by them. But covariation alone cannot explain misrepresentation. Suppose you judge that the cat is on the mat. But the light is dim; it is really a possum. Does your judgment misrepresent the situation? Well, not if its content is fixed by whatever causes it. Possums-in-dim-light cause cat-judgments just as cats do, so on a purely causal story the content of your judgment turns out to be cats or possums-in-dim-light. But there is a cat-or-possum on the mat—there is a possum. So your judgment does not misrepresent after all. Jerry Fodor calls what I have

---

69. Ned Block, "Troubles with Functionalism," *Minnesota Studies in the Philosophy of Science* 9 (1978): 261–325.

70. William Lycan, *Consciousness* (Cambridge, Mass.: MIT Press, 1987), chap. 3.

71. Fred Dretske, *Explaining Behavior*, and "Misrepresentation," in *Belief: Form, Content, and Function*, ed. Radu Bogdan (Oxford: Oxford University Press, 1986): 17–36; Ruth Millikan, *Language, Thought and Other Biological Categories* (Cambridge, Mass.: MIT Press, 1984) and "Biosemantics," *Journal of Philosophy* 86, no. 6 (1989): 281–97. For a helpful overview of these theories see Karen Neander, "Teleological Theories of Mental Content: Can Darwin Solve the Problem of Intentionality?," in *The Oxford Handbook of Philosophy of Biology*, ed. Michael Ruse (Oxford: Oxford University Press, 2008), 381–409.

72. Dretske, *Knowledge and the Flow of Information*.

73. Paul Grice, "Meaning," *Philosophical Review* 66, no. 3 (1957): 377–88.

just described "the disjunction problem."[74] I will return to it in the fifth section of the next chapter.

Dretske, for his part, to account for the possibility of misrepresentation, supplemented Gricean natural meaning with the notion of proper function. He points out that we can construct systems capable of misrepresentation if we assign a function to one of their natural information carrying capabilities. The level of mercury in a tube causally covaries with air pressure, and thus carries information about air pressure in such a way that it cannot misrepresent it. But if we assign the mercury-level in the tube the function of telling us our height above sea level, turning it into a crude altimeter, then it *can* misrepresent if, for instance, we have it in a pressurized chamber. In the case of such instruments, the ability to misrepresent depends on *our* assigning them certain functions. But Dretske, Millikan, and other proponents of teleosemantic theories think natural selection as well as artifice can assign proper functions, rendering biological systems capable of misrepresentation and fixing their content. The oft-discussed example is a frog snapping at flies. The frog's perceptual states have the function of indicating the presence of frog food because it was their success at delivering food to the frog that ensured their survival and proliferation through natural selection. Accordingly the patterns of retinal firing that causally co-vary with little black things whizzing in front of the frog have as their content "frog food." If they register the presence of frog food as we toss inedible pellets in front of them they misrepresent their environment.

Now I think Aquinas accepts a theory roughly along these lines regarding cognition in general, though only in the case of sense cognition does it yield anything like the sort of "naturalized" account Dretske and Millikan propose.[75] Recall from chapter 3 (pp. 105–6) that Aquinas thinks that satisfactory explanations of natural phenomena assign all four causes: material, formal, final, and efficient. We saw his Aristo-

---

74. Jerry Fodor, "Semantics, Wisconsin Style," *Synthese* 59, no. 3 (1984): 231–50, *Psychosemantics* (Cambridge, Mass.: MIT Press, 1987), and *A Theory of Content and Other Essays* (Cambridge, Mass.: MIT Press, 1990).

75. To be clear, I am not proposing that Aquinas is a functionalist in the sense that he thinks mental states are abstract descriptions that are realized in concrete states of organisms. See note 42 in chapter 3.

telian example of the way this is done in the case of anger.[76] My view is that commentators have largely overlooked what Aquinas has to say about the final cause of cognition.[77] Thomas would consider this a serious mistake, I think, given that he calls the final cause "the cause of causes."[78] Pasnau brings up the possibility that Aquinas might respond to the Liberalism Objection by appealing to the ways that cognitive states feed into appetitive states, but does not think it can succeed due to the way Thomas's definitions of cognition and appetite are intertwined.[79] I think this approach is on the right track, but that to succeed we need to push further in considering how cognitive states are involved in the lives of their possessors more broadly.

To see how a teleofunctional interpretation of Aquinas's theory of cognition might go, begin by considering these four passages:

(4.11) By the fact that [Aristotle] explains what is the case concerning the cognition of animals by referring to the management of life, we are given to understand that cognition belongs to these animals not for the sake of cognition itself, but rather because of the need to act.[80]

(4.12) The cognition of sensible things is directed to two things. For in the first place, both in man and in other animals, it is directed to the upkeep of the body, because by knowledge of this kind, man and other animals avoid what is harmful to them, and seek those things that are necessary for the body's sustenance. In the second place, it is directed in a manner special to man to intellectual cognition, whether speculative or practical.[81]

---

76. See also In Phys 1.1.5, where Aquinas claims that while mathematics focuses on formal causes, and metaphysics on formal, efficient, and final causality, physics demonstrates through all four causes. He repeats this claim in In DT 5.3 ad 7. See also In Phys 2.11 and In Met 3.4 and 8.4 for further discussions of the way natural science must assign all four causes, unlike metaphysics.

77. An exception is Klima, who says that "cognitive intentionality is exhibited by cognitive subjects, which besides merely receiving information are capable of actively processing and utilizing it in their vital operations," in "Three Myths of Intentionality versus Some Medieval Philosophers," *International Journal of Philosophical Studies* 21, no. 3 (2013): 359–76, at 361–62. David Lang makes a similar point in "Aquinas's Impediment Argument for the Spirituality of the Human Intellect," *Medieval Philosophy and Theology* 11, no. 1 (2003): 107–24, at 113.

78. See In Sent 2.9.1.1 ad 1, SCG 3.17.4, ST 1a.5.2 ad 1, QDV 28.7, etc.

79. Pasnau, *Theories of Cognition*, 57–59.

80. In Met 1.1.14 (Marietti 8).

81. ST 2a2ae.167.2 (Leo. 10:347). See also In NE 3.19.610–11 (Leo. 47.1:182.205–11): "Animals take pleasure only in the things referring to the preservation of nature; that is why senses of

(4.13) The entire usefulness of the senses has reference to the goods of the body. But sense cognition is subordinated to intellectual cognition; thus, animals devoid of understanding take no pleasure in sensing, except in regard to some benefit pertaining to the body, according as they obtain food or sexual satisfaction through sense cognition. Therefore, man's highest good, his felicity, does not lie in his sensitive part.[82]

(4.14) The senses that are actualized through external media ... namely smell, hearing and sight, are in those among the animals that advance—that is, that move by progressive motion—for one common cause, namely for the cause of health, that is, so that they might cognize what is necessary from a distance just as by taste and touch they know it when present ... so that sensing from a distance they might pursue suitable food and avoid whatever is bad and harmful. For instance, a sheep flees the wolf as something harmful, but a wolf pursues a sheep that is seen, heard or smelled as suitable food.[83]

One thing that all of these passages make clear is that animals have senses at least in part so that they can feed and reproduce. These "vegetative" powers are, of course, fundamental to the life of any mortal being. We mortals feed to maintain ourselves in "being and due quantity," Aquinas thinks, but because we cannot keep this up forever, we reproduce so that our being might be preserved, not numerically but at least specifically, in our progeny.[84] Of course, as 4.12 and 4.14 suggest, to successfully feed and reproduce we need to deal with potential harms as well. In general, then, we might say that animals have senses in order to navigate the four Fs of survival. Another thing claimed in the first three passages is that human animals have senses for a further reason beyond the four Fs: namely for the sake of intellectual cognition, which Aquinas

---

this kind were given them. But senses have been given to men for the perception of sensible things leading in turn to a cognition of reason."

82. SCG 3.33.4 (Leo. 14:89).

83. In DSS 1/2.7 (Leo. 45.2:13.144–56). A similar passage appears in In DA 3.17.852 (Leo. 45.1:253.76–86): "Nature has adapted the bodies of mobile animals for movement; and they move for the sake of obtaining the food which keeps them alive. And to this end they require sense-awareness; otherwise they would not perceive the harmful things to which their movement sometimes brings them, and thus they would die and the very purpose of their movements would be frustrated. For they move about in order to get food, and could not get it otherwise." QDV 18.7 ad 7 (Leo. 22.2:557.179–82) expresses a similar view about the estimative power: "brute animals receive their natural estimative abilities for the sake of cognizing the harmful and the helpful."

84. In DA 2.7.316–17.

links in 4.13 to our felicity. I will return to the teleology of human cognition shortly. For now, provisionally, a teleofunctional interpretation of Aquinas's cognitive theory would add to the descriptions canvassed at the beginning of this chapter a requirement that cognitive states are capable of bringing about further activities in their possessors: appetitive states, at least, but also in many cases motions toward or away from goods or harms.[85]

Before I explain how this teleofunctional interpretation might provide Aquinas a response to the Liberalism Objection, let me suggest that his account of cognition is not just teleofunctional but also teleosemantic. Not only is the sense cognition of nonhuman animals oriented toward certain life-preserving activities, but also its content is fixed in part by the life-preserving activities it makes possible. Consider the last sentence of 4.14: the sheep not only flees the wolf, but flees the wolf *as something harmful*. Likewise, the wolf pursues the sheep *as suitable food*. A further passage makes this point even more explicitly, adding in addition an important distinction between the ways the human cogitative power and the natural estimative power of nonhuman animals apprehend their objects:

(4.15) Therefore what is not cognized by a proper sense, if it is something universal, is apprehended by the intellect . . . but if it is apprehended in a singular [way], as for example when I see a colored object I perceive this man or this animal, an apprehension of this sort happens in man through the cogitative power, which is also called the particular reason, since it collects individual intentions [*intentionum individualium*] just as universal reason collects universal notions [*rationum universalium*]. Nevertheless, this power is still in the sensitive part, since the sensitive power at its highest point participates to some degree in the intellectual power in man, in whom sense is conjoined to intellect. But in an irrational animal the apprehension of an individual intention happens through the natural estimative [power], according to which a sheep through hearing or sight cognizes its young, or something of this sort. Nevertheless, the cogitative and estimative powers are related differently to [the intentions of individuals], for the cogitative apprehends an individual as existing under a common nature which contains it, inasmuch as it is united to an intellect

---

85. See In DA 3.15, esp. par. 831 for a discussion of the way cognition and appetite together produce local motion.

in the same subject; whence it cognizes this man precisely as this man, and this stone precisely as this stone. But the estimative does not apprehend any individual according as it is under a common nature, but only according as it is the goal or principle of some action or passion, just as a sheep cognizes this lamb, not inasmuch as it is this lamb, but inasmuch as it is something it should give milk, and this plant inasmuch as it is its food. Whence any other individual to which its action or passion does not extend is not cognized at all by its natural estimative [power]. For the natural estimative [power] is given to animals that by it they might be ordered in their proper actions or passions, pursuing or fleeing.[86]

Here we find Aquinas expressing same idea as in 4.14, that nonhuman animals cognize objects *as* things to be pursued, fled, nursed, eaten, etc. The sheep cognizes "thing to be eaten," or "thing to be nursed." Whatever does not factor into sheep survival and proliferation goes uncognized. In contrast, he adds here, humans cognize the same objects precisely as what they are, namely instances of kinds, because of the way our senses are hooked up to our intellects, which cognize universal notions. What this suggests is that Aquinas thinks that the content of cognition is fixed in part by the teleological roles it plays in the lives of cognizers. Nonhuman sense is geared toward life-preserving activities, whereas human sense has both this orientation and also another role in relation to the intellect. In both cases Aquinas's theory of cognition could be considered teleosemantic because of the way it indexes cognitive content to the teleological roles that cognitive states play in the lives of their possessors.

Various other texts beyond those I have cited so far support a teleosemantic reading of Aquinas's cognitive theory. For instance, in various passages Thomas contrasts the content of the calls (*voces*) by means of which nonhuman animals communicate with human language.[87] Nonhuman communication has to do with matters of survival; it expresses pain, pleasure, and related passions of the soul like anger or fear that lead the animal into action. Humans, in contrast, are capable of discussing not just the useful and harmful, but also the just and unjust, and the

---

86. In DA 2.13.398 (Leo. 45.1:121–22.182–222).
87. *Sententia libri Politicorum* (hereafter, In Pol) 1.1.36–38, In DSS 1/2.13, In Peri 1.2.5, *Expositio super Iob ad litteram* 6.2.

good and bad in general. Because the content of our communication plausibly corresponds to the content of our cognition, it seems reasonable to suppose that Aquinas is indicating in these passages a similar contrast to the one on display in 4.15. I will say more about this contrast and its significance later.

Having seen how Aquinas's cognitive theory might be considered both teleofunctional and teleosemantic, however, how does this interpretation provide a possible response to the Liberalism Objection? Simply put, Thomas can claim that the reason air, water, and other cognitive media do not themselves cognize even though they encode information about certain objects is because they cannot put the information to work in their lives. Cognitive information processing always involves at least the possibility of this taking place. Surely there are plenty of cognitive operations that never actually influence the lives of cognizers in any way, but acts of cognition must at least be capable of doing so in principle. Forms received into cognitive media such as air or water obviously cannot meet this requirement, given that air and water are nonliving. Hence Aquinas is not committed to doling out cognition to these entities after all, or to panpsychism. I will now deal with three potential objections against this proposed solution.

First, it might be pointed out that Aquinas nowhere explicitly states the solution I have suggested to the Liberalism Objection, whereas he does explicitly respond to the problem of cognitive media in the way we saw in 4.10. These points are correct, but I doubt that they represent a serious challenge to my proposal. Aquinas states in 4.10 that air and water do not cognize because they lack cognitive powers. And that is indeed what he believes. But that does not mean he would not go on to analyze the possession of cognitive powers partly in terms of their teleology. Indeed we have seen reasons for thinking that this is precisely what he does.

Second, it might be objected that even if my proposal yields the right result when it comes to cognitive media, it nonetheless makes cognition too broad because it seemingly allows plants to possess cognitive states. On my interpretation the possession of forms without matter counts as cognition just in case the forms possessed this way are able to play some roles in the lives of their possessors. Now Aquinas denies that plants receive forms without matter, as in 4.1, for reasons having to do with their anatomy. But if we understand receiving forms without matter in terms of information encoding as suggested above, then I think we would have to admit that because plants receive information of many different sorts from their environment, they receive forms without matter too. If they then go on to put this information to work—as in the case of phototropism, say—are they not then cognizers too? I think this is a bullet I have to bite. But I doubt it is too damaging a concession. Aquinas seems to have underestimated the complexity of plant anatomy—see 2.9. Given this, it is not surprising that he would deny that plants are capable of receiving forms without matter, or of responding to environmental stimuli. These assumptions again reflect limitations in his empirical science that he might plausibly jettison if "brought up to speed." Today, as far as I know, many scientists are perfectly willing to speak of plants as cognizers of a minimal sort.[88]

A third objection along the same lines would criticize my proposal for rendering cognition not too broad but too narrow, as it seemingly denies cognitive states of God. Aquinas thinks that God is maximally cognitive. Yet surely God's cognition does not lead to any sort of survival-directed behavior, or indeed any sort of behavior at all.[89] This is quite true. Nevertheless, Aquinas thinks that God is alive, and is perfectly willing to say that God's decisions to act in certain ways—for instance, to create the world the way he did—follow from his understanding.[90] Of course given divine simplicity, God's intelligence, will, and activity are all identical to his nature. But I see no reason why it should involve any greater impropriety to speak of God's cognition playing a role in his life than to speak of God in many of the other analogical ways we do.

Even if these replies to objections succeed, and Aquinas turns out to have a good response to the Liberalism Objection after all, it is important to notice that his teleofunctional or teleosemantic theory of cognition looks quite different in the case of human and nonhuman animal

---

88. See Michael Gross, "Could Plants Have Cognitive Abilities?," *Current Biology* 26, no. 5 (2016): 181–84.

89. Pasnau makes this point at *Theories of Cognition*, 50–51, citing In Sent 1.35.1.1 as evidence that Aquinas rejects any sort of behavioral criterion for cognition.

90. ST 1a.18.3, 19.3, 19.5, 47.1.

cognizers. In the case of nonhuman animals we might presumably provide a fairly exhaustive account of the ways that environmental stimuli are received as encoded information and in turn bring about appetitive states and life-preserving activities of different sorts. An account of this sort might look much like those sketched by Dretske, Millikan, and others who have tried to "naturalize" intentionality along teleofunctional or teleosemantic lines. In the case of humans, however, Aquinas thinks that sense cognition is not simply geared toward life-preserving activities, but toward operations of the intellect. In 4.11 he expresses this contrast by stating that while nonhuman animals cognize because of the need to act, humans cognize for the sake of cognition itself. That is, I take it, for the sake of knowing the truth. I think we can still regard Aquinas's theory of human cognition as teleosemantic insofar as the content of our cognition is partly fixed by its teleological aim. But the goal or purpose of human cognition is quite different than in the case of nonhuman animals. In the following section I will consider some additional distinctive features of intellectual cognition in connection with a further objection suggesting that these features render it mysterious in some obviously problematic sense.

Intellectual Cognition and the Mystery Objection

First, the objection. The charge is that Aquinas's terminology of cognition merely names the phenomenon, while leaving it in some problematic way mysterious what cognition itself involves. Regarding Aquinas's claim that cognizers possess the forms of what they cognize in an intentional or spiritual way, Peter King writes: "What is it for a form to be present only 'intentionally'? Aquinas never says, or, to the extent that he does, his account was opaque to his disciples and detractors alike, then and now. Aquinas's failure to say what intentional presence consists in makes representationality into a mystery ... centered on the non-informing presence of the form in the representer."[91]

Jeffrey Brower and Susan Brower-Toland call King's criticism of

---

91. King, "Rethinking Representation," 85. He goes on to suggest that this mystery "may well explain why Aquinas had few followers in the philosophy of psychology during the High Middle Ages."

Aquinas "the Mystery Objection."[92] As they note, mystery is not necessarily objectionable in and of itself; even if King is correct that Aquinas never explains what intentional or spiritual presence (or the rest of his cognitive terminology) consists in, this does not necessarily represent a mark against him. Their position is that Aquinas regards the intentionality of *species* as a primitive, unanalyzable feature. Thomas gives this feature various names—"receiving forms without matter," "possessing forms in an intentional or spiritual way," "representational likeness," etc.—but these are labels, not explanations. Brower and Brower-Toland think it is not obviously problematic for Aquinas to treat intentionality as primitive. They agree with King, however, that Aquinas leaves cognition unexplained, and hence in some respect mysterious. At least, they think, this is true of intellectual cognition; they set aside questions related to the senses.

From what we have seen so far, I think we can conclude that sense cognition is not unanalyzable at all on Aquinas's theory, and involves no great degree of mystery. Yet due to some of its distinctive features, Thomas would agree that intellectual cognition is indeed unanalyzable in at least one important respect, although whether this renders it mysterious in some problematic sense is open to debate. In this section I will explain these points in turn.

My claim about sense cognition is based on two assumptions. First, that Stump and Klima are correct to suppose that much of Aquinas's terminology of cognition refers to information processing. Second, that the teleological interpretation of Aquinas's cognitive theory I offered in the previous section provides a successful response to the Liberalism Objection. If these assumptions are correct, then it seems that Aquinas leaves sense cognition little more mysterious than do recent efforts to naturalize intentionality *via* the notions of information processing and goal-directedness, such as Dretske's or Millikan's.

Are the two assumptions correct? We saw in the previous section of this chapter that while Aquinas leaves the role of teleology in cognition largely tacit, there is considerable textual evidence for the interpretation I proposed. As for the suggestion that Aquinas understands cognition as a matter of information processing, he does speak of cognition in terms of

---

92. Brower and Brower Toland, "Aquinas on Mental Representation," 223.

information (*informationem*).⁹³ However, it must be admitted that Thomas gives us few concrete examples to shed light on what his cognitive terminology means. In 4.2 he offers the presence of images in a mirror as an example of one way that *species* might be present in a cognitive medium. In 4.3 he discusses Aristotle's use of the signet ring to illustrate what it means to receive forms without matter. Occasionally he likens representational similitude to the way a statue of Hercules resembles Hercules.⁹⁴ Mirrors, signet rings, and statues all certainly can serve as means of information transfer. But none of them clearly show Aquinas making the point that Klima's compact disc example nicely illustrates, namely that the sort of formal identity or similitude involved in cognitive cases need not be spatial isomorphism or pictorial resemblance. Furthermore, while in the compact disc and map examples certain natural changes correspond with the intentional or spiritual reception of the songs and subway system, it is not clear whether Aquinas thought any sort of natural changes correspond with some cases of intentional or spiritual change, such as visual cognition. Hence to some extent it remains difficult to say for sure what Aquinas might have thought about the idea of colors being received intentionally or spiritually in the eye as patterns of rod and cone hyperpolarization.

Still, as noted above, Aquinas does think that empirical investigation can reveal a fair bit about the conditions necessary for visual information transfer to take place: about the structure of visual organs, the role of light, etc. Presumably if he were writing today he would add a further analysis of the physiological processes required for the intentional or spiritual reception of forms to occur. Given that sense cognition can be explained in terms of these material- and efficient-causal factors, along with the teleological roles it plays, there is no reason to regard it as primitive, unanalyzable, or indeed as especially mysterious.

The case of intellect, however, is different. Aquinas characterizes intellect as the power that unites us to universal being (*ens universale*) through its similitude existing in the soul.⁹⁵ That intellect unites us to things in the world around us through their similitudes marks it as a

---

93. In Sent 1.34.1.3 ad 4, SCG 1.68.6 and 4.26.8, ST 1a.34.1 ad 3. He means simply that cognizers become formally identical to what they cognize.

94. See In Sent 4.50.1.4, QDV 4.4 ad 2, 23.7 ad 11, etc.

95. ST 1a.78.1.

cognitive power, as discussed above.[96] That it unites us to universal being, the "most common object," distinguishes it from the senses, which unite us only to sensible bodies, the "least common object."

By differentiating sense and intellect based on the degree to which their objects are "common" I take it Aquinas has at least two things in mind. First, intellectual cognition is universal in its scope. As we saw in 4.15, Thomas thinks the scope of what nonhuman animals cognize with their senses is fairly limited. Because humans have both senses and an intellect, our senses cognize more, but still only sensible bodies and their attributes. In contrast, our intellects apprehend not just sensible bodies but also immaterial entities, even if, in this life, they are best suited to cognizing essences existing in matter. Hence the scope of intellectual cognition is wider than that of the senses, extending to "every being, universally" (*universaliter omne ens*).[97] Second, intellectual cognition is universal in its mode. As 4.15 also makes clear, the intellect apprehends sensible bodies not as individuals but in terms of their common natures. Indeed, Aquinas claims that our intellects are only able to cognize in a universal way "directly and primarily," whereas we understand individuals as individuals only in an indirect way, "by a certain kind of reflection," namely "by turning itself toward the phantasms."[98] It is controversial what Aquinas means by these latter locutions, or whether it provides him a feasible account of the way we cognize in an individual mode.[99] It is also controversial exactly what sort of "abstractive" activity on the part of the "agent intellect" is required to render sense phantasms actually intelligible by generating from them intelligible *species*, received into the "possible intellect."[100] As noted previously,

---

96. Ibid. In contrast, the vegetative powers have as their object only the body to which the soul is itself united, as opposed to things in the world around us. Appetitive powers incline the soul towards exterior things, and the locomotive power actually moves it through space toward exterior things.

97. Ibid.

98. ST 1a.86.1 (Leo. 5:347).

99. See Peter King, "Thinking about Things: Singular Thought in the Middle Ages," in *Intentionality, Cognition and Mental Representation in Medieval Philosophy*, ed. Gyula Klima (New York: Fordham University Press, 2015), 104–21, and Therese Scarpelli Cory, "What Is an Intellectual 'Turn'? The *Liber de causis*, Avicenna and Aquinas's Turn to Phantasms," *Topicos* 45 (2013): 129–62.

100. See Cory, "Rethinking Abstractionism," for an excellent overview of the main lines of interpreting Aquinas on abstraction, along with some common criticisms of his views.

in 4.2 Aquinas compares the agent intellect's activity to the role light plays in rendering colors actually visible. I will return to this comparison in the following chapter.

Aquinas's claim that the intellect cognizes natures underlies two further features that distinguish it from the senses. First, because it is capable of cognizing its own nature, it is self-reflexive in a way that the senses are not. A sense-cognizer can sense that it senses, Thomas says, but cannot comprehend what it is to sense, and thus only reflects on itself in an incomplete way. The intellect, in contrast, is not simply aware that it engages from time to time in intellectual operations, but also apprehends the nature of such operations. Hence it "returns to its own essence by a complete return"—a phrase Aquinas borrows from the *Liber de causis*.[101] Second, because the intellect is self-reflexive in this way, it is capable of grasping the truth or falsehood of its judgments in a way that the senses are not. At several points Aquinas acknowledges that sense judgments can be true or false insofar as they either do or do not apprehend things as they are.[102] Still, he says, because a sense cannot cognize its own nature, it cannot judge whether or not it apprehends things as they are. Hence it "judges truly about things, but cannot cognize the truth by which it judges truly."[103] Interestingly, at several other points Aquinas appears to deny that nonhuman animals have opinions or beliefs capable of truth or falsehood.[104] A possible explanation is that he accepts something like Davidson's view that genuine belief requires a concept of belief.[105] If Aquinas thinks that having genuine beliefs requires a self-reflexive grasp of the notion of truth itself, then nonhuman animals will lack them. Human sense cognition, in contrast, will indeed turn out to be true or false in just the way Aquinas describes, precisely because our sense faculties

---

101. *In DC* 15.
102. ST 1a.16.2 and 17.2, QDV 1.9 and 11.
103. QDV 1.9 (Leo. 22.1:29.37–38).
104. In NE 6.2.1127 (Leo. 47.1:336.52–53): "and regarding truth it is clear indeed that it pertains neither to sense nor to appetite." In DA 3.5.649 (Leo. 45.1:195.158–63): "opinion follows belief; for it does not seem fitting that anyone should fail to believe what he opines; and thus since no beasts have belief, no beasts will have opinion." In DA 3.12.767 (Leo. 45.1:230.57–61): "to affirm or deny is proper to the intellect ... but sense does something similar to this when it apprehends something as agreeable or harmful." ST 1a.79.8 ad 3 (Leo. 5:274–75): "other animals are so far below man that they cannot attain to cognition of the truth, which reason pursues."
105. Donald Davidson, "Rational Animals," *Dialectica* 36, no. 4 (1982): 317–27.

are connected in the same cognitive subject to an intellect. Nonhuman animal cognition can indeed be true or false from our standpoint, then, but strictly speaking it is geared toward survival, not truth.

The four characteristics of intellectual cognition that I have pointed out so far—its universal scope, universal mode, self-reflexivity, and grasp of truth—by no means exhaust its important distinctive features. By means of the intellect we not only cognize a wide range of objects in a universal way, but also form judgments about them, and string judgments together into patterns of reasoning.[106] Because we cognize in a universal way, furthermore, we are free; Aquinas links our ability to make free decisions with our ability to think and deliberate about what is good for us in general terms.[107] Both freedom and rationality must surely count among the most important features of intellectual cognizers. I will not attempt to compile an exhaustive list of these features or their relationships to one another.

Instead, let me note that Aquinas ties many of the hallmarks of intellectual cognition mentioned in the previous paragraphs to its immateriality. Of particular significance for my purposes, Aquinas bases three of his arguments for the intellect's immateriality—the three types of argument I will consider in the following chapter—on the universality scope of its cognition, on its universal mode of cognition, and on its self-reflexivity.

Because of its immateriality, I think that Brower and Brower-Toland are in several important respects correct that Aquinas thinks of the intellect as primitive and unanalyzable. Most obviously, Thomas would deny that intellectual cognition has a material cause. While we can analyze sense cognition at least partly in terms of bodily parts, states, and (perhaps) processes, we cannot do so for the intellect. When it comes to the efficient cause of intellectual cognition, Aquinas thinks we can say a considerable amount about the intellect's reliance on the senses. Yet ultimately Thomas believes that intellectual cognition depends upon the abstractive activity of the agent intellect, which "is nothing other than a certain participated likeness of the uncreated light."[108] There is

---

106. See ST 1a.79.8, QDV 15.1, In DA 3.11, In PA pr.
107. See QDV 22.7, ST 1a.59.1 and 1a2ae.1.2 ad 3, SCG 2.60.5.
108. ST 1a.84.5 (Leo. 5:322).

debate about the extent to which this view commits Aquinas to a role for divine illumination in intellectual cognition.[109] At the least, Aquinas thinks our intellectual abilities (and in turn our souls themselves) must be directly created by God, rather than emerging from certain materials suitably structured or organized. As for the final cause of intellectual cognition, Aquinas's remarks about our ultimate end are well-known, and I will not repeat them here. There is a clear sense, however, in which the ultimate goal of our intellectual cognition remains unknowable to us in this life. Spelling out the ultimate goal of nonhuman animal sense cognition, in contrast, is a relatively straightforward matter. Putting these points together, Aquinas would say that the intellect cannot be analyzed at all in terms of its material cause, and cannot be analyzed in certain respects in terms of its efficient and final causes.

Does this mean that intellectual cognition is mysterious in some objectionable way? I doubt it. For one thing, as Brower and Brower-Toland point out, even if it resists analysis in the ways just mentioned, this does not mean that it cannot be further elucidated at all.[110] Spelling out the various distinctive features of intellectual cognition, together with their relationships to one another, is one way of providing this sort of elucidation. It may be that methods such as phenomenological analysis can shed further light on the nature of the intellect. Ultimately, however, because intellectual cognition is unanalyzable in the ways just mentioned owing mainly to its immateriality, whether Aquinas's account of the intellect faces a "mystery objection" will depend largely upon whether he has good reasons for thinking it is immaterial. If he does not, then we might indeed fault his account of the intellect for failing to supply certain crucial pieces of information. If he does, however, then it should not surprise us that the intellect should turn out to resist analysis in certain ways. I will turn in the following chapter to a detailed look at some of the arguments Aquinas gives for the immateriality of the intellect.

109. See Robert Pasnau, "Divine Illumination," in *The Stanford Encyclopedia of Philosophy* (2015), ed. Edward Zalta, available at plato.stanford.edu/entries/illumination/, and Gyula Klima, "The Medieval Problem of Universals," in *The Stanford Encyclopedia of Philosophy* (2013), ed. Edward Zalta, available at plato.stanford.edu/entries/universals-medieval/.

110. Brower and Brower Toland, "Aquinas on Mental Representation," 227.

5

AQUINAS'S ARGUMENTS FOR THE IMMATERIALITY OF THE HUMAN INTELLECT

In chapter 3 we saw the burden of proof that Aquinas's arguments for the human intellect's immateriality must bear. They must demonstrate that intellectual operations cannot be explained in terms of coordination between bodily parts, states, and processes, together with their efficient causal inputs and teleological outputs. In the previous chapter we saw further how Aquinas's theory of cognition in general is meant to work, in outline, together with some specifics about how sense cognition differs from intellectual operations. The aim of this chapter is to connect these pieces in order to examine various efforts that Aquinas made to show that the human intellect actually is immaterial. These efforts can be sorted into various types. None of them has "the human intellect is immaterial" as an explicitly stated conclusion. Many of them serve multiple purposes in Aquinas's philosophical psychology and metaphysics as a whole.

In the first section of this chapter I will survey a variety of different argument types along with their historical antecedents, explaining finally why I focus the remainder of the chapter on just three of them. The second section scrutinizes an argument that I take it Aquinas adapted chiefly from Aristotle, based upon the universality of the human intellect's scope of cognition. I will claim that this line of reasoning most likely fails unless it relies implicitly on the success of argumentation of a different type. In the third section I turn to an argument that Aquinas employs infrequently, but which appears to be initially promising, based upon the human intellect's self-reflexivity. Thomas draws it largely from Proclus and Avicenna. Unfortunately, I will claim, Aquinas provides us too few details as to how he understands it for us to determine with any degree of certainty whether it succeeds. In the final two sections of this chapter, I consider the argument that has occupied the bulk of commentators' attention in recent years, based upon the universality of the human intellect's mode of cognition. First I present the argument itself in Aquinas's terms, along with a few proposed interpretations that I consider unsuccessful, then I present an interpretation that might well succeed.

A word about the "success" of "interpretations" of Aquinas's arguments for the immateriality of the human intellect. In my opinion, none of these arguments, as Thomas expresses them, looks obviously sound. Of course whether or not an argument "looks sound" to someone is a highly subjective matter. It is easy enough to arrange the premises of Aquinas's arguments such that they are formally valid. Having done so, however, by my lights each has at least one premise that appears difficult (at least) to defend. It should not be at all surprising if Aquinas's arguments for the human intellect's immateriality fall short of the dialectical standard we would expect of such reasoning nowadays. Charles Kahn writes of Aristotle's arguments for the incorporeality of *nous* that they "are surprisingly weak and insubstantial, as if, surrounded by Platonists rather than materialists, he did not regard this position as controversial enough to stand in need of a real defence."[1] A very similar statement could be made about Aquinas. In his context, physicalist positions regarding the human intellect were distant history rather than live philosophical options.[2] Hence it should not surprise us if Aquinas

---

[1] Charles Kahn, "Aristotle on Thinking," in *Essays on Aristotle's De anima* (ed. Nussbaum and Rorty), 359–80, at 375–76.

[2] This situation changed, arguably, with John Buridan's highly influential reasoning on behalf of Alexander of Aphrodisias's psychology in the mid-fourteenth century. By the end of the fourteenth century one finds Biagio Pelicani di Parma, at least, willing to claim in his own voice that the human soul is not immortal after all. See Olaf Pluta, "Materialism in the Philosophy of Mind: Nicholas of Amsterdam's *Quaestiones De anima*," in *Mind, Cognition and Representation: The Tradition of Commentaries on Aristotle's De anima*, ed. Paul Bakker and Johannes Thijssen (Aldershot: Ashgate, 2007), 109–26; Henrik Lagerlund, "John Buridan and the Problems of Dualism in the Early Fourteenth Century," *Journal of the History of Philosophy* 42, no. 4 (2004):

does not devote as much energy to refuting them as one might expect of an antiphysicalist writing in a contemporary setting. Because none of Thomas's arguments are obviously sound, to render any of them even plausible requires, in my estimation, a considerable amount of interpretative legwork. The more a commentator presents her own interpretative gloss on Aquinas's text, of course, the more controversial it becomes whether her "reconstruction" accurately reflects Thomas's own views. The twin challenges for any viable presentation of Aquinas's arguments, then, are to depict them both as philosophically plausible and as plausibly attributable to Thomas. Perhaps something similar could be said of efforts to interpret most arguments in the history of philosophy. It is true at least of the arguments under discussion in this chapter.

Types of Argument for the Immateriality of the Human Intellect

Commentators generally agree that Aquinas presents various different arguments for the immateriality of the human intellect, and that these arguments can be sorted into types.[3] They agree about what some of these types are, but disagree about others.[4] They also disagree about the relationships between them, with some commentators claiming that certain types of argument are dialectically dependent on others, while other commentators deny such interdependence.[5] I will begin

---

369–87; Jack Zupko, "On Buridan's Alleged Alexandrianism: Heterodoxy and Natural Philosophy in Fourteenth-Century Paris," *Vivarium* 42, no. 1 (2004): 43–57; and John Marenbon, *Medieval Philosophy: An Historical and Philosophical Introduction* (London: Routledge, 2007), 327–28.

3. See David Ruel Foster, *A Study and Critique of Thomas Aquinas' Arguments for the Immateriality of the Intellect* (PhD diss., The Catholic University of America, 1988), for the most extensive treatment of Aquinas's arguments available, summarized in "Aquinas on the Immateriality of the Intellect," *The Thomist* 55, no. 3 (1991): 415–38, and "Aquinas's Arguments for Spirit," *Proceedings of the American Catholic Philosophical Association* 65 (1991): 235–52.

4. Most commentators mention what I call below the scope and mode arguments, and many also recognize what I call the self-reflexivity argument. Foster thinks many of the arguments in *SCG* can be grouped in to two further types: those involving the way the intellect possesses its objects, and those pointing out that the intellect is able to possess opposite characteristics. None of the commentators has much to say about the "intensity argument" that Aquinas takes over from *De anima* 3.4.429a29–b5.

5. For instance, Foster's *Study and Critique* states that Aquinas's "scope argument" is dialectically dependent on the "mode argument," while Matthew Sweeney thinks it is a free-standing line of reasoning in its own right. See Sweeney, *Thomas Aquinas' Commentary on 'De anima' 429a10–429b5 and the Argument for the Immateriality of the Intellect* (PhD diss., The Catholic University of America, 1994).

here by surveying what I take to be four clear cases of distinct argument types that Aquinas employs, then consider a few other miscellaneous lines of reasoning. I will then explain why, in the remainder of this chapter, I focus on just three argument types.

A complicating factor that should be noted at the outset is that none of Aquinas's arguments have, as their explicitly stated conclusion, "therefore the human intellect is immaterial." We ran into a similar problem when it came to Aquinas's argumentation for the human soul's separability from the body in chapter 3. As we saw there, the key premise Aquinas needs in order to establish the human soul's separability from the body is that the human intellect's operations do not depend upon the body, or any of its parts. I argued that we could understand this premise as a denial that our intellectual operations can be explained in terms of coordination between bodily parts, states, and processes. Some of the arguments that I will consider in this section do indeed have as their explicit conclusion that the intellect does not operate through any corporeal organ, and is independent of the body.[6] Other arguments appear to make a weaker claim: that neither the intellect itself nor intellectual substance are bodies, and are not composed of matter and form.[7] Aquinas would say the same about the powers and substantial forms of any composite substances. They are not themselves bodies, nor composed of matter and form, because they are just forms.[8] As O'Callaghan puts it, this point would establish only a sort of "benign immateriality" about the intellect, as opposed to a "malignant immateriality," because it would be entirely acceptable to physicalists, and would not provide Aquinas with any kind of support for further claims about the separability of human souls from bodies.[9] It is true that sometimes when Aquinas argues that intellectual powers and substances are not composed of matter and form he is largely interested in challenging the position of universal hylomorphists like Avicebron that human souls and angels are indeed composed in just this way.[10] But the fact that he

6. See ST 1a.75.2, QQ 10.3.2, In Sent 2.19.1.1, In DA 2.12.377.
7. See ST 1a.75.5, QDSC 1, SCG 2.49–50.
8. He argues this, for instance, in ST 1a.75.1.
9. O'Callaghan, "The Immaterial Soul and Its Discontents," Acta Philosophica 24, no. 1 (2015): 43–66, at 59–61. "Benign," that is, from the standpoint of physicalists.
10. This is quite clearly the case in QDSC 1 and DEE 4, for example.

treats the same type of reasoning elsewhere as support for the incorruptibility of human souls and other intellectual substances indicates that he believes it can serve dual roles, both "benign" and "malignant." I will pursue this point further shortly.

The first three arguments I wish to consider here, and indeed the three to which I will devote the bulk of my attention in this chapter, appear together in a passage from Aquinas's *Sentences* commentary, in which he discusses the opinion of the "ancient naturalists" who "did not distinguish intellect from sense," and hence held that "just as a sense operation depends on the body, likewise also ... the intellectual operation depends on the body":

(5.1) Aristotle sufficiently overcame this opinion, however, showing that the intellect has an absolute act of being, not depending on the body, because of which it is said not to be the act of a body, and is said by Avicenna not to be a form submerged in matter, and in the *Book of Causes* [is said] not to be supported by the body. The middle [term] of the proof of this is taken from a consideration of its operation. For since only a *per se* existing thing can have an operation, it is necessary that what has an absolute operation also has an absolute act of being *per se*. But the intellectual operation is its own, absolutely, without any corporeal organ sharing in it, which is clear chiefly in three ways. First, since this operation is of all corporeal forms as its objects, whence it is necessary that the principle of this operation is absolute from all corporeal forms. Second, since understanding is of universals, while only individuated intentions can be received into a corporeal organ. Third, since intellect understands itself, which does not happen in any power whose operation is through a corporeal organ.[11]

What we see in the beginning of this passage is the sort of Aristotelian reasoning for the human soul's separability from the body that I discussed in the first section of chapter 3. In that respect, passage 5.1 closely resembles passage 3.1, from Aquinas's tenth quodlibetal question. In 3.1, however, Aquinas offers only a (somewhat more detailed) presentation of the argument based upon the human intellect's ability to cognize all corporeal forms as a reason for denying that it operates through any corporeal organ. In 5.1, in addition to the first argument based on the

---

11. In Sent 2.19.1.1 (Mand./Moos 2:481). Aquinas goes on to explain the reasoning behind the third argument; I will examine what he says later in this chapter.

universal scope of intellectual cognition, we get two further arguments, based respectively on the universal mode of intellectual cognition, and on its self-reflexivity. I will consider these three arguments further in turn.

The first undoubtedly has as its source Aristotle's reasoning in *De anima*. Aristotle begins by suggesting a possible comparison between sense and intellect: "if thinking is like perceiving...."[12] On Aquinas's interpretation, Aristotle's point is that the senses really do resemble the intellect in that both are passive powers in potency to receiving certain objects. The difference between the two is that while a sense power is only in potency toward receiving a limited range of objects, the intellect can understand "all sensible and bodily things."[13] Hence, because whatever is in potency to receiving something must lack that to which is in potency, the intellect cannot be a sensible or bodily thing itself.[14] I will call this reasoning "the scope argument" (SA), as it is based upon the broad scope of intellectual cognition. I doubt very much whether it succeeds. It does seem to be, however, as several commentators have noted, Aquinas's "preferred" means of showing that the human intellect uses no bodily organ in its operation insofar as he is more likely to cite it than any other argument to establish this point.[15]

The second argument Aquinas presents in passage 5.1 is based upon the mode of intellectual cognition: the intellect cognizes universals, whereas powers that operate through corporeal organs grasp only individuals. I will call this "the mode argument" (MA), as it is based upon the universal mode of intellectual cognition. Aquinas deploys this argument nearly as frequently as he does SA, although he uses it often simply

---

12. *De anima* 3.4.429a13–29.
13. In DA 3.7.680 (Leo. 45.1:203.140–41).
14. This principle is found in very similar terms in Averroes's presentation of the argument in his *Long Commentary on the De anima*: "omne recipiens aliquid necesse est ut sit denudatum a natura recepti." *Averrois Cordubensis Commentarium Magnum in Aristotelis De anima libros*, ed. F. Stuart Crawford (Cambridge, Mass.: Medieval Academy of America, 1953), 385.67–68. Compare this to Aquinas in QDA 2 (Leo. 24.1:16.186–88): "omne quod est receptivum aliquorum, et in potentia ad ea, quantum de se est, est denudatum ab eis."
15. See Foster, "Arguments for Spirit," 236; Sweeney, *Aquinas' Commentary on 'De anima'* 429a10–429b5, 4; and Henry Koren, *An Introduction to the Philosophy of Animate Nature* (St. Louis, Mo.: B. Herder, 1955), 165. Beyond passage 5.1, we find versions of this argument appearing in QQ 10.3.2, ST 1a.75.2, SCG 2.59.3 (and possibly 2.49.3, 5, and 6 as well), QDA 2 and 14, CT 1.79, In DA 3.7.677–84, and DUI 1.

to show that intellectual powers or substances are not composed of matter and form, as opposed to showing that the intellect does not operate through a bodily organ.[16] As noted above, sometimes Aquinas makes this point to refute the universal hylomorphist notion that human souls and angels have spiritual matter. O'Callaghan argues that Thomas only intends for MA to establish the benign immateriality of intellectual powers and substances, as opposed to their malignant immateriality.[17] Some support for this view comes from the *Summa theologiae*, where Aquinas presents MA alongside another line of reasoning clearly intended to demonstrate its benign immateriality alone, and not its malignant immateriality.[18] Nevertheless, in 5.1 Aquinas seems to regard SA and MA alike as capable of establishing a key premise in his reasoning for the human soul's ontological independence from the body. That is, both establish its malignant immateriality. The same seems to be true in other passages too. Aquinas helpfully clarifies his position in SCG:

(5.2) To say that the intellect is a form that does not subsist, but is immersed in matter, is the same in reality as saying that the intellect is composed from matter and form, for they differ only nominally.... If it is false that the intellect is composed of matter and form, it will be false that it is a form that is not subsistent but material.[19]

Here Aquinas's claim is that if the intellectual soul lacks hylomorphic composition, then it will also be a subsistent form with an immaterial act of being. In other words, it will be malignantly immaterial, in a way that no physicalist could countenance. Apparently, then, Aquinas does think that MA can be used to establish this conclusion in spite of O'Callaghan's concerns.

While the source of SA is clear, it is more difficult to determine what might have influenced Aquinas's presentations of MA. Aristotle claims repeatedly that all understanding is about universals (*pasa epistêmê tou katholou*), and may indicate at several points in the *De anima* that that

---

16. Beyond passage 5.1, see CT 79; QDA 1 and 14; DEE; QDSC 1; ST 1a.75.5; SCG 2.49.4, 50.3, 59.6; QDV 10.8; and In DA 2.12.377 for appearances of this type of argument.
17. O'Callaghan, "Immaterial Soul and Its Discontents," 61–62.
18. ST 1a.75.5.
19. SCG 2.51.5 (Leo. 13.386).

he means to link this claim to the intellect's nonbodily nature.[20] In *De anima* 1.5, for instance, he argues against Empedocles's view that the soul is composed of elements on the grounds that if this were true, then we could have no knowledge of "the composite whole, e.g., what god, man, flesh, bone (or any other compound) is."[21] Part of the point is that if "like is known by like," as Empedocles held, then a soul made of elements could only know elements, not compounds. But the broader point seems to be that such a soul could not know what the things he mentions *are*—that is, could not know them as kinds, or in terms of their forms. He returns to this point in *De anima* 3.4, where just after arguing that *nous* is incorporeal, he contrasts it with sense cognition. Whereas by the senses "we discriminate the hot and the cold, that is, the factors which combined in a certain ratio constitute flesh," it is by means of some other faculty (presumably *nous*) that we cognize "the essential character of flesh."[22] Aquinas, at any rate, understands Aristotle to be referring here to the intellect's ability to cognize in a universal mode.[23] So too does Averroes in his long commentary on the *De anima*, perhaps a more proximate source for Aquinas's thinking with regard to MA.[24] Averroes argues that intellectual activity somehow involves receiving forms that are universal, and that no embodied cognitive power could accomplish this. Another possible influence on Thomas's uses of MA is Avicenna, who ties intellectual abilities to immateriality much as we saw Aquinas doing in 4.1.[25] Albert the Great's *De anima* cites reasoning from both Averroes and Avicenna to show that the possible intellect is "unmixed," that is, "not mixed with the body as a form of a body, nor as a form which is a power in a body."[26]

---

20. See De anima 2.5.417b23, Metaphysics 3.6.1003a15, 11.1.1059b26, 1060b20, and Parts of Animals 1.31.87b38 for Aristotle's claim that knowledge is of universals. Walter Leszl, "Knowledge of the Universal and Knowledge of the Particular in Aristotle," Review of Metaphysics 26, no. 2 (1972): 278–313, is a detailed examination of why Aristotle adopts this view.
21. De anima 1.5.409b25–410a12. I owe this point to Foster, "Arguments for Spirit," 244–45.
22. De anima 3.4.429b10–23.
23. In DA 3.8.705–16.
24. Averroes, Long Commentary on the De anima 3.5, in Commentarium magnum (ed. Crawford), 388.
25. Avicenna, Metaphysics 8.6, in Liber de philosophia prima sive scientia divina V–X, ed. S. Van Riet (Leiden: Brill, 1980), 414.
26. Albert the Great, De anima 3.2.3, in B. Alberti Magni Opera Omnia, ed. A. Borgnet (Paris: Vives, 1890–99), 5:334.

The final argument Aquinas presents in 5.1 hinges on the intellect's ability to understand itself. He develops the argument further in the lines following 5.1 with reference to Avicenna and the *Liber de causis*.[27] Because it has to do with the intellect's ability to reflect upon its own nature, I will call it the "self-reflexivity argument" (RA). Aquinas uses this type of argument much less frequently than he does SA and MA. Indeed, he uses it with the explicit purpose of proving the intellect's nonbodily nature only once, in SCG 2.49.8, although he discusses it at greater length in his commentary on the *Liber de causis*.

Beyond the three arguments that Aquinas presents in 5.1, another he draws directly from Aristotle and uses occasionally is based upon the intellect's supposed ability to withstand intense input from its cognitive objects that would overwhelm and temporarily incapacitate any power operating through a corporeal organ. Aristotle brings up the idea initially in *De anima*, in connection with the idea that sense powers involve a sort of balance or proportion in a sense organ.[28] Upset the balance too much, and the ability to sense is destroyed. Later in the text Aristotle returns to the idea, noting we are less able to hear, see, or smell after experiencing loud sounds, bright colors, or strong smells.[29] Aquinas likens this to violently twanging a musical instrument's strings, putting it out of tune.[30] Or to employ a different illustration in keeping with the information-processing interpretation of Aquinas's cognitive theory discussed above, we might picture sense powers and their organs as something like a seismograph, with a needle neutrally balanced but capable of registering geological disturbances by moving up or down. A strong enough disturbance might move the needle too violently and damage it. In contrast to this situation with the senses, Aristotle says that "in the case of thought thinking about an object that is highly thinkable renders it more and not less able afterwards to think of objects that are less thinkable."[31] While Aquinas refers to this passage

---

27. Avicenna, *De anima* 5.2, in *Liber de anima seu sextus De naturalibus*, ed. S. Van Riet (Leiden: Brill, 1968), 93–94. Aquinas cites prop. 15 of the *Liber de causis* in the discussion immediately following passage 5.1: "omnis sciens qui scit essentiam suam, est rediens ad essentiam suam reditione completa."
28. *De anima* 2.12.424a29–32.
29. *De anima* 3.4.429a29-b5.
30. *In DA* 2.24.556.
31. *De anima* 3.4.429b2–4.

frequently, it is often unclear how he understands Aristotle's "highly thinkable" objects.[32] Aquinas, of course, distinguishes between what is most intelligible *per se*, namely God, and what is most intelligible to us, namely the natures of bodies.[33] Does he take Aristotle to mean that after thinking about objects we are easily able to understand, we can afterwards think about other things more easily? Or is it rather that after thinking about lofty objects like God, we are afterwards more easily able to think about lower objects? Certain passages make clear that Aquinas holds the latter interpretation.[34] I will call this line of reasoning the "intense objects argument" (IA).

Beyond the four we have seen so far, Aquinas offers various other arguments in SCG showing why intellectual substances are neither bodies nor composites of matter and form. This work contains by far the greatest number of arguments for these conclusions anywhere in Aquinas's corpus. Many of these arguments, however, seem to me to hinge on features that are true of cognizers in general, as opposed to specifically intellectual cognizers. If they succeeded, then, they would prove the incorporeality and immateriality of sense-cognizers as well as intellectual beings. For example, Aquinas points out that while bodies cannot receive substantial forms other than their own without being corrupted, the intellect is not corrupted when it receives the forms of whatever it cognizes.[35] Similarly, he says, the forms of contraries, as they exist in matter, are opposed to each other, whereas in the intellect they can both be present at the same time.[36] Finally, Thomas argues that while things are only received into bodies "by a quantitative commensuration," that is, by receiving certain larger shares of things of the things received into their larger parts, and smaller shares into their smaller parts, the intellect does not receive its objects this way.[37] Rather "by its whole self it understands and comprehends both whole and part, both greater and larger, alike."[38] The first of these arguments, I take it, refers simply to

32. See In Sent 3.15.2.1.2, SCG 2.82.14, ST 1a.75.3 ad 2, QDA 8 and 16 ad 5.
33. ST 1a.12.1 and 84.7.
34. QDV 13.1 ad 6 and ST 1a.88.1 ad 3. In these passages the context makes clear that the "highly intelligible" objects in question are spiritual substances.
35. SCG 2.49.3 and 2.50.5, 6, 8.
36. SCG 2.50.7. See In Met 7.6.1405.
37. SCG 2.49.2 and 2.50.2.
38. SCG 2.49.2 (Leo. 13:381).

the capacity for receiving forms alongside or in addition to their own that Aquinas characterizes in 4.1 as common to all cognizers. As for the presence of contrary forms in the intellect, it seems that the senses too can process information about opposed forms at once; does this not happen when I eat sweet-and-sour chicken, or look at a red, white, and blue flag? At any rate, 4.6 indicates that opposite colors may both be received spiritually or intentionally into a cognitive medium like air without its being immaterial (at least in any malignant sense of "immateriality"). The last argument may be inspired by one that Avicenna offers in arguing for the intellect's immateriality.[39] But I take it that this argument too hinges on the special intentional or spiritual way that cognizers in general receive forms, as opposed to some specific feature of intellectual cognizers.[40]

Other arguments Aquinas presents in SCG seem to be variants upon SA. Thomas claims that if the intellect were corporeal, then it could only know bodies, and likewise that it could only apprehend a finite number of objects.[41] The intellect, however, is capable of grasping incorporeal objects, and the number of objects it can grasp is potentially infinite. Both of these arguments point to the scope of intellectual operations as reasons for thinking they are immaterial, as SA does. I will discuss them further in the following section.

In the remainder of this chapter I will focus just on SA, MA, and RA. As I just explained, many of the other arguments Aquinas mentions in SCG seem to me either reducible to one of these, or else obviously inadequate for the purposes of proving the intellect's immateriality, as the points they make would apply equally well to sense cognition. As for IA, it also seems to me too weak to be worth discussing beyond this section. Suppose the brain were the organ of intellectual cognition. In that case, it seems to me, there would be a perfectly good explanation why intense visual, auditory, or olfactory objects overwhelm sense or-

---

39. See Avicenna, *De anima* 5.2, in *Liber De anima* (ed. Van Riet), 81–89. See also Jon McGinnis, *Avicenna* (Oxford: Oxford University Press, 2010), 120–24, for a discussion of this argument.

40. Something similar could be said of another point Aquinas makes briefly at SCG 2.49.7, namely that no two bodies can contain one other, whereas two intellects are certainly capable of understanding each other. Insofar as intellects contain each other it is only in an intentional or spiritual way, as Thomas makes clear in passage 4.5.

41. SCG 2.49.5–6 and 2.50.4.

gans while thinking about lofty matters does not overwhelm the organ of the intellect. Flash blindness, for instance, is caused by oversaturated retinal pigments. Loud noises can kill hair cells in the inner ear or damage the eardrum itself. There is no reason to suppose that thinking about God would similarly affect any part of the brain. So even if Aristotle and Aquinas have correctly observed a difference between the effects of intense sense-objects and intellectual objects, this does not provide grounds for believing that intellectual activities themselves are inexplicable in terms of coordination between bodily parts, states, and processes.[42] In the remainder of this chapter, then, I will limit myself to considering whether SA, MA, or RA are capable of doing so.

The Argument from the Scope of Intellectual Cognition

I think it highly unlikely that Aquinas's scope argument is capable of demonstrating the human intellect's immateriality. To explain why, I will begin by examining Aquinas's most complete presentation of the argument in his commentary on Aristotle's *De anima*. One of its key premises is ambiguous and can be read in two different ways. Both readings are problematic. One appears incapable of yielding Aquinas the conclusion he needs, namely that our intellectual power is ontologically independent from our bodies in its operations. The other seems simply indefensible. Either way, Aquinas's SA appears incapable of achieving its aim.

In his commentary on *De anima*, Aquinas notes while the Anaxagorean argument that Aristotle is discussing bases the intellect's incorporeality on its ability to move all things, Aristotle himself bases his argument on the intellect's ability to know all things.[43] Thomas goes on to explain Aristotle's reasoning as follows:

(5.3) Whatever is in potency to receive something must lack that to which it is in potency and which it receives, just as the pupil, which is in potency to colors and receives them, is itself lacking in any color. But our intellect so understands intelligible things that it is in potency to them and receives them, just as a sense does sensible things. Therefore it lacks all those things that it

---

42. Jaworski, *Structure and the Metaphysics of Mind*, 169, also criticizes IA along these lines.
43. *De anima* 3.4.429a13–29.

is suited to understand. Since, therefore, our intellect is suited to understand all sensible and corporeal things, it is necessary that it should lack every corporeal nature, just as the sense of sight lacks every color because it is able to cognize color. For if it had any color, that color would keep it from seeing other colors, just as a feverish tongue which has a certain bitter humor is not able to receive a sweet taste. Thus also if the intellect had any determinate nature, that nature connatural to it would keep it from cognizing other natures. And this is what [Aristotle] says: the thing appearing within will keep it from cognizing anything else and obstruct it, that is, it would impede the intellect, and will veil it and close it off from the inspection of other things. And he calls the "thing appearing within" [intus apparens] anything intrinsic connatural with the intellect [aliquid intrinsicum connaturale intellectui], which while it appears to it always impedes the intellect from understanding other things, just as if we were to say that the bitter humor is a "thing appearing within" the fevered tongue. He concludes from this not that it does not pertain to the intellect to be one thing or a determinate thing, but that it has this nature alone: that it is possible with respect to all things. And this indeed pertains to the intellect since it is not just able to cognize one genus of sensible things, like sight or hearing, or all qualities and commonly or properly sensible accidents, but universally all of sensible nature. Whence just as sight lacks a certain genus of sensible features, so too the intellect must lack the whole of sensible nature.[44]

Aquinas opens with the general principle that whatever is in potency to receiving something must lack that to which it is in potency and receives. He then claims that because the senses and intellect alike, as cognitive powers, are in potency to receiving the objects they cognize, they must alike lack these objects so as to be capable of receiving them. Two examples are the way the pupil must lack any color so as to be capable of receiving all colors and the way the tongue must lack any flavor to be capable of receiving all flavors. The scope of intellectual cognition, however, is broader than that of any sense power, extending to "all sensible and corporeal things." Hence the intellect must lack any sensible or corporeal nature. That is, he goes on to explain, it must be incorporeal, and cannot operate through any bodily organ, because then it would have a certain sensible nature, namely as form of the organ through

44. In DA 3.7.680–81 (Leo. 45.1:203–4.131–70).

which it operates. Hence Aquinas's argument in 5.3 looks to be as follows:

> (SA1) Whatever is in potency to receiving something must lack that to which it is in potency.
> (SA2) Cognitive powers are in potency to receiving the forms of objects they cognize.
> (SA3) Cognitive powers must lack the forms of the objects they cognize.
> (SA4) The intellect is able to cognize all sensible and corporeal things.
> (SA5) The intellect lacks any sensible or corporeal form.

Presented this way, SA appears to be valid. It is much less clear whether it is sound.

A problem that many commentators have noted stems from the distinction we saw Aquinas draw in the previous chapter between the natural mode of receiving and possessing forms and the spiritual or intentional mode of doing so that characterizes cognition.[45] When Aquinas says that "our intellect so understands intelligible things that it is in potency to them and receives them, just as a sense does sensible things," he cannot mean that the intellect or senses literally become the objects they cognize. This much is clear from passages such as 4.3–4.8. Accordingly, SA2 should be understood as:

> (SA2*) Cognitive powers are in potency to receiving the forms of objects they cognize in an intentional or spiritual way.

But the distinction between natural and intentional/spiritual form reception calls into question what Aquinas means by SA1. There seem to be three possibilities:

---

45. See Pasnau, *Aquinas on Human Nature*, 56–57; Foster, "Aquinas on Spirit," 245; Kenny, *Aquinas on Mind*, 132; John Haldane, "The Metaphysics of Intellect(ion)," *Proceedings of the American Catholic Philosophical Association* 80 (2007): 39–55, at 50; and Calvin Normore, "The Matter of Thought," in *Representation and Objects of Thought in Medieval Philosophy*, ed. Henrik Lagerlund (Aldershot: Ashgate, 2007), 117–33.

(SA1*)   Whatever is in potency to receiving something in an intentional or spiritual way must lack that to which it is in potency in an intentional or spiritual way.

(SA1**) Whatever is in potency to receiving something in an intentional or spiritual way must lack that to which it is in potency in a natural way.

(SA1***) Whatever is in potency to receiving something in a natural way must lack that to which it is in potency in a natural way.

All of these possibilities, however, seem problematic.[46]

Consider first the possibility that SA1*** is what Aquinas means. In that case the argument from SA1*** and SA2* to SA3 involves a fallacy of equivocation. The first premise, SA1***, states a true principle of physics, and the second premise, SA2*, states a true principle of cognitive psychology. Yet because the first premise involves natural form-reception and the second specifically cognitive (spiritual or intentional) form-reception, when combined they yield an invalid argument. So if SA relies on SA***, it has a fatal flaw.

Consider, then, the possibility that SA1* is what Aquinas means instead. If so, then by combining it with SA2* we get:

(SA3*) Cognitive powers must lack the forms of objects they cognize in an intentional or spiritual way.

The argument from SA1* and SA2* to SA3* would be valid, and seems reasonable enough. The idea would be that a cognizer cannot already be cognizing what it is in potency to cognizing. For instance, if I am currently seeing red, then I am not in potency to seeing red. SA3* then would have to be understood in a diachronic way: cognitive powers cannot permanently possess any of their intentional objects, or they would be "stuck" cognizing just that one thing. At any given point in time that it is active, however, a cognizer will have some intentional object or other. Combining SA3* with SA4, however, yields only:

---

46. A fourth possibility, namely that whatever is in potency to receiving something in a natural way must lack that to which it is in potency in an intentional or spiritual way, seems to me unintelligible in this context.

(SA5*) The intellect lacks any sensible or corporeal form in an intentional or spiritual way.

That is to say, the intellect cannot permanently have any sensible or corporeal form as its sole intentional object if it is truly in potency to cognizing all such forms. For instance, if I am truly in potency to cognizing all sensible or corporeal forms I cannot permanently be thinking about trout. Understood this way, SA5* seems true, but rather trivial. It says nothing interesting about the intellect's ontology, and so cannot serve as support for the intellect's ontological independence from the body. If SA relies on SA1*, then, this jeopardizes its success as well.

It seems, then, that something like SA1** is the premise that Aquinas's argument needs. Upon examining this premise, however, the problem shifts from triviality to truth. Why should it be the case that for something to receive a form in an intentional or spiritual way it must lack that form naturally speaking? The opening line of 5.3 seems on its face to recite a straightforward principle of Aristotelian physics: receivers must lack whatever forms they are in potency to receiving. But it is far from clear that the same applies to the special kind of form reception involved in cognition. A pot of water cannot literally exemplify heat if we are going to heat it up. But why could a sense organ like the eye not literally exemplify the colors it is going to receive in an intentional or spiritual way?[47] In the previous chapter I suggested that cognition can be understood in terms of information encoding. We might ask, then, why a literally colored visual organ could not encode information about colors? Or more pertinently, why could a literally corporeal intellect not

---

47. John Buridan points out that this principle does not appear to hold even in the case of sense organs: "organum sensus tactus non est sine calido, frigido, humido, et sicco, quorum ipse est perceptivus; nec lingua sine sapore, nec oculus sine colore." QDA 3.2 in Jack Zupko, *John Buridan's Philosophy of Mind: An Edition and Translation of His 'Questions on Aristotle's De anima'* [Third Redaction], with Commentary and Critical and Interpretative Essays (PhD diss., Cornell University, 1989), 11. More recently Kenny makes the same point: "the premise is false; the tongue does have a taste—a very pleasant one, as fanciers of ox tongue will agree" (*Aquinas on Mind*, 132). It is not clear to me whether these complaints find their mark. While Aquinas sometimes refers to the eye and tongue as organs of touch and taste, his discussion of sense organs in In DSS 4/5.6 locates the organ of sight near the brain, while In DSS 4/5.16 locates the organ of taste near the heart. The eye and tongue seems to serve simply as information transfer devices. The question remains, though, why the internal organs of sense cognition (whatever they are) should not literally exemplify the features they cognize.

encode information about "all sensible and corporeal things"? Why could a brain not do so? It is hard to see what the answer to these questions might be.[48] Hence if SA1** is what Aquinas means it is hard to see why he would have thought it to be true.

Some commentators on SA overlook or dismiss the interpretative quandary I have just described altogether.[49] Most who recognize it,

---

48. Caleb Cohoe argues that there is a good answer to these questions when it comes to Aristotle's understanding of cognitive intentionality and the version of SA found at De anima 3.4.429a13–27, in his "Why the Intellect Cannot Have a Bodily Organ: De anima 3.4," Phronesis 58, no. 4 (2013): 347–77. On Cohoe's understanding, undergoing an intentional or spiritual change (a "preservative change" as he calls it) is both necessary and sufficient for cognition. Only cognizers are capable of possessing forms in an intentional or spiritual way. Furthermore, forms present in cognizers as the result of intentional or spiritual changes are formally identical to their objects in a way that cannot be understood as mere representation or information encoding. If Cohoe is right about these points of Aristotle interpretation, then it may be that they provide sufficient grounds for what he calls Aristotle's "neutrality condition" (i.e., the requirement that a cognitive organ lack those forms it is able to receive and thus cognize) for this condition to function as it needs to in SA. It seems clear to me, however, that Cohoe's Aristotle differs from Aquinas in two respects just mentioned. For one thing, the fact that Aquinas thinks there are species in the media of cognition shows that the spiritual or intentional presence of forms is not sufficient for cognition, however necessary it may be. For another thing, as I read him Aquinas does understand the formal identity of cognizer and cognized form in terms of information encoding or representation. Hence, I do not believe that the interpretation of Aristotle that Cohoe presents could be pressed successfully into service defending Aquinas.

49. Examples here include Herbert McCabe, "The Immortality of the Soul," in Aquinas: A Collection of Critical Essays (ed. Kenny), 297–306, and Edward Feser, Aquinas: A Beginner's Guide (London: Oneworld, 2009), chap. 4, who seem to believe that the notion of forms existing intentionally or spiritually in the intellect is, by itself, enough to establish its immateriality. This cannot be true, given that forms are present intentionally or spiritually in cognitive media and the senses as well. Sweeney's dissertation is by far the most detailed treatment of SA that I know of. Sweeney is aware that some have raised the distinction between natural and spiritual/intentional being as a potential complication for Aquinas's argument, but he does not agree that it poses any difficulty: "There is no need to distinguish between real and intentional being or to distinguish among various types of potentiality because the argument is based on what is generically common to all potentiality. This is the principle that the receiver cannot be naturally that which it is to receive. The differences between real and intentional being are not blurred, and the differences between various types of potentiality are not ignored, because the argument is rooted in a principle that is prior to any such differentiation. One of the most fundamental aspects of Aristotelian philosophy that Aquinas incorporated is the notion of potentiality and actuality. That Aquinas should base this argument for the immateriality of the intellect on a principle underlying all potentiality is evidence of its strength" (Aquinas' Commentary, 82). I do not see how Sweeney could be right about this. Given that the argument involves cognition, and given that Aquinas repeatedly distinguishes cognitive form reception from ordinary physical cases, it seems to me that we absolutely "need to distinguish between real and intentional being" if we are going to understand what Thomas is trying to accomplish.

however, conclude that Aquinas's argument is a failure.⁵⁰ Thomas wrongly supposes that the spiritual or intentional presence of forms in cognizers requires their literal absence.

Burnyeat suggests a reason why Thomas might have made this erroneous assumption: because forms are received spiritually or intentionally in both cognitive media and sense organs, organs and media must resemble each other.⁵¹ The medium of vision cannot itself be colored for the simple reason that, if it were, then we would see its color when we look at it, rather than seeing something else's color through it. The same point applies to the media of most other senses: still air is necessary to hear sounds, odorless air to smell, and a flavorless palate to taste. The case of touch is special, Aquinas says, because its medium cannot completely lack its own temperature and texture.⁵² To the extent that objects we touch share the same temperature and texture as our skin, we simply cannot sense them. Burnyeat suggests that Aquinas's insistence on the colorlessness of sense organs is based upon parallel reasoning. If the pupil of the eye had its own color, then we would always see that color, rather than seeing other things' colors through it. And similarly with the other senses.

It may be that Burnyeat's suggestion is correct as an interpretation of Aquinas's thinking. Thomas does indeed believe that light must enter the eye just as it illuminates the visual medium. For this to happen, there must be transparent water in the eye.⁵³ Thomas's best-known presentation of SA in his *Summa theologiae* likens the way a color present in the eye would prohibit us from seeing any other color to the way a color present in a glass vase prevents us from seeing other colors through it.⁵⁴ Likewise in 5.3 and elsewhere he mentions that a bitter coating on the tongue prevents us from tasting other flavors. Aquinas recites Avicenna's view that the organs of corporeal powers are media between the powers themselves and their objects.⁵⁵ In one way, then, it seems plausible to suppose that Thomas's reason for thinking that cognitive

---

50. See the works cited in note 45.
51. Burnyeat, *Aquinas on Spiritual Change*, 133.
52. In DA 2.23.547–58.
53. In DSS 4/5.5.
54. ST 1a.75.2.
55. In Sent 2.19.1.1, shortly after passage 5.1.

powers must lack whatever features they are going to cognize is that he thinks of them as resembling cognitive media.[56]

If this indeed what Aquinas thinks, however, it seems philosophically misguided. It makes sense that media must lack certain features in order for those features to pass through them to a cognizer. But it seems unreasonable to say this about cognizers themselves without further ado. Again, the question is why, supposing that cognition involves a sort of information processing, the information processor itself must lack the features about which it processes information in order to do its job. Aquinas thinks the "principle of vision"—that is, the central visual information processing unit—is located "near the brain, where the two nerves proceeding from the eyes come together."[57] This information processing unit must surely have a nature such that it can track visual input about colors. But why could it not do so while being colored itself? It seems unreasonable to insist that it could not without any further explanation. Of course, the fact that something seems unreasonable to us is no guarantee that Aquinas did not believe it.

A few commentators have suggested ways of salvaging Aquinas's reasoning in 5.3, even while recognizing that cognizers receive the forms they cognize only intentionally or spiritually, not naturally. One strategy is to reduce SA to MA by highlighting Aquinas's claim that the intellect cognizes sensible or corporeal *natures*, then denying that corporeal cognizers apprehend natures, but rather only cognize particulars.[58] As far as I can tell, Aquinas thinks that SA and MA are two distinct types of argument.[59] Readers who think that SA is indeed reducible to MA, how-

---

56. Further support for this interpretation might be taken from In DA 3.12.773, in which Aquinas describes how air, spiritually changed by color, affects the pupil by imprinting on it the likeness of some color, which in turn affects the common sense. Something similar happens in the case of hearing and the other senses. This suggests that the reason the pupil cannot be colored, or the ear contain moving air, is that the common sense would then perceive the pupil's color, or the ear's sound, rather than colors or sounds external to these organs. The question, however, is why the common sense organ itself must be a certain way to apprehend its various objects.

57. In DSS 4/5.6 (Leo. 45.2:29.93–94).

58. This is the strategy suggested in Kenneth Schmitz, "Purity of Soul and Immortality," The Monist 69, no. 3 (1986): 396–415.

59. Foster, "Aquinas's Arguments for Spirit," agrees that they are distinct in Aquinas, but argues that Aristotle meant for the two lines of reasoning to work together, noting the antecedents to the De anima 3.4 argument earlier in the text (1.2 and 1.5).

ever, can skip to the final two sections of this chapter, in which I discuss the latter argument further. A second strategy is to jettison the claim that cognizers must literally lack the features they are able to cognize, then to argue that there is some special reason why an intellect capable of cognizing all corporeal and sensible things must literally lack any of their forms. Why must this be?

Richard Connell's proposal is that any corporeal cognizer is constrained to cognize only a determinate and limited range of objects, whereas the intellect is "ordered to an undetermined or unlimited range of objects."[60] When Aquinas likens a corporeal intellect to a feverish tongue he is merely indicating that both are restricted in terms of their ability to receive.[61] The question for Connell, however, is why a corporeal intellect could cognize only a determinate or limited range of corporeal forms. It is true that the exterior senses are limited to cognizing only forms of a certain sort: colors, sounds, smells, tastes, or temperatures/textures. But the power of *phantasia*, which Aquinas thinks uses a bodily organ, is able to imagine features of any of these kinds, along with the substantial features of corporeal things.[62] Connell does not make it clear why an intellect operating through patterns of neural activity, say, could not cognize the full range of sensible or corporeal forms.

Klima, on the other hand, offers an intriguing suggestion as to why the intellect could not cognize all sensible or corporeal forms by means of a subset of these forms, such as neural firing patterns.[63] For the intellect to operate this way, he argues, would generate a version of Russell's paradox. Consider: if the intellect cognizes all corporeal forms by

---

60. Richard Connell, "The 'Intus Apparens' and the Immateriality of the Intellect," *New Scholasticism* 32, no. 2 (1958): 151–86, at 176.

61. Sweeney, *Aquinas' Commentary*, 123–24, argues that Connell's interpretation cannot adequately accommodate the parallel that Aquinas's argument seems to rely on between the corporeal intellect and the flavorful tongue/colored pupil.

62. This is a point some of Aquinas's medieval critics make; see Roger Marston, QDA 7, in Fr. *Rogeri Marston, O.F.M. Quaestiones Disputatae*, ed. College of St. Bonaventure (Florence: Ad Aquas Claras, 1932), 362: "nam instantia est manifesta de imaginatione: nam ipsa potest omnia corpora et quanta imaginari et eius obiectum proprium est quantitas, quam etiam apprehendit, et tamen ipsa est in organo vere quanto, et tali organo utitur in sua operatione."

63. Gyula Klima, "Reply to Bob Pasnau on Aquinas's Proofs of the Immateriality of the Intellect," in *The Immateriality of the Human Mind, the Semantics of Analogy, and the Conceivability of God*, ed. Gyula Klima and Alexander Clayton (Newcastle-upon-Tyne: Cambridge Scholars Press, 2011), 49–60.

means of a subset of corporeal forms, such as neural firing patterns, then it would have to cognize its own forms (i.e., the firing patterns) as well. For that to be true, however, some of the intellect's forms would have to be capable of cognizing themselves. Otherwise for each neural firing pattern there would have to be another pattern cognizing it, and so on into infinity, exhausting all of the intellect's cognitive forms without ever cognizing anything other than itself. Supposing there are some self-cognizing forms, then, call the set of all and only the *non-self-cognizing* forms N. Surely we are able to form a concept of N; we are certainly able to discuss it intelligibly. The "Russellian question," Klima says, is whether our concept of N is itself self-cognizing. If it is, then it is not the concept of *only* non-self-cognizing forms, for it is not itself non-self-cognizing. If it is not, then it is not the concept of *all* non-self-cognizing forms, as it leaves itself out. To extricate ourselves from this contradiction, Klima thinks, we must reject the assumption that got it started, namely that we cognize all corporeal forms by means of a subset of those forms.

I will leave it for the reader to judge whether this bit of reasoning succeeds. Klima acknowledges that it is not an argument Aquinas himself presents. It seems to me that it could not represent an accurate depiction of Aquinas's reasoning in passages like 5.3 for at least two reasons. First, Aquinas clearly means his argument to trade on a parallel between the intellect and the senses. For Aquinas it is apparently for the same reason that the pupil of the eye must lack all colors that the intellect must lack any corporeal nature of its own. But Klima's Russellian argument clearly could not apply to sense-powers; there is no reason to suppose that our eyes are capable of seeing sets, much less the set of all and only those colors that cannot see themselves. For another thing, Aquinas maintains that the intellect is capable of cognizing itself and its own cognitive forms (intelligible *species*).[64] But according to Klima's reasoning, whatever enables us to cognize forms within a certain range cannot itself be within that range. It would seem then that whatever enables the cognition of intelligible *species* could not itself *be* an intelligible species. This again seems like a conclusion Thomas could not accept.

Perhaps there is a way of developing Aquinas's SA in which it turns

64. ST 1a.87 and QDV 10.8–9.

out to be sound. Some have proposed a resemblance between SA and arguments that J. R. Lucas and Roger Penrose have developed based on Gödel's incompleteness theorem.[65] It is true that these arguments, like Aristotle's and Aquinas's, trade on the notion that corporeal cognizers are somehow limited in terms of what they can comprehend, whereas intellectual cognition is potentially infinite in scope. Lucas's and Penrose's arguments are controversial in their own right, however, and I doubt that the parallels between their reasoning and SA extend very far. I will not pursue further the proposal that SA might be developed along Gödelian lines.

Many of Aquinas's medieval critics raised as an objection against SA the fact that the human intellect cognizes itself. If a cognizer must really lack all the forms it is able to cognize, how could it ever cognize its own form? I will not consider here whether SA can be defended against this objection, because, as I have explained, even setting the objection aside I think it is unlikely that SA succeeds. I bring it up, however, because the argument that I will consider in the following section trades on the same phenomenon the objection highlights, namely the human intellect's ability to cognize itself.

The Argument from the Self-Reflexivity of Intellectual Cognition

According to Calvin Normore, there is a tradition of interpreting Aristotle's presentation of the scope argument in De Anima 3.4 in which what the intellect could not understand, if it were corporeal, is its own nature.[66] Aquinas does not seem to have followed this tradition in his own interpretation of Aristotle. But he does argue in several passages that the human intellect's immateriality can be demonstrated based upon its ability to reflect on itself. I call this Aquinas's "reflexivity argument," or RA. Because this type of argument appears only infrequently in Thomas's corpus, I will begin by presenting every instance of RA that I know of. I will then explain why, given what we know of Aquinas's the-

---

65. See Pasnau, *Aquinas on Human Nature*, 56, and Freddoso, "No Room at the Inn," 19, for this suggestion.
66. See Normore, "The Matter of Thought," who traces this line of interpretation to Alexander of Aphrodisias.

ory of self-knowledge, his terse formulations of RA simply do not provide us with sufficient information to say whether they succeed or not.

We have already seen how Aquinas's first presentation of RA begins, in 5.1: "intellect understands itself, which does not happen in any power whose operation is through a corporeal organ." He goes on to explain the reasoning behind this claim as follows:

(5.4) The reason for this is that, as Avicenna claims, the organ of any power operating through a corporeal organ must be a medium between it and its object. For vision does not cognize anything unless its *species* is first received into the pupil. Whence, since it is not possible that a corporeal organ should be a medium between a certain power and the essence of that power itself, it will not be possible that any power operating by the mediation of a corporeal organ cognizes itself. And the *Book of Causes* touches on this argument in its fifteenth proposition: "every knower that knows its own essence returns to its own essence by a complete return." And something is said to return completely to its essence, as the Commentator explains there, whose essence stands fixed [*fixa stans*], and is not supported by something else [*super aliud delata*].[67]

In SCG we find a similar line of reasoning, appealing this time however to Aristotle's conception of self-motion:

(5.5) The action of a body never reflects back on the agent itself, for it was shown in the *Physics* that no body is moved by itself except according to some part, namely when one of its parts moves and another is moved. The intellect, however, reflects upon itself by acting, for it understands itself not just in part, but as a whole. So it is not a body.[68]

The final set of passages in which Thomas presents reasoning along these lines in his commentary on the *Liber de causis*:

(5.6) First [Proclus] pursues [the intellect's] incorporeity, saying "the intellect is indeed incorporeal, which its conversion to itself makes clear." The intellect's conversion to itself consists in its understanding itself, "for no body is converted to itself." And he proved this above stating in proposition fifteen that "everything that is converted to itself is incorporeal." Which he proves thus: "no body is indeed apt to be converted to itself. For if what is converted

67. In Sent 2.19.1.1 (Mand./Moos 2.481–82).
68. SCG 2.49.8 (Leo. 13:381), on Aristotle, Physics 7.1 and 8.4.

to something is joined with that to which it is converted, therefore clearly because all the parts of a body that is converted to itself are joined to all [the other parts], which is impossible in all divisible things because of the separation of these parts, with some lying in other places than others."[69]

Most of the argument expressed here is presented in Proclus's words, not Aquinas's, but it is recognizable as the same type of reasoning as Thomas uses in 5.4, partly because both passages make reference to proposition 15 of the *Liber de causis*. The argument in 5.5 eschews neo-Platonic sources in favor of Aristotle, but seems to be driving at the same point. All three arguments could be represented in the following way:

(RA1) Nothing corporeal is capable of self-reflexivity.
(RA2) Self-cognition requires self-reflexivity.
(RA3) No self-cognizers are corporeal.
(RA4) The human intellect is able to cognize itself.
(RA5) The human intellect is not corporeal.

Expressed in this way the argument looks to be valid. Is it sound?

I take it that RA4 is fairly uncontroversial, and that the controversial question the argument raises is what kind of self-reflexivity is required for self-cognition, yet unavailable to anything corporeal. One might worry that RA equivocates on the term "self-reflexivity" in something like the way SA seemed to equivocate on "receiving forms." In SA2 the sort of form-reception in question was specifically cognitive, yet reading SA1 in a specifically cognitive way seemed to yield a conclusion weaker than Aquinas needed, whereas reading it in a straightforwardly natural way exposed the argument to a fallacy of equivocation. What Aquinas needed was a premise linking the way forms are spiritually or intentionally received in cognizers with the way the cognizers themselves literally exemplify forms. It seemed unlikely that he had a good way of defending any such premise. Turning to RA, RA2 clearly involves cognition, while RA1 does not. So is there a univocal sense of "self-reflexivity" at work in both premises?

The way that Aquinas defends RA1 in passage 5.5 makes it look as

---

69. In DC 7, in *Sancti Thomae de Aquino super Librum de causis expositio*, ed. H. D. Saffrey (Fribourg: Société Philosophique, 1954), 51.23–52.4.

though he is equivocating again. As noted, Thomas appeals to Aristotle's arguments toward the end of the *Physics* as to why no mover can move itself. Some of these arguments may well be sound. Aquinas relies on them in important ways elsewhere, for instance in his efforts to prove God's existence. Yet in 4.7 and 4.8, Aquinas appeared to distinguish ordinary natural motion from the special sort of motion involved in cognition. Again, the difference is that cognition requires receiving forms only spiritually or intentionally, as opposed to naturally. It is not clear that Aristotle's arguments from *Physics* 7 and 8, which involve natural motion, have any bearing on the sort of motion that cognition requires, even if it is self-cognition that we are talking about. If reasoning of this Aristotelian variety is all that Thomas has in mind by RA1, then it seems that RA itself may be guilty of equivocation.

Despite this obvious difficulty, some commentators who consider SA a clear failure are more optimistic about RA's prospects. Pasnau and Haldane both propose versions of RA that they think may succeed at the twin tasks I noted at the end of my introduction; that is, they are both plausibly attributable to Aquinas and plausible in their own right.[70] I think there is reason for at least a cautious optimism on both these fronts.

Pasnau and Haldane are correct, I think, to focus on self-awareness as the kind of self-cognition at stake in RA. In his most extensive discussions of self-cognition, Aquinas distinguishes both between actual and habitual self-cognition, and between singular and universal self-cognition.[71] The former distinction need not concern us here. I take it that Aquinas recognizes habitual self-cognition largely to give ample credit to the Augustinian thesis that "the mind knows itself through itself."[72] It is the sort of cognition the soul has just by possessing the sorts of intellectual powers it does. I take it, however, that RA involves some kind of actual cognition that nothing corporeal could have. Aquinas says that actual self-cognition happens in two ways: "in the first place singularly, as when Socrates or Plato perceives that he has an in-

---

70. Pasnau, *Aquinas on Human Nature*, 194, and John Haldane, *Reasonable Faith* (London: Routledge, 2010), 148, along with "(I Am) Thinking," *Ratio* 16, no. 2 (2003): 124–39.

71. ST 1a.87 and QDV 10.

72. Augustine, *De trinitate* 9.3.3; see Therese Scarpelli Cory, *Aquinas on Human Self-Knowledge* (Cambridge: Cambridge University Press, 2014), chap. 5, on habitual self-cognition.

tellectual soul because he perceives that he understands. In the second place, universally, as when we consider the nature of the human mind from a knowledge of the intellectual act."[73] He explains further that for the first sort of self-cognition "the mere presence of the mind suffices," because "the mind itself is the principle of action whereby it perceives itself, and hence [knows] itself by its own presence," but for the second sort of self-cognition "the mere presence of the mind does not suffice, but there is further required a careful and subtle inquiry."[74] It is because many do not undertake this inquiry correctly that they hold erroneous views concerning the soul's nature. It must be the first sort of actual self-cognition, "singular self-cognition," that Aquinas is concerned with in RA. This is because the second sort of self-cognition clearly involves knowledge of kinds. It is "that by which the soul is known with reference to that which is common to all souls," or "that by which the nature of the soul is known."[75] It is a soul's knowledge of what kind of thing it is. If Aquinas had this sort of self-cognition in mind in RA, then it would seemingly reduce to MA, which hinges on the inability of corporeal cognizers to understand kinds. RA would not represent a distinct line of reasoning on its own. Furthermore, the second sort of self-cognition is apparently inferential. It involves the soul *reasoning* about what kind of thing it is. But apart from the inability of corporeal cognizers to understand kinds, there is no apparent reason why a bodily intellect could not investigate its own nature by some kind of discursive process.[76] Today, presumably, this kind of discursive process of intellectual self-cognition would involve using brain-imaging technology, studying anatomy and physiology, etc. It would seem question-begging for Aquinas simply to deny that a bodily intellect could undertake such an inquiry without further ado. Hence if RA represents its own distinct, successful line of reasoning, it must hinge on some sort of singular self-cognition. Aquinas typically uses perceptual terms like *percipere* and *experiri* for this sort of

---

73. ST 1a.87.1 (Leo. 5:356).
74. Ibid.
75. QDV 10.8 (Leo. 22.2:321.203–7).
76. This is precisely the criticism that John Buridan raises against this argument; he writes that "intellect or sense ... understand [themselves] discursively, and many people call this understanding reflexively, but this sort of reflection would belong more properly to bodies than to separated substances." QDA 3.3 in Zupko, *John Buridan's Philosophy of Mind*, 25.

cognition, as opposed to terms connoting understanding, such as *intelligere* or *scire*. Hence it seems that Haldane and Pasnau are correct to call the sort of self-cognition at stake in RA self-awareness.

What is it, then, that renders corporeal cognizers incapable of self-awareness? Pasnau's proposed reconstruction of RA involves the claims that "for a cognitive capacity to be aware of itself, the whole capacity must be in contact with the whole capacity" and that "no material thing can be wholly in contact with itself in this way."[77] One might worry that these claims equivocate on the term "contact." Yes, we speak of awareness in terms of getting into cognitive "contact," but this is clearly a special use of the term. A body cannot literally touch itself in every place at once, but I see no obvious reason why a body could not be wholly in contact with itself in the special, cognitive sense. I prefer Haldane's way of putting things, then, namely that self-awareness is not "reducible to the transmission of information from one object to another, or from one part of an object to another part of that object."[78] As I understand it, this is a claim about explanation: a self-cognizer's awareness of itself cannot be explained in terms of information transfer from one part of an object to another. In effect, then, Haldane is claiming that we cannot explain self-awareness in terms of bodily parts, states, and processes. Why not?

One possibility is that the self-awareness RA involves is first-personal, and that because explanations given in bodily terms are inevitably third-personal, they cannot successfully explain this sort of self-cognition. Therese Scarpelli Cory has argued recently that Aquinas thinks a sort of "implicit self-awareness" accompanies all of our intellectual operations.[79] Whenever I think about anything, I am always aware of myself as a thinking agent. To be sure, such self-awareness remains most of the time implicit, rising only occasionally to the level of explicitly thinking about myself. Cory thinks this implicit self-awareness grounds several important features of self-awareness. It is subjective, in the sense that I am aware of myself as thinker of my thoughts, as opposed to their object(s), and it is first-personal in the sense that I am aware of myself as "I" as opposed to "it." Cory writes:

77. Pasnau, *Aquinas on Human Nature*, 196.
78. Haldane, *Reasonable Faith*, 148.
79. Cory, *Aquinas on Human Self-Knowledge*, chap. 6.

Aquinas's account of the reflexity of immaterial acts provides a ... fruitful approach to the first-personal character of experience. The first-personal character of self-awareness (whether implicit or explicit) is the experiential manifestation of the completely reflexive character of intellectual cognition.... Even in explicitly thinking about myself for Aquinas, I do not "stand outside" myself and look back on myself in a second-order act directed at a first-order act. There simply is no outside vantage point from which the intellect could look at itself as "other." Consequently, if the intellect is to cognize itself at all, it must cognize itself from the *inside*. (By analogy, one could imagine that a self-seeing eye would have to see itself from the inside, not by getting some kind of outside perspective on itself.) This necessarily "insider" character is arguably experienced as the first person, giving self-awareness the feel of intimate, privileged self-access.[80]

Cory goes on to explain why "this sort of insider self-appropriation is possible only for immaterial powers like intellect and will":

Only an indivisible and incorporeal being can be made wholly present to itself since it has no parts that get in the way of each other. What is immaterial can be placed in contact, so to speak, with the whole of itself. And in fact this complete self-reversion occurs, at least, implicitly, whenever the intellect is thinking about anything: "the intellect reflects upon itself by acting, for it understands itself not part-by-part, but according to the whole." The intellect must take a first-person perspective of itself: in perceiving itself, it cannot step outside itself and perceive itself as other, because it simply cannot leave any of itself behind to look at from outside.[81]

Readers will recognize the line Cory quotes here as one of the premises in the argument of passage 5.5. I noted earlier worries that one might have about the Aristotelian reasoning Aquinas uses there to show the impossibility of a body being placed wholly in "contact" with itself, as well as with Pasnau's use of the term. It does not seem too much of a stretch, however, to suppose that subjective, first-personal self-awareness could never be explained in third-personal terms, by invoking bodily parts, states, and processes. Indeed, that a "robust first-person perspective" such as language-users enjoy cannot be "naturalized" is a thesis Lynne

---

80. Ibid., 206.
81. Ibid., 206–7.

Rudder Baker has recently defended at book length.[82] She argues that there are first-personal properties that are neither eliminable from our ontology nor reducible to anything else. To "naturalize" these properties would involve explaining them in terms recognizable to natural science. Given that natural science is "wholly impersonal," it seems highly unlikely that this could be accomplished. Rudder Baker concludes from this that ontological naturalism is false. Her own view is that, despite this, human persons are necessarily embodied. They are "constituted" by their bodies, though not identical to them. They are also ontologically emergent. If the reasoning I presented in chapter 3 is correct, however, then Baker should not hold this set of views. If she truly believes that having a robust first-person perspective cannot be explained in bodily terms, then she should accept that it is ontologically independent from the body. In other words, it is incorporeal, just as Aquinas wants us to believe.

To summarize, I am proposing that we rephrase Aquinas's self-reflexivity argument for the immateriality of the human intellect as follows:

(RA1*) Explanations in terms of bodily parts, states, and processes are always third-personal, and hence cannot explain first-personal phenomena.
(RA2*) Self-awareness involves adopting a first-person perspective.
(RA3*) Self-awareness cannot be explained in corporeal terms.
(RA4*) The human intellect is capable of self-awareness.
(RA5*) The human intellect's acts of self-awareness cannot be explained in corporeal terms.

If this argument does indeed succeed in establishing RA5* in a way plausibly attributable to Aquinas, then Thomas has the premise he needs to establish the possibility of human souls existing in a disembodied state, namely SS2 from the end of chapter 3: "intellectual operations cannot be explained in terms of coordinated bodily parts, states, and processes." So does the reasoning from RA1* to RA5* succeed as an argument in its own right? Does it succeed as an interpretation of Aquinas?

82. Lynne Rudder Baker, *Naturalism and the First-Person Perspective* (Oxford: Oxford University Press, 2013).

Concerning the first of these questions, I cannot here defend a positive answer very far. As noted, support for RA1* can be found in Rudder Baker's work, which argues that efforts by John Perry, David Lewis, and John Searle to "naturalize" the first-person perspective do not succeed.[83] Certainly arguments like Rudder Baker's involving the first-person perspective have not received nearly as much philosophical attention as those involving other aspects of consciousness, such as its qualitative character, or "phenomenal feel." That the argument from RA1* to RA5* does not involve phenomenal consciousness is a good thing as regards the second question I just posed, namely its plausibility as an interpretation of Aquinas. King argues that the mind-body problem is not medieval, insofar as philosophers of the Middle Ages uniformly treated qualitative feels as "manifestations of the life of the living body as it goes about its business in the world, and are therefore [as] inseparable from it."[84] Aquinas would acknowledge, presumably, that there is something it is like to be a bat, but he does not think the qualitative character of bat consciousness provides any reason for supposing that it is incorporeal.[85] In contrast, he thinks that a cognitive power's awareness of itself as agent of its own activities is indeed evidence that these activities cannot be explained in corporeal terms.

Does the argument from RA1* to RA5* then plausibly capture what Aquinas is trying to accomplish in passages 5.4–5.6? Cory's work on Aquinas's theory of human self-knowledge seemingly supports the view that he is committed to RA2*. She thinks that Aquinas was aware of the phenomenon of first-person perspective-taking, and makes room for it in his theory of self-cognition. She notes that Thomas frequently uses first-personal language when talking about self-cognition, for example, "by one and the same operation I understand an intelligible [object], and also understand myself to understand."[86] Yet she acknowledges that Thomas nowhere discusses the use of the first person in its own right. Certainly he does not make explicit that this is what he has

83. Ibid., chap. 3.
84. Peter King, "Why Isn't the Mind-Body Problem Medieval?," in *Forming the Mind: Essays on the Internal Senses and the Mind-Body Problem from Avicenna to the Medical Enlightenment*, ed. Henrik Lagerlund (Dordrecht: Springer, 2007), 187–205, at 195.
85. See also on this point Haldane, "The Metaphysics of Intellect(ion)," 43–48.
86. In Sent 1.1.2.1 ad 2 (Mand./Moos 1:38).

in mind in 5.4–5.6. I have suggested one way of developing Aquinas's argument here. But it seems equally likely to me that Thomas had something different in mind—perhaps, for instance, a version of the argument from the "unity of consciousness" that Kant calls "the Achilles of all dialectical inferences of pure psychology."[87] Perhaps Aquinas himself was unsure about how best to develop the argument. He brings up Avicenna's version alongside Proclus's in the early *Sentences* commentary. He invokes Aristotle's *Physics* in SCG, from the early 1260s. He then drops the argument entirely for a decade before returning to discuss the Proclean version in his 1272 commentary on the *Liber de causis*, which does not make clear whether Thomas himself endorses it. Given the paucity of textual evidence supporting any interpretation of RA, I conclude that whatever optimism we might feel regarding any particular reconstruction should be cautious. Yet a cautious optimism may not be out of order.

The Argument from the Mode of Intellectual Cognition I: What Will Not Work

I think there is reason for a more robust optimism about the last type of reasoning I will consider in this chapter, Aquinas's argument from the mode of intellectual cognition. I will focus in this section, however, on presenting an initial formulation of the argument, a formidable obstacle this formulation appears to face, and several interpretations of the argument that fail to surmount this obstacle. Aquinas presents versions of MA far more frequently than he does RA, and MA has received more attention in recent secondary literature than either RA or SA have. Hence I will not be able to canvas all the versions of the argument Thomas presents, nor all the interpretations that commentators have proposed. I will begin by examining just one prominent example of MA, and focus on just a few of its most prominent interpretations.

The version of MA that Aquinas offers in *Summa theologiae* is probably his best-known presentation of the argument. It runs as follows:

(5.7) Whatever is received into something else is received into it according to the mode of the recipient. Moreover, a given thing is cognized in the way that

---

87. See Kant's criticism of the second paralogism of pure reason and the essays in *The Achilles of Rationalist Psychology*, ed. Thomas Lennon and Robert Stainton (Dordrecht: Springer, 2008).

its form is [received into] a cognizer. The intellective soul, however, cognizes a thing in its nature absolutely, namely [it cognizes] a stone insofar as it is stone absolutely. Therefore the form of a stone is [received] absolutely, according to its proper formal notion, in the intellective soul. Moreover, the intellective soul is, therefore, an absolute form, not something composed from matter and form. For if the intellective soul were composed from matter and form, the forms of things would be received into it as individuals, and thus it would not cognize except in a singular way, just as happens in the sense powers, which receive the forms of things in a corporeal organ, for matter is the principle of individuation of forms. It remains, therefore, that the intellective soul and every intellectual substance that cognizes forms absolutely, lacks composition of matter and form.[88]

I think Aquinas's reasoning in this passage is represented accurately enough by the following:

(MA1) Whatever is received into something else is received into it according to the mode of the recipient.
(MA2) A given thing is cognized in the way that its form is [received into] a cognizer.
(MA3) Matter is the principle of individuation of forms.
(MA4) Intellectual cognition grasps things in an absolute, non-individual way.
(MA5) So intellectual cognition grasps things apart from matter (from MA3 and MA4).
(MA6) So intellectual cognition receives the forms of things apart from matter (from MA2 and MA5).
(MA7) Therefore, anything capable of intellectual cognition lacks matter, at least with respect to whatever part of it receives the forms by which it cognizes intellectively (from MA1 and MA6).

Three points should be noted immediately about this version of MA, based upon what we have seen of Aquinas's metaphysics and cognitive psychology so far.

First, as I explained above, while the conclusion Aquinas reaches in 5.7

---

88. ST 1a.75.5 (Leo. 5:202).

is that no intellectual substance is composed of matter and form, Thomas believes that this argument also suffices to show that our intellectual powers are incorporeal, that is, that their operations cannot be explained in bodily terms. For our purposes, this is the most significant conclusion Aquinas establishes by way of MA, because it provides him with the crucial premise he needs to demonstrate the possibility of disembodied human souls.

Second, the argument importantly invokes the notion of "receiving." It opens with what looks like a sort of metaphysical axiom about reception in general, then states a more limited principle regarding specifically cognitive form-reception. As we saw in chapter 4, Thomas has various ways of talking about cognitive form-reception and -possession. Cognizers receive and possess the forms of other things in addition to or alongside their own. They receive and possess them without their matter. They do so in an intentional or spiritual way. They receive and possess *species* that are representational likenesses of what they cognize. And so on. If we adopt Stump and Klima's proposal that all of these locutions can be understood in terms of information processing, as I have suggested we should, then cognizers receive the forms of what they cognize just insofar as they encode and utilize information about certain objects. This is important to bear in mind when considering the truth of the metaphysical axiom Aquinas states in MA1 as it bears on cases of cognition.

Third, as regards the object that Aquinas thinks intellectual cognition can apprehend, yet could not apprehend if it were a corporeal power, 5.7 refers to it as a thing "in its nature absolutely" or "according to its proper formal notion." Elsewhere, as in 5.1, Aquinas refers to such objects simply as universals.[89] To understand these statements it is important to recall what we saw of Aquinas's views on universals and individuation in chapter 2. Outside the soul, Thomas thinks, there are no universals; they are beings of reason. Nevertheless, the essences of composite substances are not intrinsically individuated. Their distinctness from one another is derivative upon their designated matter, that is, matter subject to quantitative divisions. Aquinas's claims about the

89. See QDA 1 and CT 79.

objects of intellectual cognition mean at least, then, that the intellect cognizes the essences of composite substances somehow apart from the designated matter that individuates them in reality.

What exactly it means for the intellect to cognize universals or things in their natures absolutely can be better appreciated by juxtaposing two passages from Aquinas's *De anima* commentary. The first is worth quoting at length:

(5.8) It must be considered why sense [cognizes] singulars, while knowledge [*scientia*] is of universals, and how universals are in the soul. Regarding the first point it should be known that a sense is a power in a corporeal organ, while the intellect is an immaterial power which is not the act of any corporeal organ. A given thing is received into something, however, according to the mode [of the receiver]. But cognition always happens through the cognized thing being [received] in some mode into the cognizer, namely according to its similitude. For the cognizer in act is the cognized thing itself in act. It is necessary therefore that a sense receives the similitude of the thing it senses corporeally and materially, while the intellect receives the similitude of what it understands incorporeally and immaterially. The individuation of a common nature in corporeal and material things is, however, [derived] from corporeal matter contained under determinate dimensions, whereas a universal results from abstraction from matter of this sort and material individuating conditions. It is clear therefore that the similitude of a thing received in a sense represents the thing according as it is singular, while [a similitude] received in the intellect represents a thing according to the notion of its universal nature, and that is why sense cognizes singulars, but the intellect universals, which the sciences are concerned with. Regarding the second point, however, it should be considered that "universal" can be understood in two ways. In one way the common nature itself is called universal, namely insofar as it falls under the intention of universality. In another way ["universal" is said of the common nature] in itself.... That nature, however, to which the intention of universality adheres—for instance, human nature—has a twofold act of being: one material, according as it exists in material nature, the other immaterial, according as it exists in the intellect. According to the act of being it has in material nature, therefore, the intention of universality cannot adhere to it, since it is individuated through matter. Therefore, the intention of universality adheres to it according as it is abstracted from individual matter. But it is not possible that it can really be abstracted from individual matter, as the Platonists posited, for there really exists no human nature except in this flesh and these bones, as the Philosopher proves in *Metaphysics* 7. It remains, therefore, that human nature has no existence without individuating principles except in the intellect. Nevertheless, our understanding is not false when it apprehends a common nature without its individuating principles, without which [the nature] cannot exist in the nature of things, for this understanding does not apprehend the common nature to exist without individuating principles, but apprehends the common nature without apprehending the individuating principles, and this is not false.... Therefore, the intellect abstracts a genus from its species without falsehood, insofar as it understands the nature of the genus without understanding the differences, and similarly it abstracts the species from its individuals insofar as it understands the nature of the species without understanding the individual principles.[90]

One thing this passage shows is that Aquinas thinks MA can be run in the opposite direction. That is, not only does the fact that the human intellect cognizes universals demonstrate its immateriality, but also our intellect's immateriality serves as evidence that it cognizes universals.[91] The passage also sheds crucial light on what it means to cognize universals. As Aquinas explains, while the natures of composite substances never exist apart from individuating matter outside the soul, we consider them this way by an act of intellectual abstraction. Here "abstraction" appears to mean something like "selective attention": just as we can attend to an individual human's animality while ignoring her humanity, we can attend to her humanity while ignoring her individualizing features stemming from her designated matter. Klima points out that the features in question that individualize representational likenesses in the senses are "common" sense-objects such as size, shape, and location that affect more than one sense, as opposed to the "proper" sense-objects that affect one sense alone (e.g., color affects just vision,

---

90. In DA 2.12.377–79 (Leo. 45.1:115–16.71–138).

91. Care is needed here, however, because not all immaterial cognizers grasp their objects in a universal way. Aquinas argues that God and angels cognize individual things in spite of their immateriality (see ST 1a.14.11 and 57.2, QDV 2.5 and 8.11, SCG 1.65, 2.100, etc.). The reason that God is able to do so is because his cognition is causal (see ST 1a.14.8 and QDV 2.14). God causes the existence of what he cognizes, including the existence of individuating conditions. Angelic knowledge is not causal in this way. Yet because angels cognize by means of *species* given to them directly by God, rather than abstracted from the senses, their cognition ranges over both the universal and individual features of its objects as well. See also Gyula Klima, *John Buridan* (Oxford: Oxford University Press, 2009), 82–83, for an explanation of why the human intellect's immateriality does not by itself entail the universality of its cognitive acts.

sound just hearing, etc.).[92] In the *lectio* following passage 5.8 Aquinas writes that:

(5.9) There are certain other [sense-objects] that bring about a change in the sense-power not as regards the species of the agent, but as regards its mode of action. For sensible qualities move a sense corporeally and with respect to some location, when they move [the sense] differently depending on whether they are in a larger or smaller body, or located in diverse places, namely closer by or further away, or in the same or different locations. And it is in this way that common sense-objects make a difference to the change [that takes place in] a sense.[93]

Recalling Aquinas's view that matter under determinate quantitative dimensions is what individuates forms, Klima takes 5.9 to indicate that sense cognition is singular precisely because it includes information about the spatio-temporal features of its objects, which are common sense-objects. Klima writes: "*Proper sensibilia* are individualized by their spatio-temporal determinations here and now, the *common sensibilia*. The cognition of *common sensibilia*, therefore, provides precisely that distinctive sensory information that singularizes the cognition of individualized sensible qualities, presenting the singulars having these qualities *qua* the singulars actually affecting the senses *here and now*."[94] So for the intellect to cognize universals or things in their natures absolutely is for it to cognize its objects in a way that leaves out such features as their particular spatio-temporal location, etc. That is what it means for the intellect to cognize in a "universal mode."[95] It is what Aquinas primarily

---

92. Klima, "Aquinas on the Materiality," 178–79, and "Universality and Immateriality," *Acta Philosophica* 24, no. 1 (2015): 31–42, at 39–41. See also Cory's discussion of different ways of understanding abstraction, construed as a matter of selective attention at "Rethinking Abstractionism," 609–12, which includes references to the secondary literature.
93. *In DA* 2.13.394 (Leo. 45.1:120:144–53).
94. Klima, "Aquinas on the Materiality," 179; see also Klima, "Universality and Immateriality," 40.
95. Cory, "Rethinking Abstractionism," is at pains to distance Aquinas's position on abstraction from anything having to do with the content of intellectual operations (see esp. 623–27). Instead, she argues, Thomas's frequent mentions of "the light of the agent intellect," as in passage 4.2, are to be taken fairly literally; just as physical light renders colors actually visible so too the agent intellect renders phantasms actually intelligible by "immaterializing" them. Cory makes a persuasive case for thinking that what she calls the "Active Principle Model" does indeed represent an important component of Aquinas's thought regarding intellectual abstraction; it is clearly part of his overall theory, and is something most previous

has in mind when he states in MA6 that intellectual cognition receives the forms of things apart from matter.

If this is what Aquinas means by MA6, however, then the question immediately arises how he expects this premise, in conjunction with the metaphysical axiom he offers (MA1), to yield the conclusion that the intellect is immaterial. Joseph Novak criticizes Aquinas's argument for equivocating on the term "immaterial."[96] Premise MA6 states that intellectual operations are immaterial with respect to their mode of representation, insofar as they "leave out" individualizing features stemming from designated matter. Yet MA7 claims that the intellect is immaterial ontologically speaking, that is, with respect to its mode of being. Novak thinks that Aquinas illicitly shifts from the immaterial representational mode of intentional operations to their immaterial ontological status. Robert Pasnau agrees that Thomas is guilty of this error, and calls it the "Content Fallacy": an unsupported inference from something's representational or intentional characteristics, such as its content, to what it is like in reality.[97] He gives this example: we cannot infer from "Bob is thinking about red cars" that Bob's thoughts are red. Another way Pasnau offers of stating the same objection is to say that Aquinas shifts illicitly between two senses of abstraction: abstraction in the sense of focusing our attention in such a way as to remove particularizing content representing designated matter from our intellectual concepts, and abstraction in the sense of removing intelligible *species* from matter altogether, ontologically speaking.[98] Why should the former require the

---

commentators have overlooked. Nevertheless, it also seems to me that selective attention remains another part of Aquinas's overall theory of abstraction, and part of what he means when he speaks of cognizing things "universally" or "in their natures absolutely" is "cognizing them *without* cognizing their individualizing features."

96. Novak, "Aquinas and the Incorruptibility of Soul," *History of Philosophy Quarterly* 4, no. 4 (1987): 405–21.

97. Robert Pasnau, "Aquinas and the Content Fallacy," *The Modern Schoolman* 75, no. 4 (1998): 293–314.

98. Pasnau writes: "it seems to me that [Aquinas] has fallen victim to an ambiguity in the phrase 'abstracting from the conditions of individual matter.' That phrase might mean that the agent intellect produces an entity that is immaterial rather than material by stripping away the corporeal aspects of the phantasm. Or the phrase might mean that the agent intellect changes the representational content of the phantasm, makes it so that the newly formed intelligible species no longer represents 'the conditions of individual matter.' ... It seems clear that [Aquinas] describes two different kinds of abstraction without explaining how they are linked" (*Aquinas on Human Nature*, 316).

latter? To be sure, if Aquinas can provide some good reason for thinking that the immateriality of an intellectual operation's content requires that the intellectual power itself has an immaterial act of being, then he is not guilty of any fallacy after all. The objection that Novak and Pasnau pose, in a nutshell, is that Aquinas offers no such reason, nor is he in a position to offer one.

Pasnau thinks that the Content Fallacy is rife throughout Aquinas's thought, but considers this to be surprising, given that at certain points Thomas appears to recognize it precisely as a fallacy. As an example, Pasnau notes a passage in which Aquinas explains how, despite his immateriality, God is able to cognize singulars:

(5.10) A thing is cognized insofar as it is represented in the cognizer, not insofar as it exists in the cognizer; for a similitude existing in a cognitive power is the principle of the cognition of a thing not according to the act of being it has in the cognitive power, but according to the relation it has to the thing cognized. So it is not according to the way a thing's likeness has its act of being in the intellect that the thing is cognized, but rather according to the way the thing's similitude existing in the intellect is representative of the thing. And therefore even though a similitude in the divine intellect has an immaterial act of being, nevertheless, because it is the similitude of a material thing, it is also the principle of cognizing material things, and thus of singular things too.[99]

Aquinas appears here to be explicitly attempting to rule out any direct connection between the intrinsic characteristics of a cognitive power—in this case, the immaterial act of being of the divine intellect—and the mode in which that power is able to cognize or represent its objects. Even though the divine intellect is immaterial, Aquinas is saying, it can cognize material things in a singular way as the objects of its cognitive acts. In contrast, the objection Aquinas is responding to in 5.10 looks quite a lot like MA: "nothing is cognized except in whatever way it exists in the cognizer... but things exist in God immaterially... so [God] does not cognize things that depend on matter, as singular things do."[100] The objection argues from God's immaterial nature to the non-individuality of his cognitive acs. So too does the reasoning in 5.8. MA itself runs in

---

99. QDV 2.5 ad 17 (Leo. 22.1:65.440–55), quoted in Pasnau, "Content Fallacy," 307.
100. QDV 2.5 arg. 17 (Leo. 22.1:61.166–72).

the opposite direction: from the universality of intellectual operations to the immateriality of the intellect. Yet in 5.10 Aquinas seems to say that any reasoning of this sort is flawed. Another passage that gives the same impression is from the *De ente*:

(5.11) A form is not universal insofar as it exists in the intellect, but rather insofar as it refers to things as their similitude, just as, also, if there were one corporeal statue representing many men, that image or *species* of the statue would still have a proper and singular act of being, since it would exist in this matter. It would, however, have the characteristic of community [*rationem communitatis*] insofar as it would represent many things in common.[101]

Aquinas is arguing here against the Averroist view that because the intellect cognizes in a universal way, there must be just one intellect—not many distinct intellects belonging to the many distinct humans there are. Aquinas says that Averroes's inference is no good, because an intellectual *species* "is not universal according as it exists in the intellect," but rather "insofar as it refers to things as their similitude." Here again Thomas appears to reject any direct link between the materiality or singularity of an item in terms of what it represents and the materiality or singularity of the same item in itself.[102] If a singular, material statue can nevertheless be directed toward or about many men, representing them in an absolute, non-individual way, then why could a singular, material intellectual act not do the same?[103]

---

101. DEE 3 (Leo. 43:375.110–19). Aquinas's acknowledgment of the statue's ability to represent many men shows that this is possible for corporeal objects to represent in a universal mode. Many of the words in this book accomplish the same feat. But these are examples of what John Haugeland calls "derivative intentionality": statues and written words depend for their semantic features on the original, nonderivative intentionality of intellectual states; see "The Intentionality All-Stars," in his *Having Thought: Essays in the Metaphysics of Mind* (Cambridge, Mass.: Harvard University Press, 1998), 129.

102. A further case where Aquinas appears to bar inferences from a cognitive power's intrinsic characteristics to the content of its cognitive operations appears when he is arguing against the Platonist position that our intellectual activities are not directed at bodies, but at subsistent universal Forms (for instance, in ST 1a.84.1). Plato inferred from the fact that intellect is incorporeal that its objects must be incorporeal as well. He was wrong about this. The intellect *is* incorporeal, Aquinas says, but it knows corporeal objects in an immaterial way.

103. Pasnau, "Content Fallacy," 305–6, claims that despite Aquinas's failure to notice these inconsistencies in his own thought, many of his contemporaries saw them. Pasnau cites passages from Matthew of Aquasparta, William of Ockham, and Peter John Olivi which he thinks show them identifying and criticizing the content fallacy. Two contexts where one frequently finds authors like these challenging arguments resembling MA are in disputes about

Many of Aquinas's commentators seem to overlook this question altogether. For example, E. Christian Brugger proposes a "reformulation" of MA that includes the following inference: because "the act by which a cognitive power receives information free from everything material must itself be free from everything material," and because "in the formulation of universalized concepts, the intellect receives information free from everything material," therefore "the act of concept formation ... is free from everything material."[104] The second of Brugger's premises here is unproblematic if it is construed simply to mean that acts of intellectual cognition leave out information about the designated matter of their objects. But the first premise seems questionable. Why should a cognitive power's ability to receive information that leaves out individuating features require that such operations themselves are immaterial, ontologically speaking? At one point Brugger writes: "we come now to the pivotal insight of Aquinas's argument. Just as an act receptive of information pertaining to the sensitive features of material things must

---

whether the intellect can cognize singulars and whether angels and human souls are composed of form and matter. For various reasons, many of Aquinas's contemporaries wanted to reject Thomas's view that intellectual cognition, properly speaking, always involves grasping its objects in a universal, non-individual way (see ST 1a.86.1 and QDV 10.5). Accordingly, they are critical of inferences (such as Aquinas sometimes employs) from the intellect's immaterial mode of being or operation to the universal, non-individual content of its cognitive acts; see Roger Marston, QDA 2, in *Quaestiones Disputatae* (ed. College of St. Bonaventure), 227–44, esp. 231–33. Similarly, universal hylomorphists wanted to reject Aquinas's conclusion that angels and human souls lack matter of any sort. Because Aquinas attempted to establish this conclusion based on MA, many of his contemporaries attacked it. See, for instance, Bonaventure, *In Sent* 2.17.1.2 obj. 4 and ad 4, in *Opera omnia* (ed. Collegium S. Bonaventurae), 2:413–15. The way they did so often involved calling attention to distinctions very like the one Pasnau draws between a cognitive act's intrinsic features versus its intentional features. Pasnau may be correct that Aquinas's contemporaries took him to be employing a fallacious line of argument. I think it is also possible, however, that it was because they disagreed with Aquinas in other fundamental ways that they took issue with MA. For instance, while universal hylomorphists like Bonaventure and Aquasparta denied that things possessing matter could engage in intellectual cognition (because angels and human souls do so), they presumably would have denied that anything possessing corporeal matter could do so. They would have agreed with Aquinas that intellectual cognition could not be explained in terms of bodily parts, states, and processes. What they disagreed with him about was whether this implied its immateriality. Ockham, for his part, disagreed with Aquinas fundamentally concerning universals and individuation, and presumably would have rejected MA because of its apparent commitment to common natures that all members of a given kind share.

104. E. Christian Brugger, "Aquinas on the Immateriality of Intellect: A Non-materialist Reply to Materialist Objections," *National Catholic Bioethics Quarterly* 8, no. 1 (2008): 103–19, at 113.

be an act that is materially instantiated, it follows that the act in which our intellect receives information free from everything material must be free from materiality."[105] But why does this follow? As far as I can tell, Brugger does not say.

It will not suffice to avoid the criticism that Novak and Pasnau lobby against MA simply to point out that the label "Content Fallacy" is not necessarily an apt description of their charge against him. O'Callaghan and Cory both point out that despite Aquinas's talk of "reception" in connection with cognition, Thomas does not actually think of the mind as a sort of container for thoughts, which themselves contain information about the world.[106] Rather, as Cory puts it, "[Aquinas] thinks of the mind as formally shaped according to the likeness (*species*) of the cognized object, and actualized by thinking about that object. Thus for Aquinas, one ought properly to say that 'the mind is assimilated to and engaged in thinking about some object,' rather than 'it has a thought with such-and-such content.'"[107]

Both O'Callaghan and Cory think this distinction between thought-content and thought-object makes a difference for how we understand Aquinas's argument. O'Callaghan writes: "Aquinas can only be charged with committing the Content Fallacy if he thinks that what is known or 'represented' is an immaterial universal. But he does not think that. He is clear that primarily and in the first instance what is known is the nature of material things *existing in* those material things, existing not as abstract immaterial universals, but as concrete material particular natures."[108] As 5.8 makes clear, O'Callaghan is right that Aquinas's anti-Platonism leads him to deny that there are any natures actually existing in abstraction from individuating matter. Accordingly, contrary to what some commentators on Aquinas seem to suppose, Thomas's point in MA is not that the intellect serves as a container for universal, immaterial entities, and thus must itself be immaterial.[109] Rather, Thomas thinks

---

105. Ibid., 115.
106. O'Callaghan, "Immaterial Soul and Its Discontents," 54–57; Cory, *Aquinas on Human Self-Knowledge*, 69–70.
107. Cory, *Aquinas on Human Self-Knowledge*, 70.
108. O'Callaghan, "Immaterial Soul and Its Discontents," 57.
109. David Oderberg presents in several places an argument for the intellect's immateriality that he calls "the storage problem," which is based (as he puts it) on an "*ontological*

it is our ability to think about natures in an absolute, non-individual way that proves its immateriality. As Cory notes, "the question whether Aquinas commits some fallacy" in arguments like MA "hinges on whether an intentional form's mode of representing can be controlled by its mode of existing."[110] Given this, Cory and O'Callaghan may well be correct that "the Content Fallacy" is misleading as a term for describing the objection that Novak, Pasnau, and others raise against MA.

Still, I think these critics make an important point. It seems no less objectionable to move without further ado from claims about the intellect's mode of cognizing certain objects—that is, an absolute mode—to claims about the intellect's ontological status than to move from claims about content to ontological status. Cory writes that on Aquinas's view, "if an intentional form is individuated by matter, then it must *represent individually*, that is, ... represent 'horse' in a determinate way as *this horse* or *that horse*."[111] I think she is quite correct that some such premise undergirds Aquinas's thought in MA. The question, however, is whether there is cogent reasoning supporting this premise, or whether it is something Aquinas simply assumes. If the latter is true, then it seems

---

mismatch between concepts and any putative material locus for them." See "Hylemorphic Dualism"; *Real Essentialism*, chap. 10, §5, and "Concepts, Dualism, and the Human Intellect," in *Psycho-Physical Dualism Today: An Interdisciplinary Approach*, ed. Alessandro Antonietti, Antonella Corradini, and E. J. Lowe (Lanham, Md.: Rowman and Littlefield, 2008), 211–33. The idea is that concepts are abstract and universal, whereas bodily parts, states, and processes are concrete and particular, and hence the latter could not serve as "storage facilities" for the former. To be fair, while Oderberg forwards this argument in defense of a "hylemorphic dualism" that he takes to be broadly Thomistic, it is not at all clear that he forwards this particular argument as an interpretation of MA, despite superficial similarities. Edward Feser, however, does think that MA relies on the assumption that no physical representation (such as a "neuronal firing pattern") could "count as" a universal, as it would be "just one particular material thing among others, and not universal at all" (*Aquinas: A Beginner's Guide*, 156). The trouble here is that Aquinas would say that intelligible *species* are particular too, despite their immateriality, and despite their universal mode of representation; see DEE 3 (Leo. 43.375.102–7): "although a nature that is understood has the notion of universality according as it is compared to things outside the soul, since it is the similitude of all of them, nevertheless according as it exists in this intellect or that it is a certain particular understood *species*." James Madden, likewise, thinks Aquinas's reasoning depends on universals as "constituents" of "rational intentionality"—see "Is a Thomistic Theory of Intentionality Consistent with Physicalism?," *American Catholic Philosophical Quarterly* 91, no. 1 (2017): 1–28, at 26. Again, this seems to assume that Thomas's reasoning involves the intellect somehow containing universals, as opposed to merely representing its objects in a universal way.

110. Cory, "Rethinking Abstractionism," 624n66.
111. Ibid., 624.

fair to charge Thomas with a fallacy of some sort, regardless of what we call it. Is there any reason for thinking that the former is true? Some commentators have provided explanations as to why the intellect's universal mode of representation requires its ontological immateriality. I will consider three.

First, Klima proposes a sophisticated "reconstruction" of MA much as Brugger does, which hinges on the following key premise: "Common, *per se sensibilia* can be represented as a result of the natural causality of the things having them only by the corresponding spatio-temporal properties of what represents them."[112] I noted above why Klima thinks that "common, *per se sensibilia*" are important here; it is because they include such individuating features as quantitative dimensions. Hence they must be left out of the intellect's cognitive operations such that they represent their objects in a universal mode, as opposed to an individual one. Klima needs his key premise to establish that the corporeality of a cognitive power entails that its operations include information about the quantitative dimensions of their objects, and hence represent them in an individual mode. That would entitle him to the contrapositive of this implication, namely that any cognitive operations that represent their objects in a non-individual way are incorporeal.

By way of defending his key claim, however, Klima's strategy is to point out the causal link between the common, *per se sensibilia* and the corresponding spatio-temporal features of the sense organs that receive and encode them. Klima rejects Burnyeat's "spiritualist" interpretation of Aquinas's theory of sense cognition (discussed in chapter 4), writing that "what encodes spatio-temporal features in the senses is precisely some corresponding spatio-temporal features of the sense organs. For example, the spatial arrangement of distinct patches of colour in my visual field is encoded by the spatial pattern of neurons firing in the retina of my eyes, and similar considerations apply to the other senses."[113] Because sense cognition works this way, Klima thinks, any cognition that involves spatio-temporally located changes taking place in bodily organs must also involve the encoding of information about the spatio-temporal features of its objects. He explains as follows:

112. Klima, "Aquinas on the Materiality," 177.
113. Ibid., 175.

If the external senses receive distinctive, singular information about the individuating spatio-temporal conditions of their objects precisely on account of receiving the causal impact of these objects through their own spatio-temporal features, then this seems to establish the implication that the materiality of a cognitive power entails the singularity of its cognitive act. For if sensory representation is singular precisely because it represents its object in a material fashion, encoding the distinctive, singular information about the object by its own material features, then this means that sensory representation is singular because it is material, i.e., its materiality implies its singularity.[114]

What seems questionable is the last part of this explanation. Suppose Klima is correct (and Burnyeat wrong) that Aquinas took sense cognition to involve some sort of physiological process. In that case it is reasonable to say that sense cognition is singular because it represents by means of this physiological process. That is, the physiological process somehow explains the singularity of the sense power's cognitive operation. It seems unreasonable, however, to take this causal or explanatory link as grounds for the entailment that Klima's premise needs to establish, namely that *if* a given cognitive power is corporeal, *then* it represents its objects in a singular way. In general, we cannot infer from the truth of "A because of B" that "if B then A" is also true. For instance, we cannot infer from "there was lightning because there were clouds" to "if there were clouds then there was lightning." Similarly we cannot infer from the fact that sense cognition is singular *because* it involves some corporeal process (such as retinal firing, in the case of visual cognition), that *any* cognition taking place by means of such a process must be singular. I take it that most nowadays would agree with the former claim but disagree with the latter, insisting instead that it is perfectly possible for cognitive acts taking place by means of a corporeal process, such as brain activity, to grasp their objects in precisely the absolute, non-individual way that Aquinas thinks is characteristic of intellectual acts.[115]

Klima is aware of Pasnau's charge that Aquinas commits a content

---

114. Ibid., 179.
115. One recent example of an attempt to do so is Paul Churchland's *Plato's Camera: How the Physical Brain Captures a Landscape of Abstract Universals* (Cambridge, Mass.: MIT Press, 2012).

fallacy in MA, but thinks his reconstruction is immune to any such criticism. He writes:

> It may seem an altogether plausible assumption that it is a natural necessity that any encodings generated in [a] natural process of receiving, storing, and further manipulating sensory information, as long as they have their own spatio-temporal features, will thereby encode information about the individuality of their objects, and so, in order to extract their purely universal content, the abstractive intellect ... has to strip them precisely of these material conditions; but this is all the argument assumes.[116]

He then states that in his view "this is all that is needed to address Robert Pasnau's concerns about Aquinas's apparent conflating of two radically different senses in which ... the abstractive agent intellect operates on phantasms."[117] I have a difficult time agreeing. Instead, I think, Pasnau might retort that Klima's "altogether plausible assumption" is a dubious assumption in urgent need of defense. Hence, Klima's explanation why a corporeal intellect could only cognize in an individual way seems unlikely to convince.

Also unconvincing is a second response to Pasnau's "content fallacy" on Aquinas's behalf, this one by John Haldane.[118] Haldane's proposal is that instead of "distinguishing representations as vehicles of content from representational content as such," Thomas means to identify "sensory acts with their sensuous contents," and likewise identify "intellectual acts with their conceptual contents," treating both types of cognitive acts as "pure *Vorstellungen* or cognitive presentations." On the account he is putting forward, Haldane writes, "the presentation of a material particular as content is identical with the occurrence of a material particular, a state of the sensory system of the subject. Similarly, the presentation of an abstract universal, being immaterial in content, is

---

116. Klima, "Aquinas on the Materiality," 178.
117. Ibid., 178n18. See Klima, "Universality and Immateriality," 40–41: "[Thomas] is not committed to any sort of 'content fallacy,' i.e., the blunder of inferring metaphysical features from representational features. He is merely claiming ... that any material transcoding of the originally received information about the proper *sensibilia* in the material sensory organs will also preserve, by virtue of its materiality, the same distinctive singular information that was encoded by the material features of these organs in the first place. Thus the materiality of natural, cognitive representation does entail its singularity by natural necessity, and so, the universality of mental representation should entail its immateriality by the same necessity."
118. Haldane, "Metaphysics of Intellect(ion)," 52–54.

thereby immaterial in substance." By means of such a strategy Haldane thinks that Aquinas can avoid the content fallacy. It seems quite plain, however, that the strategy accomplishes nothing of the sort. Haldane is right that if Aquinas unintentionally moves without further ado from the properties of the contents of intellectual acts to their properties as vehicles of such content, as Pasnau believes, then his argument is sunk. But it would not do Aquinas any good if, instead of making such a move unintentionally, he did so on purpose.[119] How could it be the case that the properties of intellectual acts *qua* their content are identical to their properties *qua* content bearers? Is my thought about a trout identical to a trout because that is its content? Is my mind a trout? Surely not.

A third, more plausible proposal on Aquinas's behalf is Cory's suggestion that what Thomas says about corporeal powers as "particular agents" as opposed to "universal agents" might provide the link that MA requires between the intellect's ontological status and its mode of representation.[120] In various passages, Cory notes, Aquinas claims that a form's contraction by designated matter limits the scope of its activity to a particular location.[121] In other passages, however, Thomas claims that the intellect's cognitive activity takes place by means of the forms or intelligible *species* that it has in its possession. Putting these claims together, Cory reckons, it becomes clear that only an incorporeal cognitive power can act in such a way as to represent its objects in a universal way. This is a plausible proposal insofar as it stems directly from claims that Aquinas certainly does subscribe to. Yet if it does indeed accurately depict the reasoning underlying MA in its entirety, then I think Thomas's argument is still in trouble. The problem is that while it seems plausible that corporeal agents are limited in certain respects with regard to what they can accomplish, it is not clear why corporeality should limit cognitive powers to a singular mode of representation. It is true that a hand, because it is corporeal, can only grasp an object of a certain limited size at a particular time and location. Thinking involves "grasping" objects too. But why suppose that the peculiarly cognitive way our intellectual

---

119. O'Callaghan, "Immaterial Soul and Its Discontents," 49, makes this same point.
120. Cory, "Rethinking Abstractionism," 624 and n65.
121. She cites ST 1a.115.1, but Aquinas makes the same point elsewhere, for instance in QDP 3.7.

operations grasp their objects is similarly limited? I am not sure that the passages Cory cites offer any clear answer.

Aquinas's statue example seems like a case of a perfectly corporeal object that nevertheless manages to represent in a universal way. Of course, a statue is just an artifact, and arguably whatever representative abilities it has are derivative upon the interpretative abilities of cognizers. John Buridan, however, though he seems largely to agree with Aquinas about what it means for cognitive operations to represent objects in a singular or universal mode, denies that corporeal operations are constrained to representing in a singular way. A horse has no immaterial powers or operations. Yet a thirsty horse, Buridan points out, wants simply water in general, not this or that particular water.[122] If a horse can desire water in general, however, it must be capable of cognizing water in general. So the corporeality of a cognizer is consistent with the universal mode of its operations after all.

Thus far, I have surveyed efforts by Klima, Haldane, and Cory to establish a connection between the incorporeality of intellectual operations and their universal mode of representation, none of which seemed to achieve this aim. In the following section I will propose a further reading of MA that, while somewhat adventurous, may nevertheless fulfill both desiderata for a viable interpretation of Thomas's argument.

The Argument from the Mode of Intellectual Cognition II: What Might Work

In a nutshell, my suggestion is that when Aquinas argues from the "absolute" or "universal" mode of the intellect's operations to its ontological immateriality, he has in mind not so much the fact that intellectual operations leave out the individuating features of their objects (though this is true) as the fact that they cognize objects as members of kinds at all. The universal mode of cognition at work in MA is the intellect's ability to cognize an object as an X as opposed to a Y (or whatever else). No cognition that can be explained in terms of coordination between bodily parts, states, and processes (together with efficient causal inputs

---

122. Buridan, QDA 3.3, in Zupko, *John Buridan's Philosophy of Mind*, 25. See for discussion Olaf Pluta, "John Buridan on Universal Knowledge," *Bochumer Philosophisches Jahrbuch für Antike und Mittelalter* 7, no. 1 (2002): 25–46.

and teleological outputs), is determinate, in this way, with regard to its mode of representation. Rather, the singular mode in which corporeal cognizers represent their objects is indeterminate with regard to what kind of thing they are—compatible with their objects being either Xs or Ys. Hence intellectual operations cannot be explained in corporeal terms, and have their acts of being in an immaterial mode. I am not the first to make this suggestion. Elizabeth Anscombe, Thomas Nagel, and James Ross all put forward versions of the argument from the intellect's ability to represent objects determinately as members of kinds to their immateriality.[123] Edward Feser suggests that there is at least a family resemblance between Ross's argument and MA.[124] He stops short, however, of proposing that something like Ross's reasoning might be at work in Aquinas's various presentations of MA. In this section I will offer evidence for thinking that this may well be the case. I will begin by further fleshing out the argument as it appears in Anscombe, Nagel, Ross, and others. I will then provide two related strands of textual evidence for thinking that Aquinas endorsed something like it. Finally, I will consider some objections both against the argument itself, and against the suggestion that it reflects assumptions underlying Aquinas's MA.

When my son began to collect words, right around the time he turned one, he would point his finger and holler "za!" I took this to mean "what's that?" He seemed satisfied, at any rate, if I told him the names of three or four things in the region toward which he seemed to be pointing. What was impossible to know, at that stage, was what had actually caught his eye such that he wanted to be told its name. Was he pointing at the chair, the lamp behind it, or the wall behind that? His gesture alone left it impossible to say. Ludwig Wittgenstein brings up this very issue in the *Philosophical Investigations*: "Point to a piece of paper. And now point to its shape—now to its color—now to its number (that sounds queer).—How did you do it?—You will say that you 'meant' a dif-

---

123. G. E. M. Anscombe, "Analytic Philosophy and the Spirituality of Man," in *Human Life, Action and Ethics*, ed. Mary Geach and Luke Gormally (Exeter: Imprint Academic, 2005), 3–16; Thomas Nagel, *The Last Word* (Oxford: Oxford University Press, 2001); James Ross, "Immaterial Aspects of Thought," *Journal of Philosophy* 89, no. 3 (1992): 136–50, and *Thought and World: The Hidden Necessities* (Notre Dame, Ind.: University of Notre Dame Press, 2008).

124. Edward Feser, "Kripke, Ross and the Immaterial Aspects of Thought," *American Catholic Philosophical Quarterly* 87, no. 1 (2013): 1–32.

ferent thing each time you pointed. And if I ask how that is done, you will say you concentrated your attention on the color, the shape, etc. But I ask again: how is that done?"[125] Commenting on this passage, Wittgenstein's student Elizabeth Anscombe remarks: "That a physical act is an act of pointing *at all* is not a physical characterization of it. Suppose you find a bit of straight stick. It is in a certain position and therefore pointing in a certain direction. Or rather, it is pointing in two directions, and in itself is not pointing as a man points at all."[126] Both seem to be suggesting that physical acts of pointing, qua physical, are not directed at any object in particular. They are directed at *this* as opposed to *that* only by some additional mental ingredient. Neither thinks that this fact licenses us to believe in minds or souls as spiritual substances capable of existing apart from bodies. But they do appear to think that something about the intentionality of acts like pointing cannot be explained in bodily terms.

What exactly? Above I put it in terms of representing an object as a member of a kind: as an X as opposed to a Y (or whatever else). It might sound like Wittgenstein and Anscombe have something else in mind. Must representing *this* object as opposed to *that* one involve representing an object as a member of a kind? Yes, I take it. Certainly we might be in doubt about which individual member of a kind a gesture like pointing is directed towards (i.e., this X or that other X) as opposed to what kind of thing the gesture is pointing out (i.e., the X or the Y). But such doubt presupposes the ability to cognize things as members of kinds in the first place. Henceforth I will call the determinacy with respect to the intentional object of acts like pointing or cognizing that Wittgenstein and Anscombe are concerned with "intentional determinacy."

Nagel and Ross also focus on intentional determinacy as they argue, in similar ways, that the intentionality of human thought cannot be accounted for in naturalistic or physical terms. Nagel claims that "intentionality cannot be naturalistically analyzed ... nor can it be given naturalistically sufficient conditions."[127] And Ross holds that while "[brute] animal cognition and desire from the appetite of a clam to the

---

125. Wittgenstein, *Philosophical Investigations*, 1.33 (14).
126. Anscombe, "Analytic Philosophy and the Spirituality of Man," 10–11.
127. Nagel, *The Last Word*, 42.

vision of vultures is thought to have neurobiological explanations that result from, and are perhaps theoretically reducible to, physical processes," still "one cannot explain certain truth-carrying thoughts as reductively physical ... because they require features no physical thing or process could have at all."[128] The chief "feature" that Ross has in mind, and Nagel likewise, is intentional determinacy: being directed at *this* object as opposed to *that* one. Both bring up the "plus/quus" example Kripke introduced in his discussion of Wittgenstein on rule-following to illustrate their point.[129] Nagel's argument is that "my meaning a particular mathematical function by an expression—meaning addition by 'plus,' for instance—cannot consist in any fact about my behavior, my state of mind, or my brain, since any such fact would have to be finite ... and therefore could not have the infinite normative implications of the mathematical function."[130] Ross argues similarly:

> Just as rectangular doors can approximate Euclidean rectangularity, so physical change can simulate, but not realize, pure functions. In simplest terms, that is because physical phenomena are never under a single quantitative relationship. There are no physical features by which an adding machine ... can exclude its satisfying a function incompatible with addition, say "quaddition" ... modified so that the differentiating outputs ... lie beyond the lifetime of the machine. The consequence is that a physical process is really indeterminate among incompossible pure functions.[131]

In other words, Ross is claiming, how and why an intellectual act counts as an instance of addition or *modus ponens*, as opposed to quaddition or *modus tollens*, cannot possibly be explained by any of its physical or corporeal features. He cites other "jewels of analytic philosophy" in support of this conclusion as well: for instance, the *gavagai* example Quine uses to argue for ontological indeterminacy.[132] Both Quine and "Kripken-

---

128. Ross, Thought and World, 116.
129. Saul Kripke, *Wittgenstein on Rules and Private Language* (Cambridge, Mass.: Harvard University Press, 1982). I am not suggesting that this is the use to which Kripke himself puts his plus/quus doubts, which are considerably more complex than my treatment indicates, designed to undermine the possibility of you or I determining whether we meant plus or quus in cases when we thought we were adding.
130. Nagel, *The Last Word*, 43.
131. Ross, "Immaterial Aspects," 141–42.
132. Ibid., 137 and 140; W. V. O. Quine, *Word and Object* (Cambridge, Mass.: MIT Press, 1960), chap. 2.

stein," of course, wield their reasoning to arrive at skeptical conclusions. But Ross and Nagel think arguing for semantic skepticism is self-undermining: the words and inference-patterns one deploys in arguing for something must themselves be intentionally determinate or one argues to no avail. We should instead draw a different moral from Quine's and Kripke's arguments, namely that because intentional determinacy cannot be explained physically or corporeally, the intellectual operations which exhibit it are themselves nonphysical and incorporeal.

Feser has recently defended Ross's reasoning, which he understands to run as follows: "material processes cannot be determinate ... but at least some thought processes are determinate, therefore, such thought processes are immaterial."[133] By "determinate" here Feser means intentionally determinate, that is, about or directed at this object rather than that. He thinks determinacy of this sort cannot possibly be explained by an appeal to material processes. Feser claims that Ross's argument is immune to the criticism we saw Pasnau bring against MA, and it appears that he is correct to do so.[134] It seemed problematic for Aquinas to move without further ado from the fact that intellectual operations cognize their objects in such a way as to leave out their individuating, material features to the ontological immateriality of these operations. The problem was that there is no obvious reason why a perfectly material cognizer could not represent its objects in a non-individual way. If Feser, Nagel, and Ross are correct, however, there are obvious reasons why no material process could be determinate with respect to its intentional object. Of course, there are also obvious objections one might raise against their reasoning. I brought up Dretske and Millikan's teleosemantic theory of mental content in the previous chapter. I will consider below whether their theory or some other might be capable of "naturalizing" intentional determinacy. First, however, what reasons are there for supposing that Aquinas had anything like Feser, Nagel, and Ross's argument in mind by MA?

There are at least two. First, Aquinas thinks that the physical world qua material is ontologically indeterminate. Forms, natures, or essences are what lend it determinacy. This ontological indeterminacy would

133. Feser, "Kripke, Ross and the Immaterial Aspects of Thought," 18.
134. Ibid., 18–21.

translate to intentional indeterminacy in purely corporeal cognizers. Hence, when Aquinas claims in MA that the intellect cognizes "a thing in its nature absolutely" or cognizes "universals," it is plausible to suppose that he means that the intellect cognizes things in an intentionally determinate way, while denying that any corporeal account could explain how it does so. Second, various claims that Aquinas makes about the content of purely corporeal cognition—that is, cognition in nonhuman animals—suggest that it is indeed intentionally indeterminate. To be sure, Aquinas holds that there are forms present in an intentional or spiritual way in purely corporeal cognizers, just as there are in cognitive media. To that extent, Aquinas disagrees with Brentano that intentionality is the mark of the mental. Yet there is evidence that the sort of intentionality present in anything lacking an intellect is indeterminate with respect to its objects. Again, this is because Thomas does not think that intentional determinacy can be explained in corporeal terms. I will present some textual evidence in support of these two interpretative arguments in turn.

In support of the first argument, consider first the way Aquinas describes "matter in itself" or prime matter as pure potency. Apart from form, matter is ontologically indeterminate; it is not this thing or that one. We are able to think of it as a certain thing only by a kind of analogical reasoning: "what is related to natural substances the way bronze is related to the statue, and wood to the bed, and anything material and unformed is related to form, this we call prime matter."[135] Matter in itself "is not one in the way a 'this something' [*hoc aliquid*] is [one], that is, as some determinate individual," but rather "is one insofar as it is in potency to a form."[136] I take these claims of Aquinas's to mean that while matter does indeed play a limiting or determining role insofar as it individuates forms, it is nonetheless indeterminate in and of itself. Anything corporeal inherits this indeterminacy as far as its matter is concerned. As Thomas puts it at one point: "in sensible things there is much of the nature of the infinite or indeterminate, since they have matter, which is not determined in itself to one [form], but is in potency to many forms."[137] A further set of texts to consider are those in which

---

135. In Phys 1.13.9/118 (Leo. 2:46).
136. Ibid.
137. In Met 4.12.681 (Marietti 188).

Aquinas positions his position between those of the pre-Socratic naturalists and Plato when it comes to our ability to understand the material world. Here is a representative passage:

(5.12) The first philosophers who inquired into the nature of things thought there was nothing in the world except the body, and since they saw that all bodies are in motion, and thought they were in continuous flux, they supposed that no one could have certitude about the truth of things.... Following these, however, Plato, that he might rescue our certain cognition of the truth through the intellect, posited beyond these bodies another genus of beings separated from matter and motion, which he named "species" or "ideas," through participation in which each singular and sensible thing is called "man" or "horse" or something of this sort.... But this is not necessary.... The intellect receives *species* of bodies that are material and mobile immaterially and without motion, according to its own mode, for what is received is in the recipient through the mode of the recipient. Thus it must be said that the soul through the intellect cognizes bodies by an immaterial, universal and necessary cognition.[138]

As I understand him, Aquinas agrees with Plato and the pre-Socratics alike that bodies are in flux and indeterminate as far as their matter is concerned. On the other hand, he rejects the pre-Socratic view that there is no "certitude about the truth of things," or, as he puts it elsewhere, that "whatever appears in whatever way to anyone is true." He agrees with Plato that the way to avoid pre-Socratic skepticism has to do with the stability imparted to the sensible world by forms or natures. He disagrees, of course, that these entities exist in some separate realm. Instead, he says, we must be able to receive these forms or natures "immaterially and without motion" in the intellect, so as to cognize bodies with an "immaterial, universal and necessary cognition."

Putting together what Aquinas says about the indeterminacy of matter in itself and the correct way of avoiding skepticism about our cognition of the material world, a story emerges about why Thomas thinks the human intellect must lack matter. My discussion of MA so far has left it unclear why the intellect must be immaterial, ontologically speaking, so as to represent forms without representing the individuating character-

---

138. ST 1a.84.1 (Leo. 5:313–14); see QDSC 10 ad 8, In DA 1.3.39 and 1.5.60, In DT 5.2.

istics stemming from their matter. It seems clear enough, though, that what is indeterminate (neither this nor that) in and of itself cannot represent anything in a determinate fashion (as this or that). Any account of the intellect's operations in corporeal terms would, however, inherit the sort of ontological indeterminacy Aquinas associates with matter. It would thus be unable to explain how the intellect represents this form or nature as opposed to that other one. In order to represent the stable, formal features of the physical world, then, the intellect must itself be immaterial. As I read the argument in 5.7, what Thomas thinks a corporeal intellect could not do is not so much a matter of leaving certain features out of its representations as of representing forms or natures at all. It is true that thinking about things in terms of their forms or natures requires leaving out of our consideration the individuating characteristics stemming from their matter. But the important point is that the intellect's ability to represent this or that object in an intentionally determinate fashion at all could not be explained by appeal to bodily parts, states, or processes.

Turning to the second interpretative argument I mentioned above, my claim was that there is evidence Aquinas thought the content of nonhuman animal cognition exhibits the sort of intentional indeterminacy that Ross, Nagel, and Feser believe must be found in anything explicable in corporeal terms. There is also evidence that Thomas ties the lack of intentional determinacy in nonhuman animal cognition to their corporeality and their singular mode of representation.

We have seen much of this evidence already. In passages 4.11–4.14 Aquinas makes a series of claims about why non-human animals cognize. They do so: "not for the sake of cognition itself, but because of the need to act" (4.11)," to "avoid what is harmful to them, and seek those things that are necessary for the body's sustenance" (4.12), "according as they obtain food or sexual satisfaction through sense cognition" (4.13), and "that they might pursue suitable food and avoid whatever is bad and harmful" (4.14). In addition to these passages, I also mentioned in chapter 4 various texts in which Aquinas makes claims like the following about nonhuman animal communication:

(5.13) While certain other animals make utterances [habeant vocem] only man of all animals has speech. For although certain animals produce human speech, nevertheless they do not actually speak since they do not understand what they are saying, but rather produce such utterances out of habit. There is, moreover, a difference between speech and mere utterance, for an utterance is a sign of pain or pleasure, and results from other passions like anger or fear which are all ordered toward pleasure or pain, . . . and thus other animals whom nature has brought to an awareness of their pleasures and pains signify these to one another through certain natural utterances, like the lion by its roar and the dog by barking, in the place of which we use interjections. Human speech, however, signifies what is useful and what is harmful, from which it follows that it signifies what is just and unjust. . . . And thus speech is proper to humans, since it is proper to them in comparison with other animals that they cognize the good and the bad, and likewise the unjust and other things of this sort, which they can signify in speech.[139]

Elsewhere Aquinas says that the good and bad for speculative reason is the true and false.[140] So while he does not explicitly say so in 5.13, I think we can assume that he does not think that nonhuman utterances express truth or falsehood any more than they do justice or injustice. I mentioned in chapter 4 as well Aquinas's denial in certain passages that nonhuman animals lack beliefs or opinions capable of truth or falsehood.[141] He is willing to say that the senses cognize truth and falsehood insofar as they correctly apprehend sensible things, just as is the case with the intellect.[142] Yet in one such discussion he claims:

(5.14) In no way does a sense cognize [the truth], for although sight has a similitude of a visible object, nonetheless it does not cognize the relation between the object seen and what it apprehends about that object. . . . So truth can be in a sense . . . as it may be in any true thing, but not as something cognized in a cognizer, which is what the term "truth" implies, for the perfection of the intellect is truth as cognized. And therefore, properly speaking, truth exists in the intellect composing and dividing, and not in the sense.[143]

---

139. In Pol 1.36–37 (Leo. 48:A78–79.120–46). See also the passages cited in note 87 of chapter 4.
140. See In NE 6.2.1130 and In DA 3.12.780.
141. See, for example, the passages cited in note 104 of chapter 4. Another passage affirming this view concerning nonhuman animal cognition is In Sent 1.19.5.3 ad 3 (Mand./Moos 1:496), where Aquinas claims that "if neither the [human] soul nor any created intellect existed, truth, insofar as it consists in an operation of the soul, would not exist."
142. See QDV 1.7 and 1.9.
143. ST 1a.16.2 (Leo. 4:208). I am omitting Aquinas's additional claim that the intellect

Because the senses are unable to know whether they have apprehended sensible things correctly or incorrectly, Thomas tells us here, they cannot be true or false "properly speaking." Putting together what Aquinas says in some of the passages we have seen so far, then, he thinks that the content of nonhuman animal cognition has to do with actions undertaken for the sake of survival or reproduction, and that it is not properly speaking true or false.

Elsewhere Thomas makes a related point with regard to the way that nonhuman animals are able to cognize the ends at which their actions aim:

(5.15) Cognition of the end is twofold, perfect and imperfect. Perfect cognition is that by which not only is some end and good cognized, but the universal notion of end and good [is cognized as well], and such cognition belongs only to rational nature. But imperfect cognition is that by which the end and good is cognized in a particular way, and such cognition is [present] in brute animals.[144]

Part of what Thomas is claiming in passage 5.15, as with 5.13 and 5.14, presumably has to do with the inability of corporeal entities to reflect upon themselves that I discussed earlier in this chapter. In addition, however, he ties the inability of nonhuman animals to cognize their ends "perfectly" to the particular mode of their cognitive operations. I think it likely that he would tie the inability of the sense to cognize in a way that is "properly speaking" true or false to the particular mode of their cognition as well.

At least, such seems to be his view in 4.15, which I think provides a helpful gloss on how many of the other texts that I have just cited fit together. Aquinas claims in 4.15 that because the estimative power of nonhuman animals apprehends just "individual intentions," it cognizes a given object only "as the goal or principle of some action or passion." In contrast, because the human cogitative power is "conjoined to intellect" it "apprehends an individual as existing under a common nature

---

itself is not "properly speaking" true or false either insofar as it simply knows "what a thing is," i.e., grasps a nature or essence without making any further judgments about it. See In DA 3.11 for an extensive discussion of the three "operations of the intellect." Aquinas also claims, however, that the senses do not strictly speaking make judgments either at In DA 3.12.772.

144. ST 1a2ae.11.2 (Leo. 6:91); see also ST 1a2ae.6.2 and 35.2.

which contains it." Accordingly, Thomas says, while we are able to grasp objects as this X or that Y, nonhuman animals cognize objects only as thing-to-be-suckled, thing-to-be-eaten, etc. I think the point Thomas is making here is even more radical than his words might suggest. A thing-to-be-eaten is still a thing of a certain kind: an X as opposed to a Y. I take it, however, that by saying that nonhuman animals do not cognize objects as existing under common natures, Aquinas wants to deny that this is actually how they grasp their objects at all. We might put his point as follows: instead of cognizing the world in the indicative mood—"this is my food," "this other thing is my offspring," "that is a predator," etc.—nonhuman animal cognition is a series of imperatives, such as "eat!" or "suckle!" or "flee!" Aquinas frequently attributes judgments to nonhuman animals like sheep and wolves; for example: "certain things ... have a judgment that is determined by nature to one [thing], like irrational animals, for by natural estimation the sheep judges that the wolf is harmful to it, and because of this judgment it flees, and similarly in other cases."[145] A sheep that judges "the wolf is harmful to me" would appear to be entertaining a belief or opinion that apprehends an individual as existing under the common natures "wolf" and "harmful thing." If, however, Aquinas thinks that sheep do not really have beliefs or opinions, make judgments that are properly speaking true or false, or apprehend individuals as Xs or Ys, then perhaps judging that the wolf is harmful is merely a convenient way of speaking about what the sheep is really thinking, namely "run!" Which, of course, is what Aquinas says the sheep is "determined by nature" to do as a result of its judgment. In other words, if the interpretation of 4.15 that I have suggested is correct, it would explain both why he thinks that the nonhuman animal cognition is geared toward action, as well as why nonhumans lack beliefs or opinions that could be true or false "properly speaking," cognize their ends "imperfectly," and so forth.

Importantly for my purposes, it also supports a reading of MA in terms of intentional determinacy. Aquinas denies in 5.7 that a cognizer composed of matter and form could grasp "a thing in its nature absolutely," that is, cognize "a stone insofar as it is stone." This sounds very much like his denial in 4.15 that a corporeal cognitive faculty, such as

145. SCG 2.48.6 (Leo. 13:379).

the estimative power of nonhuman animal, can grasp "an individual as existing under a common nature which contains it," that is, grasp "this man" or "this stone." But the contrast between human and nonhuman cognition that Aquinas draws in 4.15 is clearly not just between cognition that leaves out the individuating features of its objects versus cognition that includes them. Instead, it is between cognition that is intentionally determinate—directed at this X or that Y—versus cognition that lacks this feature, and is instead geared simply toward action.

Anscombe writes at one point that "the immateriality of the soul consists at bottom in the fact that you cannot specify a material character or configuration which is equivalent to truth."[146] If she means by this that our ability to cognize objects in an intentionally determinate way, so as to form genuinely true and false beliefs, cannot be explained in terms of corporeal terms, then I think Aquinas agrees. Indeed, this is the main point he is trying to make in MA: no account given in terms of coordination between bodily parts, states, and processes, together with efficient causal inputs and teleological outputs, can adequately explain the intellect's ability to represent its objects as members of kinds. It is true that cognizing "a thing in its nature absolutely" or cognizing "universals" is partly a matter of cognizing forms while leaving out the individuating features stemming from their designated matter. It is also, however, a matter of cognizing things as members of kinds, as opposed to cognizing them simply as the "goal or principle" of some activity. On my understanding, Aquinas thinks the latter sort of cognition can be explained adequately in the teleofunctional or teleosemantic way I described in the third section of chapter 4. This sort of account cannot, however, adequately explain the operations of the intellect.

An objection someone might raise against my interpretation stems from Aquinas's frequent claims that cognitive operations with a universal mode in fact represent their objects in a "confused," "indistinct," or "indeterminate" way. Commenting on Aristotle's claim at the beginning of the *Physics* that "we must advance from universals to particulars," for example, Aquinas writes:

---

146. Anscombe, "Analytic Philosophy and the Spirituality of Man," 15.

(5.16) It is innate in us to proceed from cognizing those things that are better known to us toward cognizing those things that are better known to nature. But what are better known to us are things known confusedly, such as universals. So it is necessary that we proceed from universals toward singulars.[147]

This might give the appearance that Thomas thinks that the universal mode of universal cognition renders it, in fact, intentionally indeterminate in comparison with singular cognition, whereas my interpretation takes the opposite to be the case. In fact, however, Aquinas quickly explains that the "singular cognition" at issue in 5.16 is actually cognition of species as opposed to genera. To cognize something in a more universal way in terms of its genus is indeed to cognize it confusedly; "confused" here means "in potency," and genera "contain in themselves their species in potency." It turns out, then, that the "confused" cognition Aquinas is discussing in 5.16 is still intentionally determinate in the sense I specified above. If I cognize something I see out of the corner of my eye simply as a large animal, as opposed to a donkey, I am cognizing it confusedly, in the sense that 5.16 involves. Still, I am cognizing it in an intentionally determinate way as a member of the kinds "large" and "animal." Similar comments would apply to many other passages in which Aquinas calls universal cognition confused or indistinct.

Another way in which the intellectual cognition we enjoy in this life is indeterminate, on Aquinas's account, is insofar as it is directly able only to represent individuals as members of kinds, as opposed to representing them determinately as this or that individual.[148] This is due to the fact that our intellectual activities at present always involve abstraction. Of course, we are capable of cognizing individuals intellectually as well, and Aquinas claims that this happens "indirectly, and as it were by a sort of reflection."[149] I will not add to the lengthy literature on this somewhat notorious claim here. Suffice it to say, for my purposes, that even if direct intellectual cognition is indeterminate at the individual level, requiring a "conversion to the phantasms" to represent individuals as individuals, it is still intentionally determinate in the sense that concerns me, insofar as it represents its objects as members of kinds.

147. In Phys 1.1.6 (Leo. 2:5).
148. See ST 1a.86.1 and QDV 10.5.
149. ST 1a.86.1 (Leo. 5:347).

No passages I know of in which Aquinas refers to intellectual cognition as confused, indistinct, or indeterminate pose a challenge to its determinacy in the sense required by my interpretation of MA. Doubtless there are other ways of challenging the interpretation I have offered as an accurate representation of Aquinas's views. I am going to conclude this chapter, however, by commenting briefly on whether MA as I have construed it fulfills the other objective any successful interpretation of Aquinas's arguments for the intellect's immateriality must, that is, whether it succeeds as an argument.

The view that the intentional determinacy of intellectual cognition cannot be explained in terms of bodily parts, states, and processes, together with efficient causal inputs and teleological outputs, would surely find little favor among contemporary philosophers of mind. Explaining how brains enable organisms to "integrate information" is supposed to be one of the "easy" problems of consciousness.[150] It is something that can be "naturalized."

To be sure, recent scholarship is thoroughly divided on how it should be naturalized. Jerry Fodor criticizes the teleosemantic theory of mental content favored by Dretske and Millikan on precisely the grounds that it fails to eliminate intentional indeterminacy from cognitive operations.[151] Consider the oft-cited example of a frog sitting on a lilypad snapping at flies. On the story Dretske and Millikan tell, certain processes in the frog's central nervous system—its eyes and brain—have flies as their content because they were evolved to perform a certain teleological role in the frog's life, namely, producing the snapping behavior that supplies frogs with food. Fodor points out, however, that from the point of view of the frog's survival it does not much matter whether the content of the frog's visual operations consists of flies, frog food, rapidly moving little black things, or a host of other possibilities. All that matters is that the frog's acts of sense cognition, whatever they are about, trigger the appropriate snapping behavior. The moral of the story, Fodor writes, is that:

---

150. David Chalmers, *The Conscious Mind: In Search of a Fundamental Theory* (Oxford: Oxford University Press, 1997), xi–xii.

151. See note 74 of chapter 4.

Darwin doesn't care how you describe the intentional objects of frog snaps. All that matters for selection is how many flies the frog manages to ingest in consequence of its snapping, and this number comes out exactly the same whether one describes the function of snap-guidance mechanisms with respect to a world that is populated by flies that are, de facto, ambient black dots, or with respect to a world that is populated by ambient black dots that are, de facto, flies.[152]

Fodor calls this "the disjunction problem." I think Aquinas would criticize teleosemantic theories of mental content along similar lines. The information content of frog cognition is indeed indeterminate, as frog cognition only *has* content as geared toward some life-preserving task to be performed. Intellectual cognition, in contrast, cannot share this indeterminacy, as it is geared toward knowledge of the truth.

Fodor, however, suggests a different method of naturalizing intentionality in terms of the "asymmetric dependence" of misrepresentations on accurate representations.[153] Roughly, the frog's patterns of retinal firing have flies as their content because they are caused by flies, and any nonflies that might cause them are able to do so only because flies cause them. I think Aquinas would say that Fodor's account, because it involves causal interactions between bodies, which are ontologically indeterminate insofar as far as their matter is concerned, will no more prove capable of eliminating intentional indeterminacy from the frog's cognitive operations than Dretske and Millikan's teleosemantic view.

I cannot, however, hope to defend the argument for the intellect's immateriality based upon its universal, and thus intentionally determinate, mode of cognition against all possible objections here.[154] I am content to have shown that there is at least one plausible interpretation of one of Aquinas's arguments for the immateriality of the human intellect that is not obviously broken-backed. No argument for such a controversial conclusion will be able to avoid relying on some controversial premises. But Aquinas's MA, construed along Ross, Nagel, and Feser's lines, seems to me at least worth debating, instead of committing an

---

152. Fodor, "A Theory of Content I: The Problem," 72–73.
153. Fodor, "A Theory of Content II: The Theory," in A *Theory of Content*, 89–136.
154. Churchland, *Plato's Camera*, offers a theory of mental content that differs from Fodor's, Dretske's, and Millikan's alike—see 90–103 for his critical discussion of their views.

obvious fallacy, as Novak, Pasnau, and various others believe. If that is correct, then it is at least open to debate whether Aquinas has indeed succeeded in showing that the intellectual power and its operations cannot be explained in corporeal terms. Combined with the reasoning I discussed in chapter 3, this claim would entitle Aquinas to a controversial conclusion indeed, namely that human souls are incorruptible, and capable of surviving in separation from the body. In the final chapter of this book I will discuss several significant implications of Aquinas's conclusion that the human intellect has its act of being in an immaterial mode for his understanding of life after death.

6

THE IMMATERIALITY OF THE HUMAN INTELLECT AND THE LIFE TO COME

Suppose the arguments of the previous chapters succeed. In that case, Aquinas has given us reason to believe that the human intellect has its act of being in an immaterial mode. It is a psychological power that inheres directly in the human soul, rather than in the composite of soul and body. As a result, the human soul itself is a form with a subsistent mode of being, and thus is corruptible neither *per se* nor *per accidens*. Human souls are incorruptible, and are capable of surviving the death of the humans themselves to whom they once belonged in a disembodied state. The reasoning underlying all of these claims regarding the human intellect's immateriality and the soul's incorruptibility stems from the impossibility of explaining how our intellectual powers operate in bodily terms. This shows that intellectual operations—together with human souls, as their subject—are ontologically independent from the body, and capable of existing in separation from it. In this final chapter I will address a series of questions related to the implications of the human intellect's immateriality and the human soul's incorruptibility for the afterlife.

An initial pair of questions: Does Aquinas think our souls are immortal? And does he think that this can be proven? In the previous three chapters I focused on showing that because the operations of our intellectual power cannot be explained in bodily terms, it is possible for our souls to exist in a disembodied state. The separability of human souls from bodies is, I claimed, at the root of Aquinas's claim that our souls are incorruptible. But just because human souls can be separated from bodies does not mean they actually will be. Does Aquinas think he can show that there actually exist human souls in separation from bodies, engaged in vital operations of intellect and will? In the first part of this chapter, I will argue that he most likely does think this can be shown, though he leaves much of his reasoning in support of the soul's immortality tacit. I will also explain why he focuses the bulk of his attention on demonstrating the possibility that human souls exist apart from bodies, rather than their actual separate existence.

In the second section I turn to a related question that has occupied considerable recent attention, namely whether Aquinas thinks human souls are, or constitute, human persons. Most commentators deny, I think rightly, that Aquinas takes human souls to be human persons. Some have suggested, however, that Thomas thinks separated human souls wholly constitute human persons, and have forwarded various lines of reasoning in support of this interpretation. I will argue that the reasons these commentators offer are unconvincing, and that in fact several compelling considerations suggest that Thomas thought human persons simply cease to exist between their deaths and the resurrection.

The final sections of this chapter concern the bearing of the human intellect's immateriality on the theological doctrine of the general resurrection. Many contemporary philosophers of religion think that God's ability to raise humans from the dead is entirely compatible with a physicalist conception of human nature. On their view, if Aquinas were entirely mistaken about the immateriality of the human intellect and the possibility of human souls existing in a separated state, God could still bring deceased humans back to life on the last day. Interestingly, many of Aquinas's fellow scholastics embraced this position, arguing that separated souls are unnecessary for the possibility of the resurrection. Is this correct? I will argue in the third section that Thomas himself disagreed with this assessment, maintaining instead that it is impossible for our lives to "straddle temporal gaps." The reason he held this view is deeply rooted in his metaphysics of individuation. I will then explain in the fourth section why some of Aquinas's contemporaries, who rejected his position on individuation, also rejected the view that separated souls play a necessary identity-preserving role between death and resurrected life. Contemporary philosophers of religion may well wish to join them. I will argue, however, that Aquinas's stance on the afterlife should remain attractive to Christian philosophers of religion on theological grounds.

Incorruptibility and Immortality

In one passage from his commentary on *De caelo*, Aquinas distinguishes the notions of incorruptibility and immortality by claiming that the former refers only to unceasing existence while the latter includes unceasing operation:

(6.1) Immortality means unceasing life, but "to live" does not just name the act of being of a living thing, but also the operation of life, just as understanding is a certain sort of life, as is sensing and other [operations] of this sort.... And to express this [Aristotle] adds this, moreover, namely that immortality is everlasting life, and because of this he does not say that God's operation is incorruptibility, which would imply just his everlasting act of being, but rather he says [that it is] immortality, which includes an everlasting operation.[1]

Based on this distinction, it might appear possible for an incorruptible thing to exist everlastingly yet inertly, while an immortal being must not just exist, but must everlastingly exercise at least one vital activity. Owens argues that on Aquinas's view, it can be shown that human souls are incorruptible but not immortal.[2] That is, it can be shown that human souls everlastingly exist, but not that they are active in any way while disembodied. Both Pasnau and John McCormick, in contrast, argue that unless Aquinas can prove that our souls are capable of operating in a disembodied state, he cannot demonstrate that they are even capable of separate existence, much less that there actually exist any separated souls.[3] I will first explain Owens's reasoning in this section, and why Pasnau and McCormick think it fails. I will then explain why, in arguing for the separability of human souls from bodies in the way we saw him do in previous

---

1. In DCM 2.4.5/334 (Leo. 3:136), quoted in Owens, "Inseparability," 267.
2. Owens, "Inseparability," 265–70.
3. Pasnau, *Aquinas on Human Nature*, 361–77; John McCormick, "Quaestiones Disputandae," *New Scholasticism* 13, no. 4 (1939): 368–74.

chapters, Aquinas has most likely given us all we need to demonstrate their immortality as well. This also explains, I think, why Aquinas directs his arguments toward proving the former claim, not the latter.

For Owens, as we saw in the first section of chapter 3, the human soul's incorruptibility means there is no "intrinsic possibility" for it to lose existence. Our souls could only cease to exist if God annihilates them, that is, ceases to sustain them in being the way he does all creation. Aquinas thinks there are good reasons for denying that God will ever annihilate any of his creatures. So there are good reasons for believing that separated souls actually exist as well.

Owens also maintains, however, that Thomas did not consider himself to be in a position to prove philosophically that our souls are immortal, that is, that separated souls are actually engaged in any vital operations. Certainly Thomas refers to human souls as immortal with some frequency.[4] In addition, the title of QDA 14 suggests that it will concern "the immortality of the human soul." Curiously, however, all of the arguments Aquinas considers in the ensuing discussion concern the soul's incorruptibility, not its immortality. The same is true of a further (probably authentic) disputed question *De immortalitate animae*.[5] According to Owens, Aquinas only ever ends an argument with the conclusion that our souls are immortal once, in the context of discussing Augustine.[6] Thomas never argues for the human soul's immortality in his own right because he does not think that it is philosophically demonstrable. One reason Thomas might well hold this view, as Owens points out, stems from Thomas's views regarding the dependence of our intellectual operations on *phantasia* or imagination. Following Aristotle, Aquinas believes that in this life all of our intellectual activities, no matter how abstract, are accompanied by phantasms of the imagination.[7] *Phantasia* operates through the brain as its instrument, however, and hence is absent in anything lacking a body. Hence, one might suppose that separated souls, lacking *phantasia* or imagination, cannot en-

---

4. See In Sent 1.19.5.3 ad 3 and 3.10.1.1.1, SCG 2.86.9 and 3.48.16, ST 2a2ae.164.1 ad 1–2, etc.

5. L. A. Kennedy, "A New Disputed Question of Saint Thomas Aquinas on the Immortality of the Soul," *Archives d'Histoire Doctrinale et Littéraire du Moyen Âge* 45 (1978): 205–23.

6. Owens, "Inseparability," 265–66; the argument in question appears in In Sent 1.19.5.3 ad 3.

7. See ST 1a.84.7 and In DA 3.12.

gage in intellectual operations either.[8] To be sure, Aquinas thinks we would be wrong to suppose this. He discusses the nature of cognition in separated souls on many occasions, and clearly believes that separated souls actually do engage in intellectual activities. Nevertheless, Owens thinks, the soul has "no natural means" of engaging in these activities; they happen only "preternaturally," and it cannot be "demonstrated metaphysically" that they will take place.[9] Hence, the immortality of the soul is not philosophically demonstrable either.

Both Pasnau and John McCormick have pointed out why Owens's interpretation—on which Aquinas demonstrates only the soul's continued existence after death, but not its continued activity—is a problematic one. Aristotle himself raises the issue of the intellect's dependence on phantasms as a potential objection against the soul's separability from the body in De anima where he writes that "if [thinking] too proves to be a form of imagination or to be impossible without imagination, it too requires a body as a condition of its existence."[10] It was in response to this assertion that we saw Aquinas distinguish in passage 3.4 between powers that depend on bodies as their instruments, as phantasia or imagination does on the brain, and powers that depend on bodies only for their objects, as intellect does on phantasms. Yet Thomas recognizes in numerous passages that someone might just as well cite the intellect's dependence on phantasms as its objects as a reason for doubting the soul's separability from the body. In SCG, for instance, Aquinas writes:

(6.2) It is impossible for there to be any substance to which no operation belongs. But every operation of the soul ends with the body.... Although understanding is not an operation exercised through any corporeal organ, nevertheless its objects are phantasms, which are related to it just as colors are related to sight. Whence, just as sight cannot see without colors, so too the intellective soul cannot understand without phantasms.... Hence it is clear, therefore, that no operation of the soul remains after death. Nor, therefore, does its substance remain, since no substance can exist without any operation.[11]

---

8. Versions of this objection appear in In Sent 1.3.1.1 arg. 5 and 2.19.1.1 arg. 6, SCG 2.80.6, QDA 14 arg. 14 and 15 arg. 4, QQ 10.3.2 arg. 1, ST 1a.75.6 arg. 3, etc.
9. Owens, "Inseparability," 268.
10. De anima 1.1.403a8–10.
11. SCG 2.80.6 (Leo. 13:504–5).

This passage quite clearly links the soul's separability from the body, and thus its incorruptibility, with its ability to operate in a separated state. No operation entails no existence.[12] *Pace* Owens, then, Aquinas cannot demonstrate that souls continue to exist in a separated state unless he can give us some reason for thinking that they continue to operate apart from the body. Because, on Owens's interpretation, Thomas does not think it can be proven that separated souls actually engage in intellectual activities, he should not hold that their incorruptibility can be proven either.

Aquinas's response to the objection posed in 6.2, along with similar objections in other works, is to point out that because separated souls will exist in a different mode, that is, separated from the body, they will understand in a different mode as well.[13] It is true that while embodied a human soul cannot understand without phantasms. But when separated from the body the soul will understand: "through itself, in the mode of substances that are totally separated from bodies ... from which, as from its superiors, it will also be able to receive a more abundant influx for the perfection of its understanding."[14] Elsewhere Aquinas explains that separated souls will understand some things through intelligible *species* they have retained from the embodied state they enjoyed previously, although because of their new, separate state, the cognitive activities they carry out by means of these *species* will no longer require accompanying phantasms.[15] They will understand other things through new *species* infused into them by God or angels. Anton Pegis points out that Aquinas shifts throughout his career from cognition in separated souls as superior to embodied cognition, to viewing it as "imperfect" and "confused" compared with understanding by "turning to phan-

---

12. Pasnau calls this the "operation/existence conditional." He writes: "Aquinas ... confirms that the soul's separate existence requires its having its own operation, independent of the body. I refer to this all-important claim as the OE conditional.... The difficulty is that Aquinas is not entitled to E until he establishes O on independent grounds.... Aquinas seems illicitly to have pulled himself up by his own bootstraps: proving E on the supposition that O, then proving O on the basis of E" (*Aquinas on Human Nature*, 368).

13. SCG 2.81.12 (Leo. 13:506): "the soul when separated from the body understands in a different mode than when united to the body, just as it also exists in a different mode, for each thing acts in the way that it exists."

14. Ibid.

15. See QDV 19.1, QDA 15–20, ST 1a.89, In Sent 3.31.2.4 and 4.50.1.1, QQ 3.9.1.

tasms."[16] Pegis thinks this reflects a growing commitment to the unity of body and soul on Aquinas's part. It is in the relatively late *Summa theologiae* that Owens finds Aquinas describing the intellectual cognition of separated souls as "preternatural" (*praeter naturam*).[17] Owens's view, as noted above, is that because it is preternatural, Aquinas does not think that any of what he has to say about the separated soul's cognitive operations can be "demonstrated metaphysically."

If this is so, however, then Aquinas's response to the objection in passage 6.2 might look pretty dubious as well. McCormick asks: "Have we a right to assert, on grounds of reason, that the human soul has a mode of operation independent of the body because it has existence independent of the body, if we cannot show, on grounds of reason also, that it has such a separate existence without having first shown that it is capable of operating in such a state of separation?"[18] The objection says that human souls cannot exist in separation from the body because no operation entails no existence, and the intellect cannot operate without phantasms. Thomas's reply is that the different mode of existence that separated souls will enjoy entails that they will cognize in a different mode as well—one that does not require phantasms. This reply seems to beg the question by presupposing the very separated existence that the objection seeks to deny.

In fact, as both McCormick and Pasnau recognize, things are not so bad for Aquinas. His reply challenges the premise of the objection in 6.2 which asserts that the intellect's objects must always be phantasms by claiming that this is true only of intellectual cognition in an embodied mode. The "gaze" of separated souls is turned not toward phantasms, but toward themselves.[19] By viewing themselves and their intelligible *species* (whether acquired previously or infused by God or angels) they are able to understand many things, at least in an imperfect and confused way. Why suppose that the mode of intellectual cognition will change in this way? Here is where I think Aquinas leaves his reason-

---

16. Anton Pegis, "The Separated Soul and Its Nature in St. Thomas," in *St. Thomas Aquinas 1274–1974: Commemorative Studies*, ed. Armand Maurer (Toronto: PIMS, 1974), 131–58, and "Between Immortality and Death," *The Monist* 58, no. 1 (1974): 1–15.

17. ST 1a.89.1.

18. McCormick, "Quaestiones Disputandae," 371.

19. Aquinas uses the term *aspectus* ("gaze") at In Sent 4.50.1.2 and QDA 17.

ing for the soul's ability to continue operating after death largely tacit.

Thomas himself cites experiences during sleep and ecstasy in which, having momentarily detached from our senses to an extent, we are more susceptible to receiving an "influx" of cognitive input from God or angels.[20] These examples are supposed to show that even in this life it is possible for the soul to cognize in a way that does not involve phantasms, making it even more likely that separated souls would cognize this way. Pasnau and McCormick think that this reasoning is plausible, though not demonstrative.[21] It becomes more plausible upon recognizing that Aquinas's description of cognition in separated souls is hardly *ad hoc*, but rather modeled on the way other separate substances operate.[22]

What Thomas leaves largely tacit is the burden of proof he faces in responding to the objection in 6.2. Aquinas needs only to show that it is equally or more plausible that separated souls might take up a different mode of understanding than that our intellects can only ever operate with phantasms as their objects. There is little or no evidence available for the latter claim, while there is more evidence that Aquinas himself cites in support of the former claim.

Consider first why one might suppose that our intellects only ever operate with phantasms as their objects. The main reason cited in passages like 6.2 is Aristotle's claim that "to the thinking soul images serve as if they were contents of perception ... and that is why the soul never thinks without an image."[23] Aquinas takes Aristotle to be drawing an analogy: sight is related to colors as intellect is related to phantasms. Aquinas draws on this analogy frequently, but also recognizes that it can only be pressed so far. An important difference between the two cases is that while colors are the *per se* objects of sight, phantasms are not what the intellect ultimately cognizes.[24] The forms, essences, or

---

20. See SCG 2.81.12, QDA 15, etc.

21. McCormick, "Quaestiones Disputandae," 371, says "these suggestions do not quite reach the dimensions of demonstration of the possibility of independent intellectual operation, but they are valuable in pointing in that direction." Pasnau, *Aquinas on Human Nature*, 373, likewise thinks that not all of Aquinas's examples "seem equally compelling," but that Thomas's "underlying point is plausible."

22. See Pasnau's helpful discussion of this point in *Aquinas on Human Nature*, 374–77.

23. *De anima* 3.7.431a15–17.

24. See ST 1a.85.2. Another important difference is that while colors are able to act directly on the senses, phantasms (being corporeal) are not by themselves able to leave an

natures of things are the proper objects of intellectual cognition.[25] A phantasm is just one sort of mediating similitude through which we think about the natures of things. The intelligible *species* we abstract from phantasms are also mediating similitudes. It does indeed seem impossible to see without colors, as colors are the *per se* objects of vision. But it does not seem equally impossible to think about the natures of things without one of the layers of mediating similitudes through which, in this life, I do so. It would be analogous to someone who has seen, throughout her life, through glasses trying to see without them. Her vision might be "imperfect" and "confused," as Thomas thinks cognition in separated souls will be, but it seems at least possible. Are there other reasons for thinking that our intellects could not possibly operate without phantasms? Aquinas thinks introspective data show that our intellectual operations always rely on phantasms in this life, but presumably this data could not serve to refute the possibility of souls cognizing in a different mode after death. He also thinks the fact that brain damage affects our ability to think, despite the fact that the brain is not the intellect's organ, demonstrates that our intellectual activities at present rely on phantasms as their objects. This again, however, would not show that intellectual activity without phantasms is impossible altogether. In fact, although Aquinas does not make this explicit, there is little or no evidence at all that our intellects are only ever able to operate with phantasms as their objects.

In contrast, Aquinas had at least one excellent reason (other than experiences of dreams or rapture) for thinking that our intellects must be capable of cognizing at least certain objects without the mediation of phantasms: our beatitude depends upon it. Aquinas argues extensively that we cannot be truly happy without beholding God in his essence.[26] We can only do so, however, insofar as God unites his own essence to our intellect as the object of its understanding.[27] This certainly is not

---

impression on the intellect (which is incorporeal), which is why the agent intellect must perform its abstractive activity in order to impress an intelligible *species* on the possible intellect. See ST 1a.85.1 ad 3 and Cory, "Rethinking Abstractionism," 619–23, for a helpful explanation.

25. See note 141 in chapter 3.
26. SCG 3.37, ST 1a.12.1 and 1a2ae.3.8, CT 1.163, etc.
27. In Sent 4.49.2.1, ST 1a.12.4, SCG 4.51. See for discussion Richard Taylor, "Arabic/Islamic Philosophy in Thomas Aquinas's Conception of the Beatific Vision in IV Sent., D. 49, Q. 2, A. 1," *The Thomist* 76, no. 4 (2012): 509–50.

to understand God through a phantasm, but it is something Aquinas is quite sure must happen. So it must be possible for our intellects to operate in a different mode than by relying on phantasms as objects of our cognitive activities.

Considering the evidence available to Aquinas for thinking that separated souls might cognize in a mode akin to that of angels, and the dearth of evidence denying this to be possible, I think Owens is mistaken: Aquinas did think himself in a position to prove that our souls are immortal, continuing everlastingly in their nonbodily operations of intellect and will. I also think that McCormick and Pasnau underestimate the strength of the reasoning Aquinas is able to muster in support of this conclusion, perhaps because he leaves much of it unexpressed.

I am less certain, however, about their proposal that unless Aquinas can demonstrate the human soul's immortality, he is not entitled to its incorruptibility either. Here I side with Owens. The opening premise of 6.2 states that "it is impossible for there to be any substance to which no operation belongs." No operation entails no existence, as I put it above. But it is unclear whether Aquinas means by this that no substance can exist unless it is actually operating, or just that no substance can exist without some ability to operate. Pasnau thinks that Aquinas means the former, citing as evidence Aquinas's occasional claims that no substance is "unoccupied" (*otiosa*) and the fact that angels, on Thomas's view, are always actually thinking.[28] What is confusing, if Pasnau is correct, is why Thomas should sometimes have thought it sufficient to deal with objections like the one in 6.2 simply by arguing that the intellect has no corporeal organ. In 3.4, for instance, Aquinas notes Aristotle's claim that phantasms are the intellect's objects, just as colors are the objects of sight. But he does not seem to think that the intellect's reliance on phantasms as objects of its operations represents any obstacle to the independence of these operations from the body. Indeed, he moves directly from claiming in 3.4 that "intellect cannot be without a body, though only as its object, not as its instrument," to claiming that "un-

---

28. See QDA 14 arg. 14 for the claim that no substance is unoccupied cited as a reason for thinking that souls cannot exist in separation from bodies, and SCG 2.97 for the claim that angels are always thinking (just as animals are always engaged in nutritive activities). See Pasnau, "Aquinas on Human Nature," 370–71.

derstanding is an operation proper to the soul alone ... and therefore an intellect is a subsistent form, while other powers are forms in matter."[29] He then explains, as we saw in 3.2, that if the intellectual soul is subsistent, possessing its own operation apart from the body, it can exist apart from the body as well. Here, it appears, all Aquinas thinks he needs to show to demonstrate that the human soul is separable from the body is that it has a power that does not operate through any bodily organ, not that this power actually operates without certain bodily objects.[30] Even supposing that a human soul could not actually function without phantasms, it might retain the ability to operate much as Moses and Pharaoh retained the ability to see even during the ninth plague of Egypt. In that sense, an operation would still "belong" to the soul, and it would still count as a subsistent, incorruptible form capable of existing apart from the body, even if it never actually thought anything at all in a disembodied state. Of course, as I have argued, Aquinas thinks he can show that the human intellect actually continues to operate even when separated from the body. But he focuses on showing that the intellect operates without a corporeal organ (and hence has a subsistent mode of being) because this is what ultimately matters for determining whether it is separable from the body (or instead corruptible just like the souls of other living things).

If I am correct about this, it would explain in part why Aquinas never provides his own arguments for the conclusion that our souls are immortal. It is not that he does not think the human soul's immortality can be proven, as Owens believes. Thomas does think he can show that we will continue to exercise our intellectual powers after death. But the fact that we will actually do this is less important, for him, than the fact

---

29. In DA 1.2.20 (Leo. 45.1:10.70–79).

30. The same seems to be true of Aquinas's responses to the objections at ST 1a.75.2 arg. 3 and QQ 10.3.2 arg. 1; in both cases his strategy is to distinguish between powers that rely on bodies as their organs or instruments and powers that rely on bodies only to provide their objects. Readers may wish at this point to refer back to my explanation in chapter 3 regarding why the involvement of phantasms as the objects of intellectual operations does not entail their dependence on the body, given OD/E. It is true that body-dependent phantasms enter into the explanation of our intellectual operations at least in this life as one of their causal inputs. But it is not true that intellectual operations themselves are explicable in terms of coordination between bodily parts, states, and processes (as the arguments I discussed in chapter 5 are meant to show).

that our souls can exist in separation from our bodies, due to their possession of certain nonbodily powers.

A further factor might also partly explain why Aquinas focused less on the human soul's immortality than on its subsistence and incorruptibility (along with the intellectual immateriality on which they depend). He might have thought of immortality as an attribute that applies primarily to complete living substances, as opposed to incomplete substances such as human souls. While he does not argue for the soul's immortality, he does argue that humans were immortal by God's grace in their prelapsarian state of innocence, and that we will rise to immortal life on the last day.[31] Brian Davies goes so far as to claim that because Thomas does not think that human souls are human beings, "Aquinas does not believe in the immortality of the soul."[32] This clearly is not quite accurate. As noted, Thomas refers to human souls as immortal with some frequency, even if it is not a claim he argues for explicitly. But Davies does raise an important question, much discussed in recent literature on Aquinas, regarding whether human souls are, or constitute, human persons. I will address this issue in the following section.

Separated Souls and Personhood

Most commentators agree that Aquinas did not think that human souls are human persons while embodied, nor that they become human persons after death. For good reason: Aquinas is rather explicit on both points. He associates the view that human souls are humans with Plato, and rejects it explicitly both before and after death.[33] Yet some com-

---

31. See *In Sent* 2.19.1.4 and ST 1a.97.1 on immortality before the Fall, and SCG 4.82 on the immortality of those rising again.

32. Brian Davies, *Aquinas: An Introduction* (London: Continuum, 2002), 114.

33. ST 1a.75.4 and SCG 2.57 reject Plato's view that embodied human souls are human persons, and *In Sent* 3.5.3.2 answers negatively the question "whether a separated soul is a person?" (attributing the view to Plato and Hugh of St. Victor). J. P. Moreland and Scott Rae defend what they call Thomistic Dualism, on which "human persons are identical to immaterial substances, namely, to souls" (*Body and Soul*, 11). They note that because "there are different opinions about the precise details of Thomas Aquinas's philosophical-theological anthropology," they "do not claim to offer a version that conforms to Aquinas's in all details," though they think their view "shares enough of the important aspects of a Thomistic approach to warrant ... using that label" (ibid., 10). I am not sure about the last of these claims, but certainly the notion that human persons are identical to souls is one important detail that in no way "conforms" to Aquinas's views. Christina Van Dyke critically discusses their view as related to

mentators have argued in recent years that Aquinas thinks that human souls come to constitute human persons after death.[34] In life, humans are constituted by both their souls and their bodies. But Aquinas seems to have agreed with contemporary metaphysicians who argue that constitution is not identity.[35] So it is entirely possible that humans come to be constituted, after death, by just their souls, and indeed there is evidence that this is indeed the view Aquinas holds, or at least this is what some recent commentators have argued. Their interpretation of Aquinas, on which humans survive their deaths, constituted by their separated souls, is usually called "survivalism" in the literature. The opposed interpretation, on which Thomas believes that humans cease to exist at death and return to life only at the resurrection, is usually called "corruptionism" or "cessationism."[36] I will use the latter term, and ar-

---

Aquinas in "Not Properly a Person: The Rational Soul and 'Thomistic Substance Dualism,'" Faith and Philosophy 26, no. 2 (2009): 186–204.

34. I do not find Stump advocating this view in "Non-Cartesian Substance Dualism and Materialism Without Reduction," Faith and Philosophy 12, no. 4 (1995): 505–31, at 519, but her later book Aquinas (published in 2003) spells out her take on Thomas's view as follows: "a human being can exist when he is composed of nothing more than one of his metaphysical components, namely his form or soul" (51). She expands on this interpretation in "Resurrection, Reassembly and Reconstitution: Aquinas on the Soul," in Die menschliche Seele: Brauchen wir den Dualismus?, ed. Bruno Niederberger and Edmund Runggaldier (Frankfurt: Ontos Verlag, 2006), 153–74. Jason Eberl concurs in "The Metaphysics of Resurrection: Issues of Identity in Aquinas," Proceedings of the American Catholic Philosophical Association 74 (2001): 215–30, at 223, that "despite the human soul's not being a substance in itself, it serves as the necessary and sufficient condition for the existence of a human substance." See also his "Do Human Persons Persist between Death and Resurrection," in Metaphysics and God: Essays in Honor of Eleanore Stump, ed. Kevin Timpe (London: Routledge, 2009), 188–205. David Oderberg defends a similar view in "Hylemorphic Dualism," in Personal Identity (ed. Miller et al.), 70–99, Real Essentialism, and "Survivalism, Corruptionism and Mereology," European Journal for Philosophy of Religion 4, no. 4 (2012): 1–26. So does Christopher Brown in Aquinas and the Ship of Theseus and "Souls, Ships and Substances: A Response to Toner," American Catholic Philosophical Quarterly 81, no. 4 (2007): 655–68.

35. See Mark Johnston, "Constitution Is Not Identity," Mind 101, no. 401 (1992): 89–105, and Lynne Rudder Baker, "Why Constitution Is Not Identity," Journal of Philosophy 94, no. 12 (1997): 599–621. Aquinas seems to distinguish between identity and constitution in various passages, such as In Met 7.17.1674 and DEE 2 (Leo. 43:372.204–7): "for man is said to be constituted from soul and body in the way that a third thing is constituted from two things, which itself is not either of them, for man is neither his soul nor his body."

36. See Patrick Toner, "St. Thomas Aquinas on Death and the Separated Soul," Pacific Philosophical Quarterly 91, no. 4 (2010): 587–99, for the terms "survivalist" and "corruptionist." I agree with the reasoning Brower gives for preferring "cessationist" at Aquinas on the Ontology of the Material World, 280. Toner also defends cessationism in "Personhood and Death in St. Thomas Aquinas," History of Philosophy Quarterly 26, no. 2 (2009): 121–38, and "St. Thomas

gue that it probably represents the correct interpretation of Aquinas's thought. The evidence for cessationism over survivalism is not overwhelming. But the reasons favoring survivalism are not as strong as its proponents suppose either, and at least two considerations suggest that Thomas thought human persons cease to exist at death.

It will be helpful first to note a distinction, drawn by Brower, between human and nonhuman versions of survivalism.[37] Suppose I survive my death, constituted now just by my separated soul. Will I then be a human being? Most survivalists seem to think Aquinas's answer is yes. Brower disagrees, however, arguing that Thomas thinks human persons survive death, but not as individual members of the human species. They will no longer be rational animals, or indeed animals of any sort. On Brower's interpretation of Aquinas's view, individuals do not have the natures they do necessarily, but rather are only necessarily disposed to possess their essential natures. So even if Socrates is not a human being when he survives death, constituted now just by his separated soul, he will remain a human person insofar as his soul retains a disposition to be reunited to the body, thus coming to constitute a human being once more. For much of what follows this distinction will not matter, but it is crucial for evaluating one bit of evidence relevant to this debate, having to do with Christ's ontological status during the Triduum.

Turning to the respective cases in favor of cessationism and survivalism, I think it must be acknowledged that many of the passages cessationists have supposed cement their interpretative case do not in fact carry the day.[38] Consider the following passages, frequently cited as evidence that Aquinas thinks humans cease to exist at death:

Aquinas on Punishing Souls," *International Journal for the Philosophy of Religion* 71, no. 2 (2012): 103–16. For three further recent defenses of cessationism see Pasnau, *Aquinas on Human Nature*, 380–93; Christopher Martin, "Is There Identity of Person between a Living Human Being and a Separated Soul?," *Studia Theologica* 6, no. 4 (2008): 249–53; Turner Nevitt, "Aquinas on the Death of Christ: A New Argument for Corruptionism," *American Catholic Philosophical Quarterly* 90, no. 1 (2016): 77–99, and Giuseppe Butera, "Incomplete Persons: Thomas Aquinas on Separated Souls and the Identity of the Human Person," in *Distinctions of Being* (ed. Zunic), 61–80. Other defenders of cessationism include Christina Van Dyke, Anthony Kenny, Brian Davies, Herbert McCabe, and Gyula Klima.

37. See Brower, *Material World*, 292.

38. Contrary to what is often supposed; see Davies, *Aquinas*, 114, who cites passage 6.3 then writes "Aquinas does not even think that I survive if my soul carries on to enjoy some kind of union with God. I can only survive my death, he thinks, if my soul is reunited with my

(6.3) A human naturally desires his own well-being [*salutem*], but the soul is just part of a human body, not the whole human, and my soul is not me, whence even if the soul obtains well-being in the other life, nevertheless neither I nor any human will do so. So since a human naturally desires well-being, even of the body, a natural desire would be frustrated.[39]

(6.4) The soul of Abraham is not, properly speaking, Abraham himself, but one of his parts, whence the life of Abraham's soul is not sufficient for Abraham himself to be alive ... but rather [for this] is required the life of the whole composite, namely of soul and body.[40]

(6.5) Concerning the union of soul and body there were two views among the ancients. One was that the soul is united to the body as a complete being, as if it were in the body like a sailor in a ship, whence ... Plato posited that a human is not something constituted from the body and the soul but is a soul clothed in a body, and according to this view the whole personality of the human would consist in the soul, so that a separated soul would truly be called a human, as Hugh of St. Victor says.... But this opinion cannot stand, since on it the body would be joined to the soul accidentally.... The other is Aristotle's view, which all the moderns follow, that the soul is united to the body as a form to matter, whence the soul is part of human nature, and not a certain nature *per se*. And because the notion of parthood is contrary to the notion of personhood ... therefore the separated soul cannot be called a person.[41]

All of these passages can be read as rejecting just the Platonic view that humans are identical to their souls, rather than the survivalist view that humans after death are constituted by their souls.[42] None suffices to settle the interpretative debate. Nevertheless, it seems to me that these passages do read more naturally on a cessationist interpretation. If Aquinas did indeed hold that humans are constituted by their souls after death, then one would expect him to say so in passages like these,

---

body, which is to say that, when it comes to our life after death, Aquinas's emphasis is firmly on the notion of bodily resurrection." Everything Davies says here is true, I think, but passage 6.3 is not conclusive evidence for a cessationist reading.

39. *Expositio super Primam Epistolam S. Pauli ad Corinthios* (hereafter, *In 1 Cor*) 15.924 (Marietti 392).

40. *In Sent* 4.43.1.1.1 ad 2 (Parma 7.2:1058).

41. *In Sent* 3.5.3.2 (Mand./Moos 3:206–7). Further texts sometimes cited along these same lines include QDA 1 and QDP 9.2 ad 14.

42. See Stump, "Resurrection, Reassembly and Reconstitution," 166–69, and Brower, *Material World*, 301–4, for examples of ways that survivalists read these passages.

rather than simply pointing out that humans are not identical to their souls. I think passages 6.3–6.5 offer at least *prima facie* support for cessationism.[43] The question, then, is whether there is overriding evidence favoring survivalism. Survivalists cite four main lines of reasoning.

First, they argue that if humans do not survive death, our identity is interrupted such that it cannot possibly be resumed at the resurrection.[44] That would pose an obvious problem for a key item of Christian dogma. I will postpone further discussion of this argument until the following section, as Aquinas's view on the possibility of temporal gaps in a thing's existence is a vexed interpretative question in its own right.

Second, as we saw in the previous section, Aquinas thinks that separated souls engage in various intellectual activities—indeed he thinks it can be proven they will do so. But as we saw in 3.5, Aquinas does not think that it is, properly speaking, souls that engage in intellectual operations in this life: "it is more correct to say that a human understands with his soul." Accordingly, survivalists reckon, there must be a human present after death as well as the proper subject for ongoing operations of thinking and willing.[45]

I am not so sure. Aquinas's point in 3.5 is that as long as the human soul has an inherent act of being as that by which the human herself subsists *per se*, its operations are indeed attributable to the whole human. Yet human souls continue to subsist and operate *per se* after death, and 3.5 provides no reason for believing that they could only do so by constituting human persons to whom they are non-identical. It is true that once we speak of separated souls thinking and willing it is natural enough to wonder *who* is performing these operations. Just who do separated souls think they are, anyway? Surely, it would seem, they are in a position to ask themselves the question. If they are able to answer

---

43. Here I am in agreement with Nevitt, who writes that "Aquinas's silence about survivalism cries out for explanation" ("Aquinas on the Death of Christ," 85).

44. This is the main line of reasoning on which Brown focuses; see *Aquinas and the Ship of Theseus*, 120–24, along with Toner's review article "Thomas versus Tibbles: A Critical Study of Christopher Brown's Aquinas and the Ship of Theseus," *American Catholic Philosophical Quarterly* 81, no. 4 (2007): 639–53, at 640–42, and Brown's reply in "Souls, Ships and Substances," 655–58.

45. See Brower, *Material World*, 285, and Stump, "Resurrection, Reassembly and Reconstitution," 155–56, for instances of this sort of argument. Brower brings up passage 3.5, i.e., ST 1a.75.2 ad 2.

it then must they not constitute persons? Again, I am not sure. For one thing, as Geach points out, "what it is like" to be a separated soul is difficult to assess given that, absent the senses, the phenomenology of their conscious experiences is bound to be radically different from our own:

> In our human life thinking and choosing are intricately bound up with a play of sensations and mental images and emotions; if after a lifetime of thinking and choosing in this human way there is left only a disembodied mind whose thought is wholly non-sensuous and whose rational choices are unaccompanied by any human feelings—can we still say there remains the same person? Surely not: such a soul is not the person who died but a mere remnant of him.[46]

I would not say that the phenomenological break between separated souls' experiences and our own is reason by itself for denying that they are persons, as Geach suggests here, but he does effectively illustrate why it is difficult to appeal to their phenomenology in support of their personhood. Furthermore, Aquinas's Boethian criterion for personhood—"individual substance of a rational nature"—is both psychological and metaphysical.[47] It is not enough that separated souls be rational. They must also be individual substances. Aquinas denies that separated souls are individual substances, insisting that souls have a substantial act of being only incompletely, as discussed in chapter 1.[48] Nowhere does he indicate that they constitute substances. So even if we might incline toward regarding separated souls as constituting persons based upon their possession of certain psychological states today, it is not clear that Thomas would do the same.

A third reason for thinking he might, however, is that he does not hesitate to call separated souls by the names of the persons they belonged to before death. The martyr Felix appeared to the people of Nola when they were besieged by barbarians.[49] We rightly invoke saints like

---

46. Geach, "Immortality," in *God and the Soul* (Notre Dame, Ind.: St. Augustine's Press, 1969), 22.

47. See *In Sent* 1.25.1.1 arg. 1 and 3.5.3.2 arg. 1, SCG 4.38.2, ST 1a.29.1 arg. 1, etc., for references to this formula from Boethius's *De duabus naturis*.

48. See ST 1a.29.1 ad 5 (Leo. 4:328): "the soul is part of the human species, and therefore even if it is separated, since it nevertheless retains the nature of unibility, it cannot be called an individual substance" and *In Sent* 3.5.3.2 ad 1 (Mand./Moos 3:207): "a separated soul, properly speaking, is not a substance of any nature."

49. *In Sent* 4.45.1.1.3, cited in Stump, *Aquinas*, 52.

Peter by name for prayer on our behalf.[50] Dives only "sees" Lazarus in the bosom of Abraham by a sort of metaphorical vision in Luke 16:23, because he lacks eyes at the time, but the events described in the story are real nonetheless.[51] Surely if Aquinas makes claims like these he must think that Felix, Peter, Dives, Lazarus, etc., are really present after death, constituted by their separated souls.

Again, however, it is not at all clear that this argument succeeds. In fact, to explain why it is justifiable to call separated souls by certain proper names Aquinas appeals at various points to synecdoche: calling a part of something by the name of the whole. When we say "Saint Peter, pray for us," we are imposing the name of the whole, "Peter," on what is, as Geach puts it, "a mere remnant of him."[52]

A fourth consideration in support of survivalism probably represents the most serious argument in its favor. As Aquinas's understanding of the story of Dives and Lazarus illustrates, God punishes or rewards separated souls based upon the sins or merits of the humans to whom they belonged before death. If separated souls did not constitute the human persons who committed the sinful or meritorious acts in question, however, it would surely be unjust for God to punish or reward them for someone else's deeds. This line of reasoning poses an especially serious problem for cessationists because, as Christina Van Dyke points out, it is not enough to respond by appealing to the difference between Aquinas's Boethian definition of personhood and our own, as I did above.[53] Even if Aquinas would not say that separated souls constitute persons because of his metaphysical criterion for personhood, *we* would surely

---

50. ST 2a2ae.83.11 ad 5. See In Sent 3.22.1.1 arg. 6 and ST 3a.50.4 arg. 2, both of which appeal to this practice as a reason for thinking that Christ must still have been human during the Triduum, a view with which Aquinas disagrees.

51. QDA 19 ad 11. See Van Dyke, "I See Dead People: Disembodied Souls and Aquinas's 'Two-Person' Problem," *Oxford Studies in Medieval Philosophy* 2 (2014): 25–45, for discussion of Aquinas's understanding of this story.

52. In Sent 3.22.11 ad 6; see ST 2a2ae.175.6 ad 1, QDV 13.5 ad 3, QDP 3.9 ad 1, etc. See Nevitt, "The Death of Christ," 97–98, for a helpful explanation of the way Aquinas employs synecdoche in this context.

53. See Van Dyke, "Dead People," 34–35. Van Dyke herself is a cessationist, and indeed seems to think survivalism is incoherent. She thinks Aquinas's best course, faced with the injustice of God punishing or rewarding souls for deeds committed by other people, is to drop the notion that separated souls exist altogether. I hope to have shown, throughout the course of this book, just what a radical reshaping of Thomas's views this proposal would involve.

tend to regard something with states of intellect and will this way. Surely it would be unjust for God to punish or reward these "persons" (in our modern sense of the term) for the deeds of some other people, whether Aquinas thinks that separated souls constitute persons or not.

Patrick Toner argues that this is not necessarily the case; in fact, the Christian doctrine of original sin, as Aquinas understands it, seems to involve God's punishing certain persons for the sins of their forefathers.[54] On Aquinas's view, when God justly metes out punishment for original sin, it is not for some sin perpetrated *by* us, but it is for sin existing *in* us.[55] The sin in question was perpetrated by Adam, but it is in us, insofar as we are born deprived of lacking the right ordering or "original justice" we had before the Fall. Similarly, Toner argues, while disembodied souls neither are human persons nor constitute human persons, the righteous or sinful deeds of human persons are clearly *in* them in the sense that they retain habits of intellect and will acquired in this life.[56] They are shaped by their careers as parts of us, and for this reason God may justly punish or reward them for our deeds. It is not as though our souls are uninvolved bystanders as we perform sinful or meritorious deeds. As far as our parts go, they are the principal metaphysical accessories to our deeds. So when they are separated, yet still marked by the habits of their embodied existence, God justly punishes or rewards them accordingly.

I have argued that at least three main lines of reasoning in support of survivalism do not in fact provide the evidence that the interpretation needs. I have also pointed out that there is *prima facie* evidence for cessationism stemming from Aquinas's failure to support survivalism when it seemingly would have made sense for him to do so. The *prima facie* evidence is not conclusive, though. Is there further evidence to be had in support of a cessationist interpretation?

Nevitt thinks that Aquinas's views on Christ's status during the Triduum provide compelling support for cessationism. Aquinas several times

---

54. Toner, "Aquinas on Punishing."
55. ST 1a2ae.87.7 cited in Toner, "Aquinas on Punishing," 108. See SCG 4.52.6, CT 1.196, and QDM 5.1 ad 11 for other passages in which Aquinas explains why God justly punishes us for original sin, though we did not commit it.
56. See Toner, "Aquinas on Punishing," 110–12, for an explanation regarding how, on Aquinas's view, sin is in the will as its subject, which is in turn in the soul as its subject.

throughout his career denies that Christ was a human during the Triduum.[57] Christ continues to exist as the second person of the Trinity, and so does the soul pertaining to the human nature he adopted, but to say that Christ was a human during the Triduum would be wrong.[58] Nevitt writes: "in order to prove survivalism false and corruptionism true, one has to find Aquinas saying that even though a separated soul exists, nevertheless a human being does not.... And that is precisely what Aquinas says about the death of Christ."[59] Brower, however, argues that Aquinas's views on Christ's death actually support his own nonhuman version of survivalism. Christ remains a person with a soul that itself remains naturally disposed to be united to matter, and thus naturally disposed to be human. Hence: "if we allow ourselves to use the term 'human person' in a broad sense to cover any person who possesses such a natural disposition, we can say that even if Christ ceases to be a human being at death, he nonetheless survives as a human person."[60] Crucial for Brower is the distinction between human beings and human persons "in a broad sense." Aquinas does make it clear that Christ ceased to be a human being after he died, but leaves it open that Christ remained a human person. The same is true of ordinary human beings, on Brower's view. Whatever one makes of this argument, what I pointed out above pertains to the passages on Christ's death, namely that because they read more naturally on a cessationist interpretation, and because Aquinas certainly does not make his commitment to survivalism explicit, they offer *prima facie* support for a view on which human persons cease to exist at death.

In addition, I believe there is at least one further consideration in support of this interpretation that, while not conclusive, at least tips the scales in its favor. Consider again 6.3, where Aquinas is commenting on Paul's claim that "if in Christ we have hope in this life only, we are of all people most to be pitied" (1 Cor 15:19). He takes Paul to be offering an argument of the following sort:

---

57. In Sent 3.22.1.1, QQ 2.1.1 and 3.2.2, ST 3a.50.4, CT 2.229.
58. At least it would be wrong to say this "simply and absolutely speaking," although we can say Christ was a dead man (*homo mortuus*) during the Triduum, i.e., a human in an equivocal sense of the term—see ST 3a.50.4 and QQ 3.2.2, along with Brower's explanation in *Material World*, 289–90.
59. Nevitt, "The Death of Christ," 89–90.
60. Brower, *Material World*, 295.

(6.6) If there is no resurrection of the dead, it follows that nothing good is possessed by men except in this life alone; and if this is so, then those who suffer many evils and tribulations in this life are more miserable. Therefore, since the apostles and Christians suffer many tribulations, it follows that they are more miserable than other men, who at least enjoy the good things of this world.[61]

A cogent enough line of reasoning. Certainly St. Paul faced many tribulations, and Christians are told they should expect to as well. If there is no resurrection, then we Christians have nothing to hope for beyond this life. Hence if our lives here are full of tribulations, we must be accounted miserable indeed. Aquinas notes, however, that someone might raise the following "doubt" against St. Paul's argument:

(6.7) What the Apostle says does not seem to be universally true, namely, that Christians are confident in this life only, because [an objector] could say that, although our bodies do not possess any good things except in this life, which is mortal, yet according to the soul they have many good things in the other life.[62]

Our hope for future glory does *not* reside solely in the resurrection, according to this objection. Our bodies may cease to exist when this life is over, yet *we* do not cease to exist, and "according to the soul" we may go on to enjoy "many good things in the other life." Passage 6.3 represents one line of reasoning that Aquinas offers against this objection, on St. Paul's behalf. Now, as mentioned, while 6.3 is very frequently cited in support of cessationism, survivalists can maintain that Aquinas is simply drawing his customary distinction between human beings and their souls, and pointing out that the salvation of the latter is not sufficient for the salvation of the former.[63]

Still, I think that the theological context tells against this reading. St. Paul and Aquinas want to defend the necessity of the resurrection. What matters to their readers, presumably, is *their* salvation—*their* hope for beatitude after death. If survivalism of any sort is true, however, then

---

61. *In 1 Cor* 15.2.923 (Marietti 391).
62. Ibid., par. 924.
63. See Brower, *Material World*, 302n34; Stump, *Aquinas*, 52–54; and Eberl, "Do Human Persons Persist?," 195–96, for discussions of this passage.

they can indeed hope to enjoy beatitude immediately after death. Aquinas makes clear that immediately after death souls will receive punishment or reward, and on the survivalist view the human persons constituted by the souls presumably do so as well.[64] In that case, however, neither St. Paul's words nor Aquinas's seem to carry much punch. Sure, human beings might require resurrection for salvation. But why should we care about their salvation, provided that we ourselves are able to experience beatitude after death in a disembodied state? In contrast, if cessationism is true, we really do need to be raised again from the dead to be saved, because we do not exist at all until God raises us on the last day. That would indeed explain the tremendous importance that St. Paul and Aquinas alike attach to the bodily resurrection.

Survivalists might, of course, attempt to account for the importance of the resurrection in alternative ways. They might point to what we saw Aquinas say in the previous section about the "imperfect" and "confused" mode of separated souls' cognition. The resurrection is important, they might claim, so that our cognition might be perfect and crisply focused. They might also cite Aquinas's claim that "since the human soul is naturally united to a body, it naturally desires union with the body, so the will cannot be perfectly at rest unless the soul is rejoined to a body."[65] B. Carlos Bazan thinks Aquinas's insistence that souls need bodies to be perfectly happy is Thomas's "highest encomium of the human body."[66] Yet such passages are hard to square with his view that souls experience punishment or reward immediately after death. For some happy souls, the reward in question is the beatific vision, which perfectly satisfies all natural desires.[67] If I am able to experience the beatific vision in heaven, constituted by my separated soul, it is difficult for me to see why I would want my body back. I do not take this last argument I have offered for cessationism to be conclusive, but I do think the

---

64. SCG 4.91.
65. CT 1.151 (Leo. 42:139.7–11); see SCG 4.79.
66. B. Carlos Bazan, "The Highest Encomium of the Human Body," in *Littera, sensus, sententia: studi in onore del Prof. Clemente J. Vansteenkiste*, ed. A. Lobato (Milan: Massimo, 1991), 99–116.
67. See Christina Van Dyke, "Aquinas's Shiny Happy People," *Oxford Studies in Philosophy of Religion* 6 (2014): 269–91, for an illuminating critical discussion of the implications of Aquinas's "all-sufficiency thesis": the view that the beatific vision perfectly satisfies all our natural desires.

burden is on survivalists to provide as robust an explanation why disembodied human persons need their bodies back as cessationism offers us.

Separated Souls and the Resurrection I: Aquinas's Position

Most of this book's first five chapters were spent analyzing and defending one claim of Aquinas's—that the human intellect is immaterial—and showing how this claim supports the further conclusion that human souls are incorruptible, and hence capable of surviving in a disembodied state. In this chapter I have argued so far that Aquinas believes that souls are not only incorruptible but also immortal—actively engaged in operations of intellect and will even while disembodied. Nevertheless, he denied that separated souls either are or constitute persons. You and I will not survive our deaths, even though our souls will. One good reason for believing that Thomas thinks we cease to exist at death is that this best explains the tremendous importance he assigns to the doctrine of the resurrection.

In this book's last two sections, I will consider what bearing any of what I have said so far has on the possibility of the resurrection. Suppose that Aquinas is wrong. Suppose it cannot be demonstrated that human intellects are immaterial, or human souls incorruptible and immortal. Indeed, suppose that none of these claims are true. Would these suppositions affect God's ability to raise us from the dead in any significant way? Does Aquinas think they would?

Perhaps surprisingly, the answers to both of these questions are controversial. I will argue in this section that the answer to the latter question is probably "yes." Although the evidence is less conclusive than most recent commentators have supposed, Aquinas most likely believed that without separated souls persisting between death and resurrection, even God could not raise us from the dead. As for the former question, the answer is even less clear. I will explain why even though Aquinas's theory of individuation supplies the ingredients for an argument against the possibility of what is sometimes called "temporally gappy" existence, it did not convince many of his fellow scholastics. Nor, I think, is Aquinas's view likely to win over much contemporary support, although whether it should is, perhaps, open to further debate.

Let me begin by returning to the first line of reasoning in support of survivalism that I mentioned in the previous section. It hinges on the supposed impossibility of God's bringing things like humans back once they have ceased to exist. According to this argument, Aquinas does not believe that things can exist for a while, cease to exist for a while, then resume existence as numerically the same things they were before—even by God's power. It is metaphysically impossible that their existence should include temporal "gaps." Yet according to cessationists, Thomas also believed that humans cease to exist at their death. Should he not, then, have denied that God could bring them back as numerically the same individuals they were previously at the resurrection? The argument for survivalism based on the possibility of resurrection (SPR), can be represented as follows:

(SPR1) If cessationism is true, then the possibility of resurrection entails the possibility of temporally gappy existence.
(SPR2) Temporally gappy existence is impossible.
(SPR3) The resurrection is possible.
(SPR4) The possibility of resurrection does not entail the possibility of temporally gappy existence (from SPR2 and SPR3).
(SPR5) Cessationism is false (from SPR1 and SPR4).

Because Aquinas is clearly committed to SPR3 as a tremendously important item of Christian dogma, cessationists must reject SPR1, SPR2, or both. In fact, I think, to understand how Aquinas would respond to this argument it is important to recognize a distinction he implicitly draws between two different senses in which a thing's existence might be temporally gappy: a weaker sense and a stronger sense. If we read SPR1 and SPR2 as claims about the weaker sort of gappy existence, then Aquinas thinks the first is true but the second false. If these premises are claims about the stronger sort of gappy existence, then the reverse is the case: SPR1 is false, and SPR2 true.

To appreciate the distinction between the weaker and stronger kinds of gappy existence Aquinas recognizes, consider one objection Aquinas considers against the possibility of the resurrection, together with his response:

(6.8) What is not continuous seems not to be the same in number, which indeed is clear not just in the cases of magnitudes and motions, but also in qualities and forms, for if after being healthy someone gets sick, then returns to health, they will not return to numerically the same health. Moreover, it is clear that a human's act of being is removed at death, since corruption is a change from being to non-being. Therefore it is impossible that a human's act of being be restored the same in number, nor therefore will the human be the same in number, for things are the same in number whose act of being is the same.[68]

(6.9) What was said in the objection—that the act of being is not one because it is not continuous—rests on a false foundation. For it is clear that the act of being of matter and form is one, since matter only has an act of being in act through form. The rational soul differs in this respect from other forms, nevertheless, since the act of being of other forms is only had in conjunction with matter, for they exceed matter neither in their act of being nor in their operation. But it is clear that the rational soul exceeds matter in its operation, for it has a certain operation without the participation of a bodily organ, namely understanding. Whence its act of being is not just had in conjunction with matter. Therefore the act of being that belonged to the composite remains in it [the rational soul] after the body is dissolved, and once the body is restored at the resurrection, it is brought back to the same act of being that remained in the soul.[69]

Both the objection and the reply treat continuity in a thing's act of being as the decisive factor when it comes to its numerical identity over time. Aquinas's reply points out that a substance's act of being is continuous so long as its substantial form continues to exist, regardless of whether the substance itself continues to exist or not. This might sound odd. How could a substance's act of being remain if the substance to which it formerly belonged does not? Aquinas's reply also recalls passage 1.2, namely that composite substances, their substantial forms, and their matter all share the same act of being, but in different modes. Generally speaking, the substantial forms of composite substances have an act of being only in an inherent mode, as that by which the substances themselves exist. The composite substances themselves possess the same act

---

68. SCG 4.80.3 (Leo. 15:251).
69. SCG 4.81.11 (Leo. 15:253).

of being in a subsistent mode. Yet because of the human intellect's immateriality, human souls have their act of being in a subsistent mode as well as an inherent one, and are thus able to persist after the corruption of the humans themselves with the same acts of being as we formerly possessed. Following Aristotle, Aquinas thinks a living thing's act of being is just its life.[70] Hence, he would say that our souls continue on with our lives even while we no longer possess them. Again, this might sound odd, but as far as I can tell it is not incoherent, or obviously false.

Readers may recall from chapter 2 these four important features of Aquinas's thought concerning the respective identity-determining roles of forms and matter in composite substances. First, a composite substance's essence is primarily responsible for locating it in its kind. Second, such essences are themselves composed of a substantial form and prime matter, and within an essence it is primarily the form (of the part) that does the identity-determining work at the kind-level. Third, at the individual-level it is a composite substance's prime matter, as designated by certain quantitative dimensions, that determines which member of its kind it is. Fourth, because the quantitative dimensions of a composite substance obviously fluctuate considerably over its career, Aquinas is best understood as claiming that designated matter individuates forms at their origin, but that the forms themselves subsequently maintain substances' individual identity over time.

Putting these claims together, it is reasonable to suppose that on Aquinas's view, a composite substance persists as an individual member of its kind just as long as its essence does. That is, it lasts as long as its substantial form, individuated by its designated matter, continues to possess its act of being in an inherent mode. Generally speaking, if a substantial form should cease to inhere in matter, it would simply cease to exist altogether. Yet the human soul retains its act of being in a subsistent mode even after it ceases to inhere. It remains the sort of form apt to bring a human into existence by inhering in prime matter, and retains the individuation it received from designated matter at its origin. Hence, upon rejoining it to matter at the resurrection, God is able to bring about numerically the same human who previously died and ceased to exist for a time.

70. See note 17 in chapter 1.

A glance at the objections and replies bookending passages 6.8 and 6.9 in SCG confirm this interpretation. According to one objection:

(6.10) It is impossible for something to be one and the same in number whose essential principles cannot be the same in number, for having varied the essential principles, the essence of the thing—through which it is one and the same thing—is also varied.... Yet it seems that many of the essential principles of a human return to nothingness at death.... Therefore it seems impossible for a human to rise again numerically the same.[71]

Another focuses on the impossibility of our rising with the same bodies we had while living:

(6.11) If the same human body is restored to life, by the same reasoning it is necessary that whatever was in the human's body must also be restored the same. But for this to happen something very unseemly would follow ... on account of the hair, nails and bits which are clearly removed by daily trimming, and also because of other parts of the body which are digested out of sight by the action of the natural heat. If all of this were restored to the human rising again an unseemly size would result.[72]

Aquinas's response to the first of these objections (6.10) points out that in fact, "none of a human's essential principles fall entirely into nothingness at death." That is because:

(6.12) The rational soul which is a human's form remains after death ... and the matter which was subject to such a form remains as well, under the same dimensions through which it was the matter of some individual. Hence from the conjunction of numerically the same soul to numerically the same matter a human is restored.[73]

His response to the second objection (6.11) is similarly direct:

(6.13) In a human's body while he lives there are not always the same material parts, but only [sameness] according to species, while according to his matter his parts flow and ebb, nor because of this is there any obstacle to his remaining one human in number from the beginning of his life to its end. An example of this can be taken from fire which while it burns continuously is called

71. SCG 4.80.2 (Leo. 15:251).
72. Ibid., par. 4.
73. SCG 4.81.6 (Leo. 15:252).

one in number because its species remains, although wood is consumed and new wood put on. It is also this way in the human body, for the form and species of his singular parts remains continuously through his whole life, but the matter of his parts is digested through the action of natural heat, and is generated anew by food.... Thus therefore it is not required for a man to rise the same in number that whatever was in him materially according to the whole time of his life should be resumed, but just as much as suffices to complete his due quantity, and especially ... what was most perfectly consistent with his form and species of humanity.[74]

Aquinas makes clear in passage 6.13 that the persistence of a human's essence—her "form and species"—is sufficient for her numerical identity over time even as she cycles in and out new bits of matter. In 6.12, furthermore, he argues that none of a human's "essential principles" cease to exist at death: both its form and matter remain. That our substantial forms are capable of existing in a disembodied state has been a central focus of this book. The claim that our matter continues to exist "under the same dimensions" has seemed problematic to some commentators, as the dimensions of our bodies typically begin to alter rapidly after death as they decompose. I take Aquinas to mean, however, no more than that prime matter remains, and can resume our particular dimensions once rejoined to our soul, which retains its individuality even after death. As Thomas puts it in 6.13, such matter is only needed as is "perfectly consistent with [our] form and species of humanity." Hence, although our essences themselves cease to exist at death when the composite substances signified by the term "human" are corrupted, our essential principles remain. If God rejoins them, numerically the same humans return to life.

Here then is the distinction between the weaker and stronger senses of gappy existence that I mentioned earlier. A thing's existence would be gappy in a strong sense just in case it existed for a time, ceased to exist for a time, then returned to existence, while its act of being also ceased altogether with the thing itself. In contrast, a thing's existence counts as gappy in a weak sense just in case the thing in question exists for a time, ceases to exist for a time, then returns to existence, while its act of being

---

74. Ibid., par. 12 (Leo. 15:254).

continues all the while in the possession of its substantial form. As far as I can tell, humans are the only sort of thing that Aquinas thinks are capable of existing in this latter gappy way. We are able to do so due to our unique substantial forms, which possess their acts of being (while we are alive) in dual modes: both a material and an immaterial mode, and thus in both an inherent and a subsistent mode as well.

Returning to SPR, if we read it as involving the weaker sort of gappy existence, Aquinas would agree with the first premise, but reject the second. He would accept SPR1 because, according to cessationism, humans themselves cease to exist at death, and resurrection surely requires their returning to life. Hence the possibility of resurrection, if cessationism is true, requires at least the possibility of temporally gappy existence in the weak sense. Yet in this sense Aquinas evidently thinks that temporally gappy existence is metaphysically possible, and hence rejects SPR2.

If we read SPR as involving the stronger sort of gappy existence, in contrast, Aquinas would evidently reject its first premise. Even if cessationism is true, the possibility of the resurrection need not involve the possibility that a thing exists for a time, ceases to exist completely (together with its act of being), then returns to existence. That is because God might resurrect us instead by restoring to us an act of being that has continued, even in our absence, in the possession of our separated souls. The fact that Aquinas mentions separated souls in his replies to objections like those in passages 6.8 and 6.9, furthermore, has suggested to most recent commentators that they are a necessary ingredient in Thomas's story about the possibility of the resurrection.[75] That is to say, if we read SPR as making claims about the stronger sort of gappy existence, then Aquinas agrees with SPR2. Not even God could resurrect us if we ceased to exist completely at death. Our souls must persist in a disembodied state, preserving our acts of being, until the day of resurrection.

Interestingly, many of Aquinas's contemporaries rejected this view. Scotus and Ockham, to name just two, both believed that our souls would in fact exist in a disembodied state after death. They denied, how-

---

75. See Stump, *Aquinas*, 169; Pasnau, *Aquinas on Human Nature*, 393, and Christina Van Dyke, "Human Identity, Immanent Causal Relations, and the Principle of Non-Repeatability: Thomas Aquinas on the Bodily Resurrection," *Religious Studies* 43, no. 4 (2007): 373–94, at 388.

ever, that the persistence of souls after death is in any way required for God to be capable of resurrecting us. God could do so even if we should cease to exist entirely at death—body, soul, and all.[76]

What is more, some of Thomas's Renaissance interpreters took Aquinas himself to have agreed with Scotus and Ockham on this matter. Contrary to what most recent commentators suppose, both John Capreolus and Sylvester Ferrara read Aquinas as having held God is capable of restoring things like us to existence even if we are utterly "reduced to nothingness."[77] They base their interpretation largely on one of Aquinas's quodlibetal questions, which asks "whether, if something were reduced to nothingness, God could restore it the same in number." The body of the article reads as follows:

(6.14) It must be said that we should note a certain difference among things that can be reduced to nothingness. For there are some things whose unity has continuity of duration in its very notion, as is clear in the case of motion and time. Therefore an interruption of such things is indirectly contrary to their numerical unity. And things that imply a contradiction are not contained among the number of things that are possible for God, since they fall short of the notion of being. Therefore if things of this sort are reduced to nothingness, God cannot restore them the same in number. For this would require contradictories to be true at the same time—namely, that an interrupted motion should be one. But there are other things whose unity does not have continuity of duration in its very notion, as is the case with the unity of permanent things, unless *per accidens*, inasmuch as their act of being is subject to motion. For in this way things of this sort are measured by time, and their act of being is one and continuous according to the unity and continuity

---

76. See Marilyn McCord Adams, "The Resurrection of the Body according to Three Medieval Aristotelians: Thomas Aquinas, John Duns Scotus, William Ockham," *Philosophical Topics* 20, no. 2 (1998): 1–34, for discussion of Scotus's and Ockham's views, along with references. On Scotus, see also Richard Cross, "Identity, Origin and Persistence in Duns Scotus' Physics," *History of Philosophy Quarterly* 16, no. 1 (1999): 1–18.

77. See my "Mind the Gap? The Principle of Non-Repeatability and Aquinas's Account of the Resurrection," *Oxford Studies in Medieval Philosophy* 3 (2015): 99–127, for references to Capreolus and Ferrara. Nevitt argues that Capreolus and Ferrara read Aquinas correctly in "Don't Mind the Gap: A Reply to Adam Wood," *Oxford Studies in Medieval Philosophy* 4 (2016). Klima largely agrees with the interpretation I suggest here, and for some of the same reasons. See his "The Problem of 'Gappy Existence' in Aquinas' Metaphysics and Theology" in *The Metaphysics of Personal Identity*, ed. Klima, Alexander Hall, and Stephen Ogden (Newcastle upon Tyne: Cambridge Scholars Publishing, 2016), 119–34, along with Nevitt's response, "Annihilation, Re-Creation and Intermittent Existence in Aquinas," in the same volume, 101–18.

of time. And since an agent by nature cannot produce such things without motion, it's for that reason that a natural agent cannot restore things of this sort numerically the same if they were reduced to nothingness, or if they were corrupted substantially. But God could restore things of this sort, and do so without motion, since it is in his power to produce an effect without the intermediate causes. Therefore he can repair some things the same in number even if they have elapsed into nothingness.[78]

Two things are immediately obvious here. First, there are some things that even God's power could not restore. With respect to such things, Aquinas endorses what Christina Van Dyke has called "the principle of non-repeatability"; once gone, they are gone forever.[79] Second, however, the non-repeatability principle Aquinas endorses is clearly not maximum-strength, for he also clearly believes that there are certain things God could restore even if they were reduced to nothingness. Capreolus and Ferrara both think that humans fall into the latter category of things. It is true that no natural process could restore humans from total destruction. That is because natural processes always involve motion. Motions are successive entities, which exist in part at one time and in part at others, as opposed to permanent entities, which exist "all at once" (*totum simul*).[80] Because their existence is stretched out in time, the unity of a successive entity includes "continuity of duration in its very notion." If continuity of a motion is interrupted by rest, then the motion itself is gone forever. The principle of non-repeatability does indeed apply to successive entities. Accordingly, because natural processes could not repeat numerically the same motion by which I came about in the first place once this motion ceased, they could not restore me once I am gone. God, however, produces things without motion. And humans themselves are not successive entities. So God can restore things like us even if we are reduced utterly to nothingness.

Capreolus and Ferrara acknowledge that things will not actually transpire this way. Aquinas describes the way God will in fact resurrect

---

78. QQ 4.3.2 (Leo. 25.2:325.25–54).
79. Van Dyke, "Principle of Non-Repeatability," 377–79.
80. See for this formulation SCG 1.55 and 66; In Sent 1.8.2.2; ST 1a.7.4 ad 1 and 1a.10.5 ad 2. Robert Pasnau has helpful discussions of the permanent/successive distinction in *Metaphysical Themes*, chap. 18, and "On Existing All at Once," in *God, Eternity and Time*, ed. C. Tapp and E. Runggaldier (Farnham: Ashgate, 2011), 11–28.

us in passages like 6.9 and 6.12, both of which discuss reuniting separated souls with matter. The point of 6.14, however, is that God need not resurrect us this way. He is quite capable of doing so even if our souls cannot survive in a separated state at all. Or so Capreolus and Ferrara believe Aquinas taught.

For my part, I agree that passage 6.14 hinges on distinctions between the repeatability of permanent versus successive entities, and between what God versus natural agents are able to accomplish. But I think that Capreolus and Ferrara overlook a further crucial distinction Thomas draws. Immediately after distinguishing permanent from successive entities on the grounds that the unity of the former "does not have continuity of duration in its very notion," Aquinas adds "unless *per accidens*, inasmuch as their act of being is subject to motion. For in this way things of this sort are measured by time, and their act of being is one and continuous according to the unity and continuity of time." As I understand him, Thomas is distinguishing here between two different kinds of permanent entities: those whose act of being is "subject to motion," and hence "measured by time," and those whose act of being is not subject to motion. The latter include incorruptible beings like angels and celestial bodies, whose existence is measured not by time, on Aquinas's view, but by what he calls the *aevum*. Unlike temporal existence, aeviternal existence does not unfold part by part, such that some parts are "before" and others are "after." It happens "all at once." As a result, its unity does not require continuity in the way that temporal existence does. Incorruptible beings continue to exist so long as God does not annihilate them, and Aquinas thinks that God would never annihilate anything he has made. Nevertheless, 6.14 is claiming that if God were to annihilate the angel Gabriel, say, he could subsequently bring Gabriel back. Not so with human beings. The unity of a human's act of being—her life—requires temporal continuity. If it is interrupted it cannot be resumed, even by God's power. Even God could not restore us from utter nothingness. Hence the persistence of our acts of being in the possession of our separated souls is necessary for the possibility of the resurrection after all.

Textual evidence supporting my proposed interpretation of 6.14 over Capreolus and Ferrara's is not overwhelming, but a few texts point in its direction. In several questions dealing with the possibility of the resurrection, for instance, Aquinas acknowledges that certain of our accidents that have their acts of being only in a material mode, and hence cannot survive the body's corruption, cannot be restored the same in number at the resurrection.[81] He explains, in each case, why it will not affect the numerical identity of the humans rising again that these accidental features will be numerically distinct from those they possessed before death. Aquinas also appears to assert that substances that are totally destroyed cannot be restored in responding to a somewhat arcane question of eucharistic theology, namely whether it is possible to generate anything from a eucharistic host. Can I generate ashes from a host by burning it? Seemingly so, but it is hard to explain how, given that a consecrated host transforms from bread into the incorruptible body and blood of Christ. One suggestion is that when a host is burned, the bread returns, and ashes are generated from its corruption. Yet Aquinas rules out this possibility partly on the grounds that there is no way for the bread that was there before the host was consecrated to return. Suppose the bread were annihilated at the consecration. In that case, Aquinas says, "it could not return the same in number, since what falls into nothingness does not return the same in number."[82] This is true, he adds, "unless perhaps the substance in question is said to return because God creates a new substance in place of the first."[83] Creating a new (and different) substance that closely resembles the first is, of course, something God can do. Bringing back the old substance from total destruction is not.

In addition to the limited textual evidence favoring an interpretation on which Aquinas considered separated souls necessary for the possibility of the resurrection, there is good reason to believe he was philosophically committed to this view because of his views on individuation. I mentioned in chapter 2 that Aquinas's position on individuation shares similarities with Kripke's "origins essentialism" insofar as Thomas thinks that a composite substance's spatio-temporal origins mark it as this individual member of its kind as opposed to any other.

---

81. QDA 19 ad 13, In Sent 4.44.4.4.1 ad 6 and 4.44.1.1.2 ad 3, CT 1.154, SCG 4.81.7.
82. ST 3a.77.5 (Leo. 12:200).
83. Ibid.

Could a human have a certain set of spatio-temporal origins, cease to exist for a time, then reoriginate at a different time and place? No, as far as I can tell, given the way Aquinas thinks about individuation. What would settle the question whether the later human was really the first reoriginating or rather a numerically distinct human altogether? Thomas's answer seems to be: "whether the later human's act of being is continuous between her initial origin and her resurrection." Consider again the objection in passage 6.6 and Aquinas's reply in 6.7. The objection claims first that continuity in a thing's act of being is required for its numerical sameness, and second that because a human's act of being ceases at death, it cannot be restored at the resurrection. Aquinas's reply challenges the second claim, not the first. Why? In his *Physics* commentary Aquinas identifies three requirements for a motion to be numerically one.[84] First, the subject of motion must remain the same—motions cannot be transferred between one mover and another. Second, it must remain the same kind of motion generically and specifically. Third, its temporal continuity must not be interrupted by rest. Aquinas writes:

(6.15) For the continuity and unity of a motion it is required that it should be one with regard to time, such that no immobility or rest intervenes. Since the motion should cease at some time in which it was not moved, it would follow that it would rest at that time, and if rest is interposed there will be many motions and not one, for motions of which there is rest in the middle are many and not one. Whence if there is some motion that is interrupted by rest it will be neither one nor continuous. If there is time in the middle, however, it is interrupted by rest, as was shown, whence the continuity of motion requires that there be one continuous time.[85]

Although he does not make this explicit, I take it that the reason Aquinas insists on this last requirement for the unity of motions has to do with the way he thinks they are individuated. The individual identity of *this* motion as opposed to *that* other one stems not just from its subject but also from its temporal origins. Now a human's act of being is not itself a motion or operation.[86] But insofar as we are corruptible, changeable things, our lives are still subject to time and measured by it. Hence

---

84. In Phys 5.6.5/699.
85. In Phys 5.7.2/704 (Leo. 2:252).
86. In Sent 4.49.1.2.3 ad 2 and ST 1a.18.1 ad 2 and 18.2.

it seems reasonable to suppose that the same continuity requirements would apply to human lives as apply to motions. Just as an interrupted motion loses its numerical unity, so too would an interrupted human life. That is why Aquinas insists in 6.9 that a human's act of being does not cease at death, but rather continues on in the possession of her soul.

Note that on the reading of 6.14 I have offered, a similar continuity requirement would not hold for incorruptible beings like angels or celestial bodies. As I explained in chapter 2, these entities are individuated differently from sublunary, corruptible substances like ourselves. A celestial body's individuation, for instance, depends not on its spatiotemporal origins but on its "using up" all the matter of a kind suitable for its form when it first comes into being. If, *per impossibile*, God should annihilate a celestial body and then recreate it, it is possible that the later-originating body is numerically identical to the earlier one. The same is not true of human beings, according to Aquinas's position.

Separated Souls and the Resurrection II: Is Aquinas's Position Correct?

In the previous section I focused on arguing that Aquinas himself thought that separated souls are necessary if God is able to resurrect us. Aquinas thinks that humans are non-repeatable in the sense that once their act of being has ceased altogether, even God cannot bring them back numerically the same as they were previously. Having seen something of the reasoning underlying Aquinas's commitment to the principle of non-repeatability in the case of human beings, let me conclude this book with a few thoughts concerning its philosophical strength and theological attractiveness.

As I indicated, Scotus and Ockham, among others, endorse the possibility of strongly gappy existence and reject the principle of non-repeatability. Scotus writes:

Suppose God preserves something in existence at one point in time A, *and* for the whole period *up to* some other point in time B, *and* at point in time B. No one would deny, in this case, that the thing in question would be [numerically] identical at points A and B. So if God preserves a thing in existence *just* at points A and B, but does not preserve it for the period in between them, the thing in question will still be one and the same at A and B, despite its existence having been interrupted in between these two points. As proof, consider that a thing's identity at any two given points in time does not depend essentially on its preservation in the period in between either as a formal cause or as any sort of essential cause.[87]

The reasoning here obviously depends on the possibility of temporal gaps in a thing's existence. But Scotus thinks such gaps are possible in part because he denies that any of a thing's temporally indexed features plays a role in determining its identity.[88] *When* a thing exists is one of its accidental features. So given the metaphysical dependence of accidents on their substantial subjects for their identity, it cannot be that *when* a substance exists plays any role in determining *which* substance of its kind it ends up being.[89] Ockham, for his part, takes individuality to be primitive, so on his view it is not clear that there are any further factors in terms of which we could analyze whether a human coming to life at the resurrection is numerically the same as one who previously passed away.[90] Ockham sees no reason that things in general could not be brought back from destruction, or interrupted motions restored. I take it part of the reason both he and Scotus disagree with Aquinas on this score stems from their different views on individuation.

Many contemporary philosophers of religion side with Scotus and Ockham against Aquinas on this issue. Trenton Merricks, for instance, thinks (much like Ockham) that identity over time is primitive and unanalyzable.[91] As a result, there can be no good reason for doubting that bringing deceased humans back to life is a miracle God could accomplish, even if the humans in question are totally destroyed by death—body, soul, and all. Others think that Merricks is wrong that no criteria for identity over time are available, but think that the criteria we can identify might be satisfied even on a physicalist account of human

---

87. Scotus, *Ord.* 4.43.1 in *Opera omnia*, ed. L. Wadding (Paris: Vives, 1639/1891–95), 20:7.

88. See Scotus, *Ord.* 2.2.1.4.180 in *Opera omnia*, ed. C. Balic et al. (Vatican City: Typis Polyglottis Vaticanis, 1950–), 7:235, for his most explicit statement of this view. See Cross, "Identity, Origin and Persistence," for further analysis of Scotus's argument.

89. See Scotus, *Quaestiones super libros Metaphysicorum Aristotelis* 7.13.20, 24, and 26 in *Opera philosophica*, ed. G. Etzkorn et al. (St. Bonaventure, N.Y.: The Franciscan Institute, 1997–2006), 4:223–27.

90. See Jorge Gracia's epilogue to *Individuation in Scholasticism*, 543–50, at 548.

91. See Trenton Merricks, "There Are No Criteria of Identity over Time," *Nous* 32, no. 1 (1998): 106–24.

nature. Dean Zimmerman, for instance, thinks that for a material object like a human being to persist through time requires continuous "immanent causal connections" between our earlier and later temporal stages.[92] He sees no reason why such causal connections could not straddle temporal gaps. Hence, on the metaphysical "just-so story" Zimmerman calls "the Falling Elevator Model" of resurrection, God grants each atom of a soon-to-be-deceased human's body a miraculous fissioning power, which, when activated, results in two human bodies. One immediately goes on to die. We mourn over it, bury it, etc. The other does not appear until the day of resurrection, when he quickly undoes whatever damage was about to kill the human off. And there is the human herself, good as new, back from the dead. No separated souls are needed on this account of Zimmerman's, only immanent causal connections straddling temporal gaps.

Aquinas might complain that it is just as impossible for causal connections to straddle temporal gaps as it is for there to be action at a spatial distance. Yet as is well-known, many of Aquinas's contemporaries criticized his views regarding action at a distance, arguing that it is possible after all, and indeed that it frequently takes place even in the physical world.[93] As far as I know, Zimmerman is correct that contemporary physics generally treats action at a spatial distance as possible. I am less sure about action at a temporal distance. But I know of no general argument—and certainly no argument of Aquinas's—against its possibility. Without one, it appears that even if Aquinas thought separated souls are necessary for God's ability to resurrect us, as I have argued he

92. Zimmerman criticizes Merricks's "identity mysticism" along these lines in "Criteria of Identity and the 'Identity Mystics,'" *Erkenntnis* 48, nos. 2/3 (1998): 281–301, and argues that diachronic identity requires immanent causal connections at "The Compatibility of Materialism and Survival: The 'Falling Elevator' Model," *Faith and Philosophy* 16, no. 2 (1999): 194–212, and "Bodily Resurrection: The Falling Elevator Model Revisited," in *Personal Identity and Resurrection*, ed. Georg Gasser (Farnham: Ashgate, 2010), 33–50.

93. For a critical examination of Aquinas's arguments for the impossibility of action at a distance see Francis Kovach, "Aquinas's Theory of Action at a Distance: A Critical Analysis," in his *Scholastic Challenges to Some Mediaeval and Modern Ideas* (Stillwater, Okla.: Western Publications, 1987), 149–77, and "Action at a Distance in St. Thomas Aquinas," in *Thomistic Papers* 2, ed. L. A. Kennedy and Jack Marler (Houston, Tex.: Center for Thomistic Studies, 1986), 85–132. Christopher Decaen presents a more sympathetic assessment of Aquinas's views in "The Impossibility of Action at a Distance," in *Wisdom's Apprentice: Thomistic Essays in Honor of Lawrence Dewan, O.P.*, ed. Peter Kwasniewski (Washington, D.C.: The Catholic University of America Press, 2007), 173–200.

does, contemporary philosophers of religion are under no philosophical obligation to agree. Thomas's reasons for holding the view he does are rooted in a metaphysics of individuation that philosophers today are not obliged to accept.

That being said, I think Aquinas's stance on the afterlife should be considered a highly attractive option by many Christian philosophers of religion on theological grounds. Consider again Zimmerman and Merricks. The former is, in fact (as far as I know), a dualist, who says "I do not wish to rely upon the Falling Elevator Model as a mechanism for *my* survival. I hope, like the Apostle Paul, that one can be absent from this body yet present with the Lord, even before a general resurrection returns us all to a more natural, embodied state."[94] The Apostle's Creed affirms the "communion of saints," and many Christian traditions take this affirmation, along with Paul's words about being present with the Lord, to mean that the deceased remain in some way, awaiting the resurrection. On Aquinas's view, even though separated souls are not humans, deceased humans do indeed remain in *some* way, given that their souls continue to exist in a separated state, carrying on with their lives even while they themselves are no longer present. Employing the practice of synecdoche, we can even refer to these souls using the names of the humans to whom they once belonged, and to whom they will belong again after the resurrection. This much should go some way toward satisfying dualists who hope to be present with the Lord, and interpret the communion of saints in a traditional way. Merricks, for his part, rejects dualist accounts of the afterlife partly on the grounds that they do not sufficiently explain the central importance of the resurrection in the Christian tradition.[95] I agree with Merricks that the importance of the resurrection is certainly something any theologically satisfactory account of the afterlife must be able to explain. Yet as I explained in the previous section, Aquinas's account makes it quite clear why the resurrection is so important. Without it you and I have no hope of an afterlife. I might be present with the Lord in a metaphorical way insofar as

---

94. Zimmerman, "Personal Identity and Resurrection," 50.
95. Trenton Merricks, "The Resurrection of the Body and the Life Everlasting," in *Reason for the Hope Within*, ed. Michael Murray (Grand Rapids, Mich.: Eerdmans, 1998), 261–86, at 280–83.

my former substantial form (my soul) survives in a disembodied state. Yet because I myself do not survive, my hope for eternal life hinges on God someday resurrecting me. Because Aquinas's stance on the afterlife seems capable of meeting the concerns of both dualists and their opponents, it should be considered an attractive option for Christian philosophers of religion.

Of course, if the reasoning of Aquinas's that I traced throughout this book's first five chapters is cogent, then Thomas had good reasons for believing that our souls are capable of existing in a disembodied state, whether or not this is strictly speaking necessary, either for the possibility of the resurrection, or on theological grounds. These reasons are based upon the immateriality of the human intellect; I hope this book has made it clear why. I also hope to have clarified what exactly Aquinas meant by the human intellect's immateriality, and why he thought it has this status. Some of Aquinas's thought on these issues depends, of course, on deeply rooted metaphysical commitments that I have only been able to introduce here, without defending them fully. In a finite project I trust that this is not a surprising or disappointing result.

SELECTED BIBLIOGRAPHY

Adams, Marilyn McCord. *William Ockham*. Notre Dame, Ind.: University of Notre Dame Press, 1987.

———. "The Resurrection of the Body according to Three Medieval Aristotelians: Thomas Aquinas, John Duns Scotus, William Ockham." *Philosophical Topics* 20, no. 2 (1992): 1–34.

Ackrill, J. L. "Aristotle's Distinction between *Energeia* and *Kinesis*." In *New Essays on Plato and Aristotle*, edited by R. Bambrough, 121–41. London: Routledge, 1965.

Albert the Great. *Opera omnia*. Edited by A. Borgnet. Paris: Vives, 1890–99.

Anscombe, G. E. M. "Analytic Philosophy and the Spirituality of Man." In *Human Life, Action and Ethics*, edited by Mary Geach and Luke Gormally, 3–16. Exeter: Imprint Academic, 2005.

Aquinas, Thomas. *Sancti Thomae Aquinatis Doctoris Angelici Opera omnia iussu impensaque Leonis XIII P.M. edita*. Rome: Commisio Leonina, 1882–.

———. *Sancti Thomae Aquinatis Opera omnia t. 7/2: Commentum in quartum librum Sententiarum magistri Petri Lombardi*. Parma: Petrus Fiaccadoris, 1858.

———. *Scriptum super libros Sententiarum*. Edited by P. Mandonnet and M. F. Moos. Paris: P. Lethielleux, 1929–47.

———. *S. Thomas Aquinatis In duodecim libros Metaphysicorum Aristotelis expositio*. Edited by M. R. Cathala and R. M. Spiazzi. Rome: Marietti, 1971.

———. *S. Thomae Aquinatis Quaestiones disputatae, t. 2: Quaestiones disputatae de potentia*. Edited by P. M. Pession. Rome: Marietti, 1965.

———. *S. Thomae Aquinatis Super Epistolas S. Pauli lectura, t. 1: Super primam Epistolam ad Corintios lectura*. Edited by R. Cai. Rome: Marietti, 1953.

———. *S. Thomae Aquinatis Super librum De Causis expositio*. Edited by H. D. Saffrey. Louvain: Société Philosophique, 1954.

Aristotle. *The Complete Works of Aristotle*. Edited by Jonathan Barnes. Princeton, N.J.: Princeton University Press, 1984.

Arlig, Andrew. "Medieval Mereology." In *The Stanford Encyclopedia of Philosophy* (2015), edited by Edward Zalta. Available at https://plato.stanford.edu/entries/mereology-medieval/.

Armstrong, David. *Universals: An Opinionated Introduction*. Boulder, Colo.: Westview, 1989.
Averroes. *Averrois Cordubensis Commentarium Magnum in Aristotelis De anima libros*. Edited by F. Stuart Crawford. Cambridge, Mass.: Medieval Academy of America, 1953.
Avicenna. *De anima*. In *Liber de anima seu sextus De naturalibus*, edited by S. Van Riet. Leiden: Brill, 1968.
———. *Logica*. In *Opera philosophica*. Venice, 1508.
———. *Metaphysics*. In *Liber de Philosophia Prima sive Scientia Divina V–X*, edited by S. Van Riet. Leiden: Brill, 1980.
Bacon, Roger. *Communia naturalium*. In *Opera hactenus inedita Rogeri Baconi*, edited by Robert Steele. Oxford: Oxford University Press, 1909–40.
Baker, Lynne Rudder. "Why Constitution Is Not Identity." *Journal of Philosophy* 94, no. 12 (1997): 599–621.
———. "Non-Reductive Materialism." In *The Oxford Handbook of Philosophy of Mind*, edited by Brian McGlaughlin, Ansgar Beckermann, and Sven Walter, 109–27. Oxford: Oxford University Press, 2009.
———. *Naturalism and the First-Person Perspective*. Oxford: Oxford University Press, 2013.
Baldner, Stephen. "St. Albert the Great and St. Thomas on the Presence of Elements in a Compound." *Sapientia* 54 (1999): 41–57.
———. "Thomas Aquinas on Celestial Matter." *The Thomist* 68, no. 3 (2004): 431–67.
Barnes, Jonathan. "Aristotle's Concept of Mind." *Proceedings of the Aristotelian Society* 72, no. 1 (1972): 101–14.
———. *Porphyry*. Oxford: Oxford University Press, 2003.
Bazan, B. Carlos. "The Highest Encomium of the Human Body." In *Littera, sensus, sententia: studi in onore del Prof. Clemente J. Vansteenkiste*, edited by A. Lobato, 99–116. Milan: Massimo, 1991.
———. "The Human Soul: Form or Substance? Thomas Aquinas' Critique of Eclectic Aristotelianism." *Archives D'Histoire Doctrinale et Litteraire du Moyen Age* 64 (1997): 96–126.
Bechtel, William. "Reducing Psychology While Maintaining Its Autonomy Via Mechanistic Explanations." In *The Matter of the Mind: Philosophical Essays on Psychology, Neuroscience and Reduction*, edited by M. Schouton and Huib Looren de Jong, 172–98. Malden, Mass.: Blackwell, 2007.
Beckermann, Ansgar. "What Is Property Physicalism?" In *The Oxford Handbook of Philosophy of Mind*, edited by Brian McGlaughlin, Ansgar Beckermann, and Sven Walter, 152–72. Oxford: Oxford University Press, 2009.
Bedau, Mark. "Weak Emergence." In *Philosophical Perspectives*, vol. 11: *Mind, Causation and World*, edited by James Tomberlin, 375–99. Malden, Mass.: Blackwell, 1997.
Bennett, M. R., and P. M. S. Hacker. *Philosophical Foundations of Neuroscience*. Malden, Mass.: Blackwell, 2003.
Beuchot, Mauricio. "Chrysostum Javellus and Francis Sylvester Ferrara." In *Individuation in Scholasticism: The Later Middle-Ages and the Counter-Reformation*,

1150–1650, edited by Jorge Gracia, 457–74. Buffalo: State University of New York Press, 1994.
Block, Ned. "Troubles with Functionalism." *Minnesota Studies in the Philosophy of Science* 9 (1978): 261–325.
Bobik, Joseph. *Aquinas on Matter and Form and the Elements*. Notre Dame, Ind.: University of Notre Dame Press, 1998.
Boethius. *Second Commentary on Porphyry's Isagoge*. In *Five Texts on the Mediaeval Problem of Universals*, translated by P. V. Spade, 20–25. Indianapolis, Ind.: Hackett, 1994.
Bolton, Robert. "Perception Naturalized in Aristotle's *De anima*." In *Metaphysics, Soul, and Ethics in Ancient Thought: Themes from the Work of Richard Sorabji*, edited by Ricardo Salles, 209–44. Oxford: Oxford University Press, 2005.
Bonaventure. *Opera omnia*. Edited by Collegium S. Bonaventurae. Ad Aquas Claras: Ex Typographia Collegii S. Bonaventurae, 1882–1902.
Braine, David. *The Human Person: Animal and Spirit*. Notre Dame, Ind.: University of Notre Dame Press, 1994.
Brock, Stephen. *The Philosophy of Saint Thomas Aquinas*. Eugene, Ore.: Cascade Books, 2015.
Brower, Jeffrey. "Matter, Form and Individuation." In *The Oxford Handbook of Aquinas*, edited by Brian Davies and Eleonore Stump, 83–103. Oxford: Oxford University Press, 2012.
———. *Aquinas's Ontology of the Material World: Change, Hylomorphism and Material Objects*. Oxford: Oxford University Press, 2014.
———. "Medieval Theories of Relations." In *The Stanford Encyclopedia of Philosophy* (2015), edited by Edward Zalta. Available at https://plato.stanford.edu/archives/win2015/entries/relations-medieval/.
———. "Aquinas on the Problem of Universals." *Philosophy and Phenomenological Research* 92, no. 3 (2016): 715–35.
Brower, Jeffrey, and Susan Brower-Toland. "Aquinas on Mental Representation: Concepts and Intentionality." *Philosophical Review* 117, no. 2 (2008): 193–243.
Brown, Christopher. "Aquinas on the Individuation of Non-Living Substances." *Proceedings of the American Catholic Philosophical Association* 75 (2001): 237–54.
———. *Aquinas and the Ship of Theseus: Solving Puzzles about Material Objects*. London: Continuum, 2005.
———. "Souls, Ships and Substances: A Response to Toner." *American Catholic Philosophical Quarterly* 81, no. 4 (2007): 655–68.
Brugger, E. Christian. "Aquinas on the Immateriality of Intellect." *National Catholic Bioethics Quarterly* 8, no. 1 (2008): 103–19.
Burnyeat, Miles. "Is an Aristotelian Philosophy of Mind Still Credible? A Draft." In *Essays on Aristotle's De anima*, edited by Martha Nussbaum and Amelie Oksenberg Rorty, 15–26. Oxford: Oxford University Press, 1992.
———. "Aquinas on 'Spiritual Change' in Perception." In *Ancient and Medieval Theories of Intentionality*, edited by Dominik Perler, 129–54. Dordrecht: Springer, 2001.
Butera, Giuseppe. "Incomplete Persons: Thomas Aquinas on Separated Souls and the Identity of the Human Person." In *Distinctions of Being: Philosophical*

Approaches to Reality, edited by Nikolag Zunic, 61–80. Washington, D.C.: American Maritain Association Publications, 2013.

Callus, D. A. "The Origins of the Problem of the Unity of Form." *The Thomist* 24, no. 2 (1961): 257–85.

Caston, Victor. "The Spirit and the Letter: Aristotle on Perception." In *Metaphysics, Soul and Ethics: Themes From the Work of Richard Sorabji*, edited by Ricardo Salles, 245–320. Oxford: Oxford University Press, 2004.

Casey, Gerard. "Immateriality and Intentionality." In *At the Heart of the Real*, edited by F. O'Rourke, 97–112. Dublin: Irish Academic Press, 1992.

Chalmers, David. *The Conscious Mind: In Search of a Fundamental Theory*. Oxford: Oxford University Press, 1997.

Charlton, William. "Aristotle and the Principle of Individuation." *Phronesis* 17, no. 3 (1972): 239–49.

Churchland, Paul. *Plato's Camera: How The Physical Brain Captures a Landscape of Abstract Universals*. Cambridge, Mass.: MIT Press, 2012.

Cohen, Sheldon M. "St. Thomas Aquinas on the Immaterial Reception of Sensible Forms." *The Philosophical Review* 91, no. 2 (1982): 193–209.

Cohoe, Caleb. "Why the Intellect Cannot Have a Bodily Organ: De anima 3.4." *Phronesis* 58, no. 4 (2013): 347–77.

Connell, Richard. "The 'Intus Apparens' and the Immateriality of the Intellect." *New Scholasticism* 32, no. 2 (1958): 151–86.

Corkum, Phil. "Aristotle on Ontological Dependence." *Phronesis* 53, no. 1 (2008): 65–92.

Correia, Fabrice. *Existential Dependence and Cognate Notions*. Munich: Philosophia Verlag, 2005.

Craver, Carl, and Gualtiero Piccinini. "Integrating Psychology and Neuroscience: Functional Analyses as Mechanism Sketches." *Synthese* 183, no. 3 (2011): 283–311.

Cross, Richard. "Is Aquinas's Proof for the Indestructibility of the Soul Successful?" *The British Journal for the History of Philosophy* 5, no. 1 (1997): 48–76.

———. *The Physics of Duns Scotus*. Oxford: Oxford University Press, 1998.

———. "Identity, Origin and Persistence in Duns Scotus' Physics." *History of Philosophy Quarterly* 16, no. 1 (1999): 1–18.

Cummins, Robert. "Functional Analysis." *The Journal of Philosophy* 72, no. 20 (1975): 741–65.

Cunningham, Francis. *Essence vs. Existence in Thomism: A Mental vs. the "Real" Distinction?* Lanham, Md.: University Press of America, 1988.

Dales, Richard. *The Problem of the Rational Soul in the Thirteenth Century*. Leiden: Brill, 2005.

Davidson, Donald. "Rational Animals." *Dialectica* 36, no. 4 (1982): 317–27.

———. "Mental Events." In his *Essays on Actions and Events*, 207–25. Oxford: Oxford University Press, 2001.

Davies, Brian. *Aquinas: An Introduction*. London: Continuum, 2002.

———. "Kenny on Aquinas on Being." *Modern Schoolman* 82, no. 2 (2005): 111–29.

Decaen, Christopher. "Elemental Virtual Presence in St. Thomas." *The Thomist* 64, no. 2 (2000): 271–300.

———. "The Impossibility of Action at a Distance." In *Wisdom's Apprentice: Thomistic Essays in Honor of Lawrence Dewan, O.P.*, edited by Peter Kwasniewski, 173–200. Washington, D.C.: The Catholic University of America Press, 2007.

Dewan, Lawrence. *Form and Being: Studies in Thomistic Metaphysics*. Washington, D.C.: The Catholic University of America Press, 2006.

Dretske, Fred. *Knowledge and the Flow of Information*. Cambridge: Cambridge University Press, 1981.

———. "Misrepresentation." In *Belief: Form, Content and Function*, edited by Radu Bogdan, 17–36. Oxford: Oxford University Press, 1986.

———. *Explaining Behavior: Reasons in a World of Causes*. Cambridge, Mass.: MIT Press, 1988.

———. *Naturalizing the Mind*. Cambridge, Mass.: MIT Press, 1995.

Eberl, Jason. "The Metaphysics of Resurrection: Issues of Identity in Aquinas." *Proceedings of the American Catholic Philosophical Association* 74 (2001): 215–30.

———. "Do Human Persons Persist between Death and Resurrection?" In *Metaphysics and God: Essays in Honor of Eleonore Stump*, edited by Kevin Timpe, 188–205. London: Routledge, 2009.

Edwards, Sandra. "The Realism of Aquinas." In *Thomas Aquinas: Contemporary Philosophical Perspectives*, edited by Brian Davies, 97–116. Oxford: Oxford University Press, 2002.

Evans, C. Stephen. "Separable Souls: Dualism, Selfhood and the Possibility of Life after Death." *Christian Scholars' Review* 34, no. 3 (2005): 327–40.

Everson, Stephen. *Aristotle on Perception*. Oxford: Oxford University Press, 1996.

Feser, Edward. *Philosophy of Mind: A Short Introduction*. Oxford: Oneworld, 2005.

———. *Aquinas: A Beginner's Guide*. Oxford: Oneworld, 2009.

———. "Kripke, Ross and the Immaterial Aspects of Thought." *American Catholic Philosophical Quarterly* 87, no. 1 (2013): 1–32.

Fine, Kit. "Ontological Dependence." *Proceedings of the Aristotelian Society* 95, no. 3 (1995): 269–90.

———. "Things and Their Parts." *Midwest Studies in Philosophy* 23 (1999): 61–74.

Fodor, Jerry. "Semantics, Wisconsin Style." *Synthese* 59, no. 3 (1984): 231–50.

———. *Psychosemantics*. Cambridge, Mass.: MIT Press, 1987.

———. *A Theory of Content and Other Essays*. Cambridge, Mass.: MIT Press, 1990.

Foster, David Ruel. "A Study and Critique of Thomas Aquinas' Arguments for the Immateriality of the Intellect." PhD diss., The Catholic University of America, 1988.

———. "Aquinas on the Immateriality of the Intellect." *The Thomist* 55, no. 3 (1991): 415–38.

———. "Aquinas's Arguments for Spirit." *Proceedings of the American Catholic Philosophical Association* 65 (1991): 235–52.

Fox, John. "Truthmaker." *Australasian Journal of Philosophy* 65, no. 2 (1987): 188–207.

Freddoso, Alfred. "No Room at the Inn: Contemporary Philosophy of Mind Meets Thomistic Philosophical Anthropology." *Acta Philosophica* 24, no. 1 (2015): 15–30.

Galluzo, Gabriele. "Aquinas on Common Nature and Universals." *Recherches de Théologie et Philosophie Médiévales* 71, no. 1 (2004): 131–71.

Geach, Peter. *God and the Soul*. South Bend, Ind.: St. Augustine's Press, 1969.

Geiger, Louis. "Abstraction et séparation d'après S. Thomas. In *De trinitate* q. 5, a. 3." *Revue des sciences philosophiques et theologiques* 31 (1947): 3–40.

George, Marie. "On the Meaning of 'Immanent Activity' according to Aquinas." *The Thomist* 78, no. 4 (2014): 537–55.

Gilson, Etienne. *Being and Some Philosophers*. Toronto: PIMS, 1952.

———. "Quasi definitio substantiae." In *St. Thomas Aquinas 1274–1974: Commemorative Studies*, edited by Armand Maurer et al., 1:111–29. Toronto: PIMS, 1974.

Gracia, Jorge. "Cutting the Gordian Knot of Ontology: Thomas's Solution to the Problem of Universals." In *Thomas Aquinas and His Legacy*, edited by D. Gallagher, 16–36. Washington, D.C.: The Catholic University of America Press, 1994.

———. *Individuation in Scholasticism*. Albany: State University of New York Press, 1994.

Grice, Paul. "Meaning." *The Philosophical Review* 66, no. 3 (1957): 377–88.

Gross, Michael. "Could Plants Have Cognitive Abilities?" *Current Biology* 26, no. 5 (2016): 181–84.

Hacker, P. M. S. *The Intellectual Powers: A Study of Human Nature*. Oxford: Wiley Blackwell, 2013.

Haldane, John. "Aquinas on Sense Perception." *The Philosophical Review* 92, no. 2 (1983): 233–39.

———. "(I Am) Thinking." *Ratio* 16, no. 2 (2003): 124–39.

———. "The Metaphysics of Intellect(ion)." *Proceedings of the American Catholic Philosophical Association* 80 (2007): 39–55.

———. *Reasonable Faith*. London: Routledge, 2010.

Hamlyn, D. W. *Sensation and Perception*. New York: Humanities Press, 1961.

Hasker, William. *The Emergent Self*. Ithaca, N.Y.: Cornell University Press, 1999.

Haugeland, John. "The Intentionality All-Stars." In his *Having Thought: Essays in the Metaphysics of Mind*, 127–70. Cambridge, Mass.: Harvard University Press, 1998.

Heil, John. *The Universe as We Find It*. Oxford: Oxford University Press, 2012.

Henninger, Mark. *Relations: Medieval Theories: 1250–1325*. Oxford: Oxford University Press, 1989.

Hochschild, Joshua. "Kenny and Aquinas on Individual Essences." *Proceeding of the Society for Medieval Logic and Metaphysics* 6 (2006): 45–56.

———. "Form, Essence, Soul: Distinguishing Principles of Thomistic Metaphysics." In *Distinctions of Being: Philosophical Approaches to Reality*, edited by Nikolag Zunic, 21–35. Washington, D.C.: American Maritain Association Publications, 2013.

Hoffman, Paul. "St. Thomas Aquinas on the Halfway State of Sensible Being." *The Philosophical Review* 99, no. 1 (1990): 73–92.

———. "Aquinas on Spiritual Change." *Oxford Studies in Medieval Philosophy* 2 (2015): 98–103.

Inman, Ross. "Essential Dependence, Truthmaking and Mereology: Then and

Now." In *Metaphysics: Aristotelian, Scholastic, Analytic*, edited by Lukas Novak, Daniel D. Novotny, Prokop Sousedik, and David Svoboda, 73–90. Frankfurt: Ontos Verlag, 2012.

Jacobs, Nathan. "Are Created Spirits Composed of Matter and Form: A Defense of Pneumatic Hylomorphism." *Philosophia Christi* 14, no. 1 (2012): 79–108.

Jaworski, William. *Structure and the Metaphysics of Mind: How Hylomorphism Solves the Mind-Body Problem*. Oxford: Oxford University Press, 2016.

Johnston, Mark. "Constitution Is Not Identity." *Mind* 101, no. 401 (1992): 89–105.

———. "Hylomorphism." *The Journal of Philosophy* 103, no. 12 (2006): 652–98.

Jordan, Mark. *Ordering Wisdom: The Hierarchy of Philosophical Discourses in Aquinas*. Notre Dame, Ind.: University of Notre Dame Press, 1986.

———. "Medicine and Natural Philosophy in Aquinas." In *Thomas von Aquin*, edited by Albert Zimmerman, Miscellanea Medievalia 19, 233–46. Berlin: De Gruyter, 1988.

Kahn, Charles. "Aristotle on Thinking." In *Essays on Aristotle's De anima*, edited by Martha Nussbaum and Amelie Oksenberg Rorty, 359–80. Oxford: Oxford University Press, 1992.

Kemp, Simon, and Garth Fletcher. "The Medieval Theory of the Interior Senses." *American Journal of Psychology* 106, no. 4 (1993): 559–76.

Kennedy, L. A. "A New Disputed Question of Saint Thomas Aquinas on the Immortality of the Soul." *Archives d'Histoire Doctrinale et Littéraire du Moyen Âge* 45 (1978): 205–23.

Kenny, Anthony. "Intellect and Imagination in Aquinas." In *Aquinas: A Collection of Critical Essays*, edited by Kenny, 273–93. Garden City, N.J.: Anchor Books, 1969.

———. "The Homunculus Fallacy." In *Interpretations of Life and Mind*, edited by M. Grene, 65–83. London: Routledge, 1971.

———. *The Metaphysics of Mind*. Oxford: Oxford University Press, 1989.

———. *Aquinas on Mind*. London: Routledge, 1993.

———. "Body, Soul and Intellect in Aquinas." In his *Essays on the Aristotelian Tradition*, 76–91. Oxford: Oxford University Press, 2000.

———. *Aquinas on Being*. Oxford: Oxford University Press, 2002.

———. "Intentionality: Aquinas and Wittgenstein." In *Thomas Aquinas: Contemporary Philosophical Perspectives*, edited by Brian Davies, 243–56. Oxford: Oxford University Press, 2002.

Kim, Jaegwon. *Supervenience and Mind*. Cambridge: Cambridge University Press, 1993.

———. "Emergence: Core Ideas and Issues." *Synthese* 151, no. 3 (2006): 547–59.

King, Peter. "The Problem of Individuation in the Middle Ages." *Theoria* 66, no. 2 (2000): 159–84.

———. "Rethinking Representation in the Middle Ages: A Vade-Mecum to Mediaeval Theories of Mental Representation." In *Representation and Objects of Thought in Medieval Philosophy*, edited by Henrik Lagerlund, 83–102. Aldershot: Ashgate, 2007.

———. "Why Isn't the Mind-Body Problem Medieval?" In *Forming the Mind: Essays on the Internal Senses and the Mind/Body Problem from Avicenna to the Medical En-

lightenment, edited by Henrik Lagerlund, 187–206. Dordrecht: Springer, 2007.
———. "The Inner Cathedral: Mental Architecture in High Scholasticism." *Vivarium* 46, no. 3 (2008): 253–74.
———. "Medieval Intentionality and Pseudo-Intentionality." *Quaestio* 10 (2010): 25–44.
———. "Thinking About Things: Singular Thought in the Middle Ages." In *Intentionality, Cognition and Mental Representation in Medieval Philosophy*, edited by Gyula Klima, 104–21. New York: Fordham University Press, 2015.
Klima, Gyula. "The Changing Role of *Entia Rationis* in Medieval Semantics and Ontology: A Comparative Study With a Reconstruction." *Synthese* 96, no. 1 (1993): 25–58.
———. "The Semantic Principles Underlying Saint Thomas Aquinas's Metaphysics of Being." *Medieval Philosophy and Theology* 5, no. 1 (1996): 87–141.
———. "Ockham's Semantics and the Ontology of the Categories." In *The Cambridge Companion to Ockham*, edited by Paul Spade, 118–42. Cambridge: Cambridge University Press, 1999.
———. "Man = Body + Soul: Aquinas's Arithmetic of Human Nature." In *Thomas Aquinas: Contemporary Philosophical Perspectives*, edited by Brian Davies, 257–74. Oxford: Oxford University Press, 2002.
———. "Aquinas' Theory of the Copula and the Analogy of Being." *Logical Analysis and the History of Philosophy* 5 (2002): 159–76.
———. "Tradition and Innovation in Medieval Theories of Mental Representation." *Proceedings of the Society for Medieval Logic and Metaphysics* 4 (2004): 4–11.
———. "On Kenny on Aquinas on Being: A Critical Review of *Aquinas on Being* by Anthony Kenny." *International Philosophical Quarterly* 44, no. 4 (2004): 567–80.
———. "Thomas of Sutton on Individuation." *Proceedings of the Society for Medieval Logic and Metaphysics* 5 (2006): 70–78.
———. "Aquinas on the Materiality of the Human Soul and the Immateriality of the Human Intellect." *Philosophical Investigations* 32, no. 2 (2009): 163–82.
———. *John Buridan*. Oxford: Oxford University Press, 2009.
———. "Reply to Bob Pasnau on Aquinas's Proofs of the Immateriality of the Intellect." In *The Immateriality of the Human Mind, the Semantics of Analogy, and the Conceivability of God*, edited by Klima and Alexander Clayton, 49–60. Newcastle-upon-Tyne: Cambridge Scholars Press, 2011.
———. "The Medieval Problem of Universals." In *Stanford Encyclopedia of Philosophy* (2013), edited by Edward Zalta. Available at http://plato.stanford.edu/entries/universals-medieval/.
———. "Three Myths of Intentionality Versus Some Medieval Philosophers." *International Journal of Philosophical Studies* 21, no. 3 (2013): 359–76.
———. "Semantic Content in Aquinas and Ockham." In *Linguistic Content: New Essays on the History of Philosophy of Language*, edited by Margaret Cameron and Robert Stainton, 121–35. Oxford: Oxford University Press, 2015.
———. "Universality and Immateriality." *Acta Philosophica* 24, no. 1 (2015): 31–42.
———. "The Problem of 'Gappy Existence' in Aquinas' Metaphysics and Theology." In *The Metaphysics of Personal Identity*, edited by Klima, Alexander Hall,

and Stephen Ogden, 119–34. Newcastle-upon-Tyne: Cambridge Scholars Publishing, 2016.

Knasas, John. "Aquinas on the Cognitive Soul: Physics, Metaphysics or Both?" *American Catholic Philosophical Quarterly* 77, no. 4 (1998): 501–27.

Koons, Robert. "Staunch vs. Faint-Hearted Hylomorphism: Toward an Aristotelian Account of Composition." *Res Philosophica* 91, no. 2 (2014): 151–77.

Koren, Henry. *An Introduction to the Philosophy of Animate Nature*. St. Louis, Mo.: B. Herder, 1955.

Koslicki, Kathrin. *The Structure of Objects*. Oxford: Oxford University Press, 2008.

———. "Varieties of Ontological Dependence." In *Metaphysical Grounding: Understanding the Structure of Reality*, edited by Fabrice Correia and Benjamin Schnieder, 186–213. Cambridge: Cambridge University Press, 2012.

———. "Ontological Dependence: An Opinionated Survey." In *Varieties of Dependence: Ontological Dependence, Grounding, Supervenience, Response-Dependence*, edited by Benjamin Schnieder, Miguel Hoeltje, and Alex Steinberg, 31–64. Munich: Philosophia Verlag, 2013.

Kovach, Francis. "Action at a Distance in St. Thomas Aquinas." In *Thomistic Papers 2*, edited by L. A. Kennedy and Jack Marler, 85–132. Houston, Tex.: Center for Thomistic Studies, 1986.

———. "Aquinas's Theory of Action at a Distance: A Critical Analysis." In *Scholastic Challenges to Some Mediaeval and Modern Ideas*, 149–77. Stillwater, Okla.: Western Publications, 1987.

Kripke, Saul. *Naming and Necessity*. Princeton, N.J.: Princeton University Press, 1980.

———. *Wittgenstein on Rules and Private Language*. Cambridge, Mass.: Harvard University Press, 1982.

Künzle, Pius. *Das Verhältnis der Seele zu Ihren Potenzen*. Freiburg: Universitätsverlag, 1956.

Lagerlund, Henrik. "John Buridan and the Problems of Dualism in the Early Fourteenth Century." *Journal of the History of Philosophy* 42, no. 4 (2004): 369–87.

Lang, David. "Aquinas's Impediment Argument for the Spirituality of the Human Intellect." *Medieval Philosophy and Theology* 11, no. 1 (2003): 107–24.

Lee, Patrick, and Robert George. *Body-Self Dualism in Contemporary Ethics and Politics*. Cambridge: Cambridge University Press, 2009.

Leftow, Brian. "Souls Dipped in Dust." In *Soul, Body and Survival: Essays on the Metaphysics of Human Persons*, edited by Kevin Corcoran, 120–38. Ithaca, N.Y.: Cornell University Press, 2001.

———. "Aquinas on Attributes." *Medieval Philosophy and Theology* 11, no. 1 (2003): 1–41.

———. "Soul, Mind, and Brain." In *The Waning of Materialism*, edited by Robert Koons and George Bealer, 395–415. Oxford: Oxford University Press, 2010.

Leszl, Walter. "Knowledge of the Universal and Knowledge of the Particular in Aristotle." *Review of Metaphysics* 26, no. 2 (1972): 278–313.

Lewis, David. *On the Plurality of Worlds*. Oxford: Blackwell, 1986.

Lisska, Anthony. *Aquinas's Theory of Perception: An Analytic Reconstruction*. Oxford: Oxford University Press, 2016.

Lloyd, A. C. "Aristotle's Principle of Individuation." *Mind* 79, no. 316 (1970): 519–29.

Lonergan, Bernard. *Verbum: Word and Idea in Aquinas*. Notre Dame, Ind.: University of Notre Dame Press, 1967.

Lottin, Odon. *Psychologie et morale aux XIIe et XIIIe siècles*, vol. 1. Louvain: Duculot, 1942.

Lowe, E. J. *The Possibility of Metaphysics*. Oxford: Clarendon, 1998.

Lycan, William. *Consciousness*. Cambridge, Mass.: MIT Press, 1987.

MacDonald, Cynthia, and Graham MacDonald. "Emergence and Downward Causation." In *Emergence in Mind*, edited by Cynthia MacDonald and Graham MacDonald, 139–68. Oxford: Oxford University Press, 2010.

Machamer, Peter, Lindley Darden, and Carl Craver. "Thinking About Mechanisms." *Philosophy of Science* 67, no. 1 (2000): 1–25.

Madden, James. *Mind, Matter and Nature: A Thomistic Proposal for the Philosophy of Mind*. Washington, D.C.: The Catholic University of America Press, 2013.

———. "Is a Thomistic Theory of Intentionality Consistent With Physicalism?" *American Catholic Philosophical Quarterly* 91, no. 1 (2017): 1–28.

Marenbon, John. *Medieval Philosophy: An Historical and Philosophical Introduction*. London: Routledge, 2007.

Marmodoro, Anna. "Aristotle's Hylomorphism Without Reconditioning." *Philosophical Inquiry* 36, no. 1–2 (2013): 5–22.

Marston, Roger. *Quaestiones disputatae*. Edited by the Collegium S. Bonaventurae. Ad Aquas Claras: Ex Typographia Collegii S. Bonaventurae, 1932.

Martin, Christopher. "Is There Identity of Person Between a Living Human Being and a Separated Soul?" *Studia Theologica* 6, no. 4 (2008): 249–53.

Maurer, Armand. "Form and Essence in the Philosophy of St. Thomas." *Mediaeval Studies* 13, no. 1 (1951): 165–76.

———. *St. Thomas Aquinas, The Division and Methods of the Sciences: Questions V and VI of His Commentary on the De trinitate of Boethius Translated With Introduction and Notes*. Toronto: PIMS, 1963.

McCabe, Herbert. "Categories." In *Aquinas: A Collection of Critical Essays*, edited by Anthony Kenny, 54–92. Garden City, N.J.: Anchor Books, 1969.

———. "The Immortality of the Soul." In *Aquinas: A Collection of Critical Essays*, edited by Anthony Kenny, 297–306. Garden City, N.J.: Anchor Books, 1969.

———. *On Aquinas*. Edited by Brian Davies. London: Continuum, 2008.

McCormick, Bruce. "Quaestiones Disputatae." *New Scholasticism* 13, no. 4 (1939): 368–74.

McDaniel, Kris. "A Return to the Analogy of Being." *Philosophy and Phenomenological Research* 81, no. 3 (2010): 688–717.

McGinn, Colin. "Can We Solve the Mind-Body Problem?" *Mind* 98, no. 391 (1989): 349–66.

McGinnis, Jon. *Avicenna*. Oxford: Oxford University Press, 2010.

McGlaughlin, Brian. "The Rise and Fall of British Emergentism." In *Emergence or Reduction? Essays on the Prospects of Nonreductive Physicalism*, edited by Ansgar

Beckermann, Hans Flohr, and Jaegwon Kim, 45–93. Berlin: De Gruyter, 1992.
McMahon, William. "The Medieval Sufficientiae: Attempts at a Definitive Division of the Categories." *Proceedings of the Society for Medieval Logic and Metaphysics* 2 (2002): 12–25.
Merricks, Trenton. "There Are No Criteria of Identity over Time." *Nous* 32, no. 1 (1998): 106–24.
———. "The Resurrection of the Body and the Life Everlasting." In *Reason For the Hope Within*, edited by Michael Murray, 261–86. Grand Rapids, Mich.: Eerdmans, 1999.
Miller, Fred. "Aristotle on the Separability of Mind." In *The Oxford Handbook of Aristotle*, edited by Christopher Shields, 306–39. Oxford: Oxford University Press, 2012.
Millikan, Ruth. *Language, Thought and Other Biological Categories*. Cambridge, Mass.: MIT Press, 1984.
———. "Biosemantics." *The Journal of Philosophy* 86, no. 6 (1989): 281–97.
Moreland, J. P., and Scott Rae. *Body and Soul: Human Nature and the Crisis in Ethics*. Downers Grove, Ill.: Intervarsity Press, 2000.
Nagel, Ernest. *The Structure of Science: Problems in the Logic of Scientific Explanation*. New York: Harcourt, 1961.
Nagel, Thomas. *The Last Word*. Oxford: Oxford University Press, 2001.
Neander, Karen. "Teleological Theories of Mental Content: Can Darwin Solve the Problem of Intentionality?" In *The Oxford Handbook of Philosophy of Biology*, edited by Michael Ruse, 381–409. Oxford: Oxford University Press, 2008.
Nevitt, Turner. "Annihilation, Re-Creation and Intermittent Existence in Aquinas." In *The Metaphysics of Personal Identity*, edited by Gyula Klima, Alexander Hall, and Stephen Ogden, 101–18. Newcastle-upon-Tyne: Cambridge Scholars Publishing, 2016.
———. "Aquinas on the Death of Christ: A New Argument for Corruptionism." *American Catholic Philosophical Quarterly* 90, no. 1 (2016): 77–99.
———. "Don't Mind the Gap: A Reply to Adam Wood." *Oxford Studies in Medieval Philosophy* 4 (2016).
Normore, Calvin. "The Matter of Thought." In *Representation and Objects of Thought in Medieval Philosophy*, edited by Henrik Lagerlund, 117–33. Aldershot: Ashgate, 2007.
Novak, Joseph A. "Aquinas and the Incorruptibility of the Soul." *History of Philosophy Quarterly* 4, no. 4 (1987): 405–21.
Nussbaum, Martha, and Amelie Oksenberg Rorty. *Essays on Aristotle's De anima*. Oxford: Oxford University Press, 1992.
O'Callaghan, John. "Aquinas, Cognitive Theory, and Analogy: A Propos of Robert Pasnau's Theories of Cognition in the Later Middle Ages." *American Catholic Philosophical Quarterly* 76, no. 3 (2002): 451–82.
———. *Thomist Realism and the Linguistic Turn: Toward a More Perfect Form of Existence*. Notre Dame, Ind.: University of Notre Dame Press, 2003.
———. "The Immaterial Soul and Its Discontents." *Acta Philosophica* 24, no. 1 (2015): 43–66.

O'Connor, Timothy, and Hong Yu Wong. "The Metaphysics of Emergence." Nous 39, no. 4 (2005): 658–78.
Oderberg, David. "Hylemorphic Dualism." In *Personal Identity*, edited by Ellen Frankel Paul, Fred D. Miller, and Jeffrey Paul, 70–99. Cambridge: Cambridge University Press, 2005.
———. *Real Essentialism*. London: Routledge, 2007.
———. "Concepts, Dualism, and the Human Intellect." In *Psycho-Physical Dualism Today: An Interdisciplinary Approach*, edited by Alessandro Antonietti, Antonella Corradini, and E. J. Lowe, 211–33. Lanham, Md.: Rowman and Littlefield, 2008.
———. "Survivalism, Corruptionism and Mereology." *European Journal for Philosophy of Religion* 4, no. 4 (2012): 1–26.
Owens, Joseph. "Common Nature: A Point of Comparison between Thomistic and Scotistic Metaphysics." *Mediaeval Studies* 19, no. 1 (1957): 1–14.
———. *An Elementary Christian Metaphysics*. Houston, Tex.: Center for Thomistic Studies, 1963.
———. "Aquinas on the Inseparability of the Soul from Existence." *New Scholasticism* 61, no. 3 (1987): 249–70.
———. "Thomas Aquinas: Dimensive Quantity as Individuating Principle." *Mediaeval Studies* 50, no. 1 (1988): 279–310.
Page, Ben, and Anna Marmodoro. "Aquinas on Forms, Substances and Artifacts." *Vivarium* 54, no. 1 (2016): 1–21.
Panaccio, Claude. "Aquinas on Intellectual Representation." In *Ancient and Medieval Theories of Intentionality*, edited by Dominik Perler, 185–202. Dordrecht: Springer, 2001.
Pasnau, Robert. *Theories of Cognition in the Later Middle Ages*. Cambridge: Cambridge University Press, 1997.
———. "Aquinas and the Content Fallacy." *Modern Schoolman* 75, no. 4 (1998): 293–314.
———. *Thomas Aquinas on Human Nature*. Cambridge: Cambridge University Press, 2002.
———. "What Is Cognition? A Reply to Some Critics." *American Catholic Philosophical Quarterly* 76, no. 3 (2002): 483–90.
———. *Metaphysical Themes 1274–1671*. Oxford: Oxford University Press, 2011.
———. "On Existing All at Once." In *God, Eternity and Time*, edited by C. Tapp and E. Runggaldier, 11–28. Farnham: Ashgate, 2011.
———. "Response to Arlig and Symington." In *Metaphysical Themes: Medieval and Modern*, edited by Gyula Klima and Alexander Hall, 57–74. Newcastle-upon-Tyne: Cambridge Scholars Publishing, 2014.
———. "Divine Illumination." In *The Stanford Encyclopedia of Philosophy* (2015), edited by Edward Zalta. Available at https://plato.stanford.edu/entries/illumination/.
Pasnau, Robert, and Christopher Shields. *The Philosophy of Aquinas*. Boulder, Colo.: Westview, 2003.
Pawl, Tim. "A Thomistic Account of Truthmakers for Modal Truths." PhD diss., St. Louis University, 2008.

———. "A Thomistic Truthmaker Principle." *Acta Philosophica* 25, no. 1 (2016): 45–64.
Pegis, Anton. *St. Thomas and the Problem of the Soul in the Thirteenth Century*. Toronto: PIMS, 1934.
———. "The Separated Soul and Its Nature in St. Thomas." In *St. Thomas Aquinas 1274–1974: Commemorative Studies*, edited by Armand Maurer, 131–58. Toronto: PIMS, 1974.
———. "Between Immortality and Death." *The Monist* 58, no. 1 (1974): 1–15.
Peterson, Linda. "Cardinal Cajetan and Giles of Rome." In *Individuation in Scholasticism, the Later Middle-Ages and the Counter-Reformation, 1150–1650*, edited by Jorge Gracia, 431–56. Buffalo: State University of New York Press, 1994.
Pimentel, Stephen. "Formal Identity as Isomorphism in Thomistic Philosophy of Mind." *Proceedings of the American Catholic Philosophical Association* 80 (2007): 115–26.
Pini, Giorgio. "Scotus's Realist Conception of the Categories: His Legacy to Late Medieval Debates." *Vivarium* 43, no. 1 (2005): 63–110.
———. "The Individuation of Angels from Bonaventure to Duns Scotus." In *A Companion to Angels in Medieval Philosophy*, edited by Tobias Hoffman, 79–116. Leiden: Brill, 2012.
Plato. *Complete Works*. Edited by John Cooper. Indianapolis, Ind.: Hackett, 1997.
Pluta, Olaf. "John Buridan on Universal Knowledge." *Bochumer Philosophisches Jahrbuch für Antike und Mittelalter* 7, no. 1 (2002): 25–46.
———. "Materialism in the Philosophy of Mind: Nicholas of Amsterdam's Quaestiones De anima." In *Mind, Cognition and Representation. The Tradition of Commentaries on Aristotle's De anima*, edited by Paul Bakker and Johannes Thijssen, 109–26. Aldershot: Ashgate, 2007.
Porphyry. *Isagoge*. In *Five Texts on the Mediaeval Problem of Universals*, translated by Paul V. Spade, 1–19. Indianapolis, Ind.: Hackett, 1994.
Quine, W. V. O. *Word and Object*. Cambridge, Mass.: MIT Press, 1960.
Rea, Michael. "Hylomorphism Reconditioned." *Philosophical Perspectives* 25, no. 1 (2011): 341–58.
Ross, James. "Immaterial Aspects of Thought." *Journal of Philosophy* 89, no. 3 (1992): 136–50.
———. *Thought and World: The Hidden Necessities*. Notre Dame, Ind.: University of Notre Dame Press, 2008.
Rota, Michael. "Substance and Artifact in Thomas Aquinas." *History of Philosophy Quarterly* 21, no. 3 (2004): 241–59.
Ryle, Gilbert. *The Concept of Mind*. New York: Barnes and Noble, 1949.
Scarpelli Cory, Therese. "What Is an Intellectual 'Turn'? The *Liber de causis*, Avicenna and Aquinas's Turn to Phantasms." *Topicos* 45 (2013): 129–62.
———. *Aquinas on Human Self-Knowledge*. Cambridge: Cambridge University Press, 2014.
———. "Rethinking Abstractionism: Aquinas's Intellectual Light and Some Arabic Sources." *Journal of the History of Philosophy* 53, no. 4 (2015): 607–46.
Schaffer, Jonathan. "On What Grounds What." In *Metametaphysics: New Essays*

on the Foundations of Ontology, edited by David Chalmers, David Manley, and Ryan Wasserman, 347–83. Oxford: Oxford University Press, 2009.

Schmitz, Kenneth. "Purity of Soul and Immortality." The Monist 69, no. 3 (1986): 396–415.

Schnieder. Brad. "A Certain Kind of Trinity: Dependence, Substance, Explanation." Philosophical Studies 129, no. 2 (2006): 393–419.

Scotus, John Duns. Opera omnia. Edited by L. Wadding. Paris: Vives, 1639/1891–95.

———. Opera omnia. Edited by C. Balíc et al. Vatican City: Typis Polyglottis Vaticanis, 1950–.

———. Opera philosophica. Edited by G. Etzkorn et al. St. Bonaventure, N.Y.: The Franciscan Institute, 1997–2006.

Sharpe, Kevin. "Thomas Aquinas and Non-Reductive Physicalism." Proceedings of the American Catholic Philosophical Association 79 (2005): 217–25.

Shields, Christopher. Aristotle. London: Routledge, 2007.

———. "Aristotle on Action: The Peculiar Motion of Aristotelian Souls." Aristotelian Society Supplementary Volume 81, no. 1 (2007): 139–61.

Siger of Brabant. Quaestiones de anima intellectiva. In Siger de Brabant et l'Averroisme Latin au XIIIme siecle, vol. 2, edited by Pierre Mandonnet. Louvain: Institut Superieur de Philosophie de l'Universite, 1911.

Sisko, John. "Material Alternation and Cognitive Capacity in Aristotle's 'De Anima.'" Phronesis 41, no. 2 (1996): 138–57.

Sorabji, Richard. "Intentionality and Physiological Processes: Aristotle's Theory of Sense-Perception." In Essays on Aristotle's De anima, edited by Martha Nussbaum and Amelie Oksenberg Rorty, 195–225. Oxford: Oxford University Press, 1992.

Spade, Paul Vincent. Five Texts on the Medieval Problem of Universals. Indianapolis, Ind.: Hackett, 1994.

———. "Degrees of Being, Degrees of Goodness: Aquinas on Levels of Reality." In Aquinas's Moral Theory: Essays in Honor of Norman Kretzmann, edited by Eleonore Stump and Scott MacDonald, 254–76. Ithaca, N.Y.: Cornell University Press, 1999.

———. "Binarium Famosissimum." In The Stanford Encyclopedia of Philosophy (2008), edited by Edward Zalta. Available at http://plato.stanford.edu/entries/binarium/.

Spencer, Joshua. "Ways of Being." Philosophical Compass 7, no. 12 (2012): 910–18.

Spruit, Leon. Species Intelligibilis: From Perception to Knowledge. Leiden: Brill, 1994.

Stein, Nathanael. "Causation and Explanation in Aristotle." Philosophy Compass 6, no. 10 (2011): 699–707.

Stoljar, Daniel. Physicalism. London: Routledge, 2010.

———. "Physicalism." In The Stanford Encyclopedia of Philosophy (2015), edited by Edward Zalta, available at http://plato.stanford.edu/entries/physicalism/.

Stump, Eleonore. "Non-Cartesian Substance Dualism and Materialism without Reduction." Faith and Philosophy 12, no. 4 (1995): 505–31.

———. Aquinas. New York: Routledge, 2003.

———. "Resurrection, Reassembly, and Reconstitution: Aquinas on the Soul." In *Die menschliche Seele: Brauchen wir den Dualismus?*, edited by Bruno Niederberger and Edmund Runggaldier, 153–74. Frankfurt: Ontos Verlag, 2006.

———. "Substance and Artifact in Aquinas' Metaphysics." In *Knowledge and Reality*, edited by T. M. Crisp et al., 63–79. Dordrecht: Springer, 2006.

———. "Emergence, Causal Powers and Aristotelianism in Metaphysics." In *Powers and Capacities in Philosophy: The New Aristotelianism*, edited by John Greco and Ruth Groff, 48–68. London: Routledge, 2013.

Sweeney, Matthew. "Thomas Aquinas' Commentary on 'De anima' 429a10–429b5 and the Argument for the Immateriality of the Intellect." PhD diss., The Catholic University of America, 1994.

Symington, Paul. "Thomas Aquinas on Establishing the Identity of Aristotle's Categories." In *Medieval Commentaries on Aristotle's Categories*, edited by Lloyd Newton, 119–44. Leiden: Brill, 2008.

———. *On Determining What There Is: The Identity of Ontological Categories in Aquinas, Scotus and Lowe*. Frankfurt: Ontos Verlag, 2010.

Turner, Jason. "Ontological Pluralism." *Journal of Philosophy* 107, no. 1 (2010): 5–34.

Taylor, Richard. "Arabic/Islamic Philosophy in Thomas Aquinas's Conception of the Beatific Vision in IV Sent., D. 49, Q. 2, A. 1." *The Thomist* 76, no. 4 (2012): 509–50.

Tellkamp, Jörg Alejandro. "Aquinas on Intentions in the Medium and in the Mind." *Proceedings of the American Catholic Philosophical Association* 80 (2006): 275–89.

Tkacz, Michael. "Albert the Great and the Revival of Aristotle's Zoological Research Program." *Vivarium* 45, no. 1 (2007): 30–68.

Tomarchio, John. "Aquinas's Division of Being according to Modes of Existing." *Review of Metaphysics* 54, no. 3 (2001): 585–613.

Toner, Patrick. "Thomas versus Tibbles: A Critical Study of Christopher Brown's Aquinas and the Ship of Theseus." *American Catholic Philosophical Quarterly* 81, no. 4 (2007): 639–53.

———. "Personhood and Death in St. Thomas Aquinas." *History of Philosophy Quarterly* 26, no. 2 (2009): 121–38.

———. "St. Thomas Aquinas on Death and the Separated Soul." *Pacific Philosophical Quarterly* 91, no. 4 (2010): 587–99.

———. "On Hylemorphism and Personal Identity." *European Journal of Philosophy* 19, no. 3 (2011): 454–73.

———. "St. Thomas Aquinas on Punishing Souls." *International Journal for the Philosophy of Religion* 71, no. 2 (2012): 103–16.

Tweedale, Martin. "Origins of the Medieval Theory that Sensation Is an Immaterial Reception of a Form." *Philosophical Topics* 20, no. 2 (1992): 215–31.

Tweedale, Martin, and Richard Bosley, eds. *Basic Issues in Medieval Philosophy*. Peterborough: Broadview, 2006.

Van Dyke, Christina. "Human Identity, Immanent Causal Relations, and the Principle of Non-Repeatability: Thomas Aquinas on the Bodily Resurrection." *Religious Studies* 43, no. 4 (2007): 373–94.

———. "Not Properly a Person: The Rational Soul and 'Thomistic Substance Dualism.'" *Faith and Philosophy* 26, no. 2 (2009): 186–204.

———. "Aquinas's Shiny Happy People." *Oxford Studies in Philosophy of Religion* 6 (2014): 269–91.

———. "I See Dead People: Disembodied Souls and Aquinas's 'Two-Person' Problem." *Oxford Studies in Medieval Philosophy* 2 (2014): 25–45.

Van Inwagen, Peter. *Material Beings*. Ithaca, N.Y.: Cornell University Press, 1990.

Walz, Matthew. "What Is a Power of the Soul? Aquinas's Answer." *Sapientia* 60, no. 218 (2005): 319–48.

Ward, Thomas. *John Duns Scotus on Parts, Wholes and Hylomorphism*. Leiden: Brill, 2014.

Wasserman, Gloria. "Thomas Aquinas on Truths about Non-Beings." *Proceedings of the American Catholic Philosophical Association* 80 (2006): 101–13.

Weidemann, Hermann. "The Logic of Being in Thomas Aquinas." In *Thomas Aquinas: Contemporary Philosophical Perspectives*, edited by Brian Davies, 77–96. Oxford: Oxford University Press, 2002.

Weisheipl, James. "Albertus Magnus and Universal Hylomorphism." *Southwestern Journal of Philosophy* 10, no. 3 (1979): 239–60.

White, Kevin. "Individuation in Aquinas's *Super Boetium De Trinitate*, Q. 4." *American Catholic Philosophical Quarterly* 69, no. 4 (1995): 543–56.

Wilhelmsen, Frederick. "A Note on Contraries and the Incorruptibility of the Human Soul in St. Thomas Aquinas." *American Catholic Philosophical Quarterly* 67, no. 3 (1993): 333–38.

Wimsatt, William. "Emergence as Non-Aggregativity and the Biases of Reductionisms." *Foundations of Science* 5, no. 3 (2000): 269–97.

Wippel, John. "Metaphysics and *Separatio* according to Thomas Aquinas." *Review of Metaphysics* 31, no. 3 (1978): 431–70.

———. "Thomas Aquinas on the Distinction and Derivation of the Many from the One: A Dialectic between Being and Nonbeing." *Review of Metaphysics* 38, no. 3 (1985): 563–90.

———. "Thomas Aquinas's Derivation of the Aristotelian Categories." *Journal of the History of Philosophy* 25, no. 1 (1987): 13–34.

———. *The Metaphysical Thought of Thomas Aquinas: From Finite Being to Uncreated Being*. Washington, D.C.: The Catholic University of America Press, 2000.

———. *Metaphysical Themes in Thomas Aquinas II*. Washington, D.C.: The Catholic University of America Press, 2007.

Wittgenstein, Ludwig. *Philosophical Investigations*. Translated by G. E. M. Anscombe. Oxford: Blackwell, 2001.

Wolterstorff, Nicholas. *On Universals: An Essay in Ontology*. Chicago: University of Chicago Press, 1970.

Wood, Adam. "The Faculties of the Soul and Some Medieval Mind-Body Problems." *The Thomist* 75, no. 4 (2011): 585–636.

———. "Mind the Gap? The Principle of Non-Repeatability and Aquinas's Account of the Resurrection." *Oxford Studies in Medieval Philosophy* 3 (2015): 99–127.

———. "Aquinas vs. Buridan on the Substance and Powers of the Soul." In *Ques-*

tions on the Soul by John Buridan and Others: A Companion to Buridan's Philosophy of Mind, edited by Gyula Klima, 77–94. Cham: Springer, 2017.

Zavalloni, Roberto. Richard de Mediavilla et la controverse sur la pluralité des formes. Philosophes Médiévaux 2. Louvain: Editions de L'Institut Supérieur de Philosophie, 1951.

Zimmerman, Dean. "Criteria of Identity and the 'Identity Mystics.'" Erkenntnis 48, nos. 2–3 (1998): 281–301.

———. "The Compatibility of Materialism and Survival: The 'Falling Elevator' Model." Faith and Philosophy 16, no. 2 (1999): 194–212.

———. "Bodily Resurrection: The Falling Elevator Model Revisited." In Personal Identity and Resurrection, edited by Georg Gasser, 33–50. Farnham: Ashgate, 2010.

Zupko, Jack. "John Buridan's Philosophy of Mind: An Edition and Translation of His 'Questions on Aristotle's De anima' (Third Redaction), with Commentary and Critical and Interpretative Essays." PhD diss., Cornell University, 1989.

———. "How Are Souls Related to Bodies? A Study of John Buridan." Review of Metaphysics 46, no. 3 (1993): 575–601.

———. "On Buridan's Alleged Alexandrianism: Heterodoxy and Natural Philosophy in Fourteenth-Century Paris." Vivarium 42, no. 1 (2004): 43–57.

INDEX

abstraction, 53–54, 62, 147, 189, 227–29, 251
Ackrill, J. L., 168n34
act of being (*esse*), 3, 5, 8–14, 17, 19, 26, 28–35, 37, 39–41, 43–44, 46, 54–55, 61, 63, 65, 68, 73, 81–84, 90, 93, 95–96, 103, 146, 197, 199, 226, 230–31, 254–55, 257, 270–71, 279–80, 282–84, 286, 288–89
Adams, Marilyn McCord, 284n76
afterlife, 5, 255, 257, 292–93
Albert the Great, 79, 80n92, 113n62, 114, 155n6, 157n11, 200
analogy of being, 5, 17–22
angels/intelligences, 16n20, 28–31, 38–39, 41–44, 63–65, 76, 84, 101n32, 106, 112n59, 148–49, 160–61, 168, 177, 198–99, 227n91, 232n103, 260–62, 264, 286, 289
Anscombe, G. E. M., 240–41, 250
argument from mode of intellectual operations (MA) 4, 6, 191, 194, 195nn4–5, 198–200, 211, 218, 223–54
argument from reflexivity of intellectual operations (RA) 4, 191, 194, 195n4, 198, 201, 214–23
argument from scope of intellectual operations (SA), 4, 191, 193, 195nn4–5, 198, 203–14
Aristotle, 1, 3, 12n12, 14, 18, 20–22, 25n44, 33–34, 36n72, 48–49, 60n41, 71–74, 78n86, 80n92, 81, 83, 85–87, 91, 94–96, 99, 101n32, 102, 107n54, 110n55, 111–15, 117, 119–21, 131–32, 134, 145n131, 146–48, 153–59, 167–69, 171–75, 180, 188, 193–94, 197–202, 204–5, 209n48, 211n59, 214–17, 223, 250, 257–59, 262, 264, 269, 280
Armstrong, David, 74, 75n76
artifacts, 36, 85n111, 179, 239
Augustine, 42, 79, 155n6, 217, 258
Averroes, 44, 49, 50n3, 65, 71–73, 149n144, 155n6, 157n11, 159, 198n14, 200, 231
Avicebron, 42, 65, 73–74, 77, 196
Avicenna, 49, 52–55, 62, 65, 99n26, 113n62, 159, 194, 197, 200–201, 203, 210, 215, 223

Bacon, Roger 42, 79
Baker, Lynne Rudder, 132–33, 135, 221–22
Barnes, Jonathan, 20n29, 102
Bazan, B. Carlos, 46n92, 276
Bechtel, William, 123n91
Beckermann, Ansgar, 138n122
Bennett, M. R., 101n32, 102
Block, Ned, 177
Boethius, 26, 31n58, 42–43, 52–53, 60, 80, 271–72
Bonaventure, 41, 43–44, 232n103
brain, 1–2, 4, 90, 98–99, 101, 103, 107, 109, 137n119, 173n53, 174, 203–4, 208n47, 209, 211, 236, 242, 252, 258–59, 263
Brentano, Franz, 244
Brower, Jeffrey, 6, 12n12, 29n54, 31n59, 36n73, 53n14, 57–59, 62n49, 63n52,

313

Brower, Jeffrey (cont.)
  75n76–77, 78n86, 106n51, 186–87,
  191–92, 267–70, 274–75
Brower-Toland, Susan, 186–87, 191–92
Brown, Christopher, 85n111, 115n70,
  267n34, 270n44
Brugger, E. Christian, 232–33
Burnyeat, Miles, 159n13, 171–77, 210,
  235–36

Casey, Gerard, 162n23, 163n24
Caston, Victor, 173n53, 175n58
celestial bodies, 63–64, 84–85, 94–95,
  126–27, 286, 289
cessationism, 267–68, 270, 273, 275–79,
  283
Chalmers, David, 252n150
Churchland, Paul, 236n115, 253n154
cognitive media. *See* medium of cognition
Cohen, Sheldon, 163n25, 165, 171
Cohoe, Caleb, 209n48
Connell, Richard, 212
Correia, Fabrice, 139n123
corruption, 8, 10–11, 23–24, 41, 44–45,
  63, 74, 94–97, 111n58, 120, 279–80,
  287
Cross, Richard, 12n12, 45–47, 62, 81,
  115n70, 284n76, 290n88

Davidson, Donald, 130–32, 141, 190
Davies, Brian, 9n3, 149n144, 266, 268n36,
  268n38
Decaen, Christopher, 115n70, 291n93
Descartes, René, 2, 91, 128–29, 145,
  149–50
Dewan, Lawrence, 93, 97n22
disjunction problem, 179, 253
Dretske, Fred, 142–43, 178–79, 186–87,
  243, 252–53

Eberl, Jason, 267n34, 275n63
Edwards, Sandra, 56–57
elements, 59, 85–89, 93–95, 112, 114–20,
  122, 124–27, 136, 143n130, 165–66, 200
emergence, 85n111, 111, 114–20, 125–27,
  133–45, 164, 166–67, 170, 192, 221

emergentism, 6, 15n18, 92, 110, 114, 116,
  123, 126, 132–45, 151, 164, 166
Empedocles, 85n110, 86, 88, 116–17, 127,
  134, 143n130, 156, 200
epiphenomenalism, 116, 132
essence, 3, 5, 7–8, 20n30, 28–31, 34, 39,
  43, 45, 48–52, 54, 56–57, 63–73, 75,
  80–84, 94, 109, 110n55, 121, 137,
  140–41, 144, 146, 148, 150, 160n15,
  189, 215, 225–26, 243, 248n143, 262–63,
  280–82
eucharist, 37, 76, 141n124, 287
explanation: mechanistic, 122–24, 127,
  166; and ontological dependence,
  107–45, 265n30; subjective vs. objective, 131–32

Feser, Edward, 209n49, 234n109, 240,
  243, 246, 253
Fine, Kit, 14, 15n18, 137, 141
first-person perspective, 219–22
Fodor, Jerry, 178, 252–53
form: accidental, 10–11, 39, 68, 74–79,
  83–84, 88–90, 95, 116; as delimiting/
  determining principle, 3, 8, 29–31,
  39–40, 46n91, 65; as principle of
  kind-membership, 30, 32, 51, 58; substantial, 1, 5, 10–11, 16, 24, 35, 37–41, 44,
  50, 60–69, 73–88, 111n58, 114–15, 122,
  136, 145, 196, 202, 279–80, 282–83, 293.
  See also essence; structure
Foster, David Ruel, 195nn3–5, 198n15,
  200n21, 206n45, 211n59
Freddoso, Alfred, 2n1, 214n65
functional analysis. *See* explanation,
  mechanistic

Galen, 99n26, 116, 134
gappy existence, 277–78, 282–85, 289
Geach, Peter, 9n3, 149n144, 271–72
generation, 8, 10–11, 13, 23–24, 63, 69, 74,
  94, 111n58, 112, 119–20, 125n96
Gilson, Etienne, 9n3, 31n58, 35n68
God, 5, 12, 14n17, 16n20, 28–31, 34–35,
  38–39, 41, 43, 63, 75–76, 83–84, 91, 96–
  97, 100–101, 104, 106, 112n59, 113n62,

141, 145, 148–50, 177, 185, 192, 202, 204, 217, 227n91, 230, 256–58, 260–64, 266, 268n38, 272–73, 276–91
Gracia, Jorge, 55n22, 60n42, 290n90
Grice, Paul, 178–79

Hacker, P. M. S., 101–3
Haldane, John, 163n25, 206n45, 217, 219, 220n85, 237–39
Hamlyn, D. W., 163n25
Hasker, William, 135, 137n119
Haugeland, John, 231n101
Heil, John, 25n46, 77n85
Henry of Ghent, 79n87
Hochschild, Joshua, 67n61
Hoffman, Paul, 165–67
homonymy principle, 72, 83
homunculus fallacy, 101–2
hylomorphism, 14–16, 29n55, 40–43, 50–51, 58, 95, 115n70, 134, 143n130, 163, 199

immortality, 5, 141n125, 194n2, 255–66, 277
incorporeality, 89–92, 96, 98, 100–101, 103, 107, 109, 149–50, 165–67, 194, 200, 202–5, 215, 220–22, 225–26, 231n102, 235, 238–39, 243, 263n24
incorruptibility, 4, 6, 16, 44, 47, 63, 91–98, 100, 145, 150, 164-65, 197, 254–60, 264–66, 277, 286–87, 289
indeterminacy: intentional, 240–44, 246, 250–53; ontological, 242–46
individuation, 5, 30, 32, 44, 47, 50–51, 58–64, 67, 224–26, 232n103, 256–57, 277, 280, 287–92
information processing, 152, 162–67, 172, 174, 178–80, 184–88, 201, 203, 208–9, 211, 219, 225, 228, 232–37, 252
intentional being (*esse intentionale*), 158–64, 166, 169–70, 172, 174, 176–77, 186–88, 203, 206–11, 216–17, 225, 244
intentionality, 160, 180n77, 186–87, 209n48, 231n101, 234n109, 241, 244, 253

Jaworski, William, 14, 58n33, 108n55, 115n70, 116n75, 120n86, 128, 131, 133n111, 137, 142–44, 204n42
Johnston, Mark, 14, 267n35
Jordan, Mark, 99n26, 148

Kahn, Charles, 194
Kenny, Anthony, 6, 9n3, 42n82, 59n38, 101, 103, 108, 149n144, 171, 206n45, 208n47, 209n49, 268n36
Kim, Jaegwon, 133, 141–42
King, Peter, 60n42, 80n93, 162n23, 176n62, 186, 189n99, 222n84
Klima, Gyula, 2n1, 6, 9n3, 13, 16n20, 59n38, 61n46, 68n63, 78n28, 106n51, 162, 163n24, 166, 171, 180n77, 187–89, 190n109, 212–13, 225, 227–28, 235–39, 268n36, 284n77
Knasas, John, 165, 167–70
Koons, Robert, 14, 115n70
Koslicki, Kathrin, 14, 58n33, 137, 139n123, 141
Kripke, Saul, 62, 242–43, 287

Lang, David, 180n77
Leftow, Brian, 6, 12n12, 46n91, 56–57, 106n52, 155n72
levels of composition/organization, 10n4, 78, 84–86, 88–90, 111–12, 114–15, 117, 119–20, 122–24, 127, 133, 135n118, 139, 142, 164
Lewis, David, 33n63, 222
Lonergan, Bernard, 20n30, 168n35
Lowe, E. J., 77n85
Lycan, William, 178

Madden, James, 2n1, 234n109
Marmodoro, Anna, 14, 37n73, 73n73
Marston, Roger, 212n62, 232n103
matter: designated, 50–51, 56–64, 67–68, 71, 112, 157, 225–27, 229, 232, 238, 250, 280; empirically specifiable, 10n4, 59, 62, 119; from which, 8–9; prime, 10–12, 38, 42, 45, 58–59, 61, 63–64, 68–69, 71–72, 74–75, 85n110, 86, 94, 114, 119, 244, 280, 282;

matter (cont.)
  as principle of individuation, 30, 32, 50, 58–64, 67, 224, 226–27, 233, 243, 245–46, 250, 280, 287–89; proximate/remote, 10n4, 85–86, 94; as pure potency, 12, 59, 68, 72, 74n75, 244; spiritual, 42n81, 43, 199; as subject, 9–12, 35n68, 40–41, 74
Maurer, Armand, 65n58, 73n73, 147n137
McCabe, Herbert, 6, 25n44, 149n144, 209n49, 268n36
McCormick, Bruce, 257, 259, 261–262, 264
McDaniel, Kris, 19n28
McGinn, Colin, 149
McGlaughlin, Brian, 134, 135n114
medium of cognition, 104, 155–56, 160–61, 170, 172, 174–76, 181, 184, 188, 203, 209nn48–49, 210–11, 215, 244
mereological fallacy. See homunculus fallacy
Merricks, Trenton, 290–92
Millikan, Ruth, 178–79, 186–87, 243, 252–53
mixtures/mixed bodies, 82, 85n111, 86, 112, 114, 115n70, 125, 165–66
mode of being: created/uncreated, 34; material/immaterial, 28, 38–39, 160, 199; per se/per accidens, 32, 35–38, 65, 68, 85n111, 93, 116–17, 119; real/rational, 32–34, 36–38, 54, 76, 104n42, 225; subsistent/inherent, 8, 16n20, 28, 37–38, 40, 44, 46, 81, 84, 91, 93, 103, 147, 160, 255, 265, 280, 283; substantial/accidental, 9, 24, 34
multiple realizability, 101n32, 104

Nagel, Ernest, 116, 123
Nagel, Thomas, 240–43, 246, 253
natural being (*esse naturale*), 158–60, 163, 169–70
necessitation, 120, 132–33, 143n130
Nevitt, Turner, 268n36, 270n43, 272n52, 273–74, 284n77
nominalism, 52, 54, 56–58
Normore, Calvin, 206n45, 214
Novak, Joseph, 229–30, 233–34, 254

nutrition, 81, 88, 104n42, 113, 115n73, 117–20, 122–25, 127, 138–39, 141, 164, 166, 264n28

O'Callaghan, John, 104n40, 154n5, 162n20, 176–77, 196, 199, 233–24, 238n119
Oderberg, David, 2n1, 14, 233n109, 267n34
ontological dependence, 92, 108–45, 148, 150, 152, 170, 199, 204, 208, 221, 255
organs/organic parts, 2–3, 37, 39, 49, 78, 82, 84–90, 94–96, 98–108, 119, 121–22, 127, 139, 146–47, 155, 159, 163, 170–73, 175n58, 188, 196–99, 201, 204–5, 208–12, 215, 224, 226, 235, 237, 259, 263–65, 279
origins essentialism, 62, 287
Owens, Joseph, 6, 51n6, 55n22, 59n36, 78n27, 93, 95, 97, 257–61, 264–65

Panaccio, Claude, 161n18, 162–63
Parmenides/eleatic monism, 18, 21, 26–27, 31
Pasnau, Robert, 6, 42n81, 60n40, 78n27, 80n93, 83, 85n111, 88n117, 97n22, 108n54, 126n100, 149, 162n20, 171, 173n53, 174n55, 176–77, 180, 185n89, 192n109, 206n45, 214n65, 217, 219, 229–34, 237–38, 243, 254, 257, 259–62, 264, 268n36, 283n75, 285n80
Pawl, Tim, 76
Pegis, Anton, 6, 83n100, 260–61
permanent entities, 284–86
persons/personhood, 5, 31n58, 36, 221, 266n33, 256, 266–77
phantasia. See powers, imaginative
phantasms, 100, 107, 109–10, 147n135, 148, 149n144, 156, 189, 228n95, 229n98, 237, 251, 258–65
physicalism, 2, 6, 92, 116n75, 128–33, 136, 145, 151, 164–65, 194, 196, 199, 234n109, 256, 290; eliminative, 128–29; nonreductive, 104n42, 128, 130–33; reductive, 128, 164
physiological states/processes, 98–100, 105–7, 113, 142–43, 171–75, 188, 236
Pini, Giorgio, 25n44, 64n55

Plato, 2, 17, 25–26, 51, 55–57, 74n75, 77, 217, 231n102, 245, 266, 269
Pluta, Olaf, 194n2, 239n122
Porphyry, 19, 20n29
powers, 14, 15n18, 50, 77, 79–80, 84–85, 88–89, 94–95, 110n55, 115–20, 125–26, 134n113, 135–45, 196; cogitative, 182, 248; cognitive, 100n28, 113, 167, 184, 189, 200, 205–7, 222, 230–32, 235–38; imaginative, 77, 99–100, 107, 143, 148, 212, 258–59; immaterial, 145, 220, 226, 239; incorporeal, 89–90, 96, 107n52; intellectual, 3–4, 80–82, 89–92, 98, 100, 103, 107–8, 128, 146, 166–67, 182, 188, 196, 198–99, 204, 217, 220, 225–26, 230, 254–55, 265; nutritive, 122, 127, 139, 164, 166; of the soul, 49, 78–83, 89–90, 92, 104–6, 109, 111, 127, 129, 136–38, 140–44, 146–47, 150, 165, 255; single-track vs. multi-track, 77; sense-, 79, 84, 106n48, 109, 113, 167, 170–71, 175, 182, 198, 201, 205, 213, 224, 226, 228, 236; visual, 33, 79, 83–84, 169, 174
principle of non-repeatability, 285, 289
privation, 8, 11–12, 14, 24, 32–33, 69
propria/proper accidents, 23, 80, 115n73

quiddity, 20, 28, 34–35, 43, 48–50, 65–66, 68n64, 73, 110n55, 148
Quine, W. V. O., 242–43

Rea, Michael, 14, 58n33
real definition, 108–9, 137–42, 144
real distinction: act of being vs. essence, 5, 28–29; form of the whole vs. form of the part, 64, 66, 72; souls vs. their powers, 79–83, 85
realism, 51–52, 56, 58
reduction, 116–18, 120–27, 135, 164, 166, 242
reductivism 110–11, 116, 128, 164
"referent and truthmaker" view of matter and form, 3, 13, 15–17, 39, 74–75
reflexivity, 4, 149, 190–91, 194, 195n4, 198, 201, 214–23

resurrection, 5, 256–57, 267, 269n38, 270, 275–93
Ross, James, 240–43, 246, 253
Ryle, Gilbert, 77n85, 102

Scarpelli Cory, Therese, 156n9, 189n99–100, 217n72, 219–20, 222, 228n92, 228n95, 233–34, 238–39, 265n24
Scotus, John Duns, 12n12, 25n44, 55–57, 61n45, 114n70, 283–84, 289–90
self-knowledge, 1, 149, 215, 222
separated souls, 5, 46, 89, 91–92, 95, 98, 100, 146, 147n135, 256–93
Shields, Christopher, 108n54, 131, 162n23, 169n40
Siger of Brabant, 45, 47, 81
Sorabji, Richard, 172n50
Spade, Paul Vincent, 55–57, 65n57
sparse ontology/properties, 15n18, 33, 76
species, 154–57, 160–63, 167, 169–70, 172–74, 177, 187–89, 209n48, 213, 215, 225, 227n91, 229, 231, 233, 234n109, 238, 245, 260–61, 263
spiritual being (*esse spirituale*). See intentional being (*esse intentionale*)
Stoljar, Daniel, 132–33
structure, 3, 14–16, 39–40, 49, 64, 68, 73, 82–84, 103, 108, 117, 123, 127, 134–36, 138, 140, 142, 143n130, 188, 192; overarching, 66, 68, 73, 78, 83; substructure, 50, 66, 78–79, 83–85, 88–90
"stuff and structure" view of matter and form, 3, 14–16, 39
Stump, Eleonore, 6, 14, 36n73, 40, 46n91, 59n38, 84n109, 100n28, 104n42, 126, 162, 163n24, 166, 170–71, 187, 225, 267n34, 269n42, 270n45, 271n49, 275n63, 283n75
substance dualism, 2, 92, 128–29, 133, 151
successive entities, 285–86
supervenience, 74n74, 111, 114, 119–20, 130, 132–33, 143n130
survivalism, 267–75, 278
Sweeney, Matthew, 197n5, 198n15, 209n49, 212n61
systems-level tasks, 87–90, 134, 136

Taylor, Richard, 263n27
teleofunctional accounts of mind, 153, 175–77, 180, 182, 184–86, 250
teleosemantic accounts of mental content, 142–43, 153, 176, 179, 182–86, 243, 250, 252–53
Tellkamp, Jörg Alejandro, 159n13
Tkacz, Michael, 114n66
Tomarchio, John, 21n36
Toner, Patrick, 267n36, 270n44, 273
tropes, 53, 56–58, 62
truthmaker, 3, 13–16, 39–40, 49–50, 73–79, 117
Turner, Jason, 19n28
Tweedale, Martin, 157n11, 176n62

unicity of substantial forms, 5, 65–66, 77, 114n70
universal hylomorphism, 41–43, 65n57, 74, 196, 199, 232n103
universals, 25, 34, 50–58, 63, 67, 104n42, 197–200, 225–28, 232–34, 244, 250–51

Van Dyke, Christina, 266n33, 268n36, 272, 276n67, 283n75, 285
Van Inwagen, Peter, 14
virtual presence, 15n18, 114, 120

Ward, Thomas, 114n70
Weidemann, Hermann, 9n3
Wimsatt, William, 115n72, 135
Wippel, John, 6, 12n8, 25–26, 29, 31, 35n68, 59n36, 61n46, 65n56, 73n73, 78n86, 80nn92–93, 148n138
Wittgenstein, Ludwig, 101, 149n144, 240–42

Zimmerman, Dean, 291–93
Zupko, Jack, 82n98, 195n2

Thomas Aquinas on the Immateriality of the Human Intellect was designed in Quadraat and Quadraat Sans with Maestro and Hypatia Sans display type and composed by Kachergis Book Design of Pittsboro, North Carolina. It was printed on 55-pound Natural Offset and bound by Maple Press of York, Pennsylvania.

www.ingramcontent.com/pod-product-compliance
Lightning Source LLC
Chambersburg PA
CBHW022032290426
44109CB00014B/834